The Cocker Spaniel Handbook

LINDA WHITWAM

ISBN- 13: 978-1523798209

Copyright

Contributing Authors

Haja van Wessem

Kerena Marchant

Linda Reed

Peter Harvey

Richard Preest

Stewart North

Acknowledgements

My sincere thanks go to the 40 Cocker Spaniel breeders as well as owners and canine experts who have generously contributed their time and expertise to this book. Their knowledge and love of their dogs shines through and without them **The Cocker Spaniel Handbook** would not have been possible.

Special thanks to: Alan and Carole Pitchers, Andy Platt, Barry Hutchinson, Billie Cheeseman, Caroline Bymolen, Chris Warner, Christine and Dave Grant, Christine Thomas, David and Alison Matthews, Debra Ralston, Eunice Wine, Gail Parsons, Haja van Wessem, Helen Marsden, Jackie Hornby, Jacquie Ward, Jane Minikin, Jane Seekings, Jill Gunn, Jo Oxley, Julie and Darren Summers, Kate McBride, Keith Henderson, Kerena Marchant, Kirsten Strachan, Linda Reed, Louise Massey, Lynne Waterhouse, Manda and Jacquie Smith, Maxine Shaverin, Michelle Mills, Nicola Hunter, Pat and Andrew Height, Peter Harvey and Nikki Arnold, Rachel Appleby, Richard Preest, Robert and Ruth Baldwin, Stewart North, Tracey Simpson, Wendy Roberts, Wendy Tobijanski, Dr Sara Skiwski and all the Cocker Spaniel owners who participated.

Contributors' details are listed at the back of the book.

Table of Contents

1. Meet the Cocker Spaniel

With his trademark ever-wagging tail, sunny temperament and great desire to please his owners, the Cocker Spaniel has become one of the most popular of all breeds. He is handsome, intelligent, highly affectionate and loyal, good with children and loves a challenge – both physical and mental. Given enough exercise and stimulation, the Cocker is a happy, friendly dog, who is easy to train and gets along with everybody and other dogs.

Above all, the Cocker Spaniel is adaptable. It's hard to think of another canine which can successfully fulfil so many different roles: family pet, working gundog, show dog, agility and Flyball competitor, therapy and assistance dog, sniffer dog....the Cocker excels at them all.

This busy medium sized dog - the most popular of all the Spaniels - is quite unique, not only in terms of appearance with his droopy ears and constantly wagging tail, but also in personality.

His excellent temperament has made him the dog of choice for many thousands of households and his hunting instincts mean he is popular with field sport enthusiasts as well. In the UK the Cocker is the second most popular dog after the Labrador Retriever.

Perhaps more than any other dog, he lives to please his beloved owner and is happiest doing just that – surrounded by his humans or other dogs. He does not do well when left alone; separation anxiety is not uncommon within the breed. Consider a dog less dependent on company for happiness if you are out at work all day.

The Cocker Spaniel is a hardy dog bred to flush and retrieve game for the guns. He is classed in the Gundog Group in the UK, while in the USA, the American Cocker is the smallest dog in the Sporting Group. Both are simply referred to as 'Cocker Spaniel' in their home country.

The English Cocker is one of the oldest breeds, however, his American cousin is descended from dogs imported into the States from the Britain at the end of the 19th century. The modern American Cocker is smaller with a shorter muzzle, more of a 'teddy bear' face, longer coat and mat have less of a sporting drive.

When treated well, all types of Cocker are noted for their optimistic and friendly temperament as well as their ability to get along with everybody, including children.

As a working dog, the Cocker's body and mind need to be exercised before he can relax. Originally called the 'Cocking Spaniel', he was bred to flush woodcock from cover. Working gundogs can run all day long, and even a Cocker kept as a family pet needs daily exercise to burn off excess energy before he is ready to snuggle down with his owners back at home.

He has a highly developed sense of smell – those long floppy ears help to trap the scent - and loves running through the undergrowth with his nose to the ground. No matter how well trained your Cocker is, you may find that from time to time he becomes totally and temporarily deaf as he heads off full pelt on the trail of a fascinating scent!

Many prospective owners do not realise that there are two different kinds of (English) Cocker Spaniel: the show type – pictured left - and the working type. Several of the 40 breeders involved in this book thought that the differences were so great that the Kennel Club should distinguish between them by classing them as two separate breeds.

The show Cocker is bred for the ring and has longer ears and a longer, denser coat than the working Cocker. Many owners of the show type believe that their dogs are "less hyper" than the working type – read more about what breeders say later in this chapter.

Working Cockers generally have lighter frames, proportionately longer bodies, smaller ears set higher on their heads and less coat and 'feathers'. They may be 'leggier' and are often smaller, although some can be bigger than show Cockers. Dogs that will have an active working life usually have their tails docked to three-quarters length (like the dog pictured below) - although currently this is illegal in Scotland. This is done shortly after birth.

In short, they are more suited to running through dense scrub for hours on end. They may have a high mental and physical energy drive and working Cockers can often be seen taking part in canine competitions as well as field sports. There are also variations within the working type: those bred for the shoot and those bred specifically for the sport of field trials.

Kennel Club Assured Breeder Barry Hutchinson, of Brynovation Gundogs, Gloucestershire, gives a good explanation of the differences, as he sees them: "Dogs bred for the field are required to work long, often relatively fruitless, hours with a minimum of handling in a variety of environments and in pursuit of a variety of quarry.

"By contrast, those specifically bred for field trialling are required to work under intense supervision at very high speed for short periods in a controlled environment, predominantly flushing and retrieving pheasants.

"Generally (and accepting that there will always be exceptions both ways), trialling dogs will be sleeker, highly agile and active; supremely alert and responsive and, consequently, a potential handful for the wrong type of handler. More traditional shooting dogs tend to have greater stamina, a higher tolerance for boredom, require less intensive handling and often appear to have a more relaxed, self-assured, demeanour."

Pictured is Barry's working gundog Amber Aimee.

That's not to say that a show Cocker can't flush or retrieve a bird; with proper training, some do. It does, however, mean that their natural instinct to do so - and prey drive – may not be as strong as that of a working Cocker.

The same is true the other way round; working Cockers can and do become excellent family pets – but they are generally high drive and high energy and best suited to an active household. Sadly, too many end up in rescue centres, handed in by owners who couldn't give either the time or the energy that these rewarding dogs deserve.

If you haven't already got your puppy, find out as much as you can from the breeder about what the dam and sire (parents) were bred for. If you already have your Cocker, contact the breeder to find out what type he is to help you to better understand and train him.

The Different Types of Cocker

English or American?

Wendy Tobijanski, of Janski Cocker Spaniels, Shropshire, has bred both English show-type and American Cockers for 40 years. She says: "There is not much difference between the two breeds really. Both are very much family dogs and make super pets, as well as great show dogs; obviously different pedigree lines can have different temperament traits.

"When buying a puppy, look at several adults from the same lines to gauge temperament. For showing we require dogs to be outgoing, sociable and get on well with both people and dogs; that is why I would always recommend buying from a show breeder.

"I find the Americans (pictured) tend to be more bouncy. They will jump around the house more, making sure they haven't missed anything or anyone out before settling, and therefore require a bit more exercise or would benefit from mental stimulation, like doing agility or obedience or just playing games.

"Both breeds are excellent at agility. My children have had fantastic fun with an agility course set up in the garden - great exercise for both dogs and children and something they can do together. It is really good to see a child's confidence grow as the dog learns what they want them to do and responds well, forming deep bonds between dog and child. Diet also plays a part in a dog's temperament, a lot of cheap foods contain fillers, additives and colourings, all of which a dog can be sensitive to and cause him to be hyperactive."

Working or Show?

Physically, a show Cocker is bred to display certain attributes laid down in the breed standard, such as being a particular height and weight or being well proportioned and "measuring approximately same from withers to ground as from withers to root of tail".

However, few working Cockers conform in every respect to the breed standard. This is because breeders select their working stock based on abilities such as how good the dogs are at flushing and retrieving, rather than how they look. This is why the two types of Cocker Spaniel look so different nowadays.

If you haven't already got your puppy yet, the following comments from breeders might help you to make up your mind about what type of Cocker to get. It's fair to say there is a wide range of opinions on the differences between show and working Cockers. Although they might not always agree on everything, one thing is clear: the breeders' love and passion for their Cocker Spaniels - whether show or working - shines through.

This is what breeders of **show-type** Cockers have to say:

"Dogs from working stock are bred for just that - to work. It is not just physical exercise that they need, but mental exercise as well. They have, quite naturally, a massive instinct to hunt and use their nose. They are always 'on the go' and do need more than the run in the park that the show Cocker would be satisfied with. There are lots of working-bred dogs used in agility, as this is an excellent way for the 'pet' home to give them the mental and physical exercise they need. Show Cockers are a lot calmer and a road walk or a run in the park is adequate. Working dogs are like athletes - the more exercise they get, the more they need."

"Show stock tend to be a bit more docile than workers, who appear to be hyper most of the time. Show ones still have the energy and playfulness though, and will go all day if asked, too."

"My dogs are from show stock, but exhibit many traits of working Cockers. They enjoy flushing out pheasants on a walk and if they spot water, they are in it! They love helping out at the stables all day, but then are very happy to snuggle up with us on the sofa in the evenings. I have homed a show-type pup recently who regularly goes shooting with her owners, although as she is not trained, she doesn't always get it right! I know of working-type Cockers who live happily with active families, though the working traits bred into them probably mean that they would not be as happy in a very quiet home."

Pictured is Haja van Wessem's three month-old show dog Speggle-Waggel Roisin Connor, showing the typical Cocker trait of inquisitiveness.

"There is a big difference between the two types. The best way to describe this is to tell you what we say to new potential owners. The working type is slightly smaller than the show type, they have a much shorter coat and their ears seem to be set much higher on the head.

"A show-type Cocker needs as much exercise as you want to give it. Take one for a long walk and they will run and run for as long as you want them to. Once you get home, they will relax and cuddle up for the rest of the day. If one day you can't take them out, they won't tear your house down. A working Cocker will also run as much as you want it to, but when you get home, they don't stop; they just seem to want to keep going. They tend to need more exercise than the show type."

"Dogs from working stock have a lot of energy and if they are not used for shooting, the owner needs to do other forms of serious exercise with them, such as agility or other forms of sport."

"There is a significant difference between the show type and working type; so much so that I feel they should be registered as separate types by The Kennel Club. The show type (pictured) is more suited to family homes. They are much calmer and have less energy than the working type who, in my experience, require more exercise and stimulation."

"In my experience, most workers will require more daily exercise and stimulation than most show-type Cockers, but this is like saying most men are stronger than most women – there will be many exceptions. That said, I have found that show Cockers are happy to keep going as long as their owners and some can work with the shoots as happily as their working counterparts."

"The construction of the two types is so different that they need to be considered as two breeds. Show Cockers are compact, loving and adorable. When well trained and cared for, they love and respect everyone; this is what keeps me with them."

"Yes I do think there is a difference between working and show Cockers - and the clue is in the name! I own a home boarding business and have visiting working Cockers. They are totally full on, 24/7 and require far more attention and, obviously, exercise than the show types."

This is what breeders of **working Cockers** say:

"I think there is a huge difference in the two strains. I have found show Cockers to be much more relaxed, but noisier than their working cousins. The working types are generally much busier and require more mental stimulation than the show type. Working Cockers have earned their nickname 'pocket rockets' because they are very busy little souls. Overall, the Cocker is a happy, lively, biddable, family-friendly dog. The working strain does need more mental stimulation than the show type, but can still be a wonderful addition to a knowledgeable, active family home."

"Working-type Spaniels are high drive, require a great deal of exercise and stimulation and don't

make good family pets due to this. They are best suited to active, working or sporting homes. Show Cockers are calmer and less high drive and more suited to pet homes where they don't get as much stimulation."

Our photo shows a working Cocker (right) next to a Springer Spaniel.

"They have drive, sprit, trainability, size, intelligence and are good with families, if brought up correctly. I moved into Cockers from Springers and got our first as a gift for my husband. I didn't intend to breed them, but as we fell in love with the personality, the drive and the sometimes stubborn behaviour of the Cockers, we wanted more as part of our working team. They are loyal, fun pocket rockets."

"Having never owned show stock, we cannot provide solid evidence with regard to exercise and temperament. However, with regard to exercise, it is a total myth that working Cockers need a lot of exercise. They need daily exercise, but are more than happy with a mixture of long and short walks."

"There is a massive difference; they are nearly different breeds. Working Cockers have big hearts and are rarely short on determination."

"In my opinion, the stark and very apparent differences between work and show strains of Cocker Spaniels should be recognised by The Kennel Club, and reflected in a reclassification as two separate pedigree breeds. Diversity is what attracted us to the Cocker. I have never come across a dog breed that can transverse so completely and seamlessly from an armchair to a pheasant covert, and back again just as easily. It is not just that an individual dog can be cultured to a particular lifestyle from being a puppy, an individual dog can adopt a whole variety of lifestyles at once, and move between them with absolute ease."

"I feel there is a big difference between the two types, and owners should be vetted properly for working strain as they need a lot of exercise and stimulation. Personally, I love their affectionate nature and their eagerness to please. From a pet point of view, they are very cuddly and love to be around you. Initially, I was attracted to the breed because they are good with children; they are also very good with other pets."

"I believe that dogs from working stock have much higher energy levels than show stock, but am not aware of any major differences in temperament. I think that their current popularity has a lot to do with being 'on trend' – the Duke and Duchess of Cambridge have a black working Cocker.

Having said that, I think what makes them so popular is that they do have a lovely nature – very loving, loyal and the combination of intelligence with a streak of 'madness' was a huge attraction for me. I was also looking for a dog to work on a local shoot and did not want a big dog, so the working Cocker Spaniel was ideal for me. They are fun, enthusiastic, intelligent and loyal."

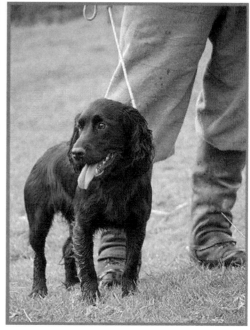

Pictured is Stewart North's Pip (Toadsspannel Foxey at Northglen).

"I would say that there is no difference in temperament. However, in terms of exercise, working Cockers have a very high hunt drive, bred in for generations and need a consistent outlet for this. The desire to cover ground and hunt out game does not make a working Cocker an ideal pet for some people, as they will inevitably want to hunt out every hedgerow, clump of grass etc. This natural instinct needs to be harnessed with training that exercises their bodies and brains, such as agility competitions, etc."

"I have three different generations of working Cockers asleep by my feet right now. In the house they are reasonably calm, outside the house they are energetic and inquisitive. They are good natured and unaggressive. I chose working Cockers because of their ability to work all day without flagging, to do what they are bred for, to be trained (fairly easily) and yet be quite happy at home in front of the fire with a warm, full belly. They are beautiful dogs, small enough to take anywhere, yet strong enough to go through anything, be it bramble or brook. They are intelligent with eyes that steal your heart, funny and clever, yet biddable with a desire to please. Mine are quite quiet, only barking if a stranger comes to the door."

"Oh, my! Absolutely there is a difference between the two types. They don't look like the same breed any more, a lot of people have suggested that they be split. I did buy a show strain and tried to train it to the gun, it completely lacked any drive, hated water and was gun shy, hence she lives with my sister as a pet!"

"I far prefer the temperaments of working Cockers. I've never had any concerns and never heard a growl between them or towards people. Exercise-wise, once the dogs are adults of over 18 months old, I think the working type needs more exercise, but also mental stimulation too. However, the more exercise they get, the more they expect. A working Cocker is cheerful and intelligent with a glint of mischief in the eye."

"There is a big difference in both temperament and exercise requirements. Working dogs have a very high working instinct and all they want to do is hunt, i.e. flush game for the guns. They are far more lively and energetic than show stock and, if not given the opportunity to use those instincts, can become a problem. I like the fact that they usually get on with everyone and everything. I think that is the reason they are popular, possibly combined with the fact they are very appealing puppies."

"The UK Kennel Club makes no distinction between show and working Cocker (English), but there is a major difference in exercise requirements and a minor difference in temperament. The working Cocker is intelligent, high energy and biddable with a massive heart."

"Show Cockers are much more laid back, shorter legged and broader bodied, the ears also sit lower. The working Cocker is the lean, longer-legged breed with masses of energy. You will be lucky to tire one out! They are lively and intelligent with a stunning character."

Cocker Character

To say all dogs of the same breed are alike would be akin to saying that all Americans are optimistic and friendly and all Brits are polite and reserved. It is, of course, a huge generalisation. There are grumpy, unfriendly Americans or rude in-your-face Brits.

However, it is also true to say that being friendly and optimistic are general American traits (just like the Cocker!), as is being polite in Britain. See **Chapter 8. Behaviour** for more information on typical Cocker Spaniel traits.

All dogs are individuals and character varies from one dog to the next. It depends to a large extent on two things. The first is his **temperament**, which he inherits - and presumably one of the reasons why you have chosen a Cocker.

The Kennel Club describes the Cocker as: "An active, happy, small dog, who quickly adapts himself to his surroundings. He is highly intelligent and affectionate, and is in his element foraging around fields and hedgerows. He also employs his retrieving instincts around the house, and can often be found with a toy or slipper in his mouth, his tail wagging furiously, waiting for praise."

However, as well as being born with the trademark physical features, your dog also inherits his temperament from his parents and ancestors. Good breeders select their breeding stock based not only on appearance, but also on what sort of disposition he or she has and, with working Cockers, how good the dam and sire are at doing a specific job.

The second important factor is **environment** – or how you rear and treat your dog. In other words, it's a combination of **Nature and Nurture**.

The first few months in a dog's life are so important. Once he has left the litter, he takes his lead from you as he learns to react to the world around him. Even though Cockers generally start out affectionate and even-tempered, it is essential to spend time getting to understand your new dog. Through training, exercise, playing, grooming and feeding a strong bond and trust will develop between the two of you.

One essential aspect of helping your dog to become a well-adjusted adult is socialisation. Introduce him to other animals and humans, as well as noises, traffic and lots of new new situations as soon as he comes home. A dog comfortable in his surroundings without fear or anxieties is less likely to display unwanted behaviour such as biting, growling, possessiveness, fear or disobedience. He also learns not to be selfish and to share you, his food and toys with others.

For the right owner, the Cocker Spaniel is a canine companion second to none, he thrives on your attention and loves to please you. Here's how some breeders sum up their trusty companions: "Bouncy, loving, enthusiastic, loyal," "Stunning," "We would not be without them," "Loving, loyal, fun and happy," "Best breed ever!" "Affectionate, happy, lively, bonkers!" "Fun, active, but gentle and loving," "Happy, intelligent and endearing," "Loving, loyal, adorable companions," "Happy, loving and biddable," "Fun, intelligent, trying, delightful," "Fun, high drive and in for the ride!"

Read on and learn more about this unique breed, how to take good care of your dog, how to socialise and train him and how to build that special bond that will become one of the most important relationships in your life...and certainly his.

2. History of the Cocker Spaniel

By Haja van Wessem

Origins

Without a doubt the Spaniel is one of the oldest breeds in history. Its origins date back over a thousand years and the breed has been recorded for posterity in literature, law and art. It is generally thought that the name 'Spaniel' derives from the word Spain, or Hispania as it used to be called.

Between 910 and 948 Wales was ruled by King Hywel Dda (Hywel the Good), who was the initiator of the codification of existing laws – i.e. he drew up a new legal code. The Spaniel was at that time already present in Wales, brought, some say, by the Spanish clan of Ebhor or Ivor many centuries before. In his Book of Laws (pictured), mammals were divided in three kinds: Birds, Beasts and Hounds, and the Hounds had three subdivisions:

> ➢ Hounds for the Scent
> ➢ Greyhounds
> ➢ Spaniels

The Greyhound and Spaniel were the favourite hunting dogs for many generations. King Hywel Dda also laid down in his Book of Laws that "*The Spaniel of the King is a pound of value.*" We have to remember that in the year AD 948, a pound could buy several wives, slaves, horses, oxen, turkeys and geese! So the Spaniel was certainly a dog of both high reputation and value at that time.

During the Crusades of 1095 to 1291, noblemen were often accompanied by huntsmen and their dogs, which interbred with dogs in the Arabian countries, and the noblemen brought these crossbreeds back to their own country. These dogs became very popular with the Royals because of their excellent hunting abilities and were also regarded as status symbols; their owners had, after all, fought for their religion.

Between the 10th and 15th centuries, these crossbreeds produced offspring with excellent hunting qualities. They spread out over the continent and developed in different ways, according to the country where they lived and the work they were asked to do. In France they became Epagneuls (French for Spaniel), in Germany Wachtelhunde, in the Netherlands they were the Spioen and in Great Britain the Spaniel.

Much of the Spaniel's history can be found in literature. Mention of a Spaniel is made in Geoffrey Chaucer's (1343-1400) *Canterbury Tales*. The Tales are about a group of pilgrims travelling together who pass the time by each telling a story, the themes of which are courtly love, treason, avarice and adultery. *The Wife of Bath's Tale* is about a woman who had been married five times (very unusual in those days) and who was looking for Husband Number Six. The storyteller compared her with a Spaniel: "*She coveteth every man that she may se: for as a spaynel she wol on hym lepe*".

A contemporary of Chaucer, Gaston III, Count of Foix, owned an estate in south west France. Between 1350 and 1390 he was the leader of a band of adventurers who travelled from the Pyrenees to Scandinavia. Between his travels he stayed on his estate, Orthez, where he dedicated himself to his three passions: weapons, love and hunting. In 1387, at over 50 years of age and finding himself too old for warfare and love, he decided to devote himself solely to the hunt.

Between 1387 and 1391 he wrote a book on hunting, *Livre de Chasse*, which was translated into English by Edmund de Langley as *The Book of Hunting*. It contained beautiful images (pictured) and was one of the first books on hunting.

De Foix, who also used the name Gaston Phébus, referred to the Spaniel: "*Another kind of hound there is that be called hounds for the hawk and Spaniels, for their kind cometh from Spain, notwithstanding that there are many in other countries. A good Spaniel should not be too rough, but his tail should be rough.*"

In 1486 the first list of domesticated dogs appeared in *The Book of St. Albans*. The book was probably meant as teaching material for the pupils of the school in the Hertfordshire town. Dame Juliana Berners (pictured), said to be Prioress of the nearby St. Mary of Sopwell Convent, is considered to be the author. In the chapter on hunting, she writes: "Thyse ben the names of houndes, fyrste there is a Grehoun, a Bastard, a Mengrell, a Mastiff, a Lemor, a Spanyel, Raches, Kenettys, Teroures, Butchers' Houndes, Myddyng dogges, Tryndel-taylles, and Prikherid currys, and smalle ladyes' poppees that bere awaye the flees." The last part refers to small lapdogs to fend off the fleas of their mistress!

In that same period, Dr John Keye (or Kaye) published *Canibus Britannicus* in Latin under his pseudonym, Dr Caius. Later it was translated into English as *Treatise of English Dogges*. Dr Caius described four kinds of dogs: the Venatici for the hunt of big game, the Aucupatorii for the hunt of small game, the Delicati such as Toy Spaniel or Comforter, and the Rustici such as the Pastoralis (herding dog) and the Villaticus (mastiff). The group of Aucupatorii he subdivided into Hispaniolus or Spainel, Setter and Aquaticus or Water Spaniel.

During the hunt, Spaniels were used to flush the game so that a bird of prey, usually a hawk, could catch the game. During Henri VIII's reign (1509-1547), large parties were held at the court with great feasts and the demand for game was inexhaustible. Partridge, quail, pheasant, rabbit and hare were caught with the snare, but demand surpassed supply. Huntsmen began to look for other means to catch the game and they discovered the use of the net.

A dog flushed the game from its cover, sat down and the huntsman threw a net over the game and the dog. The dogs they used with the net were called 'setting' or 'sitting Spaniels' and are the ancestors of our modern Setters. The dogs that were used to flush the game were called 'springing Spaniels'; this does not mean that the dogs had to spring, but rather that it was their job to make the game spring from its cover.

The first mention of a 'Cocker Spaniel' dates from William Taplin's 1803 book "*The Sporting Dictionary and Rural Repository of general information upon every subject appertaining to The Sports of the Field*". He writes: "*Spaniel is the name of a dog of which there are different kinds; and even these have been so repeatedly crossed that, unless it is in the possession of sportsmen who have been careful in preserving the purity of the breed perfectly free from casual contamination, the well-bred genuine cocking Spaniel is difficult to obtain*". Here we have the proof that the Cocker Spaniel already existed in 1803.

Dog Shows and Early Breeders

The first official dog show took place on June 28th and 29th, 1859 in Newcastle-upon-Tyne. Sixty Pointers and Setters were entered, no other breeds. The dogs were entered under the name of their owner, such as 'Mr. Murrel's Spot' and 'Mr Brown's Venus.' In 1870 it was decided that regulations were necessary and this resulted in the formation of The Kennel Club on April 4th, 1873. Since most dogs were named simply Spot, Bob, Jet and Vic, it soon became necessary to create some order among all these Spots, Bobs, Jets and Vics, so one of first tasks of The Kennel Club was to introduce a Stud Book.

Victorian gentlemen of pleasure became very interested in exhibitions as a form of instructive recreation. The new railways made travelling throughout the country possible and many of these gentlemen visited the Great Exhibition in London in 1851. In the following years, many exhibitions of various kinds were organised and more and more dog shows were held all over the country.

Around 1850 Cocker Spaniels showed little uniformity in type. They were often named after the county they lived in: Welsh Cocker, Devon Cocker, Norfolk Spaniel. To complicate matters, Land Spaniels (as opposed to Water Spaniels) were often called Field Spaniels, but the Field Spaniel as we know him today dates from a much later period.

According to the Victorian canine expert John Henry Walsh (1810-1888), who wrote under the pseudonym 'Stonehenge', there was a great variety of Cocker Spaniel colours: white, black, liver, red and white, lemon and white, liver and white and black and white. As for the body, Stonehenge describes its length as "rather more than twice his height as the shoulder." It's true to say this Cocker Spaniel didn't look much like our modern Cocker, which is a compact dog who should measure  the same from withers to ground as from withers to base of tail. Pictured is a Cocker Spaniel from 1880.

Much to the chagrin of the breeders, the Cocker disappeared from the second edition of the Stud Book, whereas the Irish Water Spaniel, Clumber Spaniel and Sussex Spaniel all had their own chapter. The Cocker was included in the Field Spaniels chapter (less than 11.5kg).

The Field Spaniel, also called Land Spaniel or Black Spaniel (pictured on the following page), was a big, black Spaniel bred from crosses between the Cocker, Norfolk and Sussex Spaniels. With his long body and short legs, this Field Spaniel became intensely popular at the exhibitions. 'Long' became the rage and breeders went to the extreme in their aim to breed long Field Spaniels. There were still Cockers around, the only difference between them and the Field Spaniel being the weight. The Field was classified as weighing more than 12kg and the Cocker less than 11.5kg. So it was possible for Field Spaniels and Cocker Spaniels to be born into a single litter, and for a dog originally registered as Cocker Spaniel to be re-registered as a Field Spaniel if he grew up and became too heavy for a Cocker.

It was around 1890 that breeders, who for the greater part also worked with their Spaniels, realised that the exaggerated 'cucumber dogs' as they were mockingly called, were unfit for work. In order to be able to retrieve game, the body of the dog should be in balance. But in these 'cucumber dogs' the centre of gravity lay much too far forwards, causing back trouble and crooked legs.

This insight led to the salvation of the Cocker. A large number of breeders decided to abandon the long-backed type and aim for a more balanced Cocker with a shorter body and longer legs. They suggested that The Kennel Club no longer have dogs judged on weight at shows, but rather on type. And in 1892 The Kennel Club took the wise decision to recognise the Field Spaniel and the Cocker Spaniel as two different breeds.

In 1902 the Cocker Spaniel Club was founded and a new breed description was issued. The length of the body was no longer mentioned, but on weight the standard stated: "It should not exceed 25lb, or 11.5kg, or be less than 20lb, or 9kg."

This marked a new era of prosperity for the Cocker Spaniel. More and more breeders discovered this attractive and talented working dog and, until the outbreak of World War I, Cockers grew in popularity, quantity and quality. Of those early breeders there are a few we should remember because they laid the basis for our Cocker as we know him today.

James Farrow was one such breeder. He bred a black dog called Obo, born on June 14th, 1879. Obo (pictured) wasn't a big dog but nevertheless was a great winner at shows. His greatest fame, however, came through his offspring, as he went on to produce a whole dynasty of winners. Farrow line bred and in-bred to this famous dog in an effort to set type. Obo probably did more for consolidating Cockers and the Cocker type than any other dog that ever lived[1]. If we go back we will find Obo in the pedigree of a great many of our modern Cockers. Obo's son, Obo II, went to the USA and became the founder of the American Cocker Spaniel.

In those days Cockers were mostly black or black and tan, but in 1900 James Farrow entered the ring with Sandy Obo, a liver roan and tan. Sandy was twice Best of Breed at Crufts. In 1902 Farrow founded the Cocker Spaniel Club of Great Britain, and in 1904 decided to retire from breeding but remained active as a judge. A contemporary of his was Richard Lloyd from Hertfordshire who started his breeding in 1870.

---

[1] Peggy Grayson in *A History of the Cocker Spaniel* (1992)

Although he used quite different lines from James Farrow, he was equally successful; the only difference between him and James Farrow being that Richard Lloyd never hesitated to sell good quality dogs to other breeders or to use stud dogs of other breeders. He was quite open about the way his dogs were bred, whereas Farrow was rather secretive about his breeding lines. Experts find it difficult to believe that a great and influential dog like Obo should have parents simply named Fred and Betty, but James Farrow never gave more information.

Prefixes in those days were not customary, but Lloyd wanted to give his dogs a 'family name' and used the word 'Little' in front of their names. The world famous prefix 'of Ware' was registered in 1906 by his son, Herbert Summers Lloyd (H.S. Lloyd), who took over the dogs after his father's death. Other famous breeders in the first decades of the 20th century were John Porter (Braeside), C.A. Philips (Rivington), R. De Courcy Peele (Bowdler) and Mrs Jamieson Higgins (Falconers). It is through the dedication of these people that the breed was in such a good state at the outbreak of World War I, which meant that after the war many breeders were able to continue where they had left off.

The period from 1920 onwards was the Golden Era for the breed. Herbert Lloyd was largely responsible for the Cocker Spaniel becoming the most successful breed in the modern era of Crufts since the Best in Show title was introduced in 1928. Of the Cocker's seven titles, all but one were from the of Ware kennel, owned and bred by him. Only four dogs have won Best in Show more than once, and three of these were Cockers owned by Lloyd: Luckystar of Ware (1930 and 1931), Exquisite Model of Ware (1938 and 1939) and, after a gap during World War II, he proved his absolute supremacy by winning again in 1948 and 1950 with Tracey Witch of Ware.

His death in 1973 was a great loss; the breed lost a successful and highly respected authority who was always willing to share his knowledge with others. His daughter Jennifer Lloyd Carey took over the kennels, later with her daughter, Paula. Herbert is pictured here with three of his dogs, including Luckystar of Ware (centre).

We have to be grateful to many breeders who bred Cockers before World War II and managed to come back after the war with dogs of great quality. Going back in the pedigrees of many solid coloured Cockers, we find Treetops Cockers, bred by Mrs Judy de Casembroot, or Sixshot Cockers, bred by Mrs Veronica Lucas-Lucas. Other renowned breeders of solids were Mrs Kay Doxford (Broomleaf) and Mrs Dorothy Hahn (Misbourne). Joe Braddon was a famous judge but also a breeder of Irish Setters and parti-coloured Cocker Spaniels. Also the Weirdene, Lochranza and Quettadene kennels know a long history.

Between 1960 and 1970 more and more successful breeders of parti-coloured Cockers came to the fore: Mrs Chadwick's Merryworth, Mr and Mrs Ron Bebb's Ronfill, Mr and Mrs Jones's Courtdale, Mr Arthur Mansfield's Lucklena, Mrs Mollie Robinson's Craigleith and Mr and Mrs Caddy's Ouaine, to name but a few. Their Champion Ouaine Chieftain was Reserve Best in Show at Crufts in 1970.

The Bitcon Cockers, mainly blue roans, were at the top for many years; the most famous being Sh Ch Bitcon Troubador who sired a great number of winning offspring at home and abroad. Mrs Denise Barney, of Cilleine fame, bred parti-coloured and solid Cockers. Her Sh Ch Cilleine Echelon was top Cocker in 1981, 1982 and 1983.

Mr and Mrs Schofield had the Scolys prefix. They bred the light blue roan Ch Scolys Starduster who became famous in his own right, but who also made his mark on the breed through his daughter Ch Bournehouse Starshine (pictured), bred by the late Gordon Williams. Starshine is considered to be the prototype for the breed. Other later kennels still successfully active nowadays are Mrs Jackie Marris-Bray's Helenwood, Mrs Susan Young's Canyonn, Mrs Sandy Platt's Charbonnel and Mrs Anne Webster's Asquannes.

Mrs Patricia Bentley has been extremely successful with her solid coloured Canigou Cockers. She started in 1968 and has since bred numerous champions. Sh Ch Canigou Cambrai (pictured, below left) was Best in Show at Crufts in 1996 and holds the record for the largest number of Championship certificates ever won by a Cocker. In 2012 three Cockers bred by her were in the top five list and two others did well at Crufts. In 1994 the orange roan Sh Ch Lynwater Dawn Shimmer, bred by Mrs Elisabeth MacLean, won the Gundog Group and in 2000 Sh Ch Wiljana Waterfall, a daughter of Sh Ch Bitcon Troubador, bred by Mrs Pamela Halkett, was Reserve Best in Show at Crufts.

Other top breeders of our time are Mrs Angela Hackett (Lindridge), Mr and Mrs Grice (Kyna), Mrs Jean Gilmore (Chavez), Mr Michael Masters (Manchela), Mrs Annie and Mrs Sue Kettle (Lujesa), Mr Andrew Jones and Mrs Jane Simmons (Shenmore) and Mrs Sarah Amos-Jones (Cassom), as well as others too numerous to mention.

The Cocker Spaniel is a gundog and has always been used as such. From the very beginning the dogs were bred and used to work in the field. In the first half of the 20th century a Cocker who won prizes at Field Trials could become Field Trial Champion (FT Ch). When his owner took him to shows and he won their prizes as well, he could become a 'full Champion' (Ch).

In 1958 The Kennel Club decided to award the title of Show Champion (Sh Ch) to a dog that had won three Challenge Certificates. This decision turned out to be of immense influence in the development of the breed, in terms of conformation, temperament and size. In many gundog breeds it has led to a divide between show type and working type.

Unfortunately, not before long that happened in Cockers too and nowadays the show Cocker and the working Cocker look very different. For a short period after 1958 the show Cocker and the working Cocker were interbred, but not so much anymore and they have become unlike each other in conformation and temperament.

The working Cocker has less feathering and shorter ears than the show type, often with a longer, lighter frame and more pointed face. Today in the UK - excluding Scotland - working dogs have a three-quarters docked tail, while show-type Cockers have full tails. Many Cockers actively work on shoots and flush out game such as pheasant, duck and woodcock. (Pictured is Cilcraig Prospect). The ultimate accolade for the working Cocker is winning the Kennel Club's Cocker Spaniel Championship, which was first held in 1925.

Nobody has been more successful at field

trialling than Ian Openshaw, of Rytex Gundogs, Shropshire. He has created a unique record in the history of gundog field trials: 100 Field Trial Champions, a phenomenal achievement which is unlikely to ever be beaten, many of them with Cocker Spaniels. Ian and wife Wendy have trained and exported Spaniels to America, Sweden, Italy, Denmark and Canada, where they have gone on to win these countries' championships.

Cocker Spaniels are extremely popular, particularly in the UK. The Kennel Club registered 22,577 Cocker puppies in 2015, making the breed the second most popular after the Labrador Retriever (32,000). The versatility of the breed means that today the dogs can be seen in a variety of roles, not only at shows, shoots and field trials, but at canine competitions such as agility and flyball, where they excel. They are also widely used as sniffer dogs by the customs and police services and their gentle nature combined with intelligence makes them eminently suitable as assistance and therapy dogs.

Few breeds can claim to have such a multitude of talents, and the Cocker Spaniel has a broad appeal. Celebrity owners, past and present, include John F. Kennedy, Bing Crosby, Lucille Ball, Rita Hayworth, Lauren Bacall, Elizabeth Taylor, Roger Daltry of The Who and, the most famous of them all today, The Duke and Duchess of Cambridge, whose beloved black Cocker, Lupo, accompanies them whenever and wherever possible.

The Cocker Spaniel has been immortalised by perhaps the greatest tribute paid to any breed in literature. Flush was a Cocker Spaniel given to poet Elizabeth Barrett Browning (1806-1861) by author and fellow dog lover Mary Russell Mitford as a gift to relieve Elizabeth's grief following the death of her beloved brother in 1840. Here is the first verse of her famous poem *Flush, My Dog*:

> *Loving friend, the gift of one,*
> *Who, her own true faith, hath run,*
> *Through thy lower nature;*
> *Be my benediction said*
> *With my hand upon thy head,*
> *Gentle fellow-creature!*

History of the American Cocker

Spaniels can be traced back to 1620 and the landing of the Mayflower, which brought a Mastiff and a Spaniel to New England. However, it's not possible to trace the ancestry of modern American Cockers to this first Spaniel, as there were no stud books until the late 19th century. Incidentally, American Cockers are simply known as 'Cocker Spaniels' in America, just as English Cockers are known as 'Cocker Spaniels' in the UK.

As we have read, the dog considered to be the founder of the modern American Cocker was a black dog called Obo II imported into the USA at the end of the 19th century. The Cocker became quite a popular dog in America and, just as in Britain, they were either classed as Field Spaniels or Cocker Spaniels, according to their body weight.

In 1881, two of the first breeders, James Watson and Clinton Wilmerding, invited a group of their Spaniel-owning friends to form what was first known as the American Cocker Spaniel Club, later the American Spaniel Club, the oldest breed club in the United States. The club's first task was to write separate breed standards for the Cocker and Field Spaniels. They received little support from Britain, where the Cocker and the Field were still interbred, and it was only after endless discussions, compromises and disagreements between themselves that separate breed standards were finally achieved.

CHAMPION OBO II
Whelped August 7, 1882. A.K.C. No. 4911. Black

The Field Spaniel had to be heavier, longer and lower on the leg than the Cocker. The Cocker was allowed to weigh between 8 and 12.5kg and the Field between 12.5 and 20kg. All colours were permitted, but "the beauty of the colour and the markings should be taken into account".

The American Kennel Club (founded in 1884) finally decided to recognise the Cocker and the Field as two different breeds, but only as far as the shows were concerned. In the Stud Book they were still registered as one breed, and it wasn't until 1905 that they began to be registered separately.

It was only in 1892 that The Kennel Club in Britain recognised the two separate breeds. However, in reality, there still was little distinction. For instance, Ch Compton Brahmin, a Cocker, was the sire of Ch Compton Bandit, a Field Spaniel with a Cocker Spaniel as his mother!

The first Cockers in America were the offspring of Obo II (pictured, above) and dogs from the Braeside kennels of John Porter in Britain. Over the years the conformation of the Cocker changed dramatically in America (see illustration, below left). Obo II was 25cm high, weighed 10kg and was 52cm long from the tip of the nose to the base of his tail; his shape was indeed the desired 'cucumber' model.

The popularity of the Cocker Spaniel increased rapidly. In 1921 the black and white Ch Midkiff Seductive, owned by W.T. Payne, was best in show at the prestigious Westminster Kennel Club Show, the American equivalent of Crufts. This success was repeated in 1940 and 1941 by the black Ch My Own Brucie, bred by the legendary Herman Mellenthin.

Cockers were long, low and heavy, but the trend for shorter bodies and longer legs became gradually more apparent, along with other influences. It's thought that the main reason for a smaller dog is that the American woodcock is smaller than the European variety, although few American Cockers are used for hunting these days.

The American breeders also did not like the 'hound-like' head of the Cocker Spaniel and

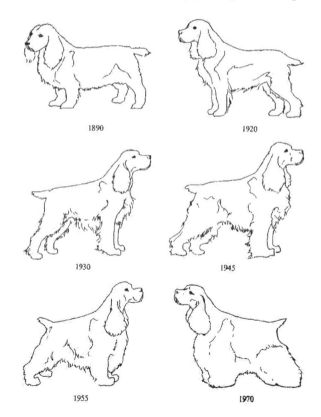

1890
1920
1930
1945
1955
1970

started to breed dogs with shorter heads. Thus, by the 1920s we again see two types of Cocker Spaniel - but this time the English Cocker type and the American Cocker type, although they were still shown and judged as one breed.

In 1930 Herman Mellenthin began breeding his My Own kennel of Cocker Spaniels. One of his bitches, Ree's Dolly, was mated to Robinhurst Foreglow's and one of the offspring of this combination was Red Brucie. Red Brucie (pictured) never became a champion and did not win prizes, but his name lives on in his offspring and in that of his three half-brothers, all of them sons of Robinhurst Foreglow. It was their influence that made the Cocker Spaniel the most popular of all dogs in the USA in 1936. Along with the four Foreglow sons, Herman Mellenthin was able to breed Cocker Spaniels which brought him and his dogs great fame. The influence of his dogs on the breed is unmistakable. He bred many famous Cockers and was the country's top breeder up to the end of World War II.

In 1935 dogs were divided by their colour, the solid ones were split into Black, Any Solid Colour other than Black (ASCOB), and particolour.

Surprisingly, it was not the breeders of the American type who sought recognition for their breed, but the breeders of the English type. They didn't like how their dogs were gradually losing ground to the American type, which was still classed as an (English) Cocker Spaniel. Fervent dog and Cocker Spaniel fancier Geraldine Dodge published a beautifully illustrated book on the English type, with which she managed to persuade the American Kennel Club to recognise the English Cocker Spaniel as a separate breed from the American version in 1946.

Other famous early breeders of American Cocker Spaniels were Arthur and Ruth Benhoff (Artru) and Mari Doty (No-Mar); later breeders who went on to produce top quality dogs include Edna Anselmi (Windy Hill), Karen and Vernon Marquez (Marquis), Laura and Kap Henson (Kaplar) and Betty Durland (Dur-Bet).

The mid and second half of the 20th century became the breed's Golden Age. The Cocker Spaniel's great popularity in the US led to frequent use of images of the breed in advertising, prints and greeting cards. And a female Cocker hit the silver screen in a big way as the demure, long-eared love interest in the 1955 Disney film 'Lady and the Tramp.'

The American Cocker was the most popular dog in the United States during the 1940s and 1950s and again during the 1980s, reigning for a total of 18 years. At the height of popularity in the 1980s, annual registrations reached almost 100,000. They are currently around 50,000 a year (fewer than 1,500 English Cockers are registered in the US each year).

The breed has also won Best in Show at Westminster four times and has been owned by

Presidents of the United States, including Richard Nixon and Harry S. Truman. Today American Cockers are the smallest dogs in the Sporting group. They have a shorter muzzle, longer and softer coat, rounder eyes, a domed skull and more clearly pronounced eyebrows than their English cousins. The roan colours are rarer in the American variety, and the buff shade, which is common in the American, is not seen at all in the English version. The American Cocker Spaniel ranked 30th in the AKC registration statistics for 2015.

Today the American Cocker's appeal is largely as a handsome and 'merry' pet, and the breed has attracted many famous owners past and present, including fashion icon Oscar de la Renta, Oprah Winfrey, George Clooney, Charlize Theron, Mariah Carey and Mentalist star Simon Baker.

The Return to the UK

Initially, a few American Cockers arrived in the UK via service personnel on American bases in the 1950s and 1960s, and several came over with embassy staff and business people returning from the US. The first American Cocker to be registered in the UK was Aramingo Argonaught, born on January 17th, 1956 and bred by Herbert L. Steinberg. Two judges confirmed that the dog was an American Cocker and not an English Cocker before the Kennel Club permitted the dog to be shown.

In the 1960s, Americans were shown as a rare breed, which meant that they did not have a show class of their own and could only be shown in variety classes. This included Aramingo Argonaught who, in 1960, had the distinction of being the first American Cocker to be shown at Crufts. It was in 1968 that the Kennel Club agreed to have the breed shown in the category "Any Variety Gundog Other than Cocker" and stated that the American Cocker was not a variety of "Spaniel (Cocker)". There were around 100 registrations from 1966 to 1968.

The American Cocker Spaniel Club of Great Britain was founded in 1967 and the first Open Show was held on August 22nd, 1970. In 1970 the breed was given a separate register in the Kennel Club Breed Supplement, it had previously been included in "Any Other Variety". The first Championship Show was held three years later.

Following the success of Am Ch Dreamridge Delegate in the Gundog Group at Crufts in 1972, the Club was informed that the breed was to be transferred to the Utility Group! This resulted in a terrific furore amongst breeders and exhibitors, both at home and overseas, and generated a tremendous amount of support from other breeds. The committee had a meeting with members of the Kennel Club in 1972, with the result that the ruling would be delayed for two years, during which time breeders were to prove the working ability of the breed and reduce the excessive coat.

The late Dick Wylde played a great part by qualifying two of his bitches to their full title and nothing more was heard of the proposed move. It has, in fact, become more common for these likeable dogs to fulfil their working potential; it is no longer an unusual sight to see the American Cocker both in the field and at trials and they are becoming a common sight in the Gamekeeper classes at Crufts. Dick Wylde's were the last full champions, until Mrs Knapper-Weijland's bitch qualified for her full title in 2007.

The breed has many followers and several breeders have produced top dogs able to win groups and Best in Shows. The American Cocker has won Top Dog All Breeds twice and the Top Gundog seven times in the Dog World and Our Dogs competition, where points are accumulated for wins at shows to find an overall champion. In 2015 there were 223 dogs registered with the Kennel Club in the UK.

3. The Breed Standard

The **breed standard** is what makes a Cocker Spaniel a Cocker Spaniel, a Great Dane a Great Dane and a Chihuahua a Chihuahua. It is a blueprint not only for the appearance of each breed, but also for character and temperament, how the dog moves and what colours are acceptable. In other words, it ensures that the Cocker Spaniel looks like a Cocker Spaniel and is "fit for function."

The breed standard is laid down by the breed societies. The UK Kennel Club - or AKC (American Kennel Club) in the US - keeps the register of pedigree (purebred) dogs. Dogs entered in conformation shows run under Kennel Club and AKC rules are judged against this ideal list of attributes. Breeders approved by the Kennel Clubs agree to produce puppies in line with the breed standard and maintain certain welfare conditions.

Kennel Club registered and Assured Breeders select only the best dogs for reproduction, based on factors such as the health, looks, temperament and the character of the parents and their ancestors. They do not simply take any available male and female and allow them to randomly breed.

They also aim to reduce or eradicate genetic illnesses. In the case of Cockers, these include eye problems and Hip Dysplasia, as well as Familial Nephropathy and Acral Mutilation Syndrome in English Spaniels, and PKF, a metabolic disorder affecting some American Cockers.

The Kennel Clubs in the UK, North America and Europe all have lists of breeders. If you have not yet got a puppy, this is a good place to start looking for one. Visit the Kennel Club website in your country for details of approved breeders.

Pictured is Dutch breeder Haja van Wessem with her multi champion show Cocker Speggle-Waggel's Xandy, aged two.

NOTE: If you are buying a Cocker from working lines specifically for the shoot or field trialling, he or she may not conform exactly to the Cocker Spaniel breed standard. This is because gamekeepers and other breeders of working Spaniels may select their breeding stock based on how good the dog is at flushing and retrieving, with less emphasis on appearance. Puppies bred from proven working dogs and field trial champions are highly sought after - regardless of whether or not they reach a specific height or have a square muzzle. However, health is still a major consideration and prospective buyers should check which tests have been carried out on a working puppy's parents.

A breed standard is an essential factor in maintaining the look and temperament of any breed. But in the past, breeders of some types of dog have concentrated too closely on the appearance of the animal without paying enough attention to soundness and health. In response, the Kennel Club set up Breed Watch, which serves as an 'early warning system' to identify points of concern for individual breeds.

Cockers in the UK - particularly working Cockers - are bred from a fairly small gene pool, compared with some other breeds. This is partly because people looking for a working Cocker have been attracted to puppies from successful field champions. The average COI (measurement of inbreeding) for Cocker Spaniels in the UK is 9%, which is relatively high. It's even higher at around 11% for working Cockers, according to breeder Kerena Marchant, of Surrey. Despite this, English Cockers are listed in the healthiest group - Category 1 - in Breed Watch, with no major points of concern.

In the UK, American Cocker Spaniels are listed in Category 2, with the following points of concern: excessively prominent eyes, incorrect bite and incorrect dentition. However, the average COI is just 4%, which means that puppies are likely to have a bigger gene pool and therefore a wider range of ancestors.

Another interesting factor with the English Cocker Spaniel is that, as mentioned, there are two distinct types: **show** and **working** Cocker. As yet the Kennel Club classes them both under one breed standard, despite working dogs often being smaller (sometimes bigger) and generally regarded as having a higher energy drive and need for mental stimulation than show Cockers.

Some breeders believe that the differences are so great that Cockers should be split into two separate breeds by the Kennel Club.

The dog pictured is an English Cocker Spaniel from working stock, also called field stock. She has a slightly docked tail. The American Cocker also has a docked tail in the US. While docking became illegal in Europe in 2007, it is still legal to dock a working Spaniel in most of Europe – but not Scotland and some Scandinavian countries.

(At the time of writing – 2016 - there is lobbying to change the law in Scotland to allow tail docking of working dogs).

Traditionally, docking was done to prevent injury as the dog ran through heavy brush to flush or retrieve game. With Spaniels, as much as three-quarters is left on – as in the photo - and the breed's trademark permanently wagging tail is still very much in evidence. English pets and show dogs have full tails.

If you are serious about getting a Cocker Spaniel, then study the breed standard before visiting any puppies, so you know what a well-bred example should look like. If you've already bought one, these are features your dog should display:

UK Breed Standard (English Cocker)

The Cocker is the smallest of all the Spaniels and classed in the Gundog Group in the UK, along with all the other Spaniels, Retrievers, Setters, Pointers, Brittanys and Hungarian Vizlas.

The Kennel Club describes them as: "Dogs that were originally trained to find live game and/or to retrieve game that had been shot and wounded.

"This group is divided into four categories - Retrievers, Spaniels, Hunt/Point/Retrieve, Pointers and Setters - although many of the breeds are capable of doing the same work as the other sub-groups. They make good companions, their temperament making them ideal all-round family dogs."

Here is the KC's description of the Cocker Spaniel: "The most popular of the Spaniel family, the Cocker is an active, happy, small dog, who quickly adapts himself to his surroundings. He is highly intelligent and affectionate, and is in his element foraging around fields and hedgerows. He also employs his retrieving instincts around the house, and can often be found with a toy or slipper in his mouth, his tail wagging furiously, waiting for praise.

"Cockers were recognised as a separate breed from Field and Springer Spaniels soon after the formation of the Kennel Club in 1873. He originated as the 'cocking Spaniel', and derived this name from flushing woodcock. As with a number of gundog breeds there is a difference between those used for work and those used for show; the show Cocker is a sturdier, heavier version of his work counterpart.

"Easy to train – his main aim in life is to please his owner – he is a busy little dog who enjoys plenty of exercise, and thrives on human companionship."

Breed Standard

General Appearance - Merry, sturdy, sporting; well balanced; compact; measuring approximately same from withers to ground as from withers to root of tail.

Characteristics - Merry nature with ever-wagging tail shows a typical bustling movement, particularly when following scent, fearless of heavy cover.

Temperament - Gentle and affectionate, yet full of life and exuberance.

Head and Skull - Square muzzle, with distinct stop set midway between tip of nose and occiput. Skull well developed, cleanly chiselled, neither too fine nor too coarse. Cheek bones not prominent. Nose sufficiently wide for acute scenting power.

Eyes - Full, but not prominent. Dark brown or brown, never light, but in the case of liver, liver roan and liver and white, dark hazel to harmonise with coat; with expression of intelligence and gentleness but wide awake, bright and merry; rims tight.

Ears - Lobular, set low on a level with eyes. Fine leathers extending to nose tip. Well clothed with long, straight silky hair.

Mouth - Jaws strong with a perfect, regular and complete scissor bite, i.e. upper teeth closely overlapping lower teeth and set square to the jaws.

Neck - Moderate in length, muscular. Set neatly into fine sloping shoulders. Clean throat.

Forequarters - Shoulders sloping and fine. Legs well boned, straight, sufficiently short for concentrated power. Not too short to interfere with tremendous exertions expected from this grand, sporting dog.

Body - Strong, compact. Chest well developed and brisket deep; neither too wide nor too narrow in front. Ribs well sprung. Loin short, wide with firm, level topline gently sloping downwards to tail from end of loin to set on of tail.

Hindquarters - Wide, well rounded, very muscular. Legs well boned, good bend of stifle, short below hock allowing for plenty of drive.

Feet - Firm, thickly padded, cat-like.

Tail - Set on slightly lower than line of back. Must be merry in action and carried level, never cocked up. Previously customarily docked.

Docked: Never too short to hide, nor too long to interfere with, the incessant merry action when working.

Undocked: Slightly curved, of moderate length, proportionate to size of body giving an overall balanced appearance; ideally not reaching below the hock. Strong at the root and tapering to a fine tip; well feathered in keeping with the coat. Lively in action, carried on a plane not higher than level of back and never so low as to indicate timidity.

Gait/Movement - True through action with great drive covering ground well.

Coat - Flat, silky in texture, never wiry or wavy, not too profuse and never curly. Well feathered forelegs, body and hindlegs above hocks.

Colour - Solid colours: Black; red; golden; liver (chocolate); black and tan; liver and tan. No white allowed except a small amount on chest.

Particolours

Bicolours: Black and white; orange and white; liver and white; lemon and white. All with or without ticking.

Tricolours: Black, white and tan; liver, white and tan.

Roans: Blue roan; orange roan; lemon roan; liver roan; blue roan and tan; liver roan and tan.

Any colour or marking other than the above is undesirable.

Size - Height approximately: dogs: 39-41 cms (15½-16 ins); bitches: 38-39 cms (15-15½,ins). Weight approximately: 13-14.5 kgs (28-32 lbs).

Faults - Any departure from the foregoing points should be considered a fault and the seriousness with which the fault should be regarded should be in exact proportion to its degree and its effect upon the health and welfare of the dog and on the dog's ability to perform its traditional work.

Note - Male animals should have two apparently normal testicles fully descended into the scrotum.

The AKC (American Kennel Club) breed standard is very similar. However, in the US, the English Cocker Spaniel is most often seen as a working dog and it is interesting to note that the AKC has more description of character:

"He is alive with energy; his gait is powerful and frictionless, capable both of covering ground effortlessly and penetrating dense cover to flush and retrieve game. His enthusiasm in the field and the incessant action of his tail while at work indicate how much he enjoys the hunting for which he was bred. His head is especially characteristic. He is, above all, a dog of balance, both standing and moving, without exaggeration in any part, the whole worth more than the sum of its parts."

When referring to gait, the American breed standard states: "The English Cocker is capable of hunting in dense cover and upland terrain. His gait is accordingly characterized more by drive and the appearance of power than by great speed. He covers ground effortlessly and with extension both in front and in rear, appropriate to his angulation.

"In the ring, he carries his head proudly and is able to keep much the same topline while in action as when standing for examination. Going and coming, he moves in a straight line without crabbing or rolling, and with width between both front and rear legs appropriate to his build and gait."

Regarding substance, the AKC says: "The English Cocker is a solidly built dog with as much bone and substance as is possible without becoming cloddy or coarse."

On temperament: "The English Cocker is merry and affectionate, of equable disposition, neither sluggish nor hyperactive, a willing worker and a faithful and engaging companion."

The tail is always docked in America. And one final point, just about everything is bigger in America than Europe - and Cockers are no exception! The height at the withers is 16-17 inches for males and 15-16 inches for females.

USA Breed Standard (American Cocker)

The American Cocker Spaniel - known simply as the Cocker Spaniel in the US - is the smallest dog in the Sporting Group. The AKC has this to say about Sporting Group dogs:

"Naturally active and alert, Sporting dogs make likeable, well-rounded companions. Remarkable for their instincts in water and woods, many of these breeds actively continue to participate in hunting and other field activities. Potential owners of Sporting dogs need to realize that most require regular, invigorating exercise."

The AKC describes the Cocker as "Happy, smart, gentle."

Breed Standard

General Appearance: He has a sturdy, compact body and a cleanly chiseled and refined head, with the overall dog in complete balance and of ideal size. He stands well up at the shoulder on straight forelegs with a topline sloping slightly toward strong, moderately bent, muscular quarters.

He is a dog capable of considerable speed, combined with great endurance. Above all, he must be free and merry, sound, well balanced throughout and in action show a keen inclination to work. A dog well balanced in all parts is more desirable than a dog with strongly contrasting good points and faults.

Size, Proportion, Substance:

Size -The ideal height at the withers for an adult dog is 15 inches and for an adult bitch, 14 inches. Height may vary one-half inch above or below this ideal. A dog whose height exceeds 15½ inches or a bitch whose height exceeds 14½ inches shall be disqualified. An adult dog whose height is less than 14½ inches and an adult bitch whose height is less than 13½ inches shall be penalized. Height is determined by a line perpendicular to the ground from the top of the shoulder blades, the dog standing naturally with its forelegs and lower hind legs parallel to the line of measurement.

Proportion -The measurement from the breast bone to back of thigh is slightly longer than the measurement from the highest point of withers to the ground. The body must be of sufficient length to permit a straight and free stride; the dog never appears long and low.

Head - To attain a well-proportioned head, which must be in balance with the rest of the dog, it embodies the following: Expression-The expression is intelligent, alert, soft and appealing.

Eyes - Eyeballs are round and full and look directly forward. The shape of the eye rims gives a slightly almond shaped appearance; the eye is not weak or goggled. The color of the iris is dark brown and in general the darker the better.

Ears - Lobular, long, of fine leather, well feathered, and placed no higher than a line to the lower part of the eye.

Skull - Rounded but not exaggerated with no tendency toward flatness; the eyebrows are clearly defined with a pronounced stop. The bony structure beneath the eyes is well chiseled with no prominence in the cheeks. The muzzle is broad and deep, with square even jaws. To be in correct balance, the distance from the stop to the tip of the nose is one half the distance from the stop up over the crown to the base of the skull.

Nose - of sufficient size to balance the muzzle and foreface, with well-developed nostrils typical of a sporting dog. It is black in color in the blacks, black and tans, and black and whites; in other colors it may be brown, liver or black, the darker the better. The color of nose harmonizes with the color of the eye rim.

Lips - The upper lip is full and of sufficient depth to cover the lower jaw.

Teeth - Teeth strong and sound, not too small and meet in a scissors bite.

Neck, Topline, Body:

Neck - The neck is sufficiently long to allow the nose to reach the ground easily, muscular and free from pendulous "throatiness." It rises strongly from the shoulders and arches slightly as it tapers to join the head.

Topline - sloping slightly toward muscular quarters.

Body - The chest is deep, its lowest point no higher than the elbows, its front sufficiently wide for adequate heart and lung space, yet not so wide as to interfere with the straightforward movement of the forelegs. Ribs are deep and well sprung. Back is strong and sloping evenly and slightly downward from the shoulders to the set-on of the docked tail. The docked tail is set on and carried on a line with the topline of the back, or slightly higher; never straight up like a Terrier and never so low as to indicate timidity. When the dog is in motion the tail action is merry.

Forequarters - The shoulders are well laid back forming an angle with the upper arm of approximately 90 degrees which permits the dog to move his forelegs in an easy manner with forward reach. Shoulders are clean-cut and sloping without protrusion and so set that the upper points of the withers are at an angle which permits a wide spring of rib. When viewed from the side with the forelegs vertical, the elbow is directly below the highest point of the shoulder blade. Forelegs are parallel, straight, strongly boned and muscular and set close to the body well under the scapulae. The pasterns are short and strong. Dewclaws on forelegs may be removed. Feet compact, large, round and firm with horny pads; they turn neither in nor out.

Hindquarters - Hips are wide and quarters well rounded and muscular. When viewed from behind, the hind legs are parallel when in motion and at rest. The hind legs are strongly boned, and muscled with moderate angulation at the stifle and powerful, clearly defined thighs. The stifle is strong and there is no slippage of it in motion or when standing. The hocks are strong and well let down. Dewclaws on hind legs may be removed.

Coat - On the head, short and fine; on the body, medium length, with enough undercoating to give protection. The ears, chest, abdomen and legs are well feathered, but not so excessively as to hide the Cocker Spaniel's true lines and movement or affect his appearance and function as a moderately coated sporting dog. The texture is most important. The coat is silky, flat or slightly wavy and of a texture which permits easy care. Excessive coat or curly or cottony textured coat shall be severely penalized. Use of electric clippers on the back coat is not desirable. Trimming to enhance the dog's true lines should be done to appear as natural as possible.

Color and Markings:

Black Variety - Solid color black to include black with tan points. The black should be jet; shadings of brown or liver in the coat are not desirable. A small amount of white on the chest and/or throat is allowed; white in any other location shall disqualify.

Any Solid Color Other than Black (ASCOB) - Any solid color other than black, ranging from lightest cream to darkest red, including brown and brown with tan points. The color shall be of a uniform shade, but lighter color of the feathering is permissible. A small amount of white on the chest and/or throat is allowed; white in any other location shall disqualify.

Parti-Color Variety -Two or more solid, well broken colors, one of which must be white; black and white, red and white (the red may range from lightest cream to darkest red), brown and white, and roans, to include any such color combination with tan points. It is preferable that the tan markings be located in the same pattern as for the tan points in the Black and ASCOB varieties. Roans are classified as parti-colors and may be of any of the usual roaning patterns. Primary color which is ninety percent (90%) or more shall disqualify.

Tan Points - The color of the tan may be from the lightest cream to the darkest red and is restricted to ten percent (10%) or less of the color of the specimen; tan markings in excess of that amount shall disqualify. In the case of tan points in the Black or ASCOB variety, the markings shall be located as follows:

1) A clear tan spot over each eye;
2) On the sides of the muzzle and on the cheeks;
3) On the underside of the ears;
4) On all feet and/or legs;
5) Under the tail;
6) On the chest, optional; presence or absence shall not be penalized.

Tan markings which are not readily visible or which amount only to traces, shall be penalized. Tan on the muzzle which extends upward, over and joins shall also be penalized. The absence of tan markings in the Black or ASCOB variety in any of the specified locations in any otherwise tan-pointed dog shall disqualify.

Gait - The Cocker Spaniel, though the smallest of the sporting dogs, possesses a typical sporting dog gait. Prerequisite to good movement is balance between the front and rear assemblies. He drives with strong, powerful rear quarters and is properly constructed in the shoulders and forelegs so that he can reach forward without constriction in a full stride to counterbalance the driving force from the rear. Above all, his gait is coordinated, smooth and effortless. The dog must cover ground with his action; excessive animation should not be mistaken for proper gait.

Temperament - Equable in temperament with no suggestion of timidity.

Disqualifications – Height: Males over 15½ inches; females over 14½ inches. Color and Markings: The aforementioned colors are the only acceptable colors or combination of colors. Any other colors or combination of colors to disqualify. Black Variety-White markings except on chest and throat. Any Solid Color Other than Black Variety-White markings except on chest and throat. Particolor Variety-Primary color ninety percent (90 percent) or more. Tan Points-(1) Tan markings in excess of ten percent (10 percent); (2) Absence of tan markings in Black or ASCOB Variety in any of the specified locations in an otherwise tan-pointed dog.

There's only a couple of slight variations in the UK breed standard for the American Cocker. The first is that the height is given as a range from 14½-15½ inches for males and from 13½-14½ inches for females, rather than an exact ideal.

The second is the tail. The UK breed standard states: "Previously customarily docked.

Docked: Docked by three fifths of tail. Set on and carried on a line with topline of back or slightly higher. Never straight up and never so low as to indicate timidity. When dog in motion, merry tail action.

Undocked: Set on a line with topline of back. Moderate length. Feathering in proportion to the coat of the dog. Thicker at the root and tapering towards the tip. Carried on a line with the topline of back, or slightly higher, but never curled over the back or so low as to indicate timidity. When dog is in motion, merry tail action."

4. Choosing a Cocker Spaniel Puppy

Are You Ready?

With their beautiful big eyes, silky soft fur and cheeky personalities there are few things more appealing than a litter of Cocker Spaniel puppies. If you go to view a litter, the pups are sure to melt your heart and it is extremely difficult – if not downright impossible - to walk away without choosing one.

However, the best way to select a puppy is with your head and not with your heart. Do your research before you visit any litters. Decide if you want a puppy bred from show lines or working lines and then select a responsible breeder with health-tested parents (of the puppy, not the breeder!) Apart from getting married or having a baby, getting a puppy is probably one of the most important, demanding, expensive and life-enriching decisions you will ever make.

Just like babies, your pup will love you unconditionally - but there is a price to pay. In return for their loyalty and devotion, you have to fulfil your part of the bargain.

In the beginning you have to be prepared to devote several hours a day to your new arrival. You have to feed him several times a day and housetrain him virtually every hour, you have to give him your attention and start to gently introduce the rules of the house as well as take care of his general health and welfare. You also have to be prepared to part with hard cash for regular healthcare and pet insurance.

Pictured is a show litter from Twizzle at seven weeks old, bred by Gail Parsons, of Gaiter Cocker Spaniels, Sussex.

If you are not prepared, or are unable, to devote the time and money to a new arrival – or if you are out at work all day – then now might not be the right time to consider getting a puppy. Cocker Spaniels need plenty of physical and mental stimulation and do not like being left alone for long periods. Separation anxiety may result and, if left too much, their naturally happy and eager-to-please temperaments can change when they become unhappy. If you are out at work all day these are not the dogs for you; they thrive on interaction, exercise and challenges.

Pick a healthy pup and he or she will probably live into the teens, so it is definitely a long-term commitment. Before taking the plunge, ask yourself some questions:

Have I Got Enough Time?

In the first days after leaving his - or her - mother and littermates, your puppy will feel very lonely and maybe even a little afraid. You and your family have to spend time with your new arrival to make him feel safe and sound. Ideally, for the first few days you will be around all of the time to help him settle and to start bonding with him. If you work, book some time off, but don't just get a puppy and leave him alone in the house a few days later.

As well as housetraining, short sessions of behaviour training are also recommended to curb puppy biting and to teach your new pup the rules of the house. Before his vaccinations have finished, start the socialisation process by taking him out of the home to see buses, trains, noisy traffic, kids, etc. - but make sure you CARRY HIM. Cocker Spaniels can be very sensitive to all sorts of things and it's important to start the socialisation process as soon as possible. The more he is introduced to at this early stage, the better.

Once he has had the all-clear after his vaccinations, get into the habit of taking him out of the house and garden or yard for a short walk every day – more as he gets older. New surroundings stimulate his interest and help to stop him from becoming bored and developing unwanted character traits. Spend some time gently brushing your puppy and checking his ears are clean to get him used to being handled and groomed right from the beginning. You'll also need to factor in time to visit the vet's surgery for regular healthcare visits and annual vaccinations.

How Long Can I Leave Him?

This is a question we get asked all of the time and one which causes a lot of debate among owners and prospective owners. All dogs are pack animals; their natural state is to be with others. Being alone is not normal for them, although many have to get used to it.

Another issue is toileting; all Cockers have smaller bladders than humans. Forget the emotional side of it, how would you like to be left for eight hours without being able to visit the bathroom? So how many hours can you leave a dog alone? Well, a useful guide comes from the canine rescue organisations. In the UK, they will not allow anybody to adopt if they are intending to leave the dog alone for more than four or five hours a day.

Dogs left alone become bored, particularly those like the Cocker which were originally bred for working, as they often have high physical and mental drives. They may become depressed and/or uncooperative. Of course, it depends on the character and temperament of your dog, but a lonely Cocker could display signs of unhappiness by being destructive, digging, chewing, barking, ignoring your commands or urinating.

A puppy or fully-grown dog must NEVER be left shut in a crate all day. It is OK to leave a puppy or adult dog in a crate if he or she is happy there, but all our breeders said the same, the door should never be closed for more than two or three hours during the day. A crate is a place where a puppy or adult should feel safe, not a prison. Ask yourself why you want a dog – is it for selfish reasons or can you really offer a good home to a young puppy - and then adult dog - for 12 to 14 years - or even longer? Would it be more sensible to wait until you are at home more?

Is My Home Suitable?

Cocker Spaniels are adaptable; they can live on a farm or in an apartment, indoors as family pets or outdoors in kennels if they are working dogs - much depends on their breeding and what they get used to as puppies. However, Cockers generally have fairly high exercise requirements – especially those bred from working Spaniels – and so all need regular access to the outdoors. More than many other breeds, the Cocker loves to run free and investigate his surroundings with his nose, so part of this time should be spent off the lead, once he as leaned the recall. Whatever type of Cocker you get, at least some of your puppy's ancestors have been bred to run all day through the undergrowth. Some Cockers end up in rescue centres due to issues related to not getting enough exercise.

Cocker Spaniels are intelligent and sensitive, and breeders find them generally easy to housetrain – provided you are diligent in the beginning. See **Chapter 6.** for more information on how to housetrain your puppy. If you are one of the few owners who lives in an apartment, it is very important to take him outside to perform his duty many times a day to start with if you don't want your pup to eliminate indoors. If you can continue to do this three or four times daily then there is no need to indoor housetrain him.

And if you live in a house with a yard or garden, don't leave your puppy unattended; dognapping is becoming increasingly common, particularly with the high price of pups. Make sure there are no poisonous plants or chemicals out there which he could eat or drink. Common plants toxic to dogs include crocus, daffodil, azalea, wisteria, cyclamen, sweet pea, lily of the valley, tulips, hyacinth and lily.

Spaniel-proofing your home should involve moving anything sharp, breakable or chewable - including your shoes - out of reach to sharp little teeth. Make sure he can't chew electrical cords – lift them off the floor if necessary, and block off any off-limits areas of the house, such as upstairs or your bedroom, with a child gate or barrier, especially as he will probably be following you around the house in the first few days. See **Chapter 5. Bringing a Puppy Home** for more details. (Pictured is an America Cocker puppy).

Family and Children

What about the other members of your family? Do they all want the puppy as well? A puppy will grow into a dog which will become a part of your family for many years to come. If you have children they will, of course, be delighted. One of the wonderful things about Cocker Spaniels is how naturally good they are with people of all ages, including children.

But remember that puppies are small and delicate, as are babies, so you should never leave babies or very small children and dogs alone together – no matter how well they get along. Small kids lack co-ordination and a young Cocker may inadvertently get poked in the eye or trodden on if you don't keep an eye on him or her. Often puppies regard children as playmates (just like a small child regards a puppy as a playmate) and so an excitable young pup might chase, jump and nip with sharp teeth. This is not aggression; this is normal play for puppies. Train yours to be gentle with your children and your children to be gentle with your dog. See **Chapter 9. Exercise and Training** on how to deal with puppy biting.

Discourage the kids from constantly picking up your gorgeous new puppy. They should learn respect for the dog, which is a living creature with his or her own needs, not a toy. Make sure your puppy gets enough time to sleep – **which is most of the time in the beginning** - so don't let your children constantly pester him. Sleep is very important to puppies, just as it is for babies. Allow your Spaniel to eat at his or her own pace uninterrupted; letting youngsters play with the dog while eating is a no-no as it may promote gulping of food or food aggression.

Doing a good impression of a sleeping mouse is this few-days-old working puppy bred by Christine Thomas, of Dodfordhills Spaniels, Worcestershire.

Another reason some dogs end up in rescue centres is that owners are unable to cope with the demands of small children AND a dog. On the other hand, it is also a fantastic opportunity for you to educate your little darlings (both human and canine) on how to get along with each other and set the pattern for wonderful life-long friendships.

Read Kerena Marchant's story in **Chapter 16. Cockers in Action** about how her young son Jordan and his working Cocker Rupert developed a special bond and went on to achieve great things together in canine agility competitions.

Single People

Many single adults own dogs, but if you live alone, having a puppy will require a lot of dedication on your part. There will be nobody to share the responsibility, so taking on a dog requires a huge commitment and a lot of your time if the dog is to have a decent life - especially on the exercise front. If you are out of the house all day as well, it is not really fair to get a puppy, or even an adult dog. Left alone all day, they will feel isolated, bored and sad. However, if you work from home or are at home all day, you're physically fit and active and you can spend time with the puppy every day, then great; your Spaniel will become your best friend.

Older People

If you are older or have elderly relatives living with you, the good news is that Cocker Spaniels are excellent company. They are gently and affectionate and love pleasing people. But, if you are older, make sure you have the energy and patience to deal with a young puppy - and even then you might want to consider a breed with lower exercise requirements. If it's companionship you're after, then there are far more suitable breeds which were bred specifically to be companions to humans and do not have the same drives and need for stimulation as a working breed such as a Spaniel. Only consider a Cocker if you are fit and active and happy to walk for an hour or two a day - whatever the weather. The Cocker doesn't care if it's raining or snowing, he just wants to be running around outside.

Dogs can be great for older people. My father is in his mid-80s, but takes his dog out walking for an hour to 90 minutes every day - a morning and an afternoon walk – even in the rain or snow. It's good for him and it's good for the dog, helping to keep both of them fit and socialised! They get fresh air, exercise and the chance to communicate with other dogs and their humans. Dogs are also great company indoors – you're never alone when you've got a dog.

Many older people get a dog after losing a loved one (a husband, wife or previous much-loved dog). A pet gives them something to care for and love, as well as a constant companion. Another factor to bear in mind is that owning a dog is not cheap, so it's important to be able to afford annual pet insurance, veterinary fees, a quality pet food, etc. The RSPCA in the UK has estimated that owning a dog costs an average of around £1,300 ($2,000) a year.

Other Animals

If you already have other pets in your household, they may not be too happy at the arrival of your new addition. While Cockers often get on well with other animals, some have a medium to strong prey drive, so it might not be a good idea to leave your hamster or pet rabbit running loose with your pup. Spend time to introduce pets to each other gradually and supervise the sessions.

Cocker puppies are naturally curious, lively and playful and they will sniff and investigate other pets. You may have to separate them to start off with, or put your boisterous puppy into a pen or crate initially to allow a cat to investigate without being mauled by the hyper active pup, which thinks the cat is a great playmate. This will also prevent your pup from being injured. If the two animals are free and the cat lashes out he or she could scratch your pup's eyes.

Just type 'Cocker Spaniel and cat' into YouTube to see some lively interactions between the two.

A timid cat might need protection from a bold, playful pup - or vice versa. A bold cat and a timid young Cocker Spaniel will probably settle down together quickest! If things seem to be going well with no aggression after one or two supervised sessions, then let them loose together.

Take the process slowly; if your cat is stressed and frightened he may decide to leave. Our feline friends are notorious for abandoning home because the food and facilities are better down the road. Until you know that they can get on, don't leave them alone together.

Cockers usually get on well with other dogs. If you already have other dogs, supervised sessions from an early age will help them to get along and for the other dogs to accept your friendly new Spaniel. If you are thinking about getting more than one pup, you might consider waiting until your first is an adolescent or adult before getting a second, so your older dog is calmer and can help train the younger one.

Coping with, training and housetraining one puppy is hard enough, without having to do it with two or more. On the other hand, some owners prefer to get the messy part over and done with in one go and get two together – but this will require a lot of your time for the first few weeks.

As with all dogs, how well they get on also depends on the temperament of the individuals. With another dog, initially introduce the two on neutral territory, rather than in areas one pet deems his own. You don't want one dog to feel he has to protect his territory. If you think there may be issues, walking the dogs parallel to each other before heading home for the first time is one way of getting them used to each other.

Some young Cockers may also have a natural tendency to chase sheep and other farm animals. If you are out walking in the countryside, start the dog off on a lead (leash) when there are other animals around. Gradually allow him off the lead, but not too far away from you. If he starts looking at or thinking about chasing the animals, use the word "No", then immediately call him back enthusiastically and give the treat. He should quickly learn not to chase and then you will be able to let him off the lead safely in fields with animals.

Show or Working Cocker?

As you've read in the first chapter, most breeders believe there is a big difference between show-type and working Cockers. All types – whether English, American, show or working - require a fair amount of exercise. After all, they were bred not as companions to humans, but to work by flushing and retrieving game. Working Spaniels are happy to run for up to eight hours a day on a shoot and in the season they will cover hundreds of miles.

All Cockers like exercise. A huge generalisation would be that if you've been out on a long walk with your dog, a show Cocker is more likely to curl up at your side and have a snooze, whereas a working Cocker may still want to be on the go, looking for mental stimulation or the next new challenge.

Both types will thrive in active families where they are getting plenty of regular daily exercise. If you are specifically looking for a gundog or intend taking part in field trials, then the working Cocker is the dog for you. If you are a less active family, then a show-type might suit you better. (Pictured below left to right: an American Cocker, an English working Cocker and a pet English show Cocker which has been clipped).

Gender and Colour

You have to decide whether you want a male or a female puppy. In terms of gender, much depends on the temperament of the individual dog - the differences WITHIN the sexes are greater than the differences BETWEEN the sexes. A couple of differences are that males are generally larger than females and on walks a male will stop frequently to mark his territory by urinating, while a female will urinate much less frequently. You might not think this is important - until you are standing in the pouring rain waiting for Jasper to do his 27th wee of the walk!

If you already have dogs or are thinking of getting more than one, you do, however, have to consider gender. You cannot expect an un-neutered male to live in a house with an unspayed female without problems. Similarly, two uncastrated males may not always get along; there might simply be too much testosterone and competition. If an existing dog is neutered (male) or spayed (female) and you plan to have your puppy neutered or spayed, then the gender should not be an issue.

Many people select a dog based on colour, and what a choice, there can be few types of dog with as many different colours and markings as Cockers. However, bear in mind that colour is not usually as important as size and temperament. We asked our breeders if there was any difference in temperament between the colours **and most thought that there wasn't.** However, there were some interesting comments:

"I have heard that solid coloured dogs, particularly reds, can suffer from 'sudden rage syndrome', but have no experience personally of this."

"I have noticed that the black dog is prone to wilfulness."

"I have found the black and tan and tricolours to be a bit calmer and laid back than the lighter American Cocker pups."

"Parti colour English Cockers seem to be 'on the go' all the while and can be more vocal than solid colours. In Americans, parti colours can be less outgoing and confident than the solids."

"With working Cockers, I have always found chocolate Cockers to be the naughty, playful and mischievous ones, lemons to be the steady ones and blacks to be the loyal, most eager to please. It's also interesting to see that the majority of Champion trials dogs are black."

"From my own experience and also from some time in Spaniel rescue, I haven't noticed differences between the colours, but those that are leggier and slimmer (especially in the workers) I have found can be more sensitive and susceptible to separation anxiety. In discussions with those who train for the forces, etc. I have found that they have concurred. Also, there are a small number of workers who have to live in a working environment and will never be pets."

"Having owned and bred English show Cocker Spaniels for 20 years, I breed only solid colours. I find them more alert and less aggressive. It depends upon the breeding, training and caring for the Cocker."

"The orange roans can have sensitive skin. Personalities are different for each colour."

"We have had Cockers for 17 years. We have only had solid colours and found no difference in temperament."

"For our second litter, we bred from our black and tan girl, the dad being black, and got seven pups. Six were black and one was red/golden. We kept the red girl. We found no real differences in temperament, but there have been situations down the years with red Cockers due to their fiery nature. Our girl has had her moments, but it's nothing to get concerned about."

"I don't think colour impacts on temperament, but there may be something in the 'naughty spots' theory!"

"In my own experience I have found the solid colours much calmer than the parti colours, with the partis (roans and with-whites) being much more lively."

"In my experience the solid coloured Cockers need a firmer hand than the parti colours."

"I have been breeding English show Cocker Spaniels for about 18 years. When I first began breeding, I had heard that the solid colours sometimes showed uncertain temperaments, called 'Cocker Rage,' especially the goldens and especially in closely-bred dogs, and this was one of the main reasons I chose to focus on the parti colours. A responsible breeder would ensure that dogs displaying undesirable temperament were not bred from."

"The blacks are definitely more stable in temperament and the chocolate/liver are more scatty and sensitive."

"I have been breeding Cockers for the last 10 years and they are working Cockers only. The solid colours seem to be the most dominantly successful in field trials. You rarely see a good blue roan or lemon roan."

"I breed English working strain Cockers: lemon and white, lemon roan, black and white, blue roan, black, liver. The black and whites and blue roans tend to be calmer than the lemon roans, although I had one litter of solid blacks and they were all full on."

"I have been breeding dogs for more than 20 years and English Cockers from working lines for six years. To my knowledge based upon my breeding lines, the dogs' colour does not affect temperament or sensitivities."

"We have been breeding dogs for over 30 years and for the last 10 years we have bred only English Cocker Spaniels. We have five males and four females, ranging in age from six months to 12 years old. They include chocolate, dark blue roan, light blue roan, black, black and tan and chocolate roan. The litters we have had have included pups with all of the above colours, plus tricolour, orange roan, gold and chocolate and tan. We have not experienced any differences between colours with regards to temperament."

One Kennel Club Assured Breeder added: "I have been involved with breeding working gundogs for nearly 30 years, but have only had Cocker Spaniels, specifically, for about the last five years. Our dogs are all working types. We have seen no evidence to support any differential in temperament caused by colouration in working Cocker Spaniels."

It's clear from these comments that there is a wide variation of opinion. The best advice is to chat to the breeder who knows his or her puppies well; discuss which puppy would best fit in with your household and lifestyle. That beautiful blue roan Cocker Spaniel with the slightly timid disposition may not be the best choice if you have a busy house full of lively kids and other pets, or that handsome lemon roan may not be the best choice if you are looking for a dog to compete in field trials.

More Than One Dog

Owning two dogs can be twice as nice - or double the trouble, and double the vet's bills. There are a number of factors to consider.

Here is some advice from one UK canine rescue organisation: "Think about why you are considering another dog. If, for example, you have a dog that suffers from separation anxiety, then rather than solving the problem, your second dog may learn from your first and you then have two dogs with the problem instead of one. The same applies if you have an unruly adolescent, cure the problem first and only introduce a second dog when your first is balanced.

"If you are tempted to buy two puppies from the same litter - DON'T! Your chances of creating a good bond with the puppies are very low and behaviour problems with siblings are very common.

"A second dog will mean double vet's fees, groomer's fees, insurance and food. You may also need a larger car, and holidays will be more problematic. Sit down with a calculator and work out the expected expense – you may be surprised. Two dogs will need training, both separately and together. If the dogs do not receive enough individual attention, they may form a strong bond with each other at the expense of their bond with you.

"Your dog may be sociable with other dogs but will not necessarily accept another dog into the household. You may find it useful to borrow a friend's dog which is familiar with your own and have a "dummy run" of life in a two-dog household. Research your considered breed well; it may be best to buy a completely different breed to add balance. If you have a very active dog, would a quieter one be best to balance his high energy or would you enjoy the challenge of keeping two high energy dogs?

"You will also need to think of any problems that may occur from keeping dogs of different sizes and ages. If you decide to purchase a puppy, you will need to think very carefully about the amount of time and energy that will be involved in caring for two dogs with very different needs. A young puppy will need to have his exercise restricted until he has finished growing and will also need individual time for training.

"Dogs of the same sex can and do live amicably in the same household, although harmony is more likely with a dog and bitch combination. If you decide to keep a dog and bitch together, then you will obviously need to address the neutering issue."

Top 10 Tips For Working Owners

We would certainly not recommend getting a Cocker Spaniel if you are out at work all day, but if you're determined to get one when you're away for several hours at a time, here are some useful points: (These presume that your Cocker is a pet and not a working dog, which may be kept outside).

1. Either come home during your lunch break to let your dog out or employ a dog walker (or neighbour) to take him out for a walk in the middle of the day.

2. Do you know anybody you could leave your dog with during the day? Consider leaving the dog with a friend, relative or neighbour who would welcome the companionship of a Cocker Spaniel without the full responsibility of ownership.

3. Take him for a walk before you go to work – even if this means getting up at the crack of dawn – and spend time with him as soon as you get home. Exercise generates serotonin in the brain and has a calming effect. A dog that has been exercised will be less anxious and more ready for a good nap.

4. Leave him in a place of his own where he feels comfortable. If you use a crate, leave the door open, otherwise his favourite dog bed or chair. If possible, leave him in a room with a view of the outside world, such as one with a patio door, this will be more interesting than staring at four blank walls.

5. Make sure that it does not get too hot during the day and there are no cold draughts in the place where you leave him.

6. Make sure he has access to water at all times. Dogs cannot cool down by sweating; they do not have many sweat glands (which is why they pant, but this is much less efficient than perspiring) and can die without sufficient water.

7. Leave toys available to play with to prevent destructive chewing (a popular occupation of bored Cockers or one suffering from separation anxiety). Stuff a Kong toy with treats to keep him occupied for a while. Choose the right size of Kong, you can even smear the inside with peanut butter or another favourite to keep him occupied for longer.

8. Consider getting a companion for your dog. This will involve even more of your time and twice the expense, and if you have not got time for one dog, you have hardly time for two. A better idea is to find someone you can leave the dog with during the day; there are also dog sitters and doggie day care for those who can afford them.

9. Consider leaving a radio or TV on very softly in the background. The 'white noise' can have a soothing effect on some pets. If you do this, select your channel carefully – try and avoid one with lots of bangs and crashes or heavy metal music!

10. Stick to the same routine before you leave your dog home alone. This will help him to feel secure. Before you go to work, get into a daily habit of getting yourself ready, then feeding and exercising your Cocker Spaniel. Dogs love routine. But don't make a huge fuss of him when you leave as this can also stress the dog; just leave the house calmly.

Similarly when you come home, your Spaniel will feel starved of attention and be pleased to see you. Greet him normally, but try not to go overboard by making too much of a fuss as soon as you walk through the door. Give him a pat and a stroke then take off your coat and do a few other things before turning your attention back to him. Lavishing your dog with too much attention the second you walk through the door may encourage needy behaviour or separation anxiety.

Puppy Stages

It is important to understand how a puppy develops into a fully grown dog. This knowledge will help you to be a good owner. The first few months and weeks of a puppy's life will have an effect on his behaviour and character for the rest of his life. This Puppy Schedule will help you to understand the early stages:

Birth to seven weeks	A puppy needs sleep, food and warmth. He needs his mother for security and discipline and littermates for learning and socialisation. The puppy learns to function within a pack and learns the pack order of dominance. He begins to become aware of his environment. During this period, puppies should be left with their mother.
Eight to 12 weeks	A puppy should not leave his mother before eight weeks. At this age the brain is fully developed and **he now needs socialising with the outside world**. He needs to change from being part of a canine pack to being part of a human pack. This period is a fear period for the puppy, avoid causing him fright and pain.

13 to 16 weeks	Training and formal obedience should begin. **This is a critical period for socialising with other humans, places and situations.** This period will pass easily if you remember that this is a puppy's change to adolescence. Be firm and fair. His flight instinct may be prominent. Avoid being too strict or too soft with him during this time and praise his good behaviour.
Four to eight months	Another fear period for a puppy is between seven to eight months of age. It passes quickly, but be cautious of fright or pain which may leave the puppy traumatised. The puppy reaches sexual maturity and dominant traits are established. Your Cocker Spaniel should now understand the following commands: 'sit', 'down', 'come' and 'stay'.

Plan Ahead

Most puppies leave the litter for their new homes when they are eight weeks or older. It is important that they have time to develop and learn the rules of the pack from their mothers. Some Spaniels take a little longer to develop physically and mentally, and a puppy which leaves the litter too early may suffer with issues, for example a lack of confidence throughout life. Breeders who allow their pups to leave early may be more interested in a quick buck than a long-term puppy placement. If you want a well-bred pup, it pays to plan ahead as good Cocker Spaniel breeders often have waiting lists.

Choosing the right breeder is one of the most important decisions you will make. Like humans, your puppy will be a product of his or her parents and will inherit many of their characteristics. His temperament and health life will be influenced by the genes of his parents. Ideally, see the puppy with the parents - or at least the mother.

It's essential you select a responsible, ethical breeder. They will have checked out the health records and temperament of the parents and will only breed from suitable stock. Good breeding comes at a price and if a puppy is being sold for less, you have to ask why. Some Cocker Spaniel breeders have their own websites and many are trustworthy and conscientious. You have to learn to spot the good ones from the bad ones.

Because of high prices, unscrupulous breeders with little knowledge of the breed have sprung up, tempted by the prospect of making easy cash. A healthy Cocker will be your trusty companion for the next decade or more, so why buy an unseen puppy, or one from a pet shop or general online ad? Good breeders do not sell their dogs on general purpose websites or in pet shops. Many reputable breeders do not have to advertise, such is the demand for their puppies - so it's up to you to do your research to find a really good one.

At the very minimum you MUST visit the breeder personally and follow our **Top 10 Tips for Selecting a Good Breeder** to help you make the right decision. Buying a poorly-bred puppy may save you a few hundred pounds or dollars in the short term, but could cost you thousands in extra veterinary bills in the long run - not to mention the terrible heartache of having a sickly dog. Rescue groups know only too well the dangers of buying a poorly-bred dog; years of problems can arise, usually health-related, but there can also be temperament issues or bad behaviour due to lack of socialisation at the breeder's.

The Kennel Club and The Cocker Spaniel Club

The UK's Kennel Club has a list of Assured Breeders for each breed. These are people who have guaranteed to produce puppies to the breed standard, in line with welfare standards, and to conform to the KC's Code of Ethics. These breeders will also have a lifetime or specified time return on all of their puppies in case things don't work out. The list can be found here: www.thekennelclub.org.uk/services/public/acbr/Default.aspx?breed=Spaniel+(Cocker).

The Cocker Spaniel Club, set up in 1902, is the parent club for the breed. The club holds shows and field trials throughout the year, details of which can be found on the website at www.thecockerspanielclub.co.uk. Member breeders have all agreed to abide by the club's Code of Ethics, which is virtually identical to the Kennel Club's. Both strongly promote animal welfare, and breeding from only the best and healthiest dogs. Here are some of the main points:

Breeders/owners will:

  ➢ Abide by all aspects of the Animal Welfare Act

  ➢ Not create demand for, nor supply, puppies that have been docked illegally

  ➢ Agree not to breed from a dog or bitch which could be in any way harmful to the dog or to the breed

  ➢ Only sell dogs where there is a reasonable expectation of a happy and healthy life and will help with the re-homing of a dog if the initial circumstances change

  ➢ Supply written details of all dietary requirements and give guidance concerning responsible ownership when placing dogs in a new home.

  ➢ Ensure that all relevant Kennel Club documents are provided to the new owner when selling or transferring a dog, and will agree, in writing, to forward any relevant documents at the earliest opportunity, if not immediately available

  ➢ Not sell any dog to commercial dog wholesalers, retail pet dealers or directly or indirectly allow dogs to be given as a prize or donation in a competition of any kind. Will not sell by sale or auction Kennel Club registration certificates as stand-alone items (not accompanying a dog)

  ➢ Not knowingly misrepresent the characteristics of the breed nor falsely advertise dogs nor mislead any person regarding the health or quality of a dog

In the USA a good place to start your search for a breeder of (English) Cockers is the American Kennel Club at http://marketplace.akc.org/puppies/english-cocker-spaniel or the English Cocker Spaniel Club of America list of breeders at www.ecsca.info/index.php/breeders/breeder-listing For American Cockers visit the AKC at http://marketplace.akc.org/puppies/cocker-spaniel or the American Spaniel Club at www.asc-cockerspaniel.org/index.php/breeders.html.

Of course, there are no cast iron guarantees that your puppy will be healthy and have a good temperament, but choosing a breeder who conforms to a code of ethics is a very good place to start. If you've never bought a puppy before, how do you avoid buying one from a 'backstreet breeder' or puppy mill?

These are people who just breed puppies for profit and sell them to the first person who turns up with the cash. Unhappily, this can end in heartbreak for a family months or years later when their puppy develops health or temperament problems due to poor breeding.

Price is a good guide, a cheap puppy usually means that corners have been cut somewhere along the line. If a puppy is advertised at a couple of hundred pounds or dollars or so, then you can bet your last penny that the dam and sire are not superb examples of their breed and they haven't been fully health tested, that the puppies are not being fed premium quality food or even kept in the house with the family where the breeder should start to socialise and housetrain them. Here's some advice on what to avoid:

Where NOT to buy a Cocker Spaniel Puppy

Due to the high cost of Cocker Spaniel puppies – as well as waiting lists for litters - unscrupulous breeders have sprung up to cash in on this highly popular breed. While new owners might think they have bagged 'a bargain,' this more often than not turns out to be false economy and an emotionally disastrous decision when the puppy develops health problems due to poor breeding, or behavioural problems due to lack of socialisation during the critical early phase of his or her life.

In September 2013 The UK's Kennel Club issued a warning of a puppy welfare crisis, with some truly sickening statistics. The situation is no better in America. The Press release stated:

As the popularity of online pups continues to soar:

> **Almost one in five pups bought (unseen) on websites or social media die within six months**

> One in three buy online, in pet stores and via newspaper adverts - outlets often used by puppy farmers – this is an increase from one in five in the previous year

> The problem is likely to grow as the younger generation favour mail order pups, and breeders of fashionable crossbreeds flout responsible steps

The Kennel Club said: "We are sleepwalking into a dog welfare and consumer crisis as new research shows that more and more people are buying their pups online or through pet shops, outlets often used by cruel puppy farmers, and are paying the price with their pups requiring long-term veterinary treatment or dying before six months old. The increasing popularity of online pups is a particular concern. Of those who source their puppies online, half are going on to buy 'mail order pups' directly over the internet."

The KC research found that:

> One third of people who bought their puppy online, over social media or in pet shops failed to experience 'overall good health'

➢ Some 12% of puppies bought online or on social media end up with serious health problems that require expensive on-going veterinary treatment from a young age

Caroline Kisko, Kennel Club Secretary, said: "More and more people are buying puppies from sources such as the internet, which are often used by puppy farmers.

"Whilst there is nothing wrong with initially finding a puppy online, it is essential to then see the breeder and ensure that they are doing all of the right things. This research clearly shows that too many people are failing to do this, and the consequences can be seen in the shocking number of puppies that are becoming sick or dying. We have an extremely serious consumer protection and puppy welfare crisis on our hands."

The research revealed that the problem was likely to get worse as mail order pups bought over the internet are the second most common way for the younger generation of 18 to 24-year-olds to buy a puppy (31%).

Marc Abraham, TV vet and founder of Pup Aid, said: "Sadly, if the 'buy it now' culture persists, then this horrific situation will only get worse. There is nothing wrong with sourcing a puppy online, but people need to be aware of what they should then expect from the breeder.

"For example, you should not buy a car without getting its service history and seeing it at its registered address, so you certainly shouldn't buy a puppy without the correct paperwork and health certificates and without seeing where it was bred. However, too many people are opting to buy directly from third parties such as the internet, pet shops, or from puppy dealers, where you cannot possibly know how or where the puppy was raised.

"Not only are people buying sickly puppies, but many people are being scammed into paying money for puppies that don't exist, as the research showed that 7% of those who buy online were scammed in this way".

The Kennel Club has launched an online video and has a Find A Puppy app to show the do's and don'ts of buying a puppy. View the video at www.thekennelclub.org.uk/paw

Caveat Emptor – Buyer Beware

Here are some signs that a puppy may have arrived via a puppy mill or a puppy broker (somebody who makes money from buying and selling puppies). Our strong advice is that if you suspect that this is the case, walk away - unless you want to risk a lot of trouble and heartache in the future. You can't buy a Rolls Royce or a Lamborghini for a couple of thousand pounds or dollars - you'd immediately suspect that the 'bargain' on offer wasn't the real thing. No matter how lovely it looked, you'd be right - and the same applies to Cockers. Here are some signs to look out for:

➢ Websites – buying a puppy from a website does not necessarily mean that the puppy will turn out to have problems. But avoid websites where there are no pictures of the home, environment and owners. If they are only showing close-up photos of cute puppies, click the **X** button

➤ Don't buy a website puppy with a shopping cart symbol next to his picture

➤ Don't commit to a website puppy unless you have seen it face-to-face. If this is not possible at the very least you must speak (on the phone) with the breeder and ask questions, don't deal with an intermediary

➤ At the breeder's you hear: "You can't see the parent dogs because……" ALWAYS ask to see the parents and at a minimum, see the mother and how she looks and behaves

➤ If the breeder says that the dam and sire are Kennel Club or AKC registered, insist on seeing the registration papers

➤ Ignore photographs of so-called 'champion' ancestors (unless you are buying from an approved breeder), in all likelihood these are fiction

➤ The puppies look small for their stated age. A committed Cocker Spaniel breeder will not let his or her puppies leave before they are eight weeks old at least

➤ The person you are buying the puppy from did not breed the dog themselves

➤ The place you meet the puppy seller is a car park, market or place other than the puppies' home

➤ The seller tells you that the puppy comes from top, caring breeders from your or another country. Not true. There are reputable, caring breeders all over the world, but not one of them sells their puppies through brokers

➤ Ask to see photos of the puppy from birth to present day. If the seller has none, there is a reason – walk away

➤ Price – if you are offered a cheap Cocker, he or she most likely comes from dubious stock. Careful breeding, taking good care of mother and puppies and health screening all add up to one big bill for breeders. Anyone selling their puppies at a knock-down price has almost certainly cut corners

➤ If you get a rescue Cocker, make sure it is from a recognised rescue group and not a 'puppy flipper' who may be posing as a do-gooder but is in fact getting dogs – including stolen ones - from unscrupulous sources

In fact the whole brokering business is just another version of the puppy mill and should be avoided at all costs. Bear in mind that for every cute puppy you see from a puppy mill or broker, other puppies have died.

Good Cocker Spaniel breeders will only breed from dogs which have been carefully selected for health, temperament, physical shape, lineage and being "fit for purpose." There are plenty out there, it's just a question of finding one. The good news is that there are signs to help the savvy buyer spot a good breeder.

Top 10 Tips for Choosing a Good Breeder

1. Good breeders either keep the dogs in the home as part of the family or, in the case of some actively working Cockers, in clean outdoor kennels - not in garages or outbuildings.

Check that the area where the puppies are kept is clean and that the puppies themselves look clean. Pictured here is a pup, complete with wet feather in mouth, bred by KC Assured Breeders Julie and Darren Summers, of Summervilles Gundogs, County Durham. Photo courtesy of http://ruralshots.com

2. Their pups appear happy and healthy. Check that the pup has clean eyes, ears, nose and bum (butt) with no discharge. The pups are alert, excited to meet new people and don't shy away from visitors.

3. A good breeder will encourage you to spend time with the puppy's parents - or at least the mother - when you visit. They want your family to meet the puppy and are happy for you to visit more than once.

4. They are very familiar with Cocker Spaniels, although they may also breed other dogs – with gundog breeders it may be Labradors.

5. Cocker Spaniels, like all purebreds, can have genetic weaknesses. Good breeders have health certificates. **See Chapter 10. Cocker Health** for details.

6. All responsible breeders should provide you with a written contract and health guarantee and allow you plenty of time to read it. They will also show you records of the puppy's visits to the vet, vaccinations, worming medication, etc. and explain what other vaccinations your puppy will need.

7. They feed their adults and puppies high quality dog food and give you some to take home and guidance on feeding and caring for your puppy. They will also be available for advice after you take your puppy home.

8. They don't always have pups available, but keep a list of interested people for the next available litter.

9. They don't over-breed, but do limit the number of litters from their dams. Over-breeding or breeding from older females can be detrimental to the female's health.

10. If you have selected a breeder and checked if/when she has puppies available, go online to the Cocker Spaniel forums before you visit and ask if anyone out there already has a dog from this breeder. If you are buying from a good breeder, the chances are someone will know this breeder or at least his or her reputation. If the feedback is negative, cancel your visit and start looking for another breeder.

And finally ... good Cocker Spaniel breeders want to know their beloved pups are going to good homes and will ask YOU a lot of questions about your suitability as owners. DON'T buy a puppy from a website or advert where a PayPal or credit card deposit secures you a puppy without any questions.

Puppies should not be regarded as must-have accessories. They are not objects, they are warm-blooded, living, breathing creatures.

A good breeder will, if asked, provide references from other people who have bought their puppies; call at least one before you commit. They will also agree to take a puppy back within a certain time frame if it does not work out for you, or if there is a health problem. Pictured is a Summerville dog in action, photo courtesy of http://ruralshots.com.

Healthy, happy puppies and adult dogs are what everybody wants. Spending hours now to find a committed breeder with well-bred Cockers is time well spent. It could save you a lot of time, money and heartache in the future and help to ensure that you and your chosen puppy are well suited and happy together for many years to come.

The Most Important Questions to Ask a Breeder

Many of these points have been covered in the previous section, but here's a reminder and checklist of the questions you should be asking.

Have the parents been health screened? Ideally you are looking for a puppy with DNA-tested parents. Ask to see original copies of health certificates. If there are no certificates available, ask what health guarantees the breeder is offering and how long they last – 12 weeks, a year, a lifetime? It will vary from breeder to breeder, but good ones will definitely give you some form of guarantee – always ask for this in writing. They will also want to be informed of any hereditary health problems with your puppy, as they may choose not to breed from the dam or sire (mother or father) again. Some breeders keep a chart documenting the full family health history of the pup.

Can you put me in touch with someone who already has one of your puppies?

Are you Kennel Club registered or a member of one of the Cocker Spaniel clubs? Not all good Cocker breeders are KC Assured Breeders or registered members of a club, but clubs are often a good place to start.

How long have you been breeding Cocker Spaniels? You are looking for someone who has a track record with the breed.

How many litters has the mother had? Females should not have litters until they are two and then only have a few litters in their lifetime, certainly not back-to-back breedings (i.e. every time she comes into season). The Kennel Club does not accept registrations from dams that have had more than four litters. Also check the age of the mother, too young or too old is not good for her health.

What happens to the female once she has finished breeding? Is she kept as part of the family, rehomed in a loving home or sent to animal rescue?

Do you breed any other types of dog? Buy from a Cocker Spaniel specialist, avoid people with a list of breeds as long as your arm. Pictured is Dutch breeder Haja Van Wessem's Multi Champion Speggle-Waggel's Roisin Connor, sire Sh.Ch. Lindridge Star Quest, dam Dutch and Multi Ch. Speggle-Waggel's Voilà.

What is so special about this litter? You are looking for a breeder who has used good breeding stock and his or her knowledge to produce healthy, handsome dogs with good temperaments. All Cocker puppies look cute, don't buy the first one you see – be patient and pick the right one. If you don't get a satisfactory answer, look elsewhere.

What do you feed your adults and puppies? A reputable breeder will feed a top quality dog food, advise that you do the same, and send some home with the puppy.

What special care do you recommend? Your Cocker Spaniel will probably need all or some of the following: regular grooming, trimming and ear cleaning.

What is the average lifespan of your dogs?

How socialised and housetrained is the puppy? Good breeders will raise their puppies as part of the household and start the socialisation and housetraining process before they leave. Even working dogs kept outside should have had some socialisation.

What healthcare have the pups had so far? Ask to see records of flea treatments, wormings and vaccinations.

Has the puppy been micro chipped?

Why aren't you asking me any questions? A responsible breeder will be committed to making a good match between the new owners and their puppies. If the breeder spends more time discussing money than the welfare of the puppy and how you will care for him, you can draw your own conclusions as to what his or her priorities are – and they probably don't include improving the breed.

If you have any doubts at all about the breeder, seller or the puppy, WALK AWAY.

TOP TIP: Take your puppy to a vet to have a thorough check-up within 48 hours of purchase. If your vet is not happy with the health of the dog, no matter how painful it may be, return the pup to the breeder. Keeping an unhealthy puppy will only cause more distress and expense in the long run.

Puppy Contracts

Ask if the puppy is being sold with a Puppy Contract. These are recommended by breed clubs around the world and protect both buyer and seller by providing information on a host of topics relating to before and after the puppy leaves the breeder. You should also have some sort of health guarantee, enabling you to return the puppy in the event of a physical and/or genetic defect.

The UK's The Royal Society for the Prevention of Cruelty to Animals (RSPCA) has a downloadable puppy contract endorsed by vets and animal welfare organisations, pictured. You can see a copy here and should be looking for something similar from the breeder or seller of the puppy: http://puppycontract.rspca.org.uk/home

Here is the Puppy Sales Contract for KC Assured Breeders **Summerville's Gundogs'** Cocker Spaniels, reproduced with kind permission of Darren and Julie Summers www.summervillesgundogs.com. You will note that there are some clauses specific to working dogs:

Section 1. Dog's Details

Breed Information: Spaniel (working cocker)

Sire: Summervilles game finder Dam: Summervilles pocket rocket

Pup's Date of Birth: Colour: Sex:

Kennel Club Details:

Registered Name: Summervilles

Registration Number:

Section 2. Details of Both Parties

Breeder: Darren and Julie Summers………………………County Durham

Purchaser's Name:

TELEPHONE *

Section 3. Health and Welfare

The Breeder has taken every care with breeding, rearing and the welfare of the dog. The dog is believed to be in good health and is sold in good faith. The Breeder makes no warranty however as to the health and disposition of the dog.

Every effort has been made to avoid any possible inherited conditions. Your pup's parents are fit for function and have followed all health test results for the breed. Hip scoring, annual eye test, glaucoma eye test, PRA clear, FN clear. Relevant, existing screening schemes have been used and copies of the relevant results are available at any time and copies will be included in your puppy pack.

The Purchaser hereby acknowledges that the Breeder has disclosed the following faults or defects in the dog ....

You will receive a copy of the vet's letter within your puppy pack. However should a defect be found and you agree to have said pup as the purchaser, you are advised to have your own vet examine the pup. This will be at the purchaser's expense.

Your puppy received its first inoculation whilst in our care and has followed a strict worming programme. Please talk to your vets about what he/she recommends for your pups future programme.

Your pup has been insured with the Kennel club and is covered for four weeks, details are in your puppy pack.

Section 4. Potential of Dog

Although any description of the dog as being of working or trial quality is given in good faith, it is a condition of this sale that no warranty can be given as to the ultimate working/trial/showing/breeding potential on maturity of the dog. (Photo: Summerville Cocker courtesy of http://ruralshots.com).

Section 5. Breeding Restrictions

Your newly purchased puppy has been sold with his/her pedigree endorsed 'progeny not eligible for registration'. This means that you will be unable to breed from the aforementioned animal and register its progeny with the Kennel Club unless the endorsement is lifted by us. Pups also endorsed not eligible for the issue of an Export Pedigree.

1. We will only consider removing these breeding restrictions only at the request of the above original Purchaser(s).

2. The pup must have had an annual eye test with certificate age minimum 12 months old and a copy of this must be forwarded to Summervilles. This must be a clear result.

3. The pup must have had a glaucoma eye examination with certificate a copy of this must be forwarded to Summervilles. This must be a clear-normal result.

4. The pup must have a full health test to prove the dog is in good condition and fit enough to be bred from, you must tell your vet what the exam is for and this should be noted in the report. A copy of this must be forwarded to Summervilles at the same time of any other documents. The pup's ID chip number must be recorded at this time by your vet.

5. The pup must have reached the minimum age of 18 months for a dog and 18 months for a bitch before we will consider removing breeding restrictions.

Only once I am satisfied with the information provided will we consider removing the breeding restrictions, we reserve the right to refuse to lift these endorsements.

By signing this contract you have agreed to these terms and conditions of this sale. And you agree we have informed you of the endorsements / breeding restrictions.

Owner(s) Signature..

Printed ....

Section 6. Tail Docking and the Puppy Purchased

If your puppy has been legally docked. You have been given a certificate proving that the puppy you have purchased was docked legally by a veterinary surgeon. You need to keep this certificate safe, as you may be called upon by the authorities to prove that the puppy was docked legally, at any time in the future. If you need to transfer ownership to another person at any time, please ensure that the certificate accompanies the sale or transfer.

At the time of docking, the breeder believed that some, or all, of the litter would be used or sold with the intention of being worked in accordance with the regulations connected to the Animal Welfare Act 2007. (Photo: Summerville Cocker courtesy of http://ruralshots.com).

The law appreciates that not every puppy docked will grow up with the necessary attributes and may never eventually work. It therefore follows that if you do not work your puppy; neither you as the owner, nor the breeder, will be liable for prosecution, provided you can produce the certificate. Information and the regulations covering this aspect, are shown on the following website: www.cdb.org/awa/index.htm

Section 7. Breeder's Condition of Sale

The Purchaser will agree to give the Breeder a regular update on the health and wellbeing of the pup, on a monthly basis for the first year of the puppy's life. This may be via the website if available, telephone, or email on .... and that the pup will be kept in the appropriate conditions for its welfare and health. Will be fed on a suitable diet for its age and condition and will receive all necessary care to maintain its good health. It is understood that if the purchaser fails any part of this contract or if the puppy is neglected or maltreated. The purchaser will surrender the above dog back to the breeder with all paperwork. This will be without financial restitution or compensation.

Section 8. Rehoming the Dog

The Purchaser(s) must agree that if, they should be in the unfortunate situation of having to rehome their dog they must return any puppy or adult dog to the breeder for rehoming. He or she must not be gifted, sold or loaned to any third party without the breeder's written permission. The purchaser understands and agrees that once the dog has been returned to the breeder, it becomes the responsibility of the breeder and that all matters concerning its future wellbeing and rehoming are to be the sole concern of the breeder. By signing the contract you agree to this condition of sale.

Section 9. Signatures, Date, Declarations

Date:

I/we confirm that I/we have read and had full explanation of all the detail and meaning of this contract prior to purchase and I/we fully understand its purpose and reason. I/we are purchasing this Cocker Spaniel for myself/ourselves and not for a third party.

All the above conditions are fully agreed:

Signed: .... Purchaser(s)...

Printed ....

I confirm that we are the Breeder of said dog:

Signed: ....

Witness name address .... Witness signature..

Top 10 Tips for Choosing a Healthy Cocker Spaniel

o   Your puppy should have a well-fed appearance. He or she should not, however, have a distended abdomen (pot belly) as this can be a sign of worms - or other illnesses such as Cushing's disease in adults. The ideal puppy should not be too thin either, you should not be able to see his ribs.

o   His nose should be cool, damp and clean with no discharge.

o   The pup's eyes should be bright and clear with no discharge or tear stain. Steer clear of a puppy which blinks a lot, this could be the sign of a problem.

o   The pup's ears should be clean with no sign of discharge, soreness or redness and no unpleasant smell. When the puppy is distracted, clap or make a noise behind him - not so loud as to frighten him - to make sure he is not deaf.

- His gums should be clean and a healthy pink colour.

- Check under the puppy's tail to make sure it is clean and there are no signs of diarrhoea.

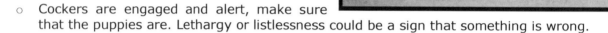

- A Cocker Spaniel's coat should be clean and silky with no signs of ticks or fleas. Red or irritated skin or bald spots could be a sign of infestation or a skin condition. Also check between the toes of the paws for signs of redness or swelling.

- Choose a puppy that moves freely without any sign of injury or lameness. It should be a fluid movement, not jerky or stiff, which could be a sign of joint problems.

- Cockers are engaged and alert, make sure that the puppies are. Lethargy or listlessness could be a sign that something is wrong.

- Finally, ask to see veterinary records to confirm your puppy has been wormed and had his first injections.

If you are unlucky enough to have a health problem with your pup within the first few months, a reputable breeder will allow you to return the pup. Also, if you get the puppy home and things don't work out for whatever reason, good breeders should also take the puppy back. Make sure this is the case before you commit.

Picking the Right Temperament

You've chosen a Cocker Spaniel, presumably, because you love these dogs, their eagerness to please, optimism, energy, friendly get-along-with-everybody nature, size, appearance and possibly their ability to perform a task. While different dogs may share many characteristics and temperament traits, each puppy also has his or her own individual character, just like humans.

Visit the breeder more than once to see how your chosen pup interacts and get an idea of his character in comparison to his littermates. Some puppies will run up to greet you, pull at your shoelaces and playfully bite your fingers. Others will be more content to stay in the basket sleeping. Watch their behaviour and energy levels. Are you an active person who enjoys masses of daily exercise or would a less hyper puppy be more suitable? Choose the puppy which will best fit in with your family and lifestyle.

A submissive dog will by nature be more passive and less energetic, a more dominant dog will usually be more energetic. They may also be more headstrong and need more patience when training or socialising with other dogs – but the rewards could be worth it.

There is no good or bad, it's a question of which type of character will best suit you and your lifestyle. Here are a couple of quick tests to try and gauge your puppy's temperament; they should be carried out by the breeder in familiar surroundings so the puppy is relaxed. It should be pointed out that there is some controversy over temperament testing as a dog's personality is formed by a combination of factors, which include inherited temperament, socialisation, training and environment (or how you treat him):

> The breeder puts the pup on his or her back on her lap and gently rests her hand on the pup's chest, or
> (S)he puts her hands under the pup's tummy and gently lifts the pup off the floor for a few seconds, keeping the pup horizontal

A puppy that struggles to get free is less patient than one which makes little effort to get away. A placid, patient dog is likely to fare better in a home with young children than an impatient one. However, if you are looking for a dog to field trial, the drive of impatient puppy might be just what is needed. Pictured is a seven-week-old American Cocker pup bred by Eunice Wine, of Blackberry Farm Enterprises, Dillwyn, Virginia, USA.

Useful Tips

Here are some other useful signs to look out for –

> Watch how your chosen pup interacts with other puppies in the litter. Does he try and dominate them, does he walk away from them or is he happy to play with his littermates? This may give you an idea of how easy it will be to socialise him with other dogs

> After contact, does the pup want to follow you or walk away from you? Not following may mean he has a more independent nature

> If you throw something for the puppy is he happy to retrieve it for you or does he ignore it? This may measure their willingness to work with humans

> If you drop a bunch of keys behind the puppy, does he act normally or does he flinch and jump away? The latter may be an indication of a timid or nervous disposition. Not reacting could also be a sign of deafness

Decide which temperament would fit in with you and your family and the rest is up to you. Whatever hereditary temperament your Cocker Spaniel has, it is true for all dogs that those that have constant positive interactions with people and other animals during the first three to four months of life will be happier and more stable. In contrast, a puppy plucked from its family too early and/or isolated at home alone for long periods will be less happy, less socialised, needier and may well display behaviour problems later on.

Puppies are like children. Being properly raised helps their confidence, sociability, stability and intellectual development. A pup raised in a comfortable, caring environment is likely to be more tolerant and accepting, and less likely to develop behaviour problems than one that isn't.

For those of you who prefer a scientific approach to choosing the right puppy, we are including the full Volhard Puppy Aptitude Test (PAT). This test has been developed by the highly respected Wendy and Jack Volhard who have built up an international reputation over the last 30 years for their contribution to dog training, health and nutrition. Their philosophy is: "We believe that one of life's great joys is living in harmony with your dog."

They have written several books and the Volhard PAT is regarded as one of the premier methods for evaluating the nature of young puppies. Jack and Wendy have also written the excellent Dog Training for Dummies book. Visit their website at www.volhard.com for details of their upcoming dog training camps, as well as their training and nutrition groups.

The Volhard Puppy Aptitude Test

Here are the ground rules for performing the test: the testing is done in a location unfamiliar to the puppies. This does not mean they have to be taken away from home. A 10-foot square area is perfectly adequate, such as a room in the house where the puppies have not been.

The puppies are tested one at a time. There are no other dogs or people, except the scorer and the tester, in the testing area:

- ✓ The puppies do not know the tester.
- ✓ The scorer is a disinterested third party and not the person interested in selling you a puppy.
- ✓ The scorer is unobtrusive and positions himself so he can observe the puppies' responses without having to move.
- ✓ The puppies are tested before they are fed. The puppies are tested when they are at their liveliest. Do not try to test a puppy that is not feeling well.
- ✓ Puppies should not be tested the day of or the day after being vaccinated.
- ✓ Only the first response counts.

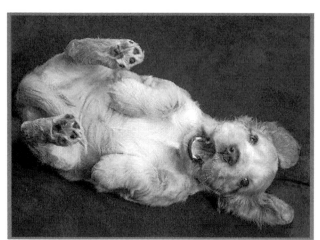

Tip: During the test, watch the puppy's tail. It will make a difference in the scoring whether the tail is up or down.

The tests are simple to perform and anyone with some common sense can do them. You can, however, elicit the help of someone who has tested puppies before and knows what they are doing.

Social Attraction - the owner or caretaker of the puppies places it in the test area about four feet from the tester and then leaves the test area. The tester kneels down and coaxes the puppy to come to him or her by encouragingly and gently clapping hands and calling. The tester must coax the puppy in the opposite direction from where it entered the test area. Hint: Lean backward, sitting on your heels instead of leaning forward toward the puppy. Keep your hands close to your body encouraging the puppy to come to you instead of trying to reach for the puppy.

Following - the tester stands up and slowly walks away encouraging the puppy to follow. Hint: Make sure the puppy sees you walk away and get the puppy to focus on you by lightly clapping your hands and using verbal encouragement to get the puppy to follow you. Do not lean over the puppy.

Restraint - the tester crouches down and gently rolls the puppy on its back for 30 seconds. Hint: Hold the puppy down without applying too much pressure. The object is not to keep it on its back but to test its response to being placed in that position.

Social Dominance - let the puppy stand up or sit and gently stroke it from the head to the back while you crouch beside it. See if it will lick your face, an indication of a forgiving nature. Continue stroking until you see a behaviour you can score. Hint: When you crouch next to the puppy avoid leaning or hovering over it. Have the puppy at your side, both of you facing in the same direction.

Tip: During testing maintain a positive, upbeat and friendly attitude toward the puppies. Try to get each puppy to interact with you to bring out the best in him or her. Make the test a pleasant experience for the puppy.

Elevation Dominance - the tester cradles the puppy with both hands, supporting the puppy under its chest and gently lifts it two feet off the ground and holds it there for 30 seconds.

Retrieving - the tester crouches beside the puppy and attracts its attention with a crumpled up piece of paper. When the puppy shows some interest, the tester throws the paper no more than four feet in front of the puppy encouraging it to retrieve the paper.

Touch Sensitivity - the tester locates the webbing of one the puppy's front paws and presses it lightly between his index finger and thumb. The tester gradually increases pressure while counting to ten and stops when the puppy pulls away or shows signs of discomfort.

Sound Sensitivity - the puppy is placed in the centre of the testing area and an assistant stationed at the perimeter makes a sharp noise, such as banging a metal spoon on the bottom of a metal pan.

Sight Sensitivity - the puppy is placed in the centre of the testing area. The tester ties a string around a bath towel and jerks it across the floor, two feet away from the puppy.

Stability - an umbrella is opened about five feet from the puppy and gently placed on the ground.

During the testing, make a note of the heart rate of the pup, this is an indication of how it deals with stress, as well as its energy level.

Puppies come with high, medium or low energy levels. You have to decide for yourself, which suits your life style. Dogs with high energy levels need a great deal of exercise, and will get into mischief if this energy is not channelled into the right direction.

Finally, look at the overall structure of the puppy. You see what you get at 49 days age (seven weeks). If the pup has strong and straight front and back legs, with all four feet pointing in the same direction, it will grow up that way, provided you give it the proper diet and environment. If you notice something out of the ordinary at this age, it will stay with puppy for the rest of its life. He will not grow out of it.

Scoring the Results

Following are the responses you will see and the score assigned to each particular response. You will see some variations and will have to make a judgment on what score to give them –

Test	Response	Score
SOCIAL ATTRACTION	Came readily, tail up, jumped, bit at hands	1
	Came readily, tail up, pawed, licked at hands	2
	Came readily, tail up	3
	Came readily, tail down	4
	Came hesitantly, tail down	5
	Didn't come at all	6
FOLLOWING	Followed readily, tail up, got underfoot, bit at feet	1
	Followed readily, tail up, got underfoot	2
	Followed readily, tail up	3
	Followed readily, tail down	4
	Followed hesitantly, tail down	5
	Did not follow or went away	6
RESTRAINT	Struggled fiercely, flailed, bit	1
	Struggled fiercely, flailed	2
	Settled, struggled, settled with some eye contact	3
	Struggled, then settled	4
	No struggle	5
	No struggle, strained to avoid eye contact	6
SOCIAL DOMINANCE	Jumped, pawed, bit, growled	1
	Jumped, pawed	2
	Cuddled up to tester and tried to lick face	3
	Squirmed, licked at hands	4
	Rolled over, licked at hands	5
	Went away and stayed away	6
ELEVATION DOMINANCE	Struggled fiercely, tried to bite	1
	Struggled fiercely	2
	Struggled, settled, struggled, settled	3
	No struggle, relaxed	4
	No struggle, body stiff	5
	No struggle, froze	6
RETRIEVING	Chased object, picked it up and ran away	1
	Chased object, stood over it and did not return	2
	Chased object, picked it up and returned with it to tester	3
	Chased object and returned without it to tester	4
	Started to chase object, lost interest	5
	Does not chase object	6
TOUCH SENSITIVITY	8-10 count before response	1
	6-8 count before response	2
	5-6 count before response	3
	3-5 count before response	4
	2-3 count before response	5
	1-2 count before response	6

SOUND SENSITIVITY	Listened, located sound and ran toward it barking	1	
	Listened, located sound and walked slowly toward it	2	
	Listened, located sound and showed curiosity	3	
	Listened and located sound	4	
	Cringed, backed off and hid behind tester	5	
	Ignored sound and showed no curiosity	6	
SIGHT SENSITIVITY	Looked, attacked and bit object	1	
	Looked and put feet on object and put mouth on it	2	
	Looked with curiosity and attempted to investigate, tail up	3	
	Looked with curiosity, tail down	4	
	Ran away or hid behind tester	5	
	Hid behind tester	6	
STABILITY	Looked and ran to the umbrella, mouthing or biting it	1	
	Looked and walked to the umbrella, smelling it cautiously	2	
	Looked and went to investigate	3	
	Sat and looked, but did not move toward the umbrella	4	
	Showed little or no interest	5	
	Ran away from the umbrella	6	

The scores are interpreted as follows:

Mostly 1s - Strong desire to be pack leader and is not shy about bucking for a promotion. Has a predisposition to be aggressive to people and other dogs and will bite. Should only be placed into a very experienced home where the dog will be trained and worked on a regular basis.

Tip: Stay away from the puppy with a lot of 1s or 2s. It has lots of leadership aspirations and may be difficult to manage. This puppy needs an experienced home. Not good with children.

Mostly 2s - Also has leadership aspirations. May be hard to manage and has the capacity to bite. Has lots of self-confidence. Should not be placed into an inexperienced home. Too unruly to be good with children and elderly people, or other animals. Needs strict schedule, loads of exercise and lots of training. Has the potential to be a great show dog with someone who understands dog behaviour.

Mostly 3s - Can be a high-energy dog and may need lots of exercise. Good with people and other animals. Can be a bit of a handful to live with. Needs training, does very well at it and learns quickly. Great dog for second-time owner.

Mostly 4s - The kind of dog that makes the perfect pet. Best choice for the first time owner. Rarely will buck for a promotion in the family. Easy to train, and rather quiet. Good with elderly people, children, although may need protection from the children. Choose this pup, take it to obedience classes, and you'll be the star, without having to do too much work!

Tip: The puppy with mostly 3's and 4's can be quite a handful, but should be good with children and does well with training. Energy needs to be dispersed with plenty of exercise.

Mostly 5s - Fearful, shy and needs special handling. Will run away at the slightest stress in its life. Strange people, strange places, different floor or surfaces may upset it. Often afraid of loud noises and terrified of thunderstorms. When you greet it upon your return, may submissively urinate. Needs a very special home where the environment doesn't change too much and where there are no children. Best for a quiet, elderly couple. If cornered and cannot get away, has a tendency to bite.

Mostly 6s – So independent that he doesn't need you or other people. Doesn't care if he is trained or not - he is his own person. Unlikely to bond to you, since he doesn't need you. A great guard dog for gas stations! Do not take this puppy and think you can change him into a lovable bundle - you can't, so leave well enough alone.

Tip: Avoid the puppy with several 6's. It is so independent it doesn't need you or anyone. He is his own person and unlikely to bond to you.

The Scores - Few puppies will test with all 2's or all 3's, there'll be a mixture of scores. For that first time, wonderfully easy to train, potential star, look for a puppy that scores with mostly 4's and 3's. Don't worry about the score on Touch Sensitivity - you can compensate for that with the right training equipment.

It's hard not to become emotional when picking a puppy - they are all so cute, soft and cuddly. Remind yourself that this dog is going to be with you for eight to 16 years. Don't hesitate to step back a little to contemplate your decision. Sleep on it and review it in the light of day.

Avoid the puppy with a score of 1 on the Restraint and Elevation tests. This puppy will be too much for the first-time owner. It's a lot more fun to have a good dog, one that is easy to train, one you can live with and one you can be proud of, than one that is a constant struggle.

Getting a Dog From a Shelter - Don't overlook an animal shelter as a source for a good dog. Not all dogs wind up in a shelter because they are bad. After that cute puppy stage, when the dog grows up, it may become too much for its owner. Or, there has been a change in the owner's circumstances forcing him or her into having to give up the dog.

Most of the time these dogs are housetrained and already have some training. If the dog has been properly socialised to people, it will be able to adapt to a new environment. Bonding may take a little longer, but once accomplished, results in a devoted companion.

So you see, it's not all about the colour or the cutest face! When getting a puppy, your thought process should run something like this:

1. Decide to get a Cocker Spaniel.
2. Decide which type of Cocker would best suit you – English or American, show or working.
3. If it's working, decide if you want a dog from gundog or field trial bloodlines (there can be a difference in temperament and drive).
4. Find a breeder with a good reputation whose dogs are health tested.

5. Find one with a litter available when you are ready for a puppy – or wait.
6. Decide on a male or female.
7. Choose one with a suitable temperament to fit in with your lifestyle.
8. Once you have decided on all the above factors, choose the colour – bear in mind that if a puppy meets all of the above criteria, colour is not important.

Some people pick a puppy based purely on how the dog looks. If coat colour, for example, is very important to you, first make sure the other boxes are ticked as well.

5. Bringing Your Puppy Home

Before you bring your precious little bundle of joy home, if your Cocker is to live in the house, it's a good idea to prepare the surroundings before he or she arrives while you still have the chance. All puppies are demanding and once they land, they will swallow up most of your time. Here's a list of things you ought to think about getting beforehand:

Puppy Checklist

- ✓ A dog bed or basket
- ✓ Bedding – old towels or a blanket which can easily be washed
- ✓ If possible, a towel or piece of cloth which has been rubbed on the puppy's mother to put in the bed
- ✓ A collar, or harness, and lead
- ✓ An identification tag for the collar or harness
- ✓ Food and water bowls, preferably stainless steel
- ✓ Lots of newspapers for housetraining
- ✓ Poo(p) bags
- ✓ Puppy food – find out what the breeder is feeding and stick with it initially
- ✓ Toys and chews suitable for puppies
- ✓ Puppy treats (preferably healthy ones, not rawhide)
- ✓ A crate if you decide to use one
- ✓ Old towels for cleaning your puppy and covering the crate
- ✓ A puppy coat if you live in a cool climate

AND PLENTY OF TIME!

Later on you'll also need a longer, stronger lead, a grooming brush and comb, dog shampoo, flea and worming products and maybe a travel crate.

Puppy Proofing Your Home

Before your puppy arrives at his or her new home, you may have to make some adjustments to make your home safe and suitable. Young Cocker puppies are small bundles of instinct and energy (when they are awake), with little common sense and even less self-control. They are extremely curious, they love to play and have a great sense of fun. They may have mad bursts of energy before they run out of steam and spend much of the rest of the day sleeping. They are like babies and it's up to you to look after them and set the boundaries – both physically and in terms of behaviour – but one step at a time.

Create an area where the puppy is allowed to go and then keep the rest of the house off-limits until housetraining is complete. This shouldn't take long; Cockers are relatively easy to housetrain, according to the breeders involved in this book. One of the biggest factors influencing the success and speed of housetraining is your commitment - another reason for taking a week or two off work when your puppy arrives home.

Like babies, most puppies are mini chewing machines and so remove anything breakable and/or chewable within the puppy's reach – including wooden furniture. Obviously you cannot remove your kitchen cupboards, doors, skirting boards and other fixtures and fittings, so don't leave him unattended for any length of time where he can chew something which is hard to replace.

A baby gate is a relatively inexpensive method of preventing a puppy from going upstairs and leaving an unwanted gift on your precious bedroom carpets. A puppy's bones are soft and recent studies have shown that if very young pups are allowed to climb or descend stairs regularly, or jump on and off furniture, they can develop joint problems later in life. This is worth bearing in mind, especially as some Cockers are prone to hip dysplasia. You can also use a baby gate or wire panels, available from pet shops, to keep the puppy enclosed in one room – preferably one with a floor which is easy to wipe clean and not too far away from a door to the garden or yard for housetraining.

You may also want to make sure your expensive oriental rugs are off limits until he or she is fully housetrained and has stopped chewing everything. Make sure you have some toys soft enough to chew and too big to swallow which are suitable for sharp little teeth. Don't give old socks, shoes or slippers or your pup will regard your footwear as fair game. Avoid rawhide chews as they can get stuck in the dog's throat.

The puppy's designated area or room should be not too hot, cold or damp and free from draughts. Puppies are sensitive to temperature fluctuations and don't do well in very hot or very cold conditions.

Just as you need a home, your puppy needs a den. This den is a haven where your puppy feels safe for the first few weeks after the traumatic experience of leaving his or her mother and littermates. Young puppies sleep for over 18 hours a day at the beginning; some may sleep for up to 22 hours a day. This is normal.

If you have young children, you must restrict the time they spend with the puppy to a few short sessions a day. Plenty of sleep is **essential** for the normal development of a young dog. You wouldn't wake a baby up every hour or so to play and shouldn't do that with a puppy. Don't invite friends round to see your new puppy for at least a day or two, preferably longer. However excited you are, your new pup needs a few days to get over the stress of leaving his mother and siblings and then to start bonding with you.

You have a couple of options with the den; you can get a dog bed or basket, or you can use a crate. Crates have long been popular in America and are becoming increasingly used in the UK, particularly as it can be quicker to housetrain a puppy using a crate.

The idea of keeping a dog in a cage like a rabbit or hamster is abhorrent to many animal-loving Brits; but they can be a useful aid if used properly. Using the crate as a prison to contain the dog for hours on end certainly is cruel, but the crate has its place as a sanctuary for your dog; a place where he or she can go. It is their own space and they know no harm will come to them in there. See **Crate Training** later in this chapter for advice on getting your Cocker used to - and even to enjoy - being in his crate.

Most puppies' natural instinct is not to soil the area where they sleep. Put plenty of newspapers down in the area next to the den and your pup should choose to go to the toilet here if you are not quick enough to take him or her outside. Of course, they may also decide to trash their designated area by chewing their blankets and shredding the newspaper – patience is the key in this situation!

If you have a garden or yard that you intend letting your puppy roam in, make sure that every little gap has been plugged. You'd be amazed at the tiny holes puppies can escape through. Also, don't leave your Cocker unattended as they can come to harm, and dogs are increasingly being targeted by thieves, who are even stealing from gardens. Make sure there are no poisonous plants which your pup might chew and check there are no low plants with sharp leaves or thorns which could cause eye or other injuries.

In order for puppies to grow into well-adjusted dogs, they have to feel comfortable and relaxed in their new surroundings and they need a great deal of sleep. They are leaving the warmth and protection of their mother and littermates and so for the first few days at least, your puppy will feel very sad. It is important to make the transition from the birth home to your home as easy as possible. Your pup's life is in your hands. How you react and interact with him in the first few days and weeks will shape your relationship and his character for the years ahead.

Breeders' Advice for New Owners

We asked a number of UK breeders what essential tips they would give and they had a wealth of advice for new and prospective owners of Cocker puppies:

Jo Oxley, Looseminxjoy Working Cocker Spaniels, Norfolk: "Really consider whether you are prepared to give them the time, then more time! Take a holiday to be with them."

Linda Reed, Delindere (English and American) Cocker Spaniels, Leicestershire: "Be patient, show them right from wrong, really reward the right behaviour and ignore the wrong, as they are very intelligent. Be aware that a pup left for long periods will become bored very quickly and will chew. Show plenty of love."

Lynne Waterhouse, Lyfora (show) Cocker Spaniels, Berkshire: "The advice I give to my puppies' new owners is to establish a routine and be consistent with discipline from day one, with all family members involved as much as possible. The poor pup will only become confused if mum and dad are housetraining and rewarding good behaviour and the children are not following the training programme. And always make sure the pup does not have access to any cleaning products, cupboards or garden chemicals, I provide a list of dangers to my new owners."

Tracey Simpson - Bravialis Gundogs, North Yorkshire: "Not letting puppies chew or find small parts that can be swallowed is the main thing. I also always advise new owners to buy a Pheromone spray. Their mothers give off calming pheromones when they feed their pups, a spray on their new bedding in their new home can help with those noisy nights."

Christine Grant, Rostreigan (show) Cocker Spaniels, Hampshire: "Be aware of all the dangers which lurk in your home and garden; electric cables, items she could swallow, poisonous plants (ivy, laburnum, oleander, the list is endless), toxic foods (onions, garlic, grapes, raisins, chocolate, etc). Block up any potential escape routes from the garden, such as broken fences, holes in hedges etc. Always accompany her into the garden to start with, anyway you need to be with her to praise when she performs as you wish her to perform."

Billie Cheeseman, BarleyCourt (working) Spaniels, Hertfordshire: "Taking a puppy home is like bringing a toddler into your home for the first time. They are into everything, everything ends up in their mouths and they don't really pay much attention (initially) to the word 'No'. My advice is

to move everything up, as you would with a toddler, don't leave small things lying around - even socks have caused puppies to choke - so when they are to be alone/unmonitored, leave them in a room where there are none of these kind of things in reach.

"There are many dangers to young puppies and equally older dogs. Some human foods are poisonous/toxic to dogs, for example raisins and chocolate. Some plants are dangerous to dogs - azaleas, for example. Small things, exposed electrical cables, phone chargers, etc. are all a potential danger to a puppy." Pictured is Billie's nine-month-old Booker.

Kennel Club Assured Breeder Peter Harvey, Grannus (show) Cocker Spaniels, Somerset: "Remove all small and damageable things from floors and tables, e.g. shoes, slippers, phones, laptops, electric cables, glass, pens etc. Close doors to no-go areas, fit child locks to fridges, cupboards containing food and cleaning products. Have an ample supply of newspapers, poo bags and bedding.

"Ensure the garden is secure and safe, remove tools, make sure things cannot fall on them. Block up holes in fences/bushes. Do not use slug pellets or other chemicals on the garden, patio or paths. Fence off flower beds, the veg patch, ponds, pools, rubbish and garden waste. I would not fit a collar until puppy is four months old; they are into everything, so can easily get it caught and cause serious harm."

Robert and Ruth Baldwin, of Annaru (show) Cocker Spaniels, South Wales: "We always say that they are likely to miss their mom and litter for a few days, but if you put the blanket in the cage with them it will help calm them down. They might cry in the night for a few days, but try not to go down and cuddle them - unless you want to do it every night. Puppies are like babies, they will chew anything and everything until they stop teething, so be careful what you leave around."

David and Alison Matthews, Tojamatt (show) Cockers, Nottinghamshire: "Give puppies plenty of opportunity to rest, they need peace and quiet. Do not over-exercise a puppy and be careful of small toys." Christine Thomas, Dodfordhills (working) Spaniels, Worcestershire: "Before bringing him home, visit them as much as possible to develop a bond, if you can."

Carole Pitchers, of Alcarbrad (working) Cocker Spaniels, Essex, agrees: "Have regular contact with your new puppy before you bring it home – I like most new owners to visit once a week, so they get to know the puppy. On the day you collect your puppy, collect as early as possible so that you have all day to settle them in. Be prepared, i.e. have a supply of puppy food and all the other essentials you will need. Establish a routine quickly - if you don't want the dog to sit on the furniture, then sit on the floor with the puppy from day one. Dangers for puppies are exactly the same as for young children. There are also the well documented issues surrounding chocolate, particularly during the Christmas period."

Pat and Andrew Height, Fourtails Cocker Spaniels, Cambridgeshire: "Be fully prepared and have all the things you need to ensure your puppy has a wonderful time in its new home. You need a nice, warm, comfortable bed for the puppy, good food and a sensible diet, as well as training from the word go and socialisation once vaccinations have taken place."

Kennel Club Assured Breeder Stewart North, Northglen Labradors and Cockers, Leicestershire, advises new owners to pay attention to: "Socialisation, immunisation, training, micro-chipping, worming, feeding, crate, kennel, grooming and exercise. And remember that not all other dogs are

nice." Kerena Marchant, of Sondes (working) Cocker Spaniels, Surrey, adds: "Don't get a working Cocker if you don't have an active lifestyle. Stimulate and play with the puppy from day one!"

Gail Parsons, of Gaiter (show) Cocker Spaniels, Sussex: "The puppy must know its place and that you are pack leader. You need to set rules and boundaries regarding eating and sleeping, and if there are children they need to be taught not to poke or pull the puppy." Did anyone tell the dogs? Our photo shows Gail's handsome quartet looking very at home on her sofa!

Helen Marsden, Finity (show) Cocker Spaniels, Hampshire: "Firstly and foremost, buy from a reputable breeder that health tests all their breeding dogs. Start as you mean to go on, a Cocker Spaniel can be headstrong and must know its boundaries from very early on. Do not allow them to go up and down the stairs or jump off furniture as this will cause joint problems later on in their lives."

Jill Gunn, Dearganach Working Cockers, Scotland: "Don't overtire your pup, and puppies are inquisitive, so ensure the environment is safe from hazards."

New breeder Jane Seekings, of Dorset, agrees: "Make the puppy feel safe, secure and loved and ensure that from the start the boundaries are set, e.g. whether the puppy allowed on the furniture, upstairs...etc. and that all members of the family know what these rules are. It is also less confusing if one person is mainly responsible for training. Finally, make sure that the garden is puppy-proof and that the puppy cannot get out or injure itself."

One North of England breeder said: "Always be calm and kind. The first few weeks' experiences are crucial in determining your puppy's temperament and responses. Ensure your puppy has a safe place to go when he is tired or you need to keep him safe, possibly in a crate. Teach small children how to handle your puppy and never leave them alone with him, as they can be overexuberant and it is very easy to cause injury. I once had a very sad fatality caused by one of my own children holding an eight-week-old puppy too tightly."

Manda and Jacquie Smith, Tassietay Working Cocker Spaniels, East Kent: "This topic could take a whole book! To be brief: as soon as you get puppy home, take him to the area you want him to use as a toilet and wait for him to wee, then praise him and take him indoors and put him in the pen for a while for him to settle.

"Offer a small meal, if he eats it, take him outside again for the toilet and then let him stay quietly in the pen for a sleep before letting him out to explore. Beware of toxic plants in the garden, for instance just chewing daffodil buds or flowers will cause extreme sickness. And make sure any prescription drugs are kept safely in a cupboard or drawer. Remember, puppies will chew everything!"

Kennel Club Assured Breeder Andy Platt, of Nithvalley Gundogs, Scotland: "Firstly, people should do a thorough self-assessment to see if they are suitable owners for a Cocker Spaniel. Hygiene is also a big thing. Many puppies carry worms and other zoological diseases that people need to be aware of when handling puppies, and especially when allowing children to handle them." Our photo shows Andy's alert working Cocker, Bailey.

Caroline Bymolen, Carto (show) Cocker Spaniels, Cambridgeshire: "First of all, make sure that you really want a pup and that you can give it the love, time and attention it needs. It is not a toy, but a living being.

"Accept that the pup will wee and poo in the house if you don't keep an eye on it, and understand that a pup cannot hold its bladder, etc. all night when young. You **will** have a dirty crate in the morning. Pups are inquisitive and will chew anything they can get hold of."

Kirsten Strachan, Lorne Working Cockers, Perthshire, Scotland: "My advice is to continue with the high quality food I have reared the pup on - I always give a puppy pack which includes a large bag of food. Then: register the pup with their vet, maintain a calm environment and ensure the pup has a den. Don't let a pup run up and downstairs or jump on and off furniture, due to his growth plates still being open and the nature/nurture argument of hip dysplasia."

Keith Henderson, of Owencraig (show) Cocker Spaniels, Dunfermline, Scotland, added: "Do not overwhelm the puppy and provide enough space to welcome the new puppy into the home." And Jackie Hornby, of Jacmist (show) Cocker Spaniels, Bedfordshire, cautioned against leaving a pup alone in the garden where he can swallow stones or bark.

Another Kennel Club Assured Breeder added: "Enjoy it, it will only be a proper puppy for a few short months, and that time is to be maximised. With the application of common sense, and reference to a wealth of freely available advice, if required, handlers should soon get to 'feel' what is right for the puppy, and have the self-confidence to act upon that."

The First Few Days

Before you collect your puppy, let the breeder know what time you will arrive and ask him or her not to feed the pup for three or four hours beforehand (unless you have a very long journey, in which case the puppy will need to eat something). He will be less likely to be car sick and should be hungry when he lands in his new home. The same applies to an adult dog moving to a new home. When you arrive, ask the breeder for an old towel which has been with the dam – you can leave one on an earlier visit to collect with the pup. Or take one with you and rub the mother with it to collect her scent and put this with the puppy for the first few days. It may help him to settle in.

Make sure you get copies of any health certificates relating to the parents. A good breeder will also have a Contract of Sale or Puppy Contract – **see Chapter 4. Choosing a Puppy** – which outlines your and their rights and responsibilities. It should also state that you can return the puppy if there are health issues within a certain time frame – although if you have picked your breeder carefully, it will hopefully not come to this. The breeder should also give you details of worming and any vaccinations. Most good breeders supply an information sheet for new owners.

You should also find out exactly what the breeder is feeding and how much. You cannot suddenly switch a dog's diet; their digestive systems cannot cope with a sudden change. In the beginning stick to whatever the puppy is used to.

The Journey Home

Bringing a new puppy home in the car can be a traumatic experience. Your puppy will be devastated at leaving his or her mother, brothers and sisters and a familiar environment. Everything will be strange and frightening and he will probably whimper and whine - or even howl or bark - on the way to his new home. If you can, take somebody with you to take care of him on that first journey. Under no circumstances have the puppy on your lap while driving. It is simply too dangerous - a little Cocker puppy is cute, lively and far too distracting.

The best and safest way to transport the pup is in a crate – either a purpose-made travel crate or a wire crate which he will use at home. Put a comfortable blanket in the bottom - preferably rubbed with the scent of the mother. See if you can get a familiar toy from the breeder as well. Ask your travel companion to sit next to the crate and talk softly to the frightened little bundle of nerves.

He or she will almost certainly cry or whimper. If you don't have a crate, your passenger may wish to hold the puppy. If so, have an old towel between the person and the pup as he may quite possibly urinate (the puppy, not the passenger!)

If you have a journey of more than a couple of hours, make sure that you take water and offer the puppy a drink en route. He may need to eliminate or have diarrhoea (hopefully, only due to nerves), but don't let him outside on to the ground in a strange place as he is not yet fully inoculated. If you have a long journey, cover the bottom of the crate with a waterproof material and put newspapers in half of it, so the pup can eliminate without staining the car seats.

Arriving Home

As soon as you arrive home, let your puppy into the garden or yard and when he 'performs,' praise him for his efforts. You must supervise him 100% of the time unless he is in a safe area, such as a puppy pen or crate.

These first few days are critical in getting your puppy to feel safe and confident in his new surroundings. Spend time with your new arrival, talk to him often in a reassuring manner. Introduce him to his den and toys, slowly allow him to explore and show him around the house – once you have puppy proofed it.

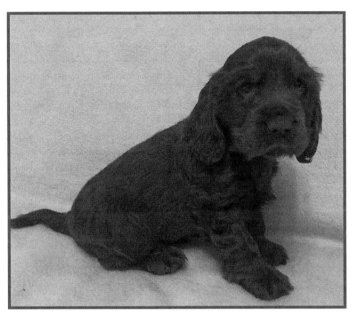

Cocker puppies are extremely curious - and amusing, you might be surprised at his reactions to everyday objects. Remember that puppies and babies explore with their mouths, so don't scold for chewing. Instead, remove objects you don't want chewed out of reach and replace them with toys he can chew.

This beautiful chocolate (also called liver) Finity show pup was bred by Helen Marsden, of Hampshire.

If you have other animals, introduce them slowly and in supervised sessions - preferably once the pup has got used to his new surroundings, not as soon as you walk through the door. Gentleness and patience are the keys to these first few days, so don't over-face your puppy. Have a special, gentle voice with which to talk to him and use his name often in a pleasant, encouraging manner. Never use his name to scold or he will associate it with bad things. The sound of his name should always make him want to pay attention to you as something good is going to happen - praise, food, play time and so on.

Resist the urge to pick the puppy up all the time. Let him explore on his own legs, encouraging a little independence. One of the most important things at this stage is to ensure that your puppy has enough sleep – **which is nearly all of the time** - no matter how much you want to play with him or watch his antics when awake.

If you haven't decided what to call your new puppy yet, 'Shadow' might be a good suggestion, as he or she will follow you everywhere! Many puppies from different breeds do this, but Cockers are devoted to their owners – both as puppies and adults. Our website receives many emails from worried new owners. Here are some of the most common concerns:

> ➢ My puppy sleeps all the time, is this normal?
> ➢ My puppy won't stop crying or whining
> ➢ My puppy is shivering
> ➢ My puppy won't eat
> ➢ My puppy is very timid
> ➢ My puppy follows me everywhere, she won't let me out of her sight

Most of the above are quite common. They are just a young pup's reaction to leaving his mother and littermates and entering into a strange new world. It is normal for puppies to sleep most of the time, just like babies. It is also normal for some puppies to whine a lot during the first few days.

Make your new pup as comfortable as possible, ensuring he has a warm (but not too hot), quiet den away from draughts, where he is not pestered by children or other pets. Handle him gently, while giving him plenty of time to sleep. During the first few nights your puppy will whine; try your best to ignore the pitiful cries.

Unless they are especially lively or dominant, most puppies will be nervous and timid for the first few days. They will think of you as their new mother and follow you around the house.

This is also quite natural, but after a few days start to leave your puppy for a few minutes at a time, gradually building up the time. Cockers, like many other breeds, can be prone to separation anxiety, particularly if they are used to being with you virtually 24/7. See **Chapter 8. Behaviour** for more information.

If your routine means you are normally out of the house for a few hours during the day, get your puppy on a Friday or Saturday so he has at least a couple of days to adjust to his new surroundings. A far better idea is to book at least a week or two off work to help your puppy settle in. If you don't work, leave your diary free for the first couple of weeks.

Helping a new pup to settle in is virtually a full-time job. However, you still need to start leaving the pup for a short time every day so he gets used to you not being there – even if you are at home all day, make the effort to go out for a short while.

The handsome young chap pictured is Gilbey's My Tonic at Lorne (Gilbey) was bred by Kirsten Strachan of Perthshire.

This is a frightening time for your puppy. Is your puppy shivering with cold or is it nerves? Avoid placing your pup under stress by making too many demands on him. Don't allow the kids to pester him and, until they have learned how to handle a dog, don't allow them to pick him up unsupervised, as they could inadvertently damage his delicate little body, as you've just read.

If your puppy won't eat, spend time gently coaxing him. If he leaves his food, take it away and try it later. Don't leave it down all of the time or he may get used to turning his nose up at it. The next time you put something down for him, he is more likely to be hungry. If your new pup is crying, it is probably for one of the following reasons:

- He is lonely
- He is hungry
- He wants attention from you
- He needs to go to the toilet

If it is none of these, then physically check him over to make sure he hasn't picked up an injury. Try not to fuss over him. If he whimpers, just reassure him with a quiet word. If he cries loudly and tries to get out of his allotted area, he probably needs to go to the toilet. Even if it is the middle of the night, get up (yes, sorry, this is best) and take him outside. Praise him if he goes to the toilet.

The strongest bonding period for a puppy is between eight and 12 weeks of age. The most important factors in bonding with your puppy are TIME spent with him and PATIENCE, even when he makes a mess in the house or chews something he shouldn't.

Remember, your pup is just a baby dog and it takes time to learn not to do these things. Spend time with your pup and you will have a loyal friend for life. Cockers are very focussed on their humans and that emotional attachment between you and your dog may grow to become one of the most important aspects of your life – and certainly his.

Where Should the Puppy Sleep?

Where do you want your new puppy to sleep? You cannot simply allow him or her to wander freely around the house. Ideally he will be in a contained area, such as a playpen or a crate, at night. While it is not acceptable to shut a dog in a cage all day, you can keep your puppy in a crate at night until he or she is housetrained. You also have to consider whether you want the pup to sleep in your bedroom or elsewhere. If your puppy is in the bedroom, try to prevent him from jumping on and off beds and/or couches or racing upstairs and downstairs until he has stopped growing, as this can damage his joints.

If he is to sleep outside your bedroom, put him in a comfortable bed of his own, or a crate – and then block your ears for the first couple of nights. He will almost certainly whine and whimper, but this won't last long and he will soon get used to sleeping on his own, without his littermates or you.

We don't recommend letting your new pup sleep on the bed. He will not be housetrained and also a puppy needs to learn his place in the household and have his own den. It's up to you whether you decide to let him on the bed when he's older. Another point to bear in mind is that if your dog is regularly exercised, his paws and coat may pick up mud, grass, brambles and other things you may not want on your bed.

While it is not good to leave a dog alone all day, it is also not healthy to spend 24 hours a day with him. He becomes too reliant on you and this increases the chance of him developing separation anxiety when you do have to leave him. A Cocker puppy used to being on his own every night is less likely to develop attachment issues, so consider this when deciding where he should sleep. Our dog sleeps in his own bed in our bedroom and has separation anxiety. Any future dogs will sleep in a separate room from us – no matter how hard that is in the beginning when the puppy is whimpering in the night.

Many owners prefer to bite the bullet right from the start by leaving the pup in a safe place downstairs or in a different room to the bedroom, so he gets used to being on his own right from the beginning. If you do this, you might find a set of earplugs very useful for helping (you) to survive the first few nights! In a moment of weakness you might consider letting the puppy sleep in the bedroom for a couple of nights until he gets used to your home, but then it is even harder to turf him out later.

If you decide you definitely do want your dog to sleep in the bedroom from day one, initially put him in a crate or similar with a soft blanket covering part of the crate. Put newspapers inside as he will not be able to last the night without urinating.

Once your dog has been housetrained and can access other areas of the house, you may reconsider where he sleeps. Some people will continue to keep him in the place where he started out; others will want the dog to sleep in a different room. But before you immediately choose the bedroom, bear in mind that Cockers scratch, snore, fart and wander about in the night...and some have a tendency to take over the bed, if allowed!

Microchipping, Vaccinations and Worming

It is **always** a good idea to have your puppy checked out by a vet within a few days of picking him up. Also, since April 2016, it is compulsory for all dogs in the UK to be microchipped and this is normally done by your vet. It is relatively quick and painless and costs around £20 ($30).

The vet inserts a tiny electronic device with a needle under the skin between your dog's shoulder blades. Once in place, your dog won't know it's there, and it should last his lifetime. If your dog is lost or stolen, it increases your chances of getting him back. Rescue centres, vets, local authorities and wardens have chip scanners so if a dog is found, they scan the chip to get its unique number. This is then matched to the owner's contact details on a database. If you move house or your details change, let the database know so that they can update their records.

Keep your away from other dogs in the waiting room as he will not be fully protected against canine diseases until the vaccination schedule is complete. All puppies need these injections; very occasionally a Cocker puppy has a reaction, but this is **very rare** and the advantages of immunisation far outweigh the disadvantages.

An unimmunised puppy is at risk every time he meets other dogs as he has no protection against potentially fatal diseases – another point is that it is unlikely a pet insurer will cover an unimmunised dog. It should be stressed that vaccinations are generally quite safe and side effects are uncommon.

If your Cocker is unlucky enough to be one of the very few that suffers an adverse reaction, here are the signs to look out for; a pup may exhibit one or more of these:

MILD REACTION - Sleepiness, irritability and not wanting to be touched. Sore or a small lump at the place where he was injected. Nasal discharge or sneezing. Puffy face and ears.

SEVERE REACTION - Anaphylactic shock. A sudden and quick reaction, usually before leaving the vet's, which causes breathing difficulties. Vomiting, diarrhoea, staggering and seizures.

A severe reaction is extremely rare. There is a far, far greater risk of your dog either being ill and/or spreading disease if he does not have the injections.

The usual schedule is for the pup to have his first vaccination at six to eight weeks of age. This will protect him from a number of diseases in one shot. In the UK these are Distemper, Canine Parvovirus (Parvo), Infectious Canine Hepatitis (Adenovirus), Leptospirosis and Kennel Cough (Bordetella). In the US this is known as DHPP. Puppies in the US also need vaccinating separately against Rabies. There are optional vaccinations for Coronavirus and - depending on where you live and if your dog is regularly around woods or forests - Lyme Disease.

The puppy requires a second vaccination around four weeks later and then maybe a third to complete his immunity, which is often from 10 to 12 weeks of age. Seven days after that he is safe to mix with other dogs. When you take your Cocker for an initial check-up within a few days of bringing him home, check with your vet exactly what shots are needed.

Diseases such as Parvo and Kennel Cough are highly contagious and you should not let your puppy mix with other dogs - unless they are your own and have already been vaccinated - until a week after he has completed his vaccinations, otherwise he will not be fully immunised. Parvovirus can also be transmitted by fox faeces.

You shouldn't take your new puppy to places where unvaccinated dogs might have been, like the local park. This does not mean that your puppy should be isolated - far from it. This is an important time for socialisation. It is OK for the puppy to mix with another dog which you 100% know has been vaccinated and is up to date with its annual boosters. Perhaps invite a friend's dog round to play in your garden to begin the socialisation process.

Once your puppy is fully immunised, you have a window of a few weeks to introduce him to as many new experiences - dogs, people, traffic, noises, other animals, etc. – This critical period before the age of four and a half or five months is when he is at his most receptive. Socialisation should not stop at that age, but continue for the rest of your Cocker's life; but it is particularly important to socialise young puppies.

Your dog will need a booster injection every year of his life. The vet should give you a record card or send you a reminder, but it's also a good idea to keep a note of the date in your diary.

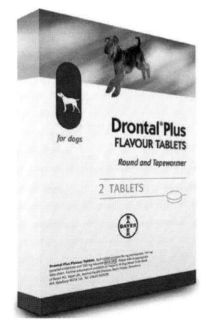

All puppies need worming. A good breeder will give the puppies their first dose of worming medication at around two weeks old, then probably again at five and eight weeks before they leave the litter. Get the details and inform your vet exactly what treatment, if any, your pup has already had. The main types of worms affecting puppies are roundworm and tapeworm. Roundworm can also be transmitted from a puppy to humans – most often children - and can in severe cases cause blindness, or miscarriage in women, so it's important to keep up to date with worming.

Worms in puppies are quite common, they are often picked up through their mother's milk. If you have children, get them into the habit of washing their hands after they have been in contact with the puppy – lack of hygiene is the reason why children are most susceptible. Most vets recommend worming a puppy once a month until he is six months old, and then around every two or three months.

If your Cocker is one of the many who is often out and about running through the woods and fields with his nose to the ground, then it is important to stick to a regular worming schedule, as he is more likely to pick up worms than one which spends more time indoors.

Fleas can pass on tapeworms to dogs, but a puppy would not normally be treated unless it is known for certain he has fleas. And then only with caution. You need to know the weight of your pet and then speak to your vet about the safest treatment to rid your puppy of the parasites.

It is not usually worth buying a cheap worming or flea treatment from a supermarket, as they are usually far less effective than more expensive vet-recommended preparations, such as Drontal. Many people living in the US have contacted our website claiming the parasite treatment Trifexis has caused severe side effects and even death to their dogs. Although this evidence is only anecdotal, you might want consider avoiding Trifexis to be on the safe side - even if your vet recommends it.

And that's it! You may not remember everything, but here are the main points again:

> Prepare for the puppy coming home
> Exercise common sense once he arrives
> Don't demand too much of him
> Allow him plenty of time for sleep

6. Crate Training and Housetraining

If you are unfamiliar with them, crates may seem like a cruel punishment for a little puppy. They are, however, becoming increasingly popular to help with housetraining and to keep the dog safe at night or when you are not there. Many breeders, trainers, behaviourists and people who show dogs use them.

Getting Your Dog Used to a Crate

If you decide to use a crate, then remember that it is not a prison to restrain the dog. It should only be used in a humane manner and time should be spent to make the puppy or adult dog feel like the crate is his own safe little haven. If the door is closed on the crate, your puppy must ALWAYS have access to water while inside. If used correctly and if time is spent getting the puppy used to the crate, it can be a valuable tool.

Cockers are sensitive dogs and they are also very attached to their humans, and so crates are not suitable for every dog; some may find them distressing. Cockers are not like hamsters or pet mice which can adapt to life in a cage. They are dogs which thrive on interaction with their humans.

Being caged all day is a miserable existence, and a crate should never be used as a means of confinement because you are out of the house all day. If you do decide to use one - perhaps to put your dog in for short periods while you leave the house, or at night - the best place for it is in the corner of a room away from cold draughts or too much heat. Remember, Cockers like to be near their family - which is you.

It is only natural for a Cocker, or any other dog, to whine in the beginning. He is not crying because he is in a cage. He would cry if he had the freedom of the room and he was alone - he is crying because he is separated from you. However, with patience and the right training he will get used to it and some come to regard the crate as a favourite place. Leave the crate where the dog can see or hear you. Some owners make the crate their dog's only bed, so he feels comfortable and safe in there.

Dogs with thick coats can overheat. When you buy a crate get a wire one (like the one pictured) which allows the air to pass through; not a plastic one which may get very hot. If you cover the crate, don't cover it 100% or you will restrict the flow of air. The crate should be large enough to allow your dog to stretch out flat on his side without being cramped, he should be able to turn round easily and to sit up without hitting his head on the top.

Depending on the adult size of your Cocker, you might want to consider a minimum of a 36 to 40 inch-wide crate or larger to allow your dog plenty of head room and space to move around easily. Crates aren't for every owner or every Cocker Spaniel, but used correctly, they can:

- Create a canine den
- Be a useful housetraining tool
- Limit access to the rest of the house while your dog learns the household rules
- Be a safe way to transport your dog in a car

If you use a crate right from Day One, cover half of it initially with a blanket to help your puppy regard it as a den. He also needs bedding and it's a good idea to put a chew in as well. A large crate may allow your dog to eliminate at one end and sleep at the other, but this may slow down his housetraining. So, if you are buying a crate which will last for a fully-grown Cocker, get

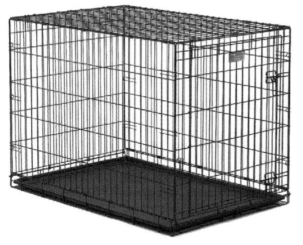

adjustable crate dividers – or make them yourself - to block part of it off while he is small so that he feels safe and secure, which he won't do in a very big crate.

Once you've got your crate, you'll need to learn how to use it properly so that it becomes a safe, comfortable den for your dog and not a prison. Here is a tried-and-tested method of getting your dog firstly to accept it, and then to actually want to spend time in there. Initially a pup might not be too happy about going inside, but he will be a lot easier to crate train than an adult dog which has got used to having the run of your house. These are the first steps:

1. Drop a few tasty puppy treats around and then inside the crate.

2. Put your puppy's favourite bedding or toy in there.

3. Keep the door open.

4. Feed your puppy's meals inside the crate. Again, keep the door open.

Place a chew or treat INSIDE the crate and close the door while your puppy is OUTSIDE the crate. He will be desperate to get in there! Open the door, let him in and praise him for going in. Fasten a long-lasting chew inside the crate and leave the door open. Let your puppy go inside to spend some time eating the chew.

IMPORTANT: Always remove your dog's collar before leaving him unattended in a crate. A collar can get caught in the wire mesh.

After a while, close the crate door and feed him some treats through the mesh while he is in there. At first just do it for a few seconds at a time, then gradually increase the time. If you do it too fast, he will become distressed. Slowly build up the amount of time he is in the crate. For the first few days, stay in the room, then gradually leave for a short time, first one minute, then three, then 10, 30 and so on.

Next Steps

5. Put your dog in his crate at regular intervals during the day - maximum two hours.

6. Don't crate only when you are leaving the house. Place the dog in the crate while you are home as well. Use it as a 'safe' zone.

7. By using the crate both when you are home and while you are gone, your dog becomes comfortable there and not worried that you won't come back, or that you are leaving him alone. This helps to prevent separation anxiety later in life.

8. Give him a chew and remove his collar, tags and anything else which could become caught in an opening or between the bars.

9. Make it very clear to any children that the crate is NOT a playhouse for them, but a 'special room' for the dog.

10. Although the crate is your dog's haven and safe place, it must not be off-limits to humans. You should be able to reach inside at any time.

The next point is important:

11. Do not let your dog immediately out of the crate if he barks or whines, or he will think that this is the key to opening the door. Wait until the barking or whining has stopped for at least 20 or 30 seconds before letting him out.

A puppy should not be left in a crate for long periods except at night time, and even then he has to get used to it first. Whether or not you decide to use a crate, the important thing to remember is that those first few days and weeks are a critical time for your puppy. Try and make him feel as safe and comfortable as you can. Bond with him, while at the same time gently and gradually introducing him to new experiences and other animals and humans.

A crate is a good way of transporting your Cocker in the car. Put the crate on the shady side of the interior and make sure it can't move around inside the car; put the seatbelt around it if necessary. If it's very sunny and the top of the crate is wire mesh, cover part of it so your dog has some shade and put the windows up and the air conditioning on. Never leave your dog unattended in a vehicle; he can quickly overheat - or be targeted by thieves.

If you are on a shoot with your working dogs, you may have to leave your dog in the car. But it's still important to ensure that the dogs are not left inside a very hot vehicle with the sun beating down – try and park in shade – and they also need access to water. Dogs overheat far sooner than humans, and what you may think is nice and warm inside the car may be intolerable for a dog. Even very fit, athletic dogs can suffer heat-related illnesses during hot summer days - and dogs can die of heatstroke within minutes.

Allowing your dog to roam freely inside the car is not a safe option, particularly if you - like me – are a bit of a 'leadfoot' on the brake and accelerator! Don't let him put his head out of the window either, he can slip and hurt himself and the wind pressure can cause an ear infection or bits of dust, insects, etc. to fly into your dog's eyes.

Special travel crates are useful for the car, or for taking your dog to the vet's or a show. Try and pick one with holes or mesh in the side (like the one pictured) to allow free movement of air, rather than a solid plastic one, in which your Cocker can become overheated.

Cocker Breeders on Crates

Traditionally crates have been more popular in America than in the UK and the rest of Europe, but opinion is slowly changing and more owners are starting to use crates on both sides of the Atlantic. This is perhaps because people's perception of a crate is shifting from regarding it as a prison to thinking of it, if used correctly, as a safe haven as well as a useful tool to help with housetraining and transportation.

Without exception, **the breeders believe that a crate should not be used for punishment or to imprison a dog for hours on end while you are away from the house.** This is cruel for any dog, but particularly a Cocker, who either wants to be with his humans or running outside with his nose to the ground.

American Cocker breeder Eunice Wine, of Blackberry Farm Enterprises, Virginia, USA, is unusual among US breeders in that she only uses a crate to transport a dog to the vet – but then her Cockers do have the run of the farm. She added: "I can't speak about crate training, but I do think that Cocker Spaniels should be with their people as much as possible." This is what the UK breeders said – and as you will read, there is a wide variety of opinions:

Caroline Bymolen, of Carto (show) Cocker Spaniels, Cambridgeshire: "We use one create for each dog. They are a safe haven if he wants to be somewhere quiet. We crate at night so they could be in there for eight hours and we don't find that to be a problem. During the day we only crate at feeding times and they come out when they have finished eating. If we go out, we try not to be too long, but if we are at a show all day we crate those that are not going - but a family member comes and lets them out during the day. Our dogs are used to this and don't seem to suffer as a result.

"As for tips, we would say first of all, that the crate should **never** be a place of punishment; it should be a nice place to be. When training during the day when you are at home always leave the door open so the pup can go in and out as he pleases. Feed the pup in the crate with the door closed and leave him there for a few minutes before letting him out. Only let him out when he is calm and quiet, not when he is over excited and crying to come out. Put him in and give him a treat. Put him in the cage and go out for short periods of time. Overall, we have found that they

soon get used to the crate and our dogs run into their own crates when we open the doors."

Manda Smith, Tassietay Working Cocker Spaniels, East Kent: "I prefer to use a pen for puppies, rather than a crate. You can put a bed in one area of the pen and newspaper over the rest, giving them a place to sleep and a place to relieve themselves. It is also less oppressive for the pup, being open at the top and usually larger than a crate. It will also be more familiar to them as the breeder will no doubt have used a pen.

"Young pups should be in the pen when you can't supervise them, but this shouldn't be for more than an hour or so at a time. Always make the crate or pen a happy, positive place to be, use treats to encourage the pup in and give them plenty of toys and stuffed Kong toys, etc. to occupy them whilst in there. Also give them a comfy bed." Pictured is Manda and Jacquie Smith's Wenji Spring Creek at Tassietay, aged 18 months.

Julie and Darren Summers, Summerville Gundogs, Country Durham: "We do crate training of our pups before they leave us. We start this from four weeks old so they grow learning the crate is nothing to fear. I have a 15-year-old dog that will still choose to lie in a crate as they learn this is their own space. However, crates are very easy to abuse and we recommend no longer than two hours at a time during the day; any longer than that and the owner needs to assess if they have time for a pup, or they need outside help to look after the pup."

Wendy Tobijanski, of Janski (English and American) Cocker Spaniels, Shropshire: "A crate can be useful, for example when travelling or in a busy household. It gives the dog somewhere safe to go away from children if they want to. The crate is a dog's bed and not a place of punishment; it should be their safe haven."

Andy Platt, Nithvalley Gundogs, Scotland: "The best tip is to make sure that the crate is not too big, so as to allow a puppy to be dirty in one corner and sleep in another. Most dogs are naturally clean if allowed frequent exercise. If a person works long hours and can't regularly walk a dog, then they shouldn't have one, simple."

Tracey Simpson, Bravialis Gundogs, North Yorkshire: "Crates are brilliant for house training. They won't mucky their bed, so always let them straight outside after they have been in their crate and you will get great results.

"I also like a crate as it gives the dog a space of its own where it can take itself off to. Also, crates work great for popping them in whilst you have guests etc. so that they don't pester or pick up bad habits, i.e. barking at the door or jumping up.

"If a Cocker has had good exercise before going in and chance to eliminate in the garden, then they can easily stay in there for four hours. Obviously, dogs work better with routines, so there's no reason they can't stay in a crate for long intervals as long as they know when they will get out."
Pictured are Tracey's lively duo, Betty and Jack, enjoying a day out on the moors.

Jane Minikin, of North Yorkshire, has been a hobby breeder of show-type Cockers for 18 years, and said: "When I first had dogs I was not keen on the idea of using a crate, but now I would not be without one. I accustom my puppies to sleep in a crate before they leave me and encourage new owners to use one. Small puppies can be kept safe in a crate and, if used sensibly, they will love their own 'special place.'

"Puppies or older dogs may need to stay in a crate to protect furniture, should they have a chewing habit and, of course, for safety when travelling.

"I often give a treat or biscuit on entering the crate when training. You should always have comfy bedding and a favourite toy or snuggle blanket in there. My dogs argue over who can use the crate now and a shout of 'bedtime' sees them rush for the crate - they love it! I think three to four hours is probably the maximum to leave a Cocker in a crate, especially if walked beforehand.

"Buy the biggest one you can accommodate. He must be able to stand and turn around and have access to water. A tip would be to always make using the crate is a pleasurable experience and build up time in there gradually."

Kirsten Strachan, Lorne Working Cockers, Perthshire, Scotland: "I have used crates, mainly to keep a pup or dog secure while say workmen, etc. are in. Crates should never be used for punishment and should be a safe 'cave' for a dog. Putting a blanket on top and all round creates a den-like environment which many enjoy."

International show champion breeder Haja van Wessem, of Speggle-Waggel Cocker Spaniels, Wassenaar, The Netherlands: "I advise the puppy buyer to use a crate during the night for the first few months and to get him used to being in a crate for shorter periods during the day. You do not leave a teething puppy alone in your sitting room if you value your possessions!

"Also a puppy needs a lot of sleep and rest and therefore needs a place where he can withdraw and be left alone. After a time he will retire to his crate without having to close it." Pictured are Haja's dogs enjoying a swim in the sea.

Helen Marsden, Finity (show) Cocker Spaniels, Hampshire: "I am a big believer in crate training and all my puppies are crate trained before leaving. All my Cockers love their crates, they are their safe havens. I don't believe a Cocker should be left too long in a crate. It should be used at night, which aids toilet training, and for leaving puppies for a short time to protect them from potential dangers whilst you are out. This only applies to puppies, and by one year old the crate may be kept as a den for the dog.

"I always offer the puppy or dog a treat when put into the crate, or a filled Kong toy to keep them entertained. I also would feed a puppy in the crate to encourage a positive experience. NEVER use the crate as a punishment, but do use it for time-out if puppy is over-tired, again with the positive reinforcement of a treat."

Jill Gunn, Dearganach Working Cockers, Scotland: "A crate should be a place of peace for the pup, where it can rest and sleep - a cover is essential to make the puppy feel safe. When you collect your puppy from the breeder, take a towel with you, let the pup lie on this on the journey home, place it in the crate and put pup in as well - DO NOT SHUT THE DOOR, let the pup come and go as he pleases, they quickly choose to take themselves off for a sleep and feel safe and at home.

"I only shut the door when I am cooking, etc. when it may be dangerous for the pup to be under my feet, or when we are having meals or out for short periods of time. As the pup grows you can extend crate time, I would never leave a pup for more than a couple of hours in a crate - take a holiday from work, this is to be your life-long friend - he is worth it."

Andrew Height, Fourtails (show) Cocker Spaniels, Cambridgeshire: "We have used crates, but the most any of ours has been left alone in there is about three hours. However, they'll happily sleep all night in a crate without any due stress. Some see the crate as a secure place, especially if you have other dogs in the house."

Kerena Marchant, Sondes (working) Cocker Spaniels, Surrey: "I use Susan Garrett's book 'Crate Games' and Absolute Dogs' boundary games. I don't think you should leave a dog in a crate for more than four hours. I don't crate mine in the house once they can be safely left – they have the run of the house. I use K9 high beds as boundaries and places of retreat. At shows the dogs are in the crates in the well-ventilated van all day and cope well."

Carole Pitchers, Alcarbrad (working) Cocker Spaniels, Essex: "We have always used crates and see them as the dogs' quiet space. We do not leave our dogs crated for any longer than three hours. Tips for crates: have a crate in a warm, quiet space (ours is in an area under our open stairs). Provide a cosy bed within the crate. Use the crate positively by giving the dog its meals within the crate. Provide treats and toys. NEVER send the dog to the crate because, in your eyes, it has been naughty."

Robert Baldwin, Annaru (show) Cockers, South Wales: "We use a large crate from about six weeks of age and suggest to all our new puppy owners to continue with this to at least one year, or as soon as they stop teething. We always say use a crate, keep it open in the day and the puppy will learn that it is his or her space to chill."

Peter Harvey, Grannus (show) Cocker Spaniels, Somerset: "Never buy one according to the 'Breed Size'. It must be large-enough for your pet to turn-around with ease when it is closed with clean and dry bedding and a supply of fresh, clean drinking water. I prefer a bottle attached to the outside which tops-up a bowl attached to the inside, ensuring it cannot spill on the bedding. Add chews which will keep them busy, toys if desired.

"I only close the door when I have visiting dogs to groom (for safety reasons), otherwise it's their bedroom with free access to the house and garden (via a dog flap). Three to four hours enclosed is the maximum I would leave them in without a break."

Hobby show Cocker breeder Maxine Shaverin, of Lancashire: "Personally, I dislike crates, although I have just bought one for my latest Cocker, who still loves to chew and has been pulling books off bookshelves, Amazon parcels off the dining table, etc. Depending on the size of the crate (and mine is as large as his pen was), I wouldn't like to leave a Cocker in one for more than four hours." (Photo library image).

Linda Reed, Delindere (English and American) Cocker Spaniels, Leicestershire: "I NEVER use a crate unless it's for travelling in the car. I think it's cruel to think that they might have to use where they sleep as a toilet. I use a pen for pups, making sure there is plenty of room for a bed and a separate toilet area."

Billie Cheeseman, BarleyCourt (working) Spaniels, Hertfordshire: "I personally feel it is a good thing to crate a puppy - as long as the crate is not abused. Dogs should not be left in a crate for hours on end (other than overnight) and the crate should not be used as a punishment. Your puppy's crate, used correctly will become his/her sanctuary, their quiet place. Also, if your pup ever needs to spend any time in the vet's, they will be in a crate/confined space, and if they are used to being crated and feel safe and secure in one, it will alleviate some of the stress involved.

"Make the crate a nice place for them to be, feed your pup in his or her crate, keep a couple of special toys for only when the pup is in his or her crate. If you lay a sheet or towel over the crate it will create a secure den-like environment for a puppy. Treat balls or other toys that keep them mentally busy are great for this. Your pup will be teething, so a hard chew will also be good. I don't put padded mattress-type beds in with young pups as they will inevitably end up in pieces. Instead, I use blankets. I also recommend buying a small plastic bed for the crate, this way if pup toilets in there, the bedding won't get wet. Put the bed in one side of the crate and the other side should be covered with newspaper or puppy pads so they can toilet on this."

Lynne Waterhouse, Lyfora (show) Cocker Spaniels, Berkshire: "I have crates available with new litters of puppies so they have been introduced to a crate prior to moving to their new homes. However, I do not close the doors so they have free access to use as they wish, and their 'toilet' area of newspapers or puppy pads is outside the crate.

"With my own dogs, I have a utility area off a kitchen which is gated and I find this suits my dogs very well. My one crate tip would be to ensure the size of the crate is adequate for your pet to move comfortably, and increase in size as your dog grows, if necessary."

Christine Thomas, Dodfordhills (working) Spaniels, Worcestershire: "Crates are the best thing since sliced bread! Associate it with quiet times and never use it for punishment. My pup goes into his crate at night by himself, it's his den - oh yes, and put a blanket on top, it makes a better den for them to sleep in.

"Gradually mine learned that the crate door didn't have to be shut (I just shut access from the kitchen to the rest of the house). You can always attach a water bowl to the side of the crate for night time. Make it cosy. Use the Vetbed fleece, well worth the investment." Pictured is a litter bred by Christine.

Jo Oxley, Looseminxjoy Working Cocker Spaniels, Norfolk: "As mine are crated from the time that they can escape from the whelping box, they consider the crate their home or nest. I leave mine in the crate overnight and find that sometimes they will put themselves to bed at night. During the day they have other beds, but sometimes choose to go into the crate."

Christine Grant, Rostreigan (show) Cocker Spaniels, Hampshire: "All my dogs are crated at night: six to seven hours maximum. My tip for using a crate as a training aid is: Don't make the crate too big initially, or she will use part of it as her toilet, which won't help train her to control her bladder and bowel. If the crate is large, make it smaller by using an upturned cardboard box."

Chris Warner, of Monwodelea Gundogs says that puppies are great chewers and he strongly recommends the use of a crate. Whereas Jane Seekings, of Dorset, says she has only ever used a crate for young puppies. Gail Parsons, Gaiter (show) Cocker Spaniels, Sussex, added: "I am not a great lover of crates, but I do use a play pen at night or if I go out to the shops. I never leave them for more than one to two hours. I do use a crate if they come in the car with me; it's safety for all concerned."

Working Gundogs breeder Stewart North, Northglen Labradors and Cockers, Leicestershire, uses crates for a maximum of two hours during daylight hours and up to 10 hours at night. David Matthews, of Tojamatt (show) Cockers, Nottinghamshire, makes an interesting point that if a crate is used properly: "It's only a bed with a door on it."

Top 10 Housetraining Tips

How easy are Cockers to housetrain? According to our breeders, pretty easy – but the dog is only as good as his or her owners. In other words, the speed and success of housetraining depends largely on one factor: the time and effort you are prepared to put in. The more vigilant you are during the early days, the quicker your dog will be housetrained. And training should always be positive and encouraging, never negative. It's as simple as that.

A broad generalisation is that the more stubborn breeds, e.g. the Bully breeds, can take a bit longer to housetrain (and I can hear breeders of Bulldogs and Frenchies rushing to their defence as I write this!). Cockers are certainly not stubborn, they are intelligent, quick, lively and eager to please. All of these traits are in the dog's favour when it comes to housetraining.

Many good breeders will already have started the process with their puppies, so when you pick up your little bundle of joy, all you have to do is ensure that you carry on the good work. Being consistent with your routines and repetitions and heeding the advice in this chapter is the quickest way to toilet train (potty train) your pup. A further piece of good news is that a puppy's instinct is not to soil his own den. From about the age of three weeks, a pup will leave his sleeping area to eliminate.

You have two more factors in your favour when it comes to housetraining: No dog wants to please his owner more than a Cocker, and puppies love treats.

If you're starting from scratch when you bring your new pup home, your new arrival thinks that the whole house is his den and doesn't realise it is not the place to eliminate. Therefore you need to gently and persistently teach him that it is unacceptable to make a mess inside the house. Cockers, like all dogs, are creatures of routine - not only do they like the same things happening at the same times every day, but establishing a regular routine with your dog also helps to speed up training and housebreaking.

Dogs are also very tactile creatures, so they will pick a toilet area which feels good under their paws. Many dogs like to go on grass - but this will do nothing to improve your lawn, so you should think carefully about what area to encourage your dog to use. You may want to consider a small patch of gravel crushed into tiny pieces in your garden.

Some breeders advise against using puppy pads for any length of time as puppies like the softness of the pads, which can encourage them to eliminate on other soft areas - such as your carpets or bed. Others love them, as you will read. Follow these tips to speed up housetraining:

1. **Constant supervision** is essential for the first week or two if you are to housetrain your puppy quickly. This is why it is important to book the week or so off work when you bring him home. Make sure you are there to take him outside regularly. If nobody is there, he will learn to urinate or poo(p) inside the house.

2. **Take your pup outside at the following times:**

- o   As soon as he wakes – every time
- o   Shortly after each feed
- o   After a drink
- o   When he gets excited
- o   After exercise or play
- o   Last thing at night
- o   Initially every hour – whether or not he looks like he wants to go

If you want the process to speed up, you should also get up during the night for the first week or two to let your pup into the garden when he whines. You may think that the above list is an exaggeration, but it isn't. Housetraining a pup is almost a full-time job for the first couple of weeks. If you are serious about housetraining your puppy quickly, then clear your diary for a few days and keep your eyes firmly glued on your pup. Learn to spot that expression or circling motion just before he makes a puddle - or worse – on your floor.

3. Take your puppy to **the same place** every time, you may need to use a lead in the beginning - or tempt him there with a treat if he is not yet lead-trained. Some say only to pick him up and dump him there in an emergency, as it is better if he learns to take himself to the chosen toilet spot. Others think it's quicker to pick them up.

Dogs naturally develop a preference for going in the same place or on the same surface - often grass or dirt. Take him to the same patch every time so he learns this is his bathroom - preferably an area in a corner of your garden or yard.

4. **No pressure – be patient.** You must allow your distracted little pup time to wander around and have a good sniff before performing his duties – but do not leave him, stay around a short distance away. Sadly, puppies are not known for their powers of concentration; it may take a while for them to select that perfect bathroom spot in the pouring rain!

5. **Housetraining is reward-based.** Praise him or give him a treat immediately when he performs his duties in the chosen spot. Cockers love praise, and reward-based training is the most successful method for this sensitive breed.

6. **Share the responsibility.** It doesn't have to be the same person that takes the dog outside all the time. In fact it's easier if there are a couple of you, as housetraining is a very time-consuming business. Just make sure you stick to the same principles and same patch of ground.

7. **Stick to the same routine.** Dogs understand and like routine. Sticking to the same one for mealtimes, short exercise sessions, play time, sleeping and toilet breaks will help to not only housetrain him quicker, but help him settle into his new home.

8. **Use your voice if you catch him in the act indoors.** A short sharp negative sound is best - NO! ACK! EH! - it doesn't matter, as long as it is loud enough to make him stop. Then start running enthusiastically towards your door, calling him to 'the chosen place' and patiently wait until he has finished what he started indoors. It is no good scolding your dog if you find a puddle or unwanted gift in the house but don't see him do it, he won't know why you are cross with him. Only use the negative sound if you catch him in the act.

9. **No punishment.** Accidents will happen at the beginning, do not punish your puppy for them. He is a baby with a tiny bladder and bowels, and housetraining takes time - it is perfectly natural to have accidents early on. Remain calm and clean up the mess with a good strong-smelling cleaner to remove the odour, so he won't be tempted to use that spot again.

Cockers have an extremely keen sense of smell; use a special spray from your vet or a hot solution of washing powder to completely eliminate the odour. Smacking or rubbing his nose in it can have the opposite effect - he will become afraid to do his business in your presence and may start going behind the couch or under the bed, rather than outside.

10. **Look for the signs.** These may be whining, sniffing the floor in a determined manner, circling and looking for a place to go, or walking uncomfortably - particularly at the rear end! Take him outside straight away. If you can help it, don't pick him up. He has to learn to walk to the door himself when he needs to go outside.

If you use puppy pads, only do so for a short time or your puppy will get used to them. You can also separate a larger crate into two areas and put a pad in one area to help housetrain your baby Cocker. He will eliminate on the pad and keep his bed clean.

If you decide to keep your puppy in a crate overnight and you want him to learn not to soil the crate right from the very beginning, you need to have the crate in the bedroom so you can hear him whine when he needs to go. Initially this might be once or twice a night. By the age of four or five months a Cocker pup should be able to last all night without needing the toilet – provided you let him out last thing at night and first thing in the morning (and don't have a lie-in!)

With a crate, remember that the door should not be closed until your puppy is happy with being inside. He needs to believe that this is a safe place and not a trap or prison. Rather than use a crate, many people prefer to section off an area inside one room or use a puppy pen to confine their pup. Inside this area is a bed and another area with pads or newspapers which the puppy can use as a toilet area.

GENERAL TIP: A trigger can be very effective to encourage your dog to perform his duties. Some people use a clicker or a bell - we used a word; well two actually. Within a week or so I trained our puppy to urinate on the command of "wee wee."

Think very carefully before choosing the word or phrase, as I often feel an idiot wandering around our garden last thing at night shouting **"Max, WEE WEE!"** in an encouraging manner - although I'm not sure that the American expression **"GO POTTY!"** sounds much better...!

Breeders' Housetraining Tips

We asked more than three dozen breeders whether they thought Cockers were easy to housetrain and if they had any tips to pass on. Here are the pick of the comments. Jo Oxley: "I have sent most of my puppies to their new owners nearly fully housetrained at eight weeks. I would say that that is pretty quick. My puppies are brought up in the house, so they do not have to learn the difference between a barn or kennel and a home. They are crated and have one area of bed and one of newspaper (increasing difficult to get hold of). Every time they are let out it is to an open door to the garden with me saying 'out, out, out' and clapping gently behind them and then scooping up any that squat and quickly putting them outside. Consistency and calmness are key."

Peter Harvey: "Breeders should have completed most of the housetraining before the puppies are sold, within the first eight weeks, this is part of the Kennel Club Regulations. Within the Puppy Pack that I give to new owners are details on continued training: Be patient and consistent, do not chastise, praise and reward, treat them with love and affection."

Kerena Marchant: "You can't generalise or be breed specific. Two of mine were raised in homes and arrived at seven weeks very advanced in training. Ghost was easier as he was a summer puppy and the door was open. Magic arrived in winter and took longer. Rupert was a nightmare as he was bred by a gamekeeper and was in an outdoor kennel; it took six months!"

Lynne Waterhouse: "As Cockers are so scent driven, they can be trained easily to 'perform' in an acceptable place in the garden if they are taken to the same spot after waking and after meals. I found my bitches slightly quicker to housetrain than my male, but it was usually a moment of excitement that caused him to have an accident; both sexes were pretty reliably housetrained from around five months."

Keith Henderson, Owencraig (show) Cocker Spaniels, Dunfermline, Scotland: "The take around four months to housetrain. Cockers are quicker than average as they are an intelligent breed. My tip is to use just one door from the home for exercise."

Linda Reed: "It depends on how much time their owner is prepared to put in. If given plenty of opportunity to 'go' outside they can be 'clean' by about four to five months old. Give plenty of praise when they 'perform' outside and just ignore any accidents indoors, but give them frequent visits outside."

Billie Cheeseman: "Housetraining is - as most training is - a matter of how much time and consistency the owner is prepared to put into the pup. My tips would be: take them out in the garden very regularly; the more regular you make it, the less accidents you will have. Go out with the pup as they are more likely to enjoy their time with you there too. I use a cue word with mine, I tell them to do 'wees' and 'poos'. This way if I am in a hurry at any point, I can ask them to go and I have found this useful. Finally don't get discouraged by the odd accident, don't make a fuss about it, just spend more time with them practising outside."

Christine Thomas: "I find working dogs are quicker than the show types. It probably takes about six to eight weeks from 12 weeks old. Take them out as much as possible, encourage and associate a word with it. Stay with them until the deed is done; don't be quick to turn around and go inside because it's cold or wet."

Maxine Shaverin: "All of my Cockers have been housetrained by about 12 weeks – faster than other breeds of dogs. One tip – try to avoid the newspaper route and start taking them outside first thing in a morning, after meals and regularly in between. I started this with my last litter at four weeks and they were virtually housetrained by eight."

Hobby breeder Debra Ralston, Staffordshire: "Cockers are very quick to train; they are trained by approximately 12 weeks old. One of our pups used to pick up the puppy pad and take it to the back door then sit on it waiting to go outside. When we opened the door he would pee! We found the males to be quicker than the females. I would recommend puppy training pads."

Stewart North says that a puppy can be trained in four weeks if he or she is fed at regular times and the owner pays attention to the pup's body clock. Jackie Hornby agrees, saying you can train Cockers in a couple of weeks if you keep near them at all times and look out for the signals, such as sniffing and looking for a place to poo.

Andrew and Pat Height: "It doesn't take long at all. Paper training and going outside can be achieved fairly quickly, in a matter of a few weeks with luck. We would say Cockers are quite quick to learn and can only compare it with Sussex Spaniels, as they are a little slower - probably because they are far more stubborn than Cockers. A tip would be to keep an eye on the pup as much as possible. The first signs of fidgeting are the signals to get him or her out for whatever they need to do."

Gail Parsons: "If the breeder starts at five weeks, then there is no reason why a puppy shouldn't be almost clean by the time it leaves to go to its new home. They are really quick learners. I have dog flaps, so all my puppies follow mum into the garden every time they have eaten and as soon as they wake up."

Jill Gunn: "Cockers are very easily housetrained - around 10 to 14 days maximum on average. New owners need to accept they will have to take the puppy outside regularly, before/after feeding/playing/sleeping, every half hour if necessary. BUT they have to be prepared to get up in the night to let the puppy out. There is no point getting a pup and expecting it to sleep eight hours plus a night; you must get up for the pup to allow it the chance to have an 'empty' and then back to bed - otherwise, don't get a pup."

Jane Seekings: "By four to five months they should be housetrained, barring the odd accident. The one tip I would give to new owners is to understand the puppy's needs and recognise the signs that he or she wants to go outside, and to realise that when they are little they will need to urinate almost every hour and go to the toilet after eating. Most accidents with me happened when I was engrossed watching the television and forgot the time, only to find a small puddle on the kitchen floor!"

Rachel Appleby, Cockerbye (show) Cocker Spaniels, Lincolnshire: "Keep calm, teach your puppy where the door is, put down paper or pads initially. They don't like being dirty and will enjoy the praise and encouragement given when they get it right. Never be angry when there is an accident, it is up to the owner to be alert to a puppy's needs."

Pictured are six of the best from Rachel, all recently groomed.

Tracey Simpson: "Working Cockers are very clever, therefore easily pick up training. I think the downside to them being so clever is they try and outsmart you sometimes, so it's important to keep them in their place and be strict.

"Some other dogs may not be so tricky to keep up with. Depending on the individual puppy, you should be able to have them without accidents within two weeks. I always recommend crate training puppies until they are around one year old. It helps with the toilet training process, as they won't mucky their bed and also dogs are derived from wolves and like to have their own dark cave, as such."

Haja van Wessem: "Sometimes puppies get the idea within two weeks, some might take months. Constant attention helps to get them housetrained quicker. Most of the times the puppies that leave the nest are already housetrained during the night. It is important that the breeders make sure that the whelping box and the puppy pen are always clean. A pup raised in dirty, messy surroundings takes longer to housetrain."

Julie and Darren Summers: "Stay calm, never lose your temper and NEVER rub a pup's nose in its business; consistency is key to toilet training. However, it all depends on the individual pup and how observant the owner is. We start all of our pups on the toilet training from approximately four weeks old; we paper train and move on to them going to a secure area on a regular basis. We them pass all this info onto our new owners, it is also written down in case they forget. We have testimonials of pups being clean after as little as a few days at their new homes. Some take a couple of weeks to a month."

Kirsten Strachan: "I'd say to allow up to the age of 20 weeks. I think Cockers are quick and many are housetrained before then. However I won't sell to people who work full-time and have young children because I have found they cannot devote the time and patience to housetraining, among other things. Patience and a regular routine are key."

Caroline Bymolen: "Be aware of the pup's actions. Take him out after feeds and when he wakes up. Walk the pup out to the garden so he knows the way, rather than carrying him. Stay with him (yes, even in the pouring rain) until he goes and then really, really praise him."

American Cocker breeder Eunice Wine added: "Our Cocker pups are trained to go outside their sleeping/eating area within a month. I can't speak of other breeds in comparison, because we've not had other puppies to train. The number one tip I give new owners is to spray the offending location where the pup has had an accident with a strong cleaner, so they do not associate that part of the house with where it is fine to have future 'accidents'.

And we love this advice from hobby breeder Wendy Roberts, of Cheshire: "My tip is get a warm dressing gown and large umbrella! Spend the time with your dog as you encourage him or her out on the lawn first thing in the morning. You know they need to wee and it's the perfect time to reward them; it starts and sets the routine. I always say 'go be clean', now I just shout it from the doorway, staying warm and dry!"

Some working Cockers kept for the shoot or field trials live in outdoor kennels, and this is the case with breeder Chris Warner: "My dogs are kennelled outside. I do housetrain them to keep the runs clean, although sometimes 'accidents' happen in the run. They will not soil their bed. I do feel, based upon my dogs' environment, they perhaps do not have the same attention to housetraining as a dog living in a house. If they were to live in the house I feel it may take longer than my current house dogs (Miniature Schnauzers). When you are undertaking housetraining, ensure that you stay outside with the dog while it toilets, as if you just put the dog outside on its own, it will just stand by the door. When it is allowed in, it will be excited to be back and have an accident."

Andy Platt, of Nithvalley Gundogs: "I don't housetrain my dogs, they live outside in kennels. But I find that they are quickly kennel clean if allowed regular exercise. Using an indoor cage (crate) is the easiest way to housetrain a dog."

And finally a word of advice from Kennel Club Assured Breeder Barry Hutchinson, of Brynovation Gundogs, Gloucestershire, who keeps his working gundogs outside: "Cocker Spaniels learn very quickly, and that is why all training must be thoroughly thought out in advance - a minor mistake on the handler's part can take a very long time to reverse. As to my personal tip regarding housetraining: Don't; buy a range of kennels instead!"

"How can you tell the dogs need to go out?"

7. Feeding a Cocker Spaniel

To keep your dog's biological machine in good working order, he or she needs the right fuel, just like a finely-tuned sports car. Feeding the correct diet is an essential part of keeping your Cocker fit and healthy.

However, the topic of feeding your dog the right diet is something of a minefield. Owners are bombarded with endless choices as well as countless adverts from dog food companies, all claiming that theirs is best.

There is not one food that will give every single dog the brightest eyes, the shiniest coat, the most energy, the best digestion, the longest life and stop him from scratching or having skin problems. Dogs are individuals, just like people, which means that you could feed a premium food to a group of dogs and find that most of them do great on it, some do not so well, while a few might even get an upset stomach or even an allergic reaction. The question is: "Which food is best for **my** Cocker Spaniel?"

If you have been given a recommended food from a breeder, rescue centre or previous owner, it is best to stick to this as long as your dog is doing well on it. A good breeder will know which food their dogs thrive on. If you do decide - for whatever reason - to change diet, then this must be done gradually. There are some things to be aware of when it comes to feeding:

1. Most Cocker Spaniels are not fussy eaters and love their food. Add to this their eagerness to please and you have a powerful training tool. You can use feeding time to reinforce a simple command on a daily basis.

2. Some dogs do not do well on diets with a high wheat or corn content.

3. Some dogs have food sensitivities or allergies, leading to skin issues and scratching/biting - more on this topic later.

4. Controlling your dog's food intake is important, as obesity can trigger or worsen numerous health conditions and shorten lives.

5. Sometimes dogs, particularly older ones, may just get bored with their diet and go off their food. This does not necessarily mean that they are ill, simply that they have lost interest and a new food should be gradually introduced.

There are many different options on the market. The most popular manufactured foods include dry complete diets, tinned food (with or without a biscuit mixer), and semi-moist. Some dog foods contain only natural ingredients. Then there is the option of feeding your dog a raw diet or a home-made diet; while a handful of owners feed vegetarian food to their dogs.

There are many different qualities of manufactured food. Often, you get what you pay for, so a more expensive food is often more likely to provide better nutrition for your dog - in terms of minerals, nutrients and high quality meats – rather than a cheap one, which will most likely contain a lot of grain and additives. However, this is not always the case - read the list of ingredients to find out. Dried foods (also called kibble) tend to be less expensive than other foods. They have improved a lot over the last few years and some of the more expensive ones are now a good choice for a healthy, complete diet. Dried foods also contain the least fat and most preservatives.

Our dog Max, who has inhalant allergies, is on a quality dried food made by James Wellbeloved who claims it is 'hypoallergenic,' i.e. good for dogs with allergies. Max does well on it, but not all dogs thrive on dried food. We tried several other foods first; it is a question of each owner finding the best one for their dog. Ask your breeder or vet if you're unsure.

TIP: Beware of buying a commercial food because it is described as 'premium' or 'natural' or both, as these terms are meaningless. Many manufacturers blithely use these words, but there are no official guidelines as to what they mean. However **"Complete and balanced"** IS a legal term and has to meet standards laid down by AAFCO (Association of American Feed Control Officials) in the USA.

Always check the ingredients on any food sack, packet or tin to see what is listed first; this is the main ingredient and it should be meat or poultry, not corn or grain. If you are in the US, look for a dog food which has been endorsed by AAFCO. In general, tinned foods are 60-70% water. Often semi-moist foods contain a lot of artificial substances and sugar - which is maybe why dogs love them!

Choosing the right food is important; it will influence your dog's health, energy levels, coat and even temperament. There are also three stages of your dog's life to consider when feeding: Puppy, Adult and Senior (also called Veteran). Some manufacturers also produce a Junior feed for adolescents. Each represents a different physical stage of life and you need to choose the right food to cope with his body during each particular phase. A pregnant female will require a special diet to cope with the extra demands on her body - this is especially important as she nears the latter stages of pregnancy - and working Cockers require extra nutrition in the shooting season.

Many Cocker owners feed their dogs twice a day, which helps to stop a hungry dog gulping food down in a mad feeding frenzy. Some owners of fussy eaters feed two different meals each day to provide variety. One meal could be dried kibble, while the other might be home-made, with fresh meat, poultry and vegetables, or a moist food. If you do this, make sure the two separate meals provide a balanced diet and that they are not too rich in protein.

We will not recommend one brand of dog food over another, but do have some general tips to help you choose what to feed. There is also some advice for owners of dogs with food allergies and intolerances. Cockers are not particularly prone to them, but they are a growing problem in the canine world generally. Sufferers may itch, lick or chew their paws and/or legs, or rub their face. They may also get frequent ear infections as well as redness and swelling on their face.

Switching to a grain-free diet can help to alleviate the symptoms, as your dog's digestive system does not have to work as hard. In the wild, a dog or wolf's staple diet would be meat with some vegetable matter from the stomach and intestines of the herbivores (plant eating animals) he ate – but no grains. Dogs do not digest corn or wheat (which are often staples of cheap commercial dog food) very efficiently. Grain-free diets still provide carbohydrates through fruits and vegetables, so your dog still gets all his nutrients.

15 Top Tips for Feeding your Cocker Spaniel

1. If you choose a manufactured food, **don't pick one where meat or poultry content is NOT the first item listed on the bag.** Foods with lots of cheap cereals or sugar are not the best choice.

2. Some dogs suffer from sensitive skin, 'hot spots' or allergies. A cheap dog food, often bulked up with grain, will only make this worse. If this is the case, bite the bullet and **choose a high quality – usually more expensive – food, or consider a raw diet.** You'll probably save money in vets' bills in the long run and your dog will be happier. A food described as 'hypoallergenic' on the sack means 'less likely to cause allergies' and is a good place to start.

3. **Feed your Cocker twice a day**, rather than once. Smaller feeds are easier to digest, and reduce flatulence and the risk of bloat from gulping food. Puppies need to be fed more often; discuss exactly how often with your breeder.

4. **Establish a feeding regime and stick to it**. Dogs like routine. If you are feeding twice a day, feed once in the morning and then again at tea-time. Stick to the same times of day. Do not give the last feed too late, or your dog's body will not have chance to process or burn off the food before sleeping. He will also need a walk or letting out in the garden or yard after his second feed to allow him to empty his bowels. Feeding at the same times each day helps your dog establish a toilet regime.

5. **Take away any uneaten food between meals.** Most Cockers are good eaters, but any dog can become fussy if food is available all day. Imagine if your dinner was left on the table for hours until you finished it. Returning to the table two or three hours later would not be such a tempting prospect, but coming back hungry for a fresh meal would be far more appetising. Also, when food is left down all day, some dogs seem to take the food for granted and lose their appetite. Then they begin to leave the food and you are at your wits' end trying to find something they will actually eat. Put the food bowl down twice a day and then take it up after 20 minutes – even if he has left some. If he is healthy and hungry, he will look forward to his next meal and soon stop leaving food. If your dog does not eat anything for a couple of days, it could well be a sign that he is not well.

6. **Do not feed too many titbits and treats between meals.** Extra weight will place extra strain on your dog's joints and organs, have a detrimental effect on his health and even his lifespan. It also throws his balanced diet out of the window. Try to avoid feeding your dog from the table or your plate, as this encourages attention-seeking behaviour and drooling.

7. **Don't give your dog cooked bones,** as these can splinter and cause him to choke or suffer intestinal problems. If your dog is a gulper, it's a good idea to avoid giving rawhide,

as dogs who rush their food have a tendency to quickly chew and swallow rawhide without first bothering to nibble it down into smaller pieces.

8. **NEVER feed the following items to your dog**: grapes, raisins, chocolate, onions, Macadamia nuts, any fruits with seeds or stones, tomatoes, avocadoes, rhubarb, tea, coffee or alcohol. ALL of these are poisonous to dogs.

9. **If you switch to a new food, do the transition gradually.** Unlike humans, dogs' digestive systems cannot handle sudden changes in diet. Begin by gradually mixing some of the new food in with the old and increase the proportion so that after seven to eight days, all the food is the new one. The following ratios are recommended by Doctors Foster & Smith Inc: Days 1-3 add 25% of the new food, Days 4-6 add 50%, Days 7-9 add 75%, Day 10 feed 100% of the new food. By the way, if you stick to the identical brand, you can change flavours in one go.

10. **Check your dog's faeces** (aka stools, poo or poop!) If his diet is suitable, the food should be easily digested and produce dark brown, firm stools. If your dog produces soft or light stools, or has a lot of gas or diarrhoea, then the diet may not suit him, so consult your vet or breeder for advice.

11. **Feed your dog in stainless steel or ceramic dishes.** Plastic bowls don't last as long and can also trigger an allergic reaction in some sensitive dogs. Ceramic bowls are best for keeping water cold.

12. **If you have more than one dog, consider feeding them separately**. Cocker Spaniels usually get on fine with other pets, especially if introduced at an early age. But feeding dogs together can sometimes lead to dog food aggression, either because he's protecting his own food or trying to eat the food designated for another pet.

13. **If you do feed leftovers, feed them as part of a balanced meal,** not as well as (unless you are feeding a raw diet). High quality dog foods already provide all the nutrients, vitamins, minerals and calories that your dog needs. Feeding titbits or leftovers may be too rich for your dog in addition to his regular diet and cause him to scratch or put on weight. You can feed your dog vegetables, such as carrots, as a healthy low-calorie treat - most dogs love 'em.

14. **Keep your dog's weight in check.** Obesity can lead to the development of serious health issues, such as diabetes, high blood pressure and heart disease. Although the weight varies from dog to dog, a general rule is that your Cocker Spaniel's

tummy should be higher than or, at worst, level with his rib cage. If his belly hangs down below it, he is overweight

15. And finally, always make sure that your dog has access to clean, fresh water. Change the water and clean the bowl regularly – it gets slimy!

Types of Dog Food

We are what we eat. And the right food is a very important part of a healthy lifestyle for dogs as well as humans. This chapter explains the main options.

Dry dog food - also called kibble, is a popular and relatively inexpensive way of providing a balanced diet. It comes in a variety of flavours and with differing ingredients to suit the different stages of a dog's life. Cheap foods are often false economy, particularly if your Cocker does not tolerate grain/cereal very well, as they often contain a lot of grain. You may also have to feed larger quantities to ensure he gets sufficient nutrients.

Canned food - another popular choice – and it's often very popular with dogs too. They love the taste and it generally comes in a variety of flavours. Canned food is often mixed with dry kibble, and a small amount may be added to a dog on a dry food diet if he has lost interest in food. It tends to be more expensive than dried food and many owners don't like the mess. These days there are hundreds of options, some are very high quality and made from natural, organic ingredients and contain herbs and other beneficial ingredients. A part-opened tin can sometimes smell when you open the fridge door. As with dry food, read the label closely. Generally, you get what you pay for and the origins of cheap canned dog food are often somewhat dubious.

Semi-Moist - These are commercial dog foods shaped like pork chops, salamis, bacon (pictured), burgers or other meaty foods and they are the least nutritional of all dog foods. They are full of sugars, artificial flavourings and colourings to help make them visually appealing. Cockers don't care what their food looks like, they only care how it smells and tastes; the shapes are designed to appeal to us humans. While you may give your dog one as an occasional treat, they are not a diet in themselves and do not provide the nutrition that your dog needs. Steer clear of them for regular feeding.

Freeze-Dried - This is made by frozen food manufacturers for owners who like the convenience – this type of food keeps for six months to a year - or for those going on a trip with their dog. It says 'freeze-dried' on the packet and is highly palatable, but the freeze-drying process bumps up the cost.

Home-Cooked - Some dog owners want the ability to be in complete control of their dog's diet, know exactly what their dog is eating and to be absolutely sure that his nutritional needs are being met. Feeding your dog a home-cooked diet is time consuming and expensive, and the difficult thing – as with the raw diet - is sticking to it once you have started out with the best of intentions. But many owners think the extra effort is worth the peace of mind. If you decide to go ahead, you should spend the time to become proficient and learn about canine nutrition to ensure your dog gets all his vital nutrients.

The Raw Diet

There is a quiet revolution going on in the world of dog food. After years of feeding dry or tinned dog food, increasing numbers of owners are now feeding a raw diet to their pets. There is anecdotal evidence that many dogs thrive on raw, although scientific proof is lagging behind. There are a number of claims made by fans of the raw diet, including:

➢ Better skin and glossier coats

➢ Reduced symptoms of - or less likelihood of – allergies, and less scratching

➢ Improved digestion

➢ Helps fussy eaters

➢ Less doggie odour and flatulence

➢ Easier weight management

➢ Improved dental health and fresher breath

➢ Less waste coming out of the dog, drier and less smelly stools, more like pellets

➢ Reduced risk of bloat (gastric torsion or twisted stomach)

➢ Overall improvement in general health and less disease

➢ Higher energy levels

➢ Most dogs love a raw diet

It's fair to say that opinion was divided among the breeders we contacted. Some found there was no need to feed a raw diet– although some had tried it and had good results - as their Cockers were thriving on commercially-prepared food, or a mixture of manufactured and home-prepared food. Others think the raw diet is the best thing since sliced bread.

A raw diet can be expensive and involves more effort on the part of the owner. It's also true to say that the Cocker Spaniel is not a breed with a history of food intolerances or skin allergies, but if your dog is unlucky enough to be a sufferer or is a fussy eater, a raw diet is worth considering. Commercial foods may contain artificial preservatives and excessive protein and fillers – causing a reaction in some dogs. Dry, canned and other styles of processed food were mainly created as a means of convenience, but unfortunately this convenience sometimes can affect a dog's health.

Some nutritionists believe that dogs fed raw whole foods tend to be healthier than those on other diets, claiming there are inherent beneficial enzymes, vitamins, minerals and other qualities in meats, fruits, vegetables and grains in their natural forms that are denatured or destroyed when cooked. Many also believe dogs are less likely to have allergic reactions to the ingredients in this diet. But, unsurprisingly, the topic is not without controversy.

Critics say that the risks of nutritional imbalance, intestinal problems and food-borne illnesses caused by handling and feeding raw meat outweigh any benefits. It's true that owners must pay strict attention to hygiene when preparing a raw diet and it may not be suitable if there are children in the household. A dog may also be more likely to ingest bacteria or parasites such as Salmonella, E.coli and Ecchinococcus.

Frozen food can be a valuable aid to the raw diet. The food is highly palatable, made from high quality ingredients and dogs usually wolf it down. The downsides are that not all pet food stores stock it and it is expensive.

There are two main types of raw diet, one involves feeding raw, meaty bones and the other is known as the BARF diet (*Biologically Appropriate Raw Food* or *Bones And Raw Food),* created by Dr Ian Billinghurst.

Raw Meaty Bones

This diet is:

➢ Raw meaty bones or carcasses, if available, should form the bulk of the diet
➢ Table scraps both cooked and raw, such as vegetables, can be fed
➢ As with any diet, fresh water should be constantly available.

NOTE: Do NOT feed cooked bones, they can splinter

Australian veterinarian Dr Tom Lonsdale is a leading proponent of the raw meaty bones diet. He believes the following foods are suitable:

➢ Chicken and turkey carcasses, after the meat has been removed for human consumption
➢ Poultry by-products, including heads, feet, necks and wings
➢ Whole fish and fish heads
➢ Sheep, calf, goat, and deer carcasses sawn into large pieces of meat and bone
➢ Other by-products, e.g. pigs' trotters, pigs' heads, sheep heads, brisket, tail and rib bones
➢ A certain amount of offal can be included in the diet, e.g. liver, lungs, trachea, hearts, tripe

He says that low-fat game animals, fish and poultry provide the best source of food for pet carnivores. If you feed meat from farm animals (cattle, sheep and pigs), avoid excessive fat and bones that are too large to be eaten.

Some of it will depend on what's available locally and how expensive it is. If you shop around you should be able to source a regular supply of suitable raw meaty bones at a reasonable price. Start with your local butcher or farm shop. When deciding what type of bones to feed your Cocker, one point to bear in mind is that dogs are more likely to break their teeth when eating large knuckle bones and bones sawn lengthwise than when eating meat and bone together.

You'll also need to think about WHERE you are going to feed your dog. A dog takes some time to eat a raw bone and will push it around the floor, so the kitchen may not be the most suitable or hygienic place. Outside is one option, but what do you do when it's raining?

Establishing the right quantity to feed is a matter of trial and error. You will reach a decision based on your dog's activity levels, appetite and body condition. High activity and a big appetite show a need for increased food, and vice versa. A very approximate guide, based on raw meaty bones, for the average dog is 15%-20% of body weight in one week, or 2%-3% a day. Table scraps should be fed as an extra component of the diet. These figures are only a rough guide and relate to adult pets in a domestic environment. Pregnant or lactating females, growing puppies and working dogs may need much more food than adult animals of similar body weight.

Dr Lonsdale says: "Wherever possible, feed the meat and bone ration in one large piece requiring much ripping, tearing and gnawing. This makes for contented pets with clean teeth. Wild carnivores feed at irregular intervals. In a domestic setting, regularity works best and accordingly I suggest that you feed adult dogs and cats once daily. If you live in a hot climate, I recommend that you feed pets in the evening to avoid attracting flies.

"I suggest that on one or two days each week your dog may be fasted — just like animals in the wild. On occasions you may run out of natural food. Don't be tempted to buy artificial food, fast your dog and stock up with natural food the next day. Puppies...sick or underweight dogs should not be fasted (unless on veterinary advice)."

Table scraps and some fruit and vegetable peelings can also be fed, but should not make up more than one-third of the diet. Liquidising cooked and uncooked scraps in a food mixer can make them easier to digest.

Things to Avoid

> ➢ Excessive meat off the bone — not balanced
> ➢ Excessive vegetables — not balanced
> ➢ Small pieces of bone — can be swallowed whole and get stuck
> ➢ Cooked bones — get stuck
> ➢ Mineral and vitamin additives — create imbalance
> ➢ Processed food — leads to dental and other diseases
> ➢ Excessive starchy food — associated with bloat
> ➢ Onions, garlic and chocolate, grapes, raisins, sultanas, currants — toxic to pets
> ➢ Fruit stones (pips) and corn cobs — get stuck
> ➢ Milk — associated with diarrhoea. Animals drink it whether thirsty or not and consequently get fat

Points of Concern

> ➢ Old dogs accustomed to processed food may experience initial difficulty when changed to a natural diet. Discuss the change with your vet first and then, if he or she agrees, switch your dog's diet over a period of a week to 10 days

> ➢ Raw meaty bones are not suitable for dogs with dental or jaw problems

- This diet may not be suitable if your dog gulps his food, as the bones can become lodged inside him; larger bones may prevent gulping

- The diet should be varied, any nutrients fed to excess can be harmful

- Liver is an excellent foodstuff, but should not be fed more than once weekly

- Other offal, e.g. ox stomachs, should not make up more than half of the diet

- Whole fish are an excellent source of food, but avoid feeding one species of fish constantly. Some species, e.g. carp, contain an enzyme which destroys thiamine (vitamin B1)

- If you have more than one dog, do not allow them to fight over the food; feed them separately if necessary

- Be prepared to monitor your dog while he eats the bones, especially in the beginning, and do not feed bones with sharp points. Take the bone off your dog before it becomes small enough to swallow

- Make sure that children do not disturb the dog when he is feeding or try to take the bone away

- Hygiene: Make sure the raw meaty bones are kept separate from human food and clean thoroughly any surface the uncooked meat or bones have touched. This is especially important if you have children. Feeding bowls are unnecessary. Your dog will drag the bones across the floor, so feed them outside if you can, or on a floor which is easy to clean

- Puppies can and do eat diets of raw meaty bones, but you should consult the breeder or a vet before embarking on this diet with a young dog

You will need a regular supply of meaty bones – either locally or online - and you should buy in bulk to ensure a consistency of supply. For this you will need a large freezer. You can then parcel up the bones into daily portions. You can also feed frozen bones; some dogs will gnaw them straight away, others will wait for them to thaw.

More information is available from the website www.rawmeatybones.com and I would strongly recommend discussing the matter with your breeder or vet first before switching to raw meaty bones.

The BARF Diet

A variation of the raw meaty bones diet is the BARF created by Dr Ian Billinghurst, who owns the registered trademark 'Barf Diet'. A typical BARF diet is made up of 60%-75% of raw meaty bones (bones with about 50% meat, such as chicken neck, back and wings) and 25%-40% of fruit and vegetables, offal, meat, eggs or dairy foods. Bones must not be cooked or they can splinter inside the dog. There is a great deal of information on the BARF diet on the internet.

One point to consider is that a raw diet is not suitable for every dog. You could consider a gradual shift and see how your dog copes with the raw bones. You might also consider feeding two different daily meals to your dog; one raw and one not - or, as some Cocker breeders feed, a mixture of raw and complete food. If you do this then research the subject, and consult your vet to make sure that the two combined meals provide a balanced diet.

NOTE: Only start a raw diet if you have done your research and are sure you have the time and money to keep it going. There are numerous websites and canine forums with information on switching to a raw diet and everything it involves.

What the Breeders Feed

We asked a large number of breeders - from those with decades of experience to new and hobby breeders - what they feed their dogs. As you might expect, there was a wide range of answers. We are not recommending one type of feeding or one brand over another, but simply present their responses. They give an excellent insight as to what issues are important when considering food and why a particular brand – or raw - has been chosen. Another factor which has been highlighted is the need for extra high quality food for working Cockers during the season. We start with those who feed a raw or part raw diet to their dogs.

Jackie Hornby, of Jacmist Cockers, Bedfordshire, has bred show Cockers for 20 years and has recently switched food: "After feeding Royal Canin for years, I started feeding raw about a year ago. I wanted to cut out preservatives, as I have done in my own diet. I now know exactly what goes in - and less comes out! I include raw poultry necks in the diet. You can feed raw at any age, unlike complete foods which have age stages and different types of food.

"I feed all of my dogs raw, from older dogs to puppies, and just add different supplements according to conditions, e.g. joint aid for old dogs, Vitamin E for breeding age bitches, and dried parsley for bitches after their seasons. The raw food keeps coats and body muscle in excellent condition, and they enjoy it along with the veg. Even fussy eaters look forward to meal times - would you want to eat the same biscuit, day in day out?"

Pictured is Jackie's Lola, aged three, who is looking rather pleased with herself, having just won the Gundog Group at a show.

Manda and Jacquie Smith, Tassietay Working Cocker Spaniels, East Kent, have bred Cockers for 10 years. Manda said: "Dogs have the same digestive system as wolves; they are designed to eat raw meat, so in my view this is what they should be fed. They have very poor ability to digest carbohydrate, even when it is processed, so it just stresses the liver and kidneys to feed grain-filled processed food.

"Our dogs are always ready for their food and can't wait for it to be served - the bowls are always licked clean in seconds. They have good coats and don't smell. Their teeth stay cleaner. They are full of energy and much healthier. My dogs don't have ear problems, which may well be due to the diet, as I am aware that toxins exit via the ears causing that horrid blackish wax. There is very little waste coming out the other end; it's small, well-formed and dry and it doesn't smell anywhere near as bad as the waste from kibble-fed dogs."

Julie Summers, of Summervilles Gundogs, County Durham, co-founded www.working cockerhealthscreendirectory.com along with Rachel Birt, of Razehaven-Dorset Gundogs. Julie said: "We feed BARF to all of our dogs and puppies. The condition of the dogs is very apparent, they are full of energy, better coats, healthier, there's less mess and the dogs' teeth are immaculate. It also works out cheaper than dried - and the dogs enjoy it more, which is important."

Kirsten Strachan, of Lorne Working Cockers, Perthshire, has 30 years' experience with the breed. She said: "I have fed raw in the past, especially when I had a larger number of dogs than I have now. I thought it was the best form of food and they really thrived on it. However, as my numbers have gone down, I have gone back to dried food with a tin of wet food through it, mainly for my own ease. I think the dogs are leaner and teeth have no plaque with raw. I have not reared pups on raw as I reckoned it was unlikely that the new owners would continue, so reared pups on Royal Canin."

Billie Cheeseman, of BarleyCourt (working) Spaniels, Hertfordshire, added: "I currently feed mine Autarky, which is a holistic food that scores quite well on the dog food comparison sites and in reviews and is within my price range. Being a multi-dog household, food doesn't last very long so it has to be affordable. I have tried more expensive higher scoring food, one in particular I had high hopes for, but it didn't suit my dogs and they were dropping weight - even after increasing the amount I was feeding them several times.

"I have come back to Autarky each time. If I had the budget and the storage space to feed raw, I definitely would give it a go. I've seen the pros and cons discussed on forums and I do personally believe it is a healthier way to feed."

Tony and Caroline Bymolen, of Carto (show) Cocker Spaniels, Cambridgeshire, said: "We feed raw meat including tripe, chicken and tripe mix, beef, salmon and tripe mix, and chicken. We also give raw chicken wings as a treat. We find a raw diet to be excellent compared with the complete kibble foods available on the market. Our dogs are fit and healthy and produce a substantially reduced quantity of stools, which are generally solid. Coat quality is very important to a show Cocker and since changing to raw, our coats have a glossy, even quality."

Pictured is their Cassom Time Lord, known as Tino at home, aged nearly four.

Kerena Marchant, of Sondes (working) Cocker Spaniels, Surrey, comes from three generations of Cocker owners and says: "It's raw all the way. Our family has fed this since I can remember; a raw diet keeps dogs in a good shape and gives them energy. It also keeps timings up at agility and flyball and keeps the vets and animal dentists away. The vet says mine are perfect weight."

Michelle Mills, of Bryntail Gundogs, Powys, Wales, added: "I feed raw, I believe it is healthier for dogs - and less mess comes out. They have good, healthy teeth from the bones we feed and good skin and hair quality."

Andrew Platt, of Nithvalley Gundogs, Scotland, feeds mainly raw: "I feed raw tripe to the adult dogs, along with sardines, chicken and beef. If I use dry food, it is the grain-free salmon and trout product, along with a squirt of salmon oil and linseed oil. The puppies only get Eukanuba until six months old when they can be wormed with Drontal Plus and Milbemax, then they can have some raw food."

Top Dutch breeder Haja Van Wessem has been breeding Cockers since 1955 and winning prizes with her Speggle-Waggel lines since 1960, including the accolades of top Cocker in both the Netherlands and Germany, Junior European Champion and Junior World Champion. She said: "I feed raw tripe and dog biscuits of a good brand. I feed the dogs twice a day because I feel it is better to divide the food into two portions and also not to let them feel hungry."

Pictured is Haja's beautiful multi champion Speggle-Waggel's Ultra Blue, aged three.

Helen Marsden, of Finity (show) Cocker Spaniels, Hampshire, said: "I have fed raw as it is the natural diet for canines. However, there are very good grain-free kibbles and also natural wet foods that come a very close second. I think a raw diet is very good and suits a lot of dogs that suffer with food intolerances/allergies. Raw-fed dogs have great coats and fantastic muscle tone. I haven't personally come across any allergy issues, but do advocate as natural a food as possible, be that grain-free, kibble or a raw diet."

New breeder Christine Thomas, Dodfordhills (working) Spaniels, Worcestershire: "If it was easy to feed, I'd prefer to feed a raw diet. I was feeding the ready prepared raw food Nutriment and my bitch was so healthy when she was eating this. She pooped less and didn't have runny stools like a lot of dry food diets. She looked healthier and had shinier fur. However, raw meat has to be handled with care and it's not easy to feed when you're going away with your dogs (i.e. it has to be kept frozen). So now I use the dry food, Proplan, which was working OK, although after six months, my bitch got bored with the lamb flavour and we have had to switch to chicken. The occasional bit of boiled meat goes down well too, as a treat."

Gail Parsons, of Gaiter (show) Cocker Spaniels, Sussex: "I have tried raw and also dry; both are excellent. Luckily, my own dogs will eat anything! Having tried raw, I find their coats are good and teeth clean. I haven't had any issues, although I would say that the dogs need more raw food than is often stated."

David and Alison Matthews, of Tojamatt Cockers, Nottinghamshire, have 17 years' experience with show Cockers: "We feed our dogs Royal Canin and fresh raw mince. We feel a combined diet give the best of both worlds and chicken wings help to keep teeth clean."

Hobby (show) breeder Jane Minikin, of North Yorkshire, who has 18 years' experience with Cockers, said: "I have always fed my adult dogs and weaned puppies on a good quality dried complete food and canned. I feed a dry diet - Royal Canin - to my breeding dogs and a working dog mix to the other adult dogs for convenience, although in the past I fed a raw diet to my breeding dogs.

"I always supplemented my in-whelp and lactating bitches with fresh and raw meat. This suited the often fussy eaters and ensured excellent quality food for growing puppies before birth and during weaning. More recently, it has become popular to feed a completely dry diet with special kibble for pregnant mums and young puppies, which I have used, but I have been looking at research which seems to show a link between some health issues and the feeding of dry diets.

"At the moment I am reconsidering how I feed my dogs. On reading recent research on the health effects of different diets, I am considering feeding a raw diet again. A raw diet needs to be fed carefully, as it is difficult to get the right balance of nutrients. In the wild, dogs would eat organ meat and bone as well as muscle meat, so feeding butcher's mince and chicken would simply not be adequate."

Jill Gunn, of Dearganach Working Cockers, Scotland, said: "I feed grain-free kibble with any household leftovers - raw carrots are a big favourite. I also feed Nature's Menu raw with kibble. Feeding is an extremely personal thing; dogs have survived for thousands of years scavenging etc., being fed rubbishy dog food and still they survive. Raw, if you can store it and understand the regime, is probably the best you can do."

Pictured in a pigeon hide is Jill's stud dog Derwach Noel of Dearganach, or Red to his friends.

Pat and Andrew Height, Fourtails (show) Cocker Spaniels: "We feed a mixture of wet food, dry food and raw food, all with bio-live yoghurt mixed in. The yoghurt helps the dogs' digestive systems and the food mixture gives them a really good glossy coat."

Barry Hutchinson, Brynovation Gundogs, Gloucestershire:" All of our adult dogs are fed Skinners Field and Trial Working 23, once per day. We also feed raw tripe, offal, eggs (with shell), raw meat and bones, as and when available. From time to time the entire kennels - excluding puppies - are left fallow (i.e. fasted) for a day. We do not set dates, but it is about quarterly. The benefit is that we have a kennel of fit and healthy dogs, but diet is only one contributor to that."

Many breeders find their dogs thrive on a complete commercial food. Wendy Tobijanski, of Janski Cocker Spaniels, Shropshire, has bred both English and American Cockers for 40 years. She said: "I feed a complete food, usually a fish or tripe based one. But I always read the label and only buy a food with few ingredients and a single known protein source. Good, natural food is very important for health. As a vegetarian I won't feed raw, although you do then know exactly what your dog is eating."

Chris Warner, of Monwodelea Gundogs, Coventry, has bred dogs for over 20 years and working Cockers for six. He said: "I feed all my dogs on a dry complete working dog food. During the working season I add raw tripe to ensure they maintain their weight and condition. A dry food is very convenient for preparation, e.g. scoops of food into bowls which can be prepared beforehand. I know of people who feed a raw diet and their dogs appear healthy and in good condition. Initially, maintaining a supply of food from a butcher and storing it put me off the diet. It can now be purchased in convenient prepared packs. The cost is a factor; the dry food is cheaper."

Wendy Roberts, of Cheshire, has bred one litter from her working dog Cockermouth Lola and said: "We have always used a dried food, currently Iams, I feel it's easier to feed and keeps their teeth clean. I believe the raw diet is very effective, although I understand the sourcing and storage is quite complicated. My dogs seem happy, healthy and weight-managed on their current food."

Alan and Carole Pitchers, Alcarbrad (working) Cocker Spaniels, Essex: "We feed CSJ Champ Dog. This is a food for working dogs, and it is a complete food with all the necessary nutrients. The dogs' coats are glossy and they all appear healthy. We don't believe that raw feeding is a good idea in the summer. If the dogs don't eat all of the meal, the raw meat attracts flies, and could lead to stomach upsets."

Peter Harvey and Nikki Arnold, of Grannus Cocker Spaniels, Somerset, have owned and bred show Cockers for 20 years, Peter said: "My dogs have a variety of tinned, complete dry food, basic biscuits, cooked veg, bones, and sometimes left-overs. They are fed twice daily."

Jane Seekings, of Dorset, is about to breed her second litter of working Cockers. She said: "For breakfast I feed working dog biscuits, as these are higher in protein than normal biscuits. For dinner I feed a mixture of these biscuits and raw meat. During the working season they also have biscuits for lunch. My personal feeling is that the mixture of biscuits and raw meat provides them with a good source of protein, vitamins and carbohydrates, which they need as active dogs."

Pictured are Jane's golden Cocker Bulbarrow Elsey (Bella) aged six and a half, and her black daughter Melbury Abbas Daisy (Daisy) aged three.

Robert and Ruth Baldwin, Annaru Cocker Spaniels, South Wales: "We feed Purina Beta Lamb and Rice dry food. That is what our first puppy, Casey, was fed on when we brought her home and we have continued with it because we have had many nice pups and no problems. I would not give my dogs raw meat."

Keith Henderson, Owencraig (show) Cocker Spaniels, Dunfermline, Scotland: "I feed James Wellbeloved because it has no cereals, artificial flavourings or colourings. I wouldn't feed a raw diet."

Maxine Shaverin, of Lancashire, has owned Cockers for more than 20 years, been involved in Cocker rescue and has bred one show litter. She said: "I feed Skinners dry complete food, although one dog does have raw mince mixed in, but this is to encourage her to eat her kibble. I personally think that raw feeding is a fad. I'm not saying that raw isn't good for dogs but I don't believe it is necessary, nor brings about the positive results as claimed. A good kibble is satisfactory and much easier for most owners to manage. My last Cocker lived until she was just short of 17 and was fed a poor kibble to start with, then Skinners. We always shared our food with her too and she was incredibly healthy, despite suspicions regarding her heritage."

Christine and Dave Grant, of Rostreigan (show) Cocker Spaniels have bred Cockers since 1997, Chris said: "I feed my dogs on a complete premium dry dog food. For many years I used Technical, but I have recently changed to Costco premium chicken dry food. My latest two litters were weaned and reared on Pets at Home Advanced Nutrition chicken for small-medium puppies, and have done extremely well. I believe dogs should be fed on a well-balanced diet that has everything they need. We should take advantage of the research and testing that has been carried out to make dog food ideal for our dogs. Besides, my dogs like it!"

And finally, we hear from American Kennel Club registered breeder Eunice Wine, of Blackberry Farm Enterprises, Virginia, USA, who has been breeding American Cockers since 2010: "We feed our Cockers a 24% protein dog food from a good brand to give them energy and to keep them healthy and with shiny coats. We can't speak about a raw diet as we use dry feed. I do give our dogs treats, and occasionally they get raw meat. However, if a Cocker is fed raw chicken, for example, he might become a chicken killer and that can be unhandy on a working farm!

Food Allergies

Symptoms

Dog food allergies affect about one in 10 dogs. They are the third most common canine allergy after atopy (inhaled or contact allergies) and flea bite allergies. Vets believe that a dog may have a genetic predisposition to a food allergy and there is a lot of research going on right now to determine what makes the immune system more likely to develop that trait. Some breeds do appear to have a higher incidence than others. The Cocker Spaniel is not regarded as particularly susceptible, but any individual dog of whatever breed can suffer from them.

One school of thought is that young puppies treated with antibiotics are possibly more likely to develop food allergies later in life because antibiotics change the environment inside the gut, which is the body's largest immune organ. The trigger would then be exposure to the allergen. For this reason, some vets recommend giving puppies probiotics (healthy bacteria) - e.g. a spoonful of yoghurt a day - up to the age of six to 12 months and varying the diet.

Food allergies affect males and females in equal measures as well as neutered and intact pets. They can start when your dog is five months or 12 years old - although the vast majority start when the dog is between two and six years old. A dog can suddenly develop a food allergy to something that he's eaten for years with no problems. It is not uncommon for dogs with food allergies to also have other types of allergies.

If your dog is not well, how do you know if the problem lies with his food or not? Here are some common symptoms of food allergies to look out for:

> ➢ Itchy skin (this is the most common). The dog may lick or chew his paws or legs and rub his face with his paws or on the furniture, carpet, etc.
> ➢ Excessive scratching
> ➢ Ear infections
> ➢ Hot patches of skin
> ➢ Hair loss
> ➢ Redness and inflammation on the chin and face
> ➢ Recurring skin infections
> ➢ Increased bowel movements (maybe twice as often as usual)
> ➢ Skin infections that clear up with antibiotics but recur when the antibiotics run out

Allergies or Intolerance?

There's a difference between dog food ***allergies*** and dog food ***intolerance***:

Typical reactions to allergies are skin problems and/or itching

Typical reactions to intolerance are diarrhoea and/or vomiting

Dog food intolerance can be compared to people who get diarrhoea or an upset stomach from eating spicy food. Both can be cured by changing to a diet specifically suited to your dog. A food allergy may be harder to get to the root cause of. As they say in the canine world: "One dog's meat is another dog's poison".

With dogs, certain ingredients are more likely to cause allergies than others. To make matters worse, dogs are often allergic to more than one ingredient. In order of the most common triggers, they are: **Beef, dairy products, chicken, wheat, eggs, corn, soya (soy), pork, rabbit and fish.**

Unfortunately, these most common offenders are also the most common ingredients in dog foods. By the way, don't think if you put your dog on a rice and lamb kibble diet that it will automatically cure the problem. It might, but then again there's a fair chance it won't. The reason lamb and rice were thought to be less likely to cause allergies is simply because they have not traditionally been included in dog food recipes - therefore fewer dogs had reactions to them.

It is also worth noting that a dog is allergic or sensitive to an **ingredient** or ingredients, not to a particular brand of dog food, so it is very important to read the label on the sack or tin. If your dog has a reaction to beef, for example, he will react to any food containing beef, regardless of how expensive it is or how well it has been prepared.

Symptoms of food allergies are well documented. Unfortunately, the problem is that these conditions may also be symptoms of other issues, such as environmental or flea bite allergies, intestinal problems, mange and yeast or bacterial infections. And if your Cocker suffers from ear infections, there could be a number of different causes, it is more likely to be a bacterial or yeast infection due to the lack of air circulation under the hairy ear flap, but a reaction to a certain type of food should also be considered.

The only way to completely cure a food allergy or intolerance is complete avoidance. This is not as easy as it sounds. First you have to be sure that your dog does have a food allergy, and then you have to discover which food is causing the reaction. You can have a blood test on your dog, but many vets now believe that this is not accurate enough. As far as I am aware, the only true way to determine exactly what your dog is allergic to is to start a food trial.

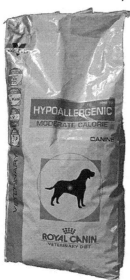

If you don't or can't do this for the whole 12 weeks, then you could try a more amateurish approach, which is eliminating ingredients from your dog's diet one at a time by switching diets – remember to do this over a period of a week to 10 days. You could also try feeding a raw diet and see how your dog responds to that. It's more time and effort on your part, but at least you know exactly what your dog is eating.

A food trial is usually the option of last resort, due to the amount of time and attention that it requires. It is also called '**an exclusion diet'** and is the only truly accurate way of finding out if your dog has a food allergy and what is causing it. Before embarking on one, try switching dog food. A hypoallergenic dog food, either commercial or home-made, is a good place to start. There are a number of these on the market and they all have the word '*hypoallergenic*' in the name.

Usually more expensive, hypoallergenic dog food ingredients do not include common allergens such as wheat protein or soya - thereby minimising the risk of an allergic reaction. Many may have less common ingredients, such as venison, duck or types of fish. Here are some things to look for in a high quality food: meat or poultry as the first ingredient, vegetables, natural herbs such as rosemary or parsley, oils such as rapeseed (canola) or salmon.

Here's what to avoid: corn, corn meal, corn gluten meal, meat or poultry by-products (as you don't know exactly what these are or how they have been handled), artificial preservatives (including BHA, BHT, Propyl Gallate, Ethoxyquin, Sodium Nitrite/Nitrate and TBHQBHA), artificial colours, sugars and sweeteners like corn syrup, sucrose and ammoniated glycyrrhizin, powdered cellulose, propylene glycol. If you can rule out all of the above, and you have tried switching diet without much success, then a food trial may be the only option left.

Food Trials

Before you embark on one of these, you need to know that they are a real pain-in-the-you-know-what to monitor. You have to be incredibly vigilant and determined, so only start one if you 100% know you can see it through to the end, or you are wasting your time. It is important to keep a diary during a food trial to record any changes in your dog's symptoms, behaviour or habits. It's even more difficult if, like a lot of Cocker owners, you have more than one dog.

A food trial involves feeding one specific food for 12 weeks, something the dog has never eaten before, such as rabbit and rice or venison and potato. Surprisingly, dogs are typically NOT allergic to foods they have never eaten before. The food should contain no added colouring, preservatives or flavourings.

There are a number of these commercial diets on the market, as well as specialised diets that have proteins and carbohydrates broken down into such small molecular sizes that they no longer trigger an allergic reaction. These are called **'limited antigen'** or **'hydrolysed protein'** diets.

Home-made diets are another option as you can strictly control the ingredients. The difficult thing is that this must be the **only thing** the dog eats during the trial. Any treats or snacks make the whole thing a waste of time. During the trial, you shouldn't allow your dog to roam freely, as you cannot control what he is eating or drinking when he is out of sight outdoors – not easy with a lively Cocker. Only the recommended diet must be fed.

Do NOT give:

> ➢ Treats
> ➢ Rawhide
> ➢ Pigs' ears
> ➢ Cows' hooves
> ➢ Flavoured medications (including heartworm treatments) or supplements
> ➢ Flavoured toothpastes and flavoured plastic toys

If you want to give a treat, use the recommended diet. (Tinned diets can be frozen in chunks or baked and then used as treats). If you have other dogs, either feed them all on the trial diet or feed the others in an entirely different location. If you have a cat, don't let the dog near the cat litter tray. And keep your pet out of the room when you are eating. Even small amounts of food dropped on the floor or licked off of a plate can ruin an elimination trial, meaning you'll have to start all over again...as I said, it isn't easy!

Of the three dozen breeders taking part in this book, only two had had a dog with a food sensitivity - one was a show Cocker and the other a working dog, and one other breeder had heard of issues. Considering the number of dogs our breeders have owned and bred between them, it is anecdotal evidence that this is not a common problem among Cockers. The pet show Cocker was born with a food intolerance, which was noticed "more or less at the time of going onto solid food as a puppy."

The breeder said: "He was sick nearly every time he ate and had a runny tummy as well. We went to our vets and they diagnosed the intolerance and said that we would have to find a food that he could eat. So, by a process of elimination, he ended up on fish and potatoes. Hypoallergenic food was just starting to get noticed and we made sure that his food was in that category. Today, he can eat a lot more variety, mainly due to the hypoallergenic qualities of the food. Now he is seven years old, it is no problem at all and he is healthy and wonderful!"

The second breeder said: "One of my puppies has been food sensitive, other than that they have been fine. It is important to feed puppies/dogs a good quality food as it will have a direct impact on their health and longevity. Some lower quality food has fillers in that can cause skin irritation, ear problems and many other symptoms. It's worth doing some research."

Tracey Simpson, of Bravialis Gundogs, North Yorkshire, added: "I have lately noticed an intolerance issue. Since the new surge to feed a raw dog food product, which I do fully support, I have noticed that puppies that have been weaned on a raw diet cannot then ever tolerate a kibble-based diet. I have had many dog owners ask for advice with it and also experienced the issue myself with my own dogs. I feed my dogs a raw diet of chicken and tripe with some vegetable. Raw food is as nature intended, I find their coats healthier and stamina better, also they poo a lot less."

Linda Reed, of Delindere Cocker Spaniels, Leicestershire, has over 30 years' experience of breeding English Cockers and 20 years' experience with American Cockers. She had this advice: "Avoid feeding beef and beef based completes as this can be too rich a diet for a Cocker and can cause hot spots and general skin irritation. I feed mine raw, unbleached tripe, natural, with all the essential vitamins and minerals. Add a good quality complete feed for crunch and roughage and you have a well-balanced diet."

Grain

Although beef is scientifically the food most likely to cause allergies in the general dog population, there is evidence to suggest that the ingredient most likely to cause a problem in many dogs is grain. Grain is wheat or any other cultivated cereal crop.

Foods that are high in grains and sugar can cause an increase in unhealthy bacteria and yeast in the stomach. This crowds out the good bacteria in the stomach and can cause toxins to occur that affect the immune system.

When the immune system is not functioning properly, the itchiness related to food allergies can cause secondary bacterial and yeast infections. These often show as ear infections, skin disorders, bladder infections and reddish or dark brown tear stains.

Symptoms of a yeast infection also include:

> ➢ Itchiness
> ➢ A musty smell
> ➢ Skin lesions or redness on the underside of the neck, the belly or paws

Although drugs such as antihistamines and steroids will temporarily help, they do not address the cause. Long term use of steroids is not recommended as it can lead to organ problems. Switching to a grain-free diet may help your dog get rid of the yeast and toxins. Some owners also feed their Cockers a daily spoonful of natural, live yoghurt, as this contains healthy bacteria and helps to balance the bacteria in your dog's digestive system (it works for humans too!).

Others have switched their dogs to a raw diet. Switching to a grain-free diet may also help to get rid of yeast and bad bacteria in the digestive system. Introduce the new food slowly and be patient, it may take two to three months for symptoms to subside – but you will definitely know if it has worked after 12 weeks.

Wheat products are known to produce flatulence in some dogs, while corn products and feed fillers may cause skin rashes or irritations. Some of the symptoms of food allergies - particularly the scratching, licking, chewing and redness - can also be a sign of inhalant or contact (environmental) allergies, which are caused by a reaction to such triggers as pollen, grass or dust. Some dogs are also allergic to flea bites. See **Chapter 11. Skin and Allergies** for more details.

If you suspect your dog has a food allergy, the first port of call should at the vet's to discuss the best course of action. Many vets' practices promote specific brands of food, which may or may not be the best for your dog. Don't buy anything without first checking every ingredient on the label.

How Much Food?

This is another question I am often asked. The answer is … there is no easy answer! The correct amount of food for your dog depends on a number of factors:

> ➢ Breed
> ➢ Gender
> ➢ Age
> ➢ Energy levels
> ➢ Amount of daily exercise
> ➢ Health
> ➢ Environment
> ➢ Number of dogs in house
> ➢ Quality of food
> ➢ Whether the dog is working

Some breeds have a higher metabolic rate than others. Cockers are generally regarded as dogs with medium to high activity levels. Very broadly, dogs bred from working English Cockers often have higher energy requirements than English show and American Cockers – although this can be misleading, as energy levels can also vary tremendously from one dog to another.

Generally, smaller dogs have faster metabolisms so require a higher amount of food per pound of body weight. Female dogs can be slightly more prone to putting on weight than male dogs. Some people say that dogs which have been spayed or neutered are more likely to put on weight, although this is disputed by others. Growing puppies and young dogs need more food than senior dogs with a slower lifestyle.

Every dog is different. You can have two Cocker Spaniels from the same litter with different temperaments and energy levels; the energetic dog will burn off more calories. Maintaining a healthy body weight for dogs – and humans – is all about balancing what you take in with how much you burn off. Certain health conditions, such as an underactive thyroid, diabetes, arthritis or heart disease, can lead to dogs putting on weight, so their food has to be adjusted accordingly.

If your dog is exercised for a couple of hours a day and has play sessions with humans or other dogs, he will need more calories than, for example, a dog who spends most of his time in a house or apartment. A Spaniel working out in the field all day will require extra nutrition to fuel his body for the several hours he is running around.

Pictured is Andy Platt's prizewinning working Cocker, Boots, looking very alert and ready for action.

Just like us, a dog kept in a very cold environment will need more calories to keep warm than a dog in a warm climate. They burn extra calories in keeping themselves warm. Here's an interesting fact: a dog kept on his own is more likely to be overweight than a dog kept with other dogs. This is because he receives all of the food-based attention.

The daily recommended amount listed on sacks or tins of cheaper commercial foods is generally too high, as much of the food is made up of cereals, which are not doing much except bulking up the weight of the food – and possibly triggering allergies.

We feed our dog a dried hypoallergenic dog food made by James Wellbeloved in England. Max has seasonal allergies which make him scratch, but he seems to do pretty well on this food.

Below we list James Wellbeloved's recommended feeding amounts, listed in kilograms and grams. (28.3g=1oz; 1kg=2.2lb). It gives a broad guideline as to the average number of **calories** dogs with **medium** energy and activity levels need. (This does not apply to working dogs during the season).

The number on the left is the dog's **adult weight** in kilograms. On the right is the amount of daily food in grams that an average dog with average energy levels requires, measured in grams (divide by 28.3 to get ounces). For example, a three-month-old Cocker pup which will grow into a 10kg (22lb) adult requires around 185g of food per day (6.5oz).

Adult Cockers vary in weight, depending on whether they are English or American (pictured), male or female, show or working stock, but most will weigh between 10kg and 15kg (33lb) when fully grown.

NOTE: These are only very general guidelines, your dog may need more or less than this. Use the chart as a guideline only and if your dog loses or gains weight, adjust his or her feeds accordingly.

Canine Feeding Chart

PUPPY

Size type	Expected adult body weight (kg)	Daily serving (g)					
		2 mths	3 mths	4 mths	5 mths	6 mths	> 6 mths
Toy	2	50	60	60	60	55	
	5	95	110	115	115	110	Change to Adult or Small Breed Adult
Small	10	155	185	195	190	185	
Medium	17	215	265	285	285	280	Change to Junior
	25	270	350	375	375	370	
	32	300	400	445	450	450	
	40	355	475	525	530	530	
	50	405	545	610	625		
	60	450	605	685			
	70	485	670				
Large	90	580					Change to Large Breed Junior

JUNIOR

Size type	Expected adult body weight (kg)	Daily serving (g)						
		6 mths	7 mths	8 mths	10 mths	12 mths	14 mths	16 mths
Medium	10	195	185	175	160			
	17	290	285	270	245	Change to Adult		
Large	25	390	380	365	330	320		
	32	445	435	415	380	365		Change to Large Breed Adult
	40	555	545	530	500	460	460	

ADULT

Size type	Bodyweight (kg)	Daily serving (g)		
		High activity	Normal activity	Low activity
Toy	2-5	60-115	55-100	45-85
Small	5-10	115-190	100-170	85-145
Medium	10-15	190-255	170-225	145-195
	15-25	255-380	225-330	195-285
Large	25-40	380-535	330-475	285-410
	40-55	535-680	475-600	410-520
	55-70	680-820	600-720	520-620
	70-90	820-985	720-870	620-750

SENIOR

Size type	Bodyweight (kg)	Daily serving (g)	
		Active	Normal
Toy	2-5	50-105	45-90
Small	5-10	105-175	90-150
Medium	10-15	175-235	150-205
	15-25	235-345	205-300
	25-40	345-495	300-425
	40-55	495-625	425-540
	55-70	625-750	540-650
Large	70-90	750-905	650-780

Overweight Dogs

It is far easier to regulate your Spaniel's weight and keep it at a healthy level than to try and slim down a voraciously hungry dog when he becomes overweight. Overweight and obese dogs are susceptible to a range of illnesses. According to James Howie, Veterinary Advisor to Lintbells, some of the main ones are:

Joint disease – excessive body weight may increase joint stress which is a risk factor in joint degeneration (arthrosis), as is cruciate disease (knee ligament rupture). Joint disease tends to lead to a reduction in exercise which then increases the likelihood of weight gain, which reduces exercise further. A vicious cycle is created. Overfeeding Cocker Spaniels while they are growing can lead to various problems, including the worsening of hip dysplasia. Weight management may be the only measure required to control symptoms in some cases.

Heart and lung problems – fatty deposits within the chest cavity and excessive circulating fat play important roles in the development of cardio-respiratory and cardiovascular disease.

Diabetes – resistance to insulin has been shown to occur in overweight dogs, leading to a greater risk of diabetes mellitus.

Tumours – obesity increases the risk of mammary tumours in female dogs.

Liver disease – fat degeneration may result in liver insufficiency.

Reduced lifespan - one of the most serious proven findings in obesity studies is that obesity in both humans and dogs reduces lifespan.

Exercise intolerance – this is also a common finding with overweight dogs, which can compound an obesity problem as fewer calories are burned off and are therefore stored, leading to further weight gain.

Most Cockers are extremely attached to their humans. However, beware of going too far in regarding your dog as a member of the family. **You have to resist those beautiful big, pleading eyes!** It has been shown that dogs regarded as 'family members' (i.e. anthropomorphosis) by the owner are at greater risk of becoming overweight. This is because attention given to the dog often results in food being given as well.

The important thing to remember is that many of the problems associated with being overweight are reversible. Increasing exercise increases the calories burned, which in turn reduces weight. If you do put your dog on a diet, the reduced amount of food will also mean reduced nutrients, so he may need a supplement during this time.

Feeding Puppies

Puppy foods

Feeding your puppy the right diet is important to help his young body and bones grow strong and healthy. Puppyhood is a time of rapid growth and development, and puppies require different levels of nutrients to adult dogs.

For the first six weeks, they need milk about five to seven times a day, which they take from their mother. Generally they make some sound if they want to feed. The frequency is reduced when the pup reaches six to eight weeks old. Pictured below is a litter bred by Wendy Tobijanski.

Cocker Spaniel puppies should stay with their mothers and littermates until at least eight weeks old. During this time, the mother is still teaching her offspring some important rules about life. Good breeders will tell you in detail what your puppy is being fed and often provide you with a sample of the food to take home.

Leaving the litter is a very stressful time for puppies and a change of diet is the last thing they need. You should continue feeding the same puppy food and at the same times as the breeder at least for the first few days – or longer - at home. Dogs do not adapt to changes in their diet or feeding habits as easily as humans.

You can then slowly change the food based on information from the breeder and your vet. This should be done very gradually by mixing in a little more of the new food each day over a period of seven to 10 days.

If at any time your puppy starts being sick, has loose stools or is constipated, slow the rate at which you are switching him over. If he continues vomiting, seek veterinary advice as he may have a problem with the food you have chosen. Puppies who are vomiting or who have diarrhoea quickly dehydrate.

Because of their special nutritional needs, you should only give your puppy a food that is approved either just for puppies or for all life stages. If a feed is recommended for adult dogs only, it won't have enough protein, and the balance of calcium and other nutrients will not be right for a pup. Puppy food is very high in calories and nutritional supplements, so you want to switch to a junior or adult food once he leaves puppyhood. Feeding puppy food too long can result in obesity and orthopaedic problems – check with your vet on the right time to switch.

Getting the amount and type of food right for your pup is important. Feeding too much will cause him to put on excess pounds, and overweight puppies are more likely to grow into overweight adults. As a very broad guideline, dogs normally mature into fully developed adults at around two years old, although some Cockers may develop a little more slowly.

DON'T:

> Feed table scraps from the table. Your puppy will get used to begging for food; it will also affect a puppy's carefully balanced diet. Pictured is Jackie Hornby's four-month-old Buddy, showing just how hard it is to resist those big brown eyes

> Feed food or uncooked meat which has gone off. Puppies have sensitive stomachs, stick to a prepared puppy food, preferably one recommended by your breeder

DO:

> Regularly check the weight of your growing pup to make sure he is within normal limits for his age. There are charts available on numerous websites, just type "puppy weight chart" into Google – you'll need to know the exact age and current weight of your puppy

> Take your puppy to the vet if he has diarrhoea or is vomiting for two days

> Remove his food after it has been down for 15 to 20 minutes. Food available 24/7 encourages fussiness

How Often?

Puppies have small stomachs but big appetites, so feed them small amounts on a frequent basis. Establishing a regular feeding routine with your puppy will also help with toilet training. Get him used to regular mealtimes and then let him outside to do his business as soon as he has finished. Puppies have fast metabolisms, so the results may be pretty quick!

You should be there for the feeds because you want him and his body on a set schedule. Smaller meals are easier for him to digest and energy levels don't peak and fall so much with frequent feeds. There is some variation between recommendations, but here's a broad guideline:

> ➢ Up to the age of three or four months, feed your puppy four times a day
> ➢ Feed him three times a day until he is six months old
> ➢ Then twice a day for the rest of his life

It's up to you to control your dog's intake and manage his or her diet. Stick to the correct amount; you're doing your pup no favours by overfeeding. Unless your puppy is particularly thin (which is highly unlikely), don't give in - no matter how much your cute Cocker pleads. You must be firm and resist the temptation to give him extra food or treats.

A very broad rule of thumb is to feed puppy food for a year, but some owners start earlier on adult food, while others delay switching until their Cocker is 18 months or even two years old. If you are not sure, consult your breeder or your vet.

TIP: Cocker Spaniels make devoted companions and normally love to please you. But if your dog is not responding well to a particular family member, a useful tactic is to get that person to feed the dog every day. The way to a dog's heart can be through his stomach.

Feeding Seniors

Once your adolescent dog has switched to an adult diet he will be on this for several years. As a dog moves towards old age, his body has different requirements to those of a young dog. This is the time to consider switching to a senior diet. Dogs are living much longer than they did 30 years ago. There are many factors contributing to this, including better vaccines and veterinary care, but one of the most important factors is better nutrition. Generally a dog is considered to be 'older' or senior if he is in the last third of his normal life expectancy.

Some owners of large breeds - such as Great Danes with a lifespan of nine years - switch their dogs from an adult to a senior diet when they are only six or seven years old. A typical Cocker Spaniel lifespan ranges from 10 to 15 years; a few live even longer.

When you change to a senior food depends on the individual dog, his or her size, energy levels and general health. Look for signs of your dog slowing down or having joint problems. That may be the time to talk to your vet about switching. You can describe any changes at your dog's annual vaccination appointment, rather than having the expense of a separate consultation.

As a dog grows older, his metabolism slows down, his joints may stiffen, his energy levels decrease and he needs less exercise, just like with humans. You may notice in middle or old age that your dog starts to put weight on. The adult diet he is on may be too rich and have too many calories, this would be the time to consider switching.

Even though he is older, keep his weight in check, as obesity in old age only puts more strain on his body - especially joints and organs - and makes any health problems even worse. Because of lower activity levels, many older dogs will gain weight and getting an older dog to slim down can be very difficult. It is much better not to let your dog get too chunky than to put him on a diet. But if he is overweight, put in the effort to shed the extra pounds. This is one of the single most important things you can do to increase your Cocker's quality AND length of life.

Other changes in canines are again similar to those in older humans and as well as stiff joints or arthritis, he might move more slowly and sleep more. Hearing and vision may not be so sharp, organs don't all work as efficiently and his teeth may have become worn down. You may also notice that your old dog isn't quite as tolerant as he used to be – particularly with boisterous puppies – dogs, as well as humans, can get grumpier with age!

Specially formulated senior diets are lower in protein and calories but help to create a feeling of fullness. Older dogs are more prone to develop constipation, so senior diets are often higher in fibre - at around 3% to 5%.

Wheat bran can also be added to regular dog food to increase the amount of fibre - but do not try this if your Cocker Spaniel has a low tolerance or intolerance to grain. If your dog has poor kidney function, then a low phosphorus diet will help to lower the workload for the kidneys.

Ageing dogs have special dietary needs, some of which can be provided in the form of supplements, such as glucosamine and chondroitin, which help joints. If your dog is not eating a complete balanced diet, then a vitamin/mineral supplement is recommended to prevent any deficiencies. Some owners also feed extra antioxidants to an older dog – ask your vet's advice on your next visit. Antioxidants are also found naturally in fruit and vegetables.

While some older dogs put on weight more easily, others have the opposite problem – they lose weight and are disinterested in food. If your old dog is losing weight and not eating well, firstly get him checked out by the vet to rule out any possible disease problems. If he gets the all-clear, your next challenge is to tempt him to eat. He may be having trouble with his teeth, so if he's on a dry food, try smaller kibble, moistening it with water or gravy and/or adding a little meat.

Our dog loved his twice daily feeds until he recently got to the age of 10 when he suddenly lost interest in his hypoallergenic kibble. We tried switching flavours within the same brand, but that didn't work. After a short while we mixed his daily feeds with a little gravy and a spoonful of tinned dog food – Bingo! He's wolfing it down again and lively as ever.

Some dogs can tolerate a small amount of milk or eggs added to their food, and home-made diets of boiled rice, potatoes, vegetables and chicken or meat with the right vitamin and mineral supplements can also work well. However, other dogs have a low tolerance to dairy products. See **Chapter 15. Caring for Older Dogs** for more information on looking after a senior.

Reading Dog Food Labels

A NASA scientist would have a hard job understanding some dog food manufacturers' labels, so it's no easy task for us lowly dog owners. Here are some things to look out for on the manufacturers' labels:

➤ The ingredients are listed by weight and the top one should always be the main content, such as chicken or lamb. Don't pick one where grain is the first ingredient, it is a poor quality feed and some dogs can develop grain intolerances or allergies - often it is specifically wheat they have a reaction to

> **Ingredients:** Chicken, Chicken By-Product Meal, Corn Meal, Ground Whole Grain Sorghum, Brewers Rice, Ground Whole Grain Barley, Dried Beet Pulp, Chicken Fat (preserved with mixed Tocopherols, a source of Vitamin E), Chicken Flavor, Dried Egg Product, Fish Oil (preserved with mixed Tocopherols, a source of Vitamin E), Potassium Chloride, Salt, Flax Meal, Sodium Hexametaphosphate, Fructooligosaccharides, Choline Chloride, Minerals (Ferrous Sulfate, Zinc Oxide, Manganese Sulfate, Copper Sulfate, Manganous Oxide, Potassium Iodide, Cobalt Carbonate), DL-Methionine, Vitamins (Ascorbic Acid, Vitamin A Acetate, Calcium Pantothenate, Biotin, Thiamine Mononitrate (source of vitamin B1), Vitamin B12 Supplement, Niacin, Riboflavin Supplement (source of vitamin B2), Inositol, Pyridoxine Hydrochloride (source of vitamin B6), Vitamin D3 Supplement, Folic Acid), Calcium Carbonate, Vitamin E Supplement, Brewers Dried Yeast, Beta-Carotene, Rosemary Extract.

➤ High up the list should be meat or poultry by-products, these are clean parts of slaughtered animals, not including meat. They include organs, blood and bone, but not hair, horns, teeth or hooves

➤ Guaranteed Analysis (pictured below) – This guarantees that your dog's food contains the labelled percentages of crude protein, fat, fibre and moisture. Keep in mind that wet and dry dog foods use different standards. (It does not list the digestibility of protein and fat and this can vary widely depending on their sources). While the guaranteed analysis is a start in understanding the food quality, be wary about relying on it too much. One pet food manufacturer made a mock product with a Guaranteed Analysis of 10% protein, 6.5% fat, 2.4% fibre, and 68% moisture - not unlike what's on many canned pet food labels – the only problem was that the ingredients were old leather boots, used motor oil, crushed coal and water!

➤ Chicken meal (dehydrated chicken) has more protein than fresh chicken, which is 80% water. The same goes for beef, fish and lamb. So, if any of these meals are number one on the ingredient list, the food should contain enough protein

➤ A certain amount of flavourings can make a food more appetising for your dog. Chose a food with a specific flavouring, like **'beef flavouring'** rather than a general **'meat flavouring',** where the origins are not so clear

➤ Find a food that fits your dog's age and size. Talk to your vet or visit an online Cocker Spaniel forum and ask other owners what they are feeding their dogs

➤ If your dog has a food allergy or intolerance to wheat, check whether the food is gluten free. All wheat contains gluten

➤ The USA's FDA says: "The term **'natural'** is often used on pet food labels, although that term does not have an official definition either. AAFCO has developed a feed term definition for what types of ingredients can be considered 'natural' and "Guidelines for Natural Claims" for pet foods. For the most part, 'natural' can be construed as equivalent to a lack of artificial flavours, artificial colours, or artificial preservatives in the product." However, as artificial flavours and colours are not used in many foods, the word 'natural' on dog food does not mean a lot, neither are there legal guidelines regarding use of the word 'organic'

> ➢ In the USA, dog food that meets minimum nutrition requirements has a label that confirms this. It states: *"[food name] is formulated to meet the nutritional levels established by the AAFCO Dog Food Nutrient Profiles for [life stage(s)]"*

> ➢ **'Complete and balanced'** DO have a legal meaning'; these are the words to look for on a packet or tin. The FDA states: "This means the product contains the proper amount of all recognized essential nutrients needed to meet the needs of the healthy animal."

Even better, look for a food that meets the minimum nutritional requirements **'as fed'** to real pets in an AAFCO-defined feeding trial, then you know the food really delivers the nutrients it claims to. AAFCO feeding trials on real dogs are the gold standard. Brands that do costly feeding trials (including Nestlé and Hill's) indicate so on the package.

NOTE: Dog food labelled **'supplemental'** isn't complete and balanced. Unless you have a specific, vet-approved need for it, it's not something you want to feed your dog for an extended period of time. Check with your vet if in doubt. If it all still looks a bit baffling, you might find the following websites very useful. I have no vested interest in either website, but have found them to be a good source of independent advice.

www.dogfoodadvisor.com provides useful information with star ratings for grain-free and hypoallergenic dog foods for USA brands. It is run by Mike Sagman who has a medical background and analyses and rates hundreds of brands of dog food based on the listed ingredients and meat content. You might be surprised at some of his findings.

In the UK there is www.allaboutdogfood.co.uk by David Jackson, who used to be employed in the dog food industry.

To recap: No single food is right for every dog; you must decide on the best for yours and tailor the food to meet your dog's energy levels and workload. If you have a puppy, initially stick to the same food that the breeder has been feeding the litter, and only change diet later and gradually. Once you have decided on a food, monitor your puppy or adult. The best test of a food is how well your dog is doing on it.

If your Cocker Spaniel is happy, alert and healthy, interested in life, has plenty of energy, is not too fat and not too thin, doesn't scratch a lot and has healthy-looking stools, then…

Congratulations, you've got it right!

8. Behaviour

Just as with humans, a dog's personality is made up of a combination of temperament and character.

Temperament is the nature – or inherited traits - a dog is born with; a predisposition to act or react in a certain way. This is why getting your puppy from a good breeder is so important. Not only will a responsible breeder produce puppies from physically healthy dams and sires, but he or she will also look at the temperament of the dogs and breed from those with good traits.

You should also think carefully about what type of Cocker you want: American or English, from working or show stock? Within working types there are dogs bred for the shoot and others which are field trial specialists, each with different traits. The differences in temperament between show and working Cockers, and shooting dogs and field trailers, have been highlighted in **Chapter 1. Meet the Cocker Spaniel.**

Character is what develops through the dog's life and is formed by a combination of temperament and environment. How you treat your dog will have a huge effect on his or her personality and behaviour. Starting off on the right foot with good routines for your puppy is very important; so treat your dog well, spend time with him and give him plenty of socialisation and exercise.

All dogs need different environments, scents and experiences to keep them stimulated and well-balanced. Spaniels are particularly scent driven and time spent off the lead, running free with his or her nose to the ground, helps to achieve that balance.

Praise good behaviour, use positive methods and keep training short and fun. At the same time, all dogs should understand the "No" (or similar) command. Just as with children, a dog has to learn boundaries to adapt successfully and be content with his or her environment.

Be consistent so your dog learns the guidelines quickly. All of these measures will help your dog grow into a happy, well-adjusted and well-behaved adult dog who is a delight to be with.

If you adopt a Cocker from a rescue centre, you may need a little extra patience. These eager-to-please people-loving dogs may also arrive with some baggage. They have been abandoned by their previous owners for a variety of reasons - or perhaps forced to produce puppies in a puppy mill - and may very well still carry the scars of that trauma.

They may feel nervous and insecure, they may be needy or aloof, and they may not know how to properly interact with a loving owner. Your time and patience is needed to teach these poor animals to trust again and to become happy in their new forever homes.

Understanding Canine Emotions

As pet lovers, we are all too keen to ascribe human traits to our dogs; this is called **anthropomorphism** – "the attribution of human characteristics to anything other than a human being." Most of us dog lovers are guilty of that, as we come to regard our pets as members of the family - and Cockers certainly regard themselves as members of the family.

An example of anthropomorphism might be that the owner of a male dog might not want to have him neutered because he will "miss sex," as a human might if he or she were no longer able to have sex. This is simply not true. A male dog's impulse to mate is entirely governed by his hormones, not emotions. If he gets the scent of a bitch on heat, his hormones (which are just chemicals) tell him he has to mate with her. He does not stop to consider how attractive she is or whether she is '**the one**' to produce his puppies. No, his reaction is entirely physical, he just wants to dive in there and get on with it!

It's the same with females. When they are on heat, a chemical impulse is triggered in their brain making them want to mate – with any male, they aren't at all fussy. So don't expect your little princess to be all coy when she is on heat, she is not waiting for Prince Charming to come along - the tramp down the road or any other scruffy pooch will do! It is entirely physical, not emotional. Food is another issue. A dog will not stop to count the calories of that lovely treat (you have to do that). No, he or she is driven by food and just thinks about getting the treat. Most non-fussy eaters will eat far too much, given the opportunity.

Cockers are very loving and extremely eager to please you, and if yours doesn't make you laugh from time to time, you must have had a humour by-pass. Those kept in the house want to spend their time with their owners. All of these characteristics add up to one thing: an extremely endearing and loving family member that it's all too easy to reward - or spoil. Treating a Cocker like a child is a habit to be avoided.

If your dog is kept indoors, it's fine to treat him like a member of the family - as long as you keep in mind that he is a canine and not a human. Understand his mind, patiently train him to learn his place in the household and that there are household rules he needs to learn – like not jumping on the couch when he's covered in mud - and you will be rewarded with a companion who is second to none and fits in beautifully with your family and lifestyle.

Dr Stanley Coren is a psychologist well known for his work on canine psychology and behaviour. He and other researchers believe that in many ways a dog's emotional development is equivalent to that of a young child. Dr Coren says: "Researchers have now come to believe that the mind of a dog is roughly equivalent to that of a human who is two to two-and-a-half years old. This conclusion holds for most mental abilities as well as emotions.

"Thus, we can look to human research to see what we might expect of our dogs. Just like a two-year-old child, our dogs clearly have emotions, but many fewer kinds of emotions than found in adult humans. At birth, a human infant only has an emotion that we might call excitement. This indicates how excited he is, ranging from very calm up to a state of frenzy. Within the first weeks of life the excitement state comes to take on a varying positive or a negative flavour, so we can now detect the general emotions of contentment and distress.

"In the next couple of months, disgust, fear, and anger become detectable in the infant. Joy often does not appear until the infant is nearly six months of age and it is followed by the emergence of shyness or suspicion. True affection, the sort that it makes sense to use the label "love" for, does not fully emerge until nine or ten months of age."

So, our Cockers can truly love us – but we knew that already!

According to Dr Coren, dogs can't feel shame, so if you are housetraining your puppy, don't expect him to be ashamed if he makes a mess in the house, he can't; he simply isn't capable of feeling shame. But he will not like it when you ignore him when he's behaving badly, and he will love it when you praise him for eliminating outdoors. He is simply responding to your reaction with his simplified range of emotions.

Dr Coren also believes that dogs cannot experience guilt, contempt or pride. I'm no psychology expert, but I'm not sure I agree. Take a Cocker to a local dog show or agility class, watch him perform and then maybe win a rosette - is the dog's delight something akin to pride? And Cockers can certainly experience joy.

They love your attention and praise at home, and just watch a working Cocker out in the field if you want to see a happy dog. When they run through the muddy undergrowth and return with a present for you in the form of a deceased bird or small mammal - isn't there a hint of pride there?

Cockers can show empathy - "the ability to understand and share the feelings of another" - and this is one reason why they make such excellent therapy and service dogs. Like many sensitive breeds, they get into tune with the rhythms of the household and pick up on the mood and emotions of the owner.

One emotion which all dogs can experience is jealousy – with Cockers this may be displayed when you give your precious attention to animals other than themselves. Or they may guard their food or be protective of a toy.

An interesting article was published in the PLOS (Public Library of Science) Journal in 2014 following an experiment into whether dogs get jealous. Building on research that shows that six-month old infants display jealousy, the scientists studied 36 dogs in their homes and video recorded their actions when their owners displayed affection to a realistic-looking stuffed canine.

Over three-quarters of the dogs were likely to push or touch the owner when they interacted with the decoy (pictured, right). The envious mutts were more than three times as likely to do this for interactions with the stuffed dog compared to when their owners gave their attention to other objects, including a book. Around a third tried to get between the owner and the plush toy, while a quarter of the put-upon pooches snapped at the dummy dog!

"Our study suggests not only that dogs do engage in what appear to be jealous behaviours, but also that they were seeking to break up the connection between the owner and a seeming rival," said Professor Christine Harris from University of California in San Diego.

The researchers believe that the dogs understood that the stuffed dog was real. The authors cite the fact that 86% of the dogs sniffed the toy's rear end during and after the experiment!

"We can't really speak of the dogs' subjective experiences, of course, but it looks as though they were motivated to protect an important social relationship. Many people have assumed that jealousy is a social construction of human beings - or that it's an emotion specifically tied to sexual and romantic relationships," said Professor Harris. "Our results challenge these ideas, showing that animals besides ourselves display strong distress whenever a rival usurps a loved one's affection."

Typical Cocker Traits

Every dog is different, of course. But within the breeds, there are some similarities. Here are some typical Cocker traits - some of them may also apply to other breeds of dog, but put them all together and you have a blueprint for the Cocker Spaniel.

1. The Cocker was originally bred as a working gundog to flush and retrieve game; many are still used for this purpose. Working dogs generally have higher exercise demands and a greater need for mental stimulation than other types of dog, such as companion dogs. Even if your Cocker is a pet, he or she still has these needs to some extent.

2. Cockers have a naturally gentle and happy temperament; the Kennel Clubs describe them as "merry", and they have a trademark constantly wagging tail. Treated well, a Cocker will generally get on well with everybody and other dogs.

3. They make wonderful companions and family dogs as long as they get enough physical and mental stimulation.

4. Cockers are intelligent, 'busy' dogs who need mental as well as physical exercise. They love to play both indoor and outdoor games and enjoy activities which challenge them, which is why working Cockers in particular excel at agility and Flyball.

5. They love water and are usually good swimmers. Cockers are generally hardy (active working dogs may be kept outside in kennels) and most do well in cold conditions and snow. Pictured is one of Julie and Darren Summers' working Cockers in action. Photo: www.ruralshots.com

6. One thing which surprises some new owners is the amount of exercise some Cockers need. It does, of course, depend on factors such as whether your dog was bred from working or

show Spaniels (workers often require more exercise and mental stimulation) but two or more hours of exercise a day is not unusual for some dogs and their owners. Much also depends on what the dog gets used to as a pup. Most are happy to chill out and snuggle up with their owners after a good exercise session.

7. An under-exercised, under-stimulated Cocker will display poor behaviour, as any dog would.

8. Cockers have a very keen sense of scent and are happiest running off the lead with their noses to the ground. They are used as sniffer dogs by police and customs services.

9. Some have a fairly strong sense of prey, so keep them on the lead around farm animals until you know they can be trained and trusted not to chase them. You may never stop some dogs chasing a squirrel or small bird.

10. Cockers of all types are quite sensitive and do not respond well to rough handling or heavy-handed training.

11. If kept in a house, they do not like being left alone for long periods. If you are away from the home a lot, consider another type of dog not so dependent on humans and activity for happiness. Cockers can develop separation anxiety, so factor in some time away from your dog every single day, starting as soon as your pup or adult dog arrives - separation anxiety is stressful for both dog and owner.

12. They are "biddable." Provided you put the time in, most are easy to train - and they can be trained to a very high level in a number of different fields. Their intelligence and eagerness to please are powerful training aids.

13. The same goes for housetraining; a Cocker can get the hang of it in a few days or a couple of weeks, provided you are extremely vigilant in the beginning.

14. Cockers are not aggressive dogs and generally get on well with other dogs, provided they have been properly socialised.

15. Some Cockers can suffer from submissive urination, especially if they are under-socialised, insecure or over-excited. Proper socialisation and plenty of exercise can help to combat this issue.

16. They are fairly high maintenance when it comes to grooming, especially show-type Cockers.

17. They love muddy puddles and running through the undergrowth and many shed a lot, so may not be the best choice for the extremely house-proud.

18. Working Cockers are better suited to active households.

19. Cockers are honest dogs, devoted to their owners and incredibly eager to please them; they will steal your heart. OK, that's not very scientific, but ask anyone who owns one!

What the Breeders Say

We asked the breeders involved in this book to describe the Cocker Spaniel temperament. If you haven't made up your mind yet what type of Cocker to get, their comments might help you decide. This is what they said:

Show Cockers

Caroline Bymolen: "Every dog is, of course, an individual and as such their temperaments are all different. However, in general, (and we talk about the show type) they are a fun-loving, affectionate and loyal breed with good temperaments. One tag line which is very apt is that they are a big dog in a small body. They are a joy to have around and we wouldn't be without them."

David Matthews: "The typical Cocker has a sound temperament. They are loveable, bright, very clever and a good size for most homes." Andrew Height: "Merry, easy to live with, loving, calm and biddable."

Haja van Wessem: "A Cocker is happy, energetic, inventive, nosy and very lovable. He is a true optimist. I was attracted by their loving temperament and optimistic nature. Life is always fun." Pictured is Haja's multi champion Speggle-Waggel's Ultra Blue, aged three.

Gail Parsons: "Cockers want to please, they are playful, a bit of a comedian and don't have a nasty bone in their body. I like their size and temperament; they are good with children and make a good, all-round family dog."

Helen Marsden couldn't agree more: "The English show-type Cocker is a happy, merry dog, always wanting to please. I got my first Cocker after having looked after others as part of my dog boarding business. English show-type Cockers are loving, loyal and biddable. A well-trained Cocker makes a great family addition, one that is good with children and other animals. They are a manageable size, easy to train and appealing to the eye."

Jackie Hornby: "They are merry, love people and children and are friendly with other dogs, cats and rabbits. I would describe them as nice little people who love to be with you at all times, very versatile; able to adapt to all conditions."

Jane Minikin: "Cockers have traditionally been described as 'merry' and I think this aptly describes their ever-wagging tail and busy, inquisitive nature. Cockers are very adaptable and are happy to be anywhere: at home, on a walk, visiting friends, on holiday, etc. and they seem to make friends with everyone. Mine even love going to the vet's to meet everyone there!

"My first Cocker came from my sister who had bred a litter from her pet bitch. We both had small children at the time and the Cockers were fantastic with them. I have never seen one of our dogs snap or snarl at a child. Equally, I have very successfully homed puppies with retired couples and into a huge variety of households. They are people dogs and love being with their owners."

Keith Henderson: "The Cocker Spaniel is very affectionate and calm, once trained, and will follow you from room to room. This medium-sized dog has an excellent temperament with children and is very easy to train."

Maxine Shaverin: "The best thing about Cockers is their overall temperament; they are very affectionate and loyal dogs and relatively easy to train. They fit into your routine happily and most seem to be comfortable with changes of routine. I like how they can be both active and lazy and, of course, they are cute too which makes them appealing to many, including those who sadly should not own one."

Rachel Appleby: "Cockers' most appealing quality is their unconditional love. They are a very human-orientated breed and want to be a full member of the family, involved in everything. They are friendly, loving, intelligent, reliable and fun; an all-round perfect dog."

Robert Baldwin: "Their temperament first attracted us to the breed; they are beautiful dogs. They are loyal and very easy to train. We had a King Charles Spaniel who lived to 17 and we bought our first Cocker when our King Charles was diagnosed terminally ill because my wife wanted a slightly larger dog. They are excellent with children and love being part of the family."

Wendy Tobijanski (English and American Cockers): "My family have had Cockers since I was a child, so I grew up with them, both as family dogs and for show and breeding. They are beautiful dogs with a lovely expression, and they are popular because they have a lovely temperament and are an easy-going dog."

Working Cockers

Alan and Carole Pitchers: "Very loving and loyal, they love to be close to you - to the extent sometimes they give the impression they want to be inside your skin. They are social dogs who get along easily with other dogs." Andy Platt: "They have big hearts and are rarely short on determination."

Barry Hutchinson: "I have never come across a dog breed that can transverse so completely and seamlessly from an armchair to a pheasant covert, and back again just as easily. It is not just that an individual dog can be cultured to a particular lifestyle from being a puppy; an individual dog can adopt a whole variety of lifestyles at once and move between them with absolute ease."

Billie Cheeseman: "Working Cockers have earned their nickname 'pocket rockets' because they are

very busy little souls. Overall, the Cocker is a happy, lively, biddable, family-friendly dog. The working strain does need more mental stimulation than the show type, but can still be a wonderful addition to a knowledgeable, active family home."

Jo Oxley: "In the house they are reasonably calm. They are good natured and unaggressive. Outside the house they are energetic and inquisitive." Christine Grant: "Friendly, eager to please, gentle, happy to walk for miles or curl up on your lap or in front of the fire." Pictured in the snow is Jo's working Cocker, Slip.

Chris Warner: "A typical Cocker's temperament could be described as playful/demanding.

Cockers can be extremely loyal, and will give full attention to the owner even when faced with many distractions. I was attracted to the breed as I wanted a fresh gundog training challenge. I had only previously trained and worked Labradors." Christine Thomas: "Lively, affectionate, eager, keen, loyal and very friendly."

Jane Seekings: "Full of energy, highly intelligent, very loyal and loving and slightly bonkers! I think that their current popularity has a lot to do with being 'on trend' – the Duke and Duchess of Cambridge have a black working Cocker Spaniel and when I was looking for owners for my puppies, there were a lot of people who wanted a black dog.

"Having said that, I think what makes them so popular is that they do have a lovely nature – very loving, loyal and the combination of intelligence with a streak of 'madness' was also a huge attraction for me. I was also looking for a dog to work on a local shoot and did not want a big dog, so the working Cocker Spaniel was ideal."

Jill Gunn: "Happy, fun, intelligent, endearing - an absolute joy. We have Labradors and on working days my oldest dog could no longer tackle big fences and obstacles. I needed a dog I could lift easily over these to send to retrieve and that's why I got my first Cocker."

Julie Summers: "They have drive, spirit, trainability and intelligence, they are a good size, and are good with families if brought up correctly. I moved into Cockers from Springers and got our first as a gift for my husband. I didn't intend to breed them from the start, but as we fell in love with the personality, the drive and sometimes stubborn behaviour of the Cockers, we wanted more as part of our working team."

Kirsten Strachan: "A working Cocker is cheerful and intelligent with a glint of mischief in the eye. What attracted me to the breed was the intelligence, temperament, physical size and easy-to-care-for coat of the working Cocker. Thirty years ago workers were a real minority and very hard to source a litter. I'd had nothing but temperament issues with show types I'd had. I saw a working one and loved everything about it, so I drove a few hundred miles to get my first when I heard there was a litter for sale."

Manda Smith: "Friendly, happy, energetic. They like lots of attention and would have you stroke them all day if they could. They are normally good with children. The working type has a very strong hunting instinct and it can be very difficult to train the recall. I like the fact that they

usually get on with everyone and everything. I think that is the reason they are popular, possibly combined with the fact they are very appealing puppies."

Michelle Mills: "They are very busy and loving and can be possessive. They are very loyal and I love their need to please you."

Kerena Marchant: "Working Cockers are high drive, busy little things that like a job to do. They are very bright and food motivated, which makes them easy to train. They are rather like kids; if it's fun, they will do it, if it's not, they can shut down. They can be destructive if bored and don't get enough exercise and stimulation. Generally they are fun-loving dogs with good temperaments."

Pictured is Jacquie Ward's Sox, of Breezybrook Gundogs, Bedfordshire, with a dummy retrieve.

Wendy Roberts: "They are willing, keen, sometimes a little overwhelmed by the need to possess (a ball or stick or even an owner), they make great pets, they are loyal, sensitive and calm - once walked and kept mentally stimulated. We have always found when we relax at night, so do they. They are truly medium size and fit most cars, can be handled easily - especially when they get muddy and need washing. They will join you on a walk, checking you're there, running to fetch balls and generally exploring the world - of which you are their centre."

Cause and Effect

As you've read, treated well, socialised and trained, well-bred Cocker Spaniels make lively and devoted canine companions and excellent working and competitive dogs. They are affectionate and sociable, they love being around people or other dogs. Once you've had one, no other dog seems quite the same. But sometimes Cockers, just like other breeds, can develop behaviour problems. There are numerous reasons for this; every dog is an individual with his or her own temperament and environment, both of which influence the way he or she interacts with you and the world. Poor behaviour may result from a number of factors, including:

> Poor breeding
> Boredom, due to lack of exercise or mental challenges
> Being left alone too long
> Lack of socialisation
> Lack of training
> Being badly treated
> A change in living conditions
> Anxiety or insecurity
> Fear
> Being spoiled

Bad behaviour may show itself in a number of different ways, such as:

> Constantly demanding attention
> Chewing or destructive behaviour
> Jumping up
> Excessive barking
> Biting or nipping
> Growling
> Soiling or urinating inside the house
> Aggression towards other dogs

NOTE: You may have heard of something called "Cocker Rage". This expression came about after World War II when certain reds and goldens were thought to suffer from Rage Syndrome, which is actually a medical condition rather than a behaviour problem. Research has been carried out over many years and, as yet, there has been no real explanation for it. The condition is not prevalent within the breed these days, according to the breeders in this book.

This chapter has looked at some familiar behaviour problems and is geared towards dogs kept in the house as pets. Although every dog is different, some common causes of unwanted behaviour are covered, along with tips to help improve the situation. The best way to avoid poor behaviour is to put in the time early on to socialise and train your dog, and nip any potential problems in the bud. If you are rehoming a dog, you'll need extra time and patience to help your new arrival unlearn some bad habits.

10 Ways to Avoid Bad Behaviour

Different dogs have different reasons for exhibiting bad behaviour. There is no simple cure for everything. Your best chance of ensuring your dog does not become badly behaved is to start out on the right foot and follow these simple guidelines:

1. **Buy from a good breeder**. They use their expertise to match suitable breeding pairs, taking into account factors such as good temperament, health and being "fit for function."

2. **Start training early** - you can't start too soon. Like babies, Cocker puppies have incredibly enquiring minds which can quickly absorb a lot of new information. You can start teaching your puppy to learn his own name as well as some simple commands as soon as you bring him home.

3. **Basic training should cover several areas:** housetraining, chew prevention, puppy biting, simple commands like 'sit', 'come', 'stay' and familiarising him with a collar or harness and lead. Adopt a gentle approach and keep training sessions short. Cockers are sensitive to you and your mood and do not respond well to harsh words or treatment. Start with five or 10 minutes a day and build up.

   Often the way a dog responds to his or her environment is a result of owner training and management – or lack of it. Puppy classes or adult dog obedience classes are a great way to start, but make sure you do your homework afterwards. Spend a few minutes each day reinforcing what you have both learned in class - owners need training as well as dogs!

4. **Start socialisation right away -** We are beginning to realise the vital role that early socialisation plays in developing a well-rounded adult dog. It is essential to expose your dog to other people, places, animals and experiences as soon as possible. Give him a few days to settle in and then start – even if this means carrying him places until his vaccination schedule is complete. Lack of socialisation is one of the major causes of unwanted behaviour traits. Exposing your dog to as many different things as possible goes a long way in helping a dog become a more stable, happy and trustworthy companion.

IMPORTANT: Socialisation does not end at puppyhood. Cockers are social creatures that thrive on sniffing, seeing, hearing and even licking. While the foundation for good behaviour is laid down during the first few months, good owners will reinforce social skills and training throughout a dog's life. Cockers love to be involved and at the centre of the action, and it is important that they learn when young that they are not also the centre of the universe. Socialisation helps them to learn their place in that universe and to become comfortable with it.

5. **Reward your dog for good behaviour.** All behaviour training should be based on positive reinforcement; so praise and reward your dog when he does something good. Play time is another form of reward. Generally,

Cockers live to please their owners, and this trait speeds up the training process. The main aim of training is to build a good understanding between you and your dog.

6. **Ignore bad behaviour**, no matter how hard this may be. If, for example, your dog is chewing his way through your shoes, couch or toilet rolls, remove him from the situation and then ignore him. For some dogs even negative attention is some attention. Or if he is constantly demanding your attention, ignore him. Remove yourself from the room so he learns that you give attention when you want to give it, not when he demands it.

The more time you spend praising and rewarding good behaviour while ignoring bad behaviour, the more likely he is to respond to you. If your pup is a chewer –and most are - make sure he has plenty of durable toys to keep him occupied. Cockers can chew their way through flimsy toys in no time.

7. **Take the time to learn what sort of temperament your dog has.** Is she by nature a nervous or confident girl? What was she like as a puppy, did she rush forward or hang back? Does she fight to get upright when on her back or is she happy to lie there? Is she a couch potato or a ball of fire?

Your puppy's temperament will affect her behaviour and how she responds to the world around her. A timid Cocker will certainly not respond well to a loud approach on your part, whereas an energetic, strong-willed one will require more patience and exercise.

8. **Exercise and stimulation -** A lack of either is another major reason for dogs behaving badly. Regular daily exercise, indoor or outdoor games and toys are all ways of stopping your dog from becoming bored or frustrated.

9. **Learn to leave your dog.** Just as leaving your dog alone for too long can lead to problems, so can being with him 100% of the time. The dog becomes over-reliant on you and then gets stressed when you leave him. This is called *separation anxiety* and something which Cockers are susceptible to. When your dog is a puppy, or when he arrives at your house as an adult, start by leaving him for a few minutes every day and gradually build it up so that after a few weeks or months you can leave him for up to four hours.

10. **Love your Cocker– but don't spoil him,** however difficult that might be. You don't do your dog any favours by giving him too many treats, constantly responding to his demands for attention or allowing him to behave as he wants inside the house.

Separation Anxiety

It's not just dogs that experience separation anxiety - people do too. About 7% of adults and 4% of children suffer from this disorder. Typical symptoms for humans are:

> ➢ Distress at being separated from a loved one
> ➢ Fear of being left alone

Our canine companions aren't much different to us. When a dog leaves the litter, his owners become his new family or pack. It's estimated that as many as 10% to 15% of dogs suffer from separation anxiety. Both male and female Cockers are susceptible because they thrive on interaction with people. It is an exaggerated fear response caused by separation from their owner.

Separation anxiety is on the increase and recognised by behaviourists as the most common form of stress for dogs. Millions of dogs suffer from separation anxiety.

It can be equally distressing for the owner - I know because our dog, Max, suffers from this. He howls whenever we leave home without him. Fortunately his problem is only a mild one. If we return after only a short while, he's usually quiet. Although if we silently sneak back home and peek in through the letterbox, he's never asleep. Instead he's waiting by the door looking and listening for our return. It can be embarrassing. Whenever I go to the Post Office, I tie him up outside and even though he can see me through the glass door, he still barks his head off - so loud that the people inside can't make themselves heard. Luckily the lady behind the counter is a dog lover and, despite the large **'GUIDE DOGS ONLY'** sign outside, she lets Max in. He promptly dashes through the door and sits down beside me, quiet as a mouse!

Tell-Tale Signs

Does your Cocker do any of the following?

> ➢ Follow you from room to room – even the toilet - whenever you're home?
> ➢ Get anxious or stressed when you're getting ready to leave the house?
> ➢ Howl, whine or bark when you leave?
> ➢ Tear up paper or chew cushions, couches or other objects?
> ➢ Dig, chew, or scratch at the carpet, doors or windows trying to join you?
> ➢ Soil or urinate inside the house, even though he is housetrained? (This **only** occurs when left alone)
> ➢ Exhibit restlessness - such as licking his coat excessively, pacing or circling?
> ➢ Greet you ecstatically every time you come home – even if you've only been out to empty the bins?
> ➢ Wait by the window or door until you return?
> ➢ Dislike spending time alone in the garden or yard?
> ➢ Refuses to eat or drink if you leave him?
> ➢ Howl or whine when one family member leaves - even though others are still in the room or car?

If so, he or she may suffer from separation anxiety. Fortunately, in many cases this can be cured.

Canine Separation Anxiety Through the Ages

Dogs are pack animals and being alone is not a natural state for them. Puppies should be patiently taught to get used to isolation slowly and in a structured way if they are to be comfortable with it. A puppy will emotionally latch on to his new owner, who has taken the place of his mother and siblings.

He will want to follow you everywhere initially and, although you want to shower him with love and attention, it's important to leave your new puppy alone for short periods in the beginning to avoid him becoming totally dependent on you. In our case, I was working from home when we got Max. With hindsight, we should have regularly left him alone for short periods more often in the critical first few months.

Adopted dogs may be particularly susceptible to separation anxiety. They may have been abandoned once already and fear it happening again.

There are several causes, one or more of which can trigger separation anxiety. These include:

> Poor socialisation with other dogs and people resulting in too much focus and dependence on you, his owner
> Boredom, Cockers are busy dogs and need physical and mental exercise
> Not being left alone for short periods when young
> Being left for too long by owners who are out of the house for much of the day
> Leaving a dog too long in a crate or confined space
> Being over-indulgent with your dog; giving him too much attention
> Making too much of a fuss when you leave and return to the house
> Mistreatment in the past, a dog from a rescue centre may have insecurities and feel anxious when left alone
> Wilful behaviour due to a lack of training

Symptoms are not commonly seen in middle-aged dogs, although dogs that develop symptoms when young may be at risk later on. Separation anxiety is, however, common in elderly dogs.

Pets age and - like humans - their senses, such as hearing and sight, deteriorate. They become more dependent on their owners and may then become more anxious when they are separated from them - or even out of view.

It may be very flattering and cute that your dog wants to be with you all the time, but insecurity and separation anxiety are forms of panic, which is distressing for your Cocker. If he shows any signs, help him to become more self-reliant and confident; he will be a happier dog.

So what can you do if your dog is showing signs of canine separation anxiety? Every dog is different, but here are tried and tested techniques which have proved effective for some dogs.

12 Tips to Combat Separation Anxiety

1. After the first few days, practise leaving your new puppy or adult dog for short periods starting with a minute or two and gradually lengthening the time you are out of sight.

2. Tire your Cocker out before you leave him alone. Take him for a walk or play a game before leaving and, if you can, leave him with a view of the outside world, e.g. in a room with a patio door or low window.

3. Keep arrivals and departures low key and don't make a big fuss. For example, when I come home, Max is hysterically happy and runs round whimpering with a toy in his mouth. I make him sit and stay and then let him out into the garden without patting or acknowledging him. I pat him several minutes later.

4. Leave your dog a "security blanket," such as an old piece of clothing you have recently worn which still has your scent on it, or leave a radio on - not too loud - in the room with the dog. Avoid a heavy rock station! If it will be dark when you return, leave a lamp on a timer.

5. Associate your departure with something good. As you leave, give your dog a rubber toy, like a Kong, filled with a tasty treat, or a frozen treat. This may take his mind off of your departure. (Some dogs may refuse to touch the treat until you return home).

6. If your dog is used to a crate, try crating him when you go out. Many dogs feel safe there, and being in a crate can also help to reduce destructiveness. Always take the collar off first. Pretend to leave the house, but listen for a few minutes. NEVER leave a dog in a crate with the door closed all day; two or three hours are long enough during the day.

    Warning: if your dog starts to show major signs of distress, remove him from the crate immediately as he may injure himself.

7. Structure and routine can help to reduce anxiety in your dog. Carry out regular activities, such as feeding and exercising, at the same time every day.

8. Dogs read body language very well, many Cockers are intuitive. They may start to fret when they think you are going to leave them. One technique is to mimic your departure routine when you have no intention of leaving. So put your coat on, grab your car keys, go out of the door and return a few seconds later. Do this randomly and regularly and it may help to reduce your dog's stress levels when you do it for real.

9. Some dogs show anxiety in new places, get him better socialised and used to different environments, dogs and people.

10. However lovable your Cocker is, if he is showing early signs of anxiety when separating from you, do not shower him with attention all the time when you are there. He will become too dependent on you.

11. If you have to leave the house for a few hours at a time, ask a neighbour or friend to call in - or drop the dog off with them.

12. Getting another dog to keep the first one company can help, but first ask yourself whether you have the time and money for two or more dogs. Can you afford double the vet's and food bills?

Sit-Stay-Down

Another technique for helping to reduce separation anxiety is to practise the common "sit-stay" or "down-stay" exercises using positive reinforcement. The goal is to be able to move briefly out of your dog's sight while he is in the "stay" position.

Through this your dog learns that he can remain calmly and happily in one place while you go about your normal daily life. You have to progress slowly with this. Get your dog to sit and stay and then walk away from him for five seconds, then 10, 15 and so on, gradually increase the distance you move away from your dog. Reward your dog with a treat every time he stays calm.

Then move out of sight or out of the room for a few seconds, return and give him the treat if he is calm, gradually lengthen the time you are out of sight. If you're watching TV with your Cocker snuggled up at your side and you get up for a snack, say 'stay' and leave the room. When you come back, give him a treat or praise him quietly.

It is a good idea to practise these techniques after exercise or when your dog is a little sleepy (but not exhausted), as he is likely to be more relaxed. Canine Separation Anxiety is NOT the result of disobedience or lack of training. It's a psychological condition; your dog feels anxious and insecure.

NEVER punish your dog for showing signs of separation anxiety – even if he has chewed your best shoes. This will only make him worse.

NEVER leave your dog unattended in a crate for long periods or if he is frantic to get out, it can cause physical or mental harm. If you're thinking of leaving an animal all day in a crate while you are out of the house, get a rabbit or a hamster - not a dog.

Excessive Barking

Dogs, especially youngsters and adolescents, sometimes behave in ways you might not want them to, until they learn that this type of unwanted behaviour doesn't earn any rewards. Cockers are not normally excessive barkers, but any dog can bark a lot, until he learns not to.

Some puppies start off by being noisy from the outset, while others hardly bark at all until they reach adolescence or adulthood. On our website we get emails from dog owners worried that their young dogs are not barking enough. However, we get many more from owners whose dogs are barking too much!

Some Cockers will bark if someone comes to the door – and then welcome them like best friends - while others remain quiet. However, they do not make good guard dogs, as they are friendly with everyone.

There can be a number of reasons a Cocker barks too much. He may be lonely, bored or demanding your attention. He may be possessive and over-protective and so barks (or howls) his head off when others are near you. Excessive, habitual barking is a problem which should be corrected early on before it gets out of hand and drives you and your neighbours nuts.

The problem often develops during adolescence or early adulthood as your dog becomes more confident. If your barking dog is an adolescent, he is probably still teething, so get him a good selection of hardy chews, and stuff a Kong toy with a treat or peanut butter to keep him occupied and gnawing. But give him these when he is quiet, not when he is barking.

Your behaviour can also encourage excessive barking. If your dog barks non-stop for several minutes and then you give him a treat to quieten him, he associates his barking with getting a nice treat. A better way to deal with it is to say in a firm voice: **"Quiet"** after he has made a few barks. When he stops, praise him and he will get the idea that what you want him to do is stop. The trick is to nip the bad behaviour in the bud before it becomes ingrained.

If he's barking to get your attention, ignore him. If that doesn't work, leave the room and don't allow him to follow you, so you deprive him of your attention. Do this as well if his barking and attention-seeking turns to nipping. Tell him to **"Stop"** in a firm voice - not shouting - remove your hand or leg and, if necessary, leave the room.

As humans, we can use our voice in many different ways: to express happiness or anger, to scold, to shout a warning, and so on. Dogs are the same; different barks and noises give out different messages. **Listen** to your dog and try and get an understanding of Cocker language. Learn to recognise the difference between an alert bark, an excited bark, a demanding bark, a nervous, high pitched bark, an aggressive bark or a plain "I'm barking 'coz I can bark" bark!

If your dog is barking at other dogs, arm yourselves with lots of treats and spend time calming your dog down. When he or she starts to bark wildly at another dog - usually this happens when your dog is on a lead – distract your dog by letting them sniff a treat in your hand. Make your dog sit down and give him or her a treat. Talk in a gentle manner and keep showing and giving your dog a treat for remaining calm and not barking. There are several videos on YouTube which show how to deal with this problem in the manner described here.

Speak and Shush!

Cockers are not good guard dogs, they couldn't care less if somebody breaks in and walks off with the family silver – they are more likely to approach the burglar for a pat or a treat. But if you do have a problem with excessive barking when somebody visits your home, the Speak and Shush technique is one way of getting a dog to quieten down.

If your Cocker doesn't bark and you want him to, a slight variation of this method can also be used to get him to bark as a way of alerting you that someone is at the door.

When your dog barks at an arrival at your house, gently praise him after the first few barks. If he persists, gently tell him that that is enough. Like humans, some dogs can get carried away with the sound of their own voice, so try and discourage too much barking from the outset. The Speak and Shush technique teaches your dog or puppy to bark and be quiet on command. Get a friend to stand outside your front door and say "Speak" - or "Woof" or "Alert." This is the cue for your accomplice to knock or ring the bell –don't worry if you both feel like idiots, it will be worth the embarrassment!

When your dog barks, praise him profusely. You can even bark yourself in encouragement…. After a few good barks, say "Shush" and then dangle a tasty treat in front of his nose. He will stop barking as soon as he sniffs the treat, because it is physically impossible for a dog to sniff and woof at the same time.

Praise your dog again as he sniffs quietly and then give him the treat. Repeat this routine a few times a day and your Cocker will quickly learn to bark whenever the doorbell rings and you ask him to speak. Eventually your dog will bark after your request but BEFORE the doorbell rings, meaning he has learned to bark on command. Even better, he will learn to anticipate the likelihood of getting a treat following your "Shush" request and will also be quiet on command.

With Speak and Shush training, progressively increase the length of required shush time before offering a treat - at first just a couple of seconds, then three, five, 10, 20, and so on. By alternating instructions to speak and shush, the dog is praised and rewarded for barking on request and also for stopping barking on request.

To get your Cocker to bark on command, you need to have some treats at the ready, waiting for that rare bark. Wait until he barks - for whatever reason - then say "Speak" or whatever word you want to use, praise him and give him a treat. At this stage, he won't know why he is receiving the treat. Keep praising him every time he barks and give him a treat. After you've done this for

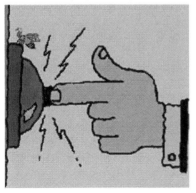

several days, hold a treat in your hand in front of his face and say "Speak." Your dog will probably still not know what to do, but will eventually get so frustrated at not getting the treat that he will bark. At which point, praise him and give him the treat. We trained our dog to do this and now he barks his head off when anybody comes to the door or whenever we give him the command: "Speak."

Always use your 'encouraging teacher voice' when training; speak softly when instructing your dog to Shush, and reinforce the Shush with whisper-praise. The more softly you speak, the more your dog will be likely to pay attention. Cockers respond very well to training when it is fun, short and reward-based.

Aggression

Some breeds are more prone to aggression than others. Fortunately, this is a problem not often seen in Cockers. However, given a certain set of circumstances, any dog can growl, bark or even bite. As well as snarling, lunging, barking or biting, you should also look out for other physical signs of aggression, such as: raised hackles, top lip curled back to bare teeth, ears up and tail raised.

All puppies bite; they explore the world with their noses and mouths. But it is important to train your cute little pup not to bite, as he may cause injury if he continues as an adult.

Any dog can bite when under stress, and, however unlikely it may seem, there are images on the internet of people - often children - who have been bitten by Cockers.

Here are some different types of aggressive behaviour:

> Growling at you or other people
> Snarling or lunging at other dogs
> Being possessive with toys
> Growling or biting if you or another animal goes near his food
> Growling if you pet or show attention to another animal
> Marking territory by urinating inside the house
> Growling and chasing other small animals
> Growling and chasing cars, joggers or strangers
> Standing in your way, blocking your path
> Pulling and growling on the lead

Cockers love to be the focus of your attention, but they can also become possessive of you, their food or toys, which in itself can lead to bullying behaviour. Aggression may be caused by a lack of socialisation, an adolescent dog trying to see how far he can push the boundaries, nervousness, being spoiled by the owner, jealousy or even fear. This fear may come from a bad experience the dog has suffered or from lack of proper socialisation.

Another form of fear-aggression is when a dog becomes over-protective/possessive of his owner, which can lead to barking and lunging at other dogs or humans.

An owner's treatment of a dog can be a further reason. If the owner has been too harsh with the dog, such as shouting, using physical violence or reprimanding the dog too often, this in turn causes poor behaviour. Aggression breeds aggression. Dogs can also become aggressive if they are consistently left alone, cooped up, under-fed or under-exercised. A bad experience with another dog or dogs can be a further cause.

Many dogs are more combative on the lead (leash). This is because once on a lead, they cannot run away and escape. Fight or flight. They know they can't run away, so they make themselves as frightening as possible. They therefore bark or growl to warn off the other dog or person.

Socialising your Cocker when young is vital. The first four to five months of a puppy's life is the critical time for socialisation.

If your dog **suddenly** shows a change of behaviour and becomes aggressive, have him checked out by a vet to rule out any underlying medical reason for the crankiness, such as earache or toothache. Raging hormones can be another reason for aggressive actions. Consider having your Cocker spayed or neutered if the vet thinks this may be the cause. A levelling-off of hormones can lead to a more laid-back dog.

Another reason for dogs to display aggression is because they have been spoiled by their owners and have come to believe that the world revolves around them. Not spoiling your dog and teaching him what is acceptable behaviour in the first place is the best preventative measure. Early training, especially during puppyhood and adolescence - before he or she develops unwanted habits - can save a lot of trouble in the future.

Professional dog trainers employ a variety of techniques with a dog which has become aggressive. Firstly they will look at the causes and then they almost always use reward-based methods to try and cure aggressive or fearful dogs.

Counter conditioning is a positive training technique used by many professional trainers to help change a dog's aggressive behaviour towards other dogs. A typical example would be a dog which snarls, barks and lunges at other dogs while on the lead. It is the presence of other dogs which is triggering the dog to act in a fearful or anxious manner.

Every time the dog sees another dog, he or she is given a tasty treat to counter the aggression. With enough steady repetition, the dog starts to associate the presence of other dogs with a tasty treat. Properly and patiently done, the final result is a dog which calmly looks to the owner for the treat whenever he or she sees another dog while on the lead. Whenever you encounter a potentially aggressive situation, divert your Cocker's attention by turning his head away from the other dog and towards you, so that he cannot make eye contact with the other dog.

Aggression Towards People

Desensitisation is the most common method of treating aggression. It starts by breaking down the triggers for the behaviour one small step at a time. The aim is to get the dog to associate pleasant things with the trigger, i.e. people or a specific person whom he previously feared or regarded as a threat. This is done through using positive reinforcement, such as praise or treats. Successful desensitisation takes time, patience and knowledge. If your dog is starting to growl at people, there are a couple of techniques you can try to break him of this bad habit before it develops into full-blown biting.

One method is to arrange for some friends to come round, one at a time. When they arrive at your house, get them to scatter kibble on the floor in front of them so that your dog associates the arrival of people with tasty treats. As they move into the house, and your dog eats the kibble, praise your dog for being a good boy or girl. Manage your dog's environment. Don't over-face him.

Most Cockers love children, but if yours is at all anxious around them, separate them or carefully supervise their time together in the beginning. Children typically react enthusiastically to dogs and some dogs may regard this as frightening or an invasion of their space.

Some dogs, particularly spoiled dogs, may show aggression towards people other than the owner. Several people have written to our website on this topic and it usually involves a partner or husband. Often the dog is jealous of the attention the owner is giving to the other person, or it could be that the dog feels threatened by him. This is, however, more common with Toy breeds. If it should arise with your Spaniel, the key is for the partner to gradually gain the trust of the dog. He or she should show that they are not a threat by speaking gently to the dog and giving treats for good behaviour. Avoid eye contact, as the dog may see this as a challenge. If the subject of the aggression lives in the house, then try letting this person give the dog his daily feeds. The way to a dog's heart is often through his stomach.

A crate is also a useful tool for removing an aggressive dog from the situation for short periods of time, allowing him out gradually and praising good behaviour. As with any form of aggression, the key is to take steps to deal with it immediately.

Coprophagia (Eating Faeces)

It is hard for us to understand why a dog would want to eat his or any other animal's faeces (stools, poop or poo, call it what you will), but it does happen. There is plenty of anecdotal evidence that some dogs love the stuff. Nobody fully understands why dogs do this, it may simply be an unpleasant behaviour trait or there could be an underlying reason.

It is also thought that the inhumane and useless housetraining technique of "sticking the dog's nose in it" when he has eliminated inside the house can also encourage coprophagia.

If your dog eats faeces from the cat litter tray - a problem several owners have contacted us about - the first thing to do is to place the litter tray somewhere where your dog can't get to it – but the cat can. Perhaps on a shelf or put a guard around it, small enough for the cat to get through but not your Cocker.

Our dog sometimes eats cow or horse manure when out in the countryside. He usually stops when we tell him to and he hasn't suffered any after effects – so far. But again, this is a very unpleasant habit as the offending material sticks to the fur around his mouth and has to be cleaned off.

Sometimes he rolls in the stuff and then has to be washed down. You may find that your Cocker will roll in fox poo to cover the fox's scent. Try and avoid areas you know are frequented by foxes if you can, as their faeces can transmit several diseases, including Canine Parvovirus or lungworm – neither of these should pose a serious health risk if your dog is up to date with vaccinations and worming medication.

Vets have found that canine diets with low levels of fibre and high levels of starch increase the likelihood of coprophagia. If your dog is exhibiting this behaviour, first check that the diet you are feeding is nutritionally complete. Look at the first ingredient on the dog food packet or tin – is it corn or meat? Does he look underweight? Check that you are feeding the right amount.

If there is no underlying medical reason, you will have to try and modify your dog's behaviour. Remove cat litter trays, clean up after your dog and do not allow him to eat his own faeces. If it's not there, he can't eat it. Don't reprimand the dog for this behaviour. A better technique is to distract him while he is in the act and then remove the offending material.

Coprophagia is sometimes seen in pups aged between six months to a year and often disappears after this age.

In extreme cases, when a dog exhibits persistent bad behaviour that the owner is unable to correct, a canine professional may be the answer. However, this is not an inexpensive option. Far better to spend time training and socialising your dog as soon as you get him or her.

Important: This chapter provides just a general overview of canine behaviour. If your Cocker exhibits persistent behavioural problems, particularly if he or she is aggressive towards people or other dogs, you should consider seeking help from a reputable canine behaviourist, such as those listed the Association of Professional Dog Trainers at http://www.apdt.co.uk (UK) or https://apdt.com (USA)

9. Exercise and Training

One thing all dogs have in common – including every Cocker Spaniel ever born - is that they need daily exercise, and the best way to give them this is through regular walks or by using them for what they were bred for; retrieving. Activities such as agility and flyball also allow the Cocker to burn off steam and fulfil its natural instinct for a challenge. Here is what daily exercise does for your dog - and you:

> ➢ It strengthens respiratory and circulatory systems
> ➢ Helps get oxygen to tissue cells
> ➢ Wards off obesity
> ➢ Keeps muscles toned and joints flexible
> ➢ Aids digestion
> ➢ Releases endorphins which trigger positive feelings
> ➢ Helps to keep dogs mentally stimulated and socialised

Whether you live in a house, an apartment or on a farm, start regular exercise patterns early so your dog gets used his daily routine and gets chance to blow off steam and excess energy. Daily exercise helps to keep your dog content, healthy and free from disease.

How Much Exercise?

Most Cockers will take as much exercise as you are prepared to give them. They are generally regarded as having medium to high exercise requirements, but there is no one-rule-fits-all solution. The amount of exercise that each individual dog needs varies tremendously. It depends on a number of issues, including temperament, natural energy levels, size, your living conditions, whether your dog is kept with other dogs and, importantly, what he gets used to.

Another major factor is whether your dog is bred from show or working stock. There are, of course, variations from one individual dog to another; however, many breeders feel that some working Cockers are happier with more exercise and mental challenges than show Cockers. After all, it makes sense. A Cocker whose parent was bred to run all day and be on the lookout for game is likely to have higher energy demands than one bred to have a calmer nature for the show ring. Working dogs have high energy drives; they are not usually couch potatoes.

That's not to say Cockers don't love snuggling up on the couch with you; they most certainly do. They just need their exercise as well.

Ideally you should have the time to exercise your dog for a minimum of an hour a day – even longer is better. You can hike with a Cocker bred from working parents all day long and still not tire him out. A fenced garden or yard where he can burn off energy between walks is an advantage, but should never be seen as a replacement for daily exercise away from the home. If you don't think you have the time or energy levels for one long or a couple of shorter walks a day, then consider getting a breed which requires less exercise. Your dog will enjoy going for walks on the lead (leash), but will enjoy it far more when he is allowed to run free. A Cocker is never happier than when running around with his nose to the ground following a scent or chasing an old stick or ball. Cockers excel at flyball, agility and other canine competitions which involve lots of energy and mental challenges.

Make sure it is safe to let your dog off the lead, away from traffic and other hazards. And do not let him run free until he has learned the recall. There is also growing concern in both the UK and North America about attacks from loose dogs in public parks and dog parks. If you are at all worried about this, avoid public areas and find woodlands, fields, a beach or open countryside where your dog can exercise safely.

Breeders on Exercise

This is what the breeders say on exercise. As you will read, there is a wide variation of opinion, but in a nutshell, your Cocker's exercise requirements will be heavily influenced by his or her ancestry and what your dog gets used to.

Andrew Height, Fourtails (show) Cocker Spaniels, Cambridgeshire: "We give ours two walks a day, morning and afternoon, total distance about three miles, on every day of the year unless the weather is really bad. They also have a paddock to run around in too whenever they want. In the summer they end up asleep in it and in the winter, it's a quick visit and back on the sofa!"

Kennel Club Assured Breeder Andy Platt, of Nithvalley Gundogs, Scotland, says: "Depending on age and stage of training, exercise can vary from one to three hours daily. We also take part in Field Trials, rough shooting, picking up and beating."

Caroline Bymolen, Carto (show) Cocker Spaniels, Cambridgeshire: "A show type Cocker needs as much exercise as you want to give it. Take one for a long walk and they will run and run for as long as you want them to. Once you get home they will relax and cuddle up for the rest of the day. If one day you can't take them out, they won't tear your house down. A working Cocker will also run as much as you want it to, but when you get home they don't stop; they just seem to want to keep going. They tend to need more exercise than a show type dog."

Kennel Club Assured Breeder Barry Hutchinson, of Brynovation Gundogs, Gloucestershire: "The more a dog is exercised, the more it needs to be exercised. One of the reasons that Cocker Spaniels are so dynamic is that they can need as little as two short walks (or freedom of a reasonably-sized garden) per day or, subject to stamina training, can work for hours at a time in hard cover in the coldest of weathers. Given that range, most owners would, surely, be hard pushed not to be satisfied, unless they were absolutely infirm - or a triathlete!"

David Matthews, Tojamatt (show) Cockers, Nottinghamshire: "It's hard to say exactly how much exercise; they're in and out all day. A good hour of walking and free running seems OK, although they will do much more."

Alan and Carole Pitchers, Alcarbrad Cocker Spaniels, Essex: "Our dogs are working stock. Having never owned show stock we cannot provide solid evidence with regard to exercise and temperament. However, with regard to exercise, it is a total myth that working Cockers need a lot of exercise. They need daily exercise, but are more than happy with a mixture of long and short walks. Our Cockers are exercised for at least 45 minutes per day, this can rise to 90 minutes some days. There are also days when we are shooting where the dogs will be working for roughly five hours."

Hobby show-type breeder Jane Minikin, of North Yorkshire: "Our Cockers live an active life with us at work in our livery yard and so are fine with a half hour run around the fields each day, and as a group they exercise themselves. For dogs leading a more sedentary life, a couple of good walks a day would be best with some ball play or chasing games off the lead preferably, especially if they have to be left at home whilst their owners are at work."

Chris Warner, Monwodelea Gundogs, Coventry: "Ours are lead walked for about 30 minutes and then allowed to free run for approximately 30 minutes." Billie Cheeseman, of BarleyCourt (working) Spaniels, Hertfordshire, also exercises her dogs for an hour a day when they are not working or training. Several other breeders also said they exercise their dogs for around an hour a day, including Helen Marsden, of Finity (show) Cocker Spaniels, Hampshire, who added: "They also get playtime with each other, the children and metal stimulation as needed." Some breeders said they exercise their dogs for two or more hours a day.

Linda Reed, Delindere (English show and American) Cocker Spaniels, Leicestershire: "Pups up to six months old get free exercise in the garden only and are taken on short 15 minute walks for socialisation. As adults they will take as much exercise as you want them to have. You will drop long before a Cocker does!"

Christine Thomas, Dodfordhills (working) Spaniels, Worcestershire: "It varies. The best type of walk for them with me is to take them through the local woods for an hour in the mornings. They have the natural instinct. Of course, when they are puppies, you have to exercise them for less time and work up. Remember that they run at least twice the amount that you walk."

Jill Gunn, of Dearganach Working Cockers, Scotland: "It varies. On working days they do full days, otherwise the exercise is broken up into five 10-15 minutes per day plus training sessions out of season."

Kennel Club Assured breeders Julie and Darren Summers, of Summervilles Gundogs, County Durham: "We walk our dog along the river Wear on a morning for approximately 70 to 80 minutes; the dogs will do triple. Any other exercise will be individual training sessions later in the day. When we are in the shooting season, the dogs will do less as they need energy for a full day's work. We work our dogs on a regular basis, and several of our Cockers work as therapy dogs that I voluntary take into care homes to bring some joy." (Stock photo).

Tracey Simpson, Bravialis Gundogs, North Yorkshire: "An hour a day, but that hour involves running and playing, not just lead walking. The more exercise the better. A hunting working Cocker Spaniel needs a lot more. They need mental stimulation and to be kept up with their training.

They should get half an hour a day of retrieving skills and gundog training, along with another half an hour to an hour of fast-paced exercise.

"Dogs sleep up to 18 hours a day, so keeping your dog fit for hunting season is very important. I keep to these exercise levels and then slowly increase the exercise a couple of months before the season begins. They need to be running for up to eight hours a day and really pushing themselves throughout the season, so by at least four weeks before the season, they need to be able to run for long periods of time. It also gets you very fit in time too! Although Cockers are very much up to the job anyway with their huge energy levels, they also need stamina and muscular strength to hunt."

Eunice Wine, of Blackberry Farm Enterprises, Virginia, USA, breeds American Cockers: "Our Cockers are allowed the free run of our farm and often run and play outside for two to three hours each day. They follow us around doing chores and swim in our pond in the summer."

A number of participating breeders said that their dogs also took part in flyball, other canine competitions or worked as therapy dogs.

Establish a Routine

Establish an exercise regime early in your dog's life. Dogs like routine. If possible, get him used to walks at the same time every day, at a time that fits in with your daily routine. For example, take your dog out after his morning feed, then perhaps for another walk in the afternoon or when you come home from work, and a short toilet trip or out in the garden last thing at night.

Daily exercise could mean a walk, a jog, playing fetch or swimming - an activity loved by most Cockers. Swimming is a great way for dogs to exercise; so much so that many veterinary practices are now incorporating small water tanks - not only for remedial therapy - but also for canine recreation. Pictures are three of Haja van Wessem's dogs enjoying a dip in the sea.

Cockers will dash in and out of the water all day if you'll let them, but remember that swimming is a lot more strenuous for a dog than walking or even running. Don't constantly throw that stick or ball into the water - your Cocker will fetch it back until he drops; the same is true if he is following you on your cycle. Overstretching him could place a strain on his heart. He should exercise within his limits.

Whatever routine you decide on, your Cocker should be getting walked at least once or twice a day and you should stick to it. If you begin by taking your dog out three times a day and then suddenly stop, he will become restless and attention-seeking because he has been used to having more exercise. Conversely, don't expect a dog used to very little exercise to suddenly go on day-long hikes; he will probably struggle. Cockers may make suitable hiking or jogging companions, but they need to build up to that amount of exercise gradually - and such strenuous activity is not suitable for puppies.

To those owners who say their dog is happy and getting enough exercise playing in the yard or garden, just show him his lead and see how he reacts. Do you think he is excited at the prospect of leaving the property and going for a walk? Of course he is. Nothing can compensate for interesting new scents, meeting other dogs, playing games, frolicking in the snow or going swimming. Cockers are energetic and love all these activities.

Exercising a dog requires a big commitment from owners – you are looking at daily walks for 10 to 15 years – occasionally more - when you get a Cocker. Don't think that as your dog gets older he won't need exercising. Older dogs need exercise to keep their body, joints and systems functioning properly. They need a less strenuous regime, but still enough to keep them physically and mentally active. Regular exercise can add months or even years to a dog's life. Look on the bright side, a brisk walk is a great way of keeping both you and your dog fit – even when it's raining or snowing.

Most Cockers love snow, but it can sometimes present problems with clumps of snow and ice building up on paws, ears, legs and tummy. Salt or de-icing products on roads and pathways can also cause irritation – particularly if he or she tries to lick it off - as they can contain chemicals which are poisonous to dogs. After a walk you can bathe your dog's paws, ears and anywhere else affected in lukewarm (NOT HOT) water to remove the snow or ice. If your dog spends a lot of time in snow, you might even invest in a pair of canine snow boots. These are highly effective in preventing snow and ice balls from forming on paws – provided you can get the boots to stay on!

Mental Stimulation

Cockers are very intelligent. This is good news when it comes to training as they generally learn quickly. But the downside is that this intelligence needs to be fed. Without mental challenges, a dog can become bored, unresponsive, destructive attention-seeking and/or needy. You should factor in play time with your Cocker – even for old dogs.

If your Cocker's behaviour deteriorates or he suddenly starts chewing things he's not supposed to or barking a lot, the first question you should ask yourself is: "Is he getting enough exercise?" Boredom through lack of exercise or mental stimulation (such being alone and staring at four walls a lot) leads to bad behaviour and it's why some Cockers end up in rescue centres, through no fault of their own. On the other hand, a Cocker at the heart of the family getting plenty of daily exercise and play time is a happy dog and a companion second to none. As well as exercise, spend a short time each day training or playing with your dog. Some breeders invent games, such as hiding things around the house or garden, to keep their dogs mentally challenged.

Exercising Puppies

There are strict guidelines to stick to with puppies, as it is important not to over-exercise young pups. Their bones and joints are developing and cannot tolerate a great deal of stress, so playing fetch for hours on end with your adolescent or baby Cocker is not a good option. You'll end up with an injured dog and a pile of vet's bills.

We are often asked how much to exercise a pup. Just like babies, Cocker puppies have different temperaments and some will be livelier and need more exercise than others. The golden rule is to start slowly and build it up. The worst danger is a combination of over exercise and overweight when the puppy is growing. Do not take him out of the yard or garden until he has completed his vaccinations and it is safe to do so – unless you carry him around to start the socialisation process. Then start with short walks on the lead every day. A good guideline is:

Five minutes of on-lead exercise per month of age

until the puppy is fully grown. That means a total of 15 minutes when he is three months (13 weeks old), 20 minutes when four months (17 weeks) old, and so on. Slowly increase the time as he gets used to being exercised on the lead and this will gradually build up his muscles and stamina. Too much walking on pavements early on places stress on young joints.

It is, however, OK for your young pup to have free run of your garden or yard (once you have plugged any gaps in the fence), provided it has a soft surface such as grass, not concrete. He will take things at his own pace and stop to sniff or rest. Once he is fully grown, your dog can go out for much longer walks. And when your little pup has grown into a beautiful adult with a skeleton capable of carrying him through a long and healthy life, it will have been worth all the effort.

A long, healthy life is best started slowly

Puppies have enquiring minds. Get your pup used to being outside the home environment and experiencing new situations as soon as he is clear after vaccinations. Start to train your puppy to come back to you so that you are soon confident enough to let him roam off the lead. Under no circumstances leave a puppy imprisoned in a crate for hours on end. Cockers are extremely sociable; they love being physically close to their humans and definitely do not like being left alone for long periods.

If you are considering getting two puppies, you might consider waiting until the first pup is older so he can teach the new arrival some good habits. Some say that if you keep two puppies from the same litter, their first loyalty may be to each other, rather than to you as their owner. (Others say this is simply untrue!)

As already outlined, your Cocker will get used to an exercise routine. If you over-stimulate and constantly exercise him as a puppy, he will think this is the norm. This is fine with your playful little pup, but may not be such an attractive prospect when your fully-grown Cocker constantly needs and demands your attention and exercise a year or two later, or your work patterns change and you have not so much time to devote to him. The key is to start a routine that you can stick to.

Exercise Tips

➢ Cockers are intelligent and love a challenge. They need to use their brains. Make time to play indoor and outdoor games - such as Fetch or Hide-The-Toy - regularly with your dog; even elderly Cockers like to play

➢ Don't strenuously exercise your dog straight after or within an hour of a meal as this can cause bloat, particularly in larger dogs. Canine

bloat causes gases to build up quickly in the stomach, blowing it up like a balloon, which cuts off normal blood circulation to and from the heart. The dog can go into shock and then cardiac arrest within hours. If you suspect this is happening, get the dog to a vet immediately

➤ If you want your dog to fetch a ball, don't fetch it back yourself or he will never learn to retrieve. Train him when he's young by giving him praise or a treat when he brings the ball or toy back to your feet

➤ Do not throw a ball or toy repeatedly for a dog; he will do it to please you and because it's great fun. Stop the activity after a while - no matter how much he begs you to throw it again. He may become over-tired, damage his joints, pull a muscle, strain his heart or otherwise injure himself. Keep an eye out for heavy panting and other signs of over-exertion or overheating

➤ The same goes for swimming, which is an exhausting exercise for a dog. Repeatedly retrieving from water may cause him to overstretch himself and get into difficulties. A short swim is an excellent form of exercise for your dog and gentle swimming is a good low-impact activity for older Cockers

➤ Follow the tips earlier in this chapter and/or invest in a set of doggie boots if your Cocker spends a lot of time in snow. It can actually be quite painful for your dog when his legs and ears become covered in snowballs. Never use hot water to wash off snowballs and salt

➤ Some dogs, particularly adolescent ones, may try to push the boundaries when out walking on the lead. If your Cocker stops dead and stares at you or tries to pull you in another direction, ignore him. Do not return his stare, just continue along the way you want to go, not him!

➤ Exercise older dogs more gently - especially in cold weather when it is harder to get their bodies moving. Have a cool-down period at the end of the exercise to reduce stiffness and soreness; it helps to remove lactic acids from the dog's body, and our 11-year-old dog loves a body massage

➤ Vary your exercise route – it will be more interesting for both of you

➤ If exercising off-lead at night, buy a battery-operated flashing collar for your dog

➤ Make sure your dog has constant access to fresh water. Dogs can't sweat much, they need to drink water to cool down

Admittedly, when it is pouring down with rain, freezing cold (or scorching hot), the last thing you want to do is to venture outdoors with your dog. But the lows are more than compensated for by the highs. Exercise helps you to bond with your dog, keeps you both fit; you see different places and meet new companions - both canine and human. In short, it enhances both your lives.

Socialisation

Your adult dog's character will depend largely on two things. The first is his temperament, which he is born with, and presumably one of the reasons you have chosen a Cocker. (The importance of picking a good breeder who selects breeding stock based on temperament, physical characteristics and health cannot be over-emphasised). The second factor is environment – or how you bring him up and treat him. In other words, it's a combination of **nature and nurture**. And one absolutely essential aspect of nurture is socialisation.

Scientists have come to realise the importance that socialisation plays in a dog's life. We also now know that there is a fairly small window which is the optimum time for socialisation - and this is up to the age of up to around four months (14-16 weeks) of age - depending on which study you read.

Most young animals, including dogs, are naturally able to get used to their everyday environment until they reach a certain age. When they reach this age they become much more suspicious of things they haven't yet experienced. This is why it often takes longer to train an older dog. Our photo shows Jane Minikin's Elsie (Elsie Rock Chick) aged 12 weeks getting acquainted with an equine friend.

The age-specific natural development allows a puppy to get comfortable with the normal sights, sounds, people and animals that will be a part of his life. It ensures that he doesn't spend his life jumping in fright or growling at every blowing leaf or bird in song. The suspicion that dogs develop in later puppyhood – after the critical window - also ensures that they do react with a healthy dose of caution to new things that could really be dangerous - Mother Nature is clever!

Socialisation means learning to be part of society, or integration. When we talk about socialising puppies, it means helping them learn to be comfortable within a human society that includes many different types of people, environments, buildings, sights, noises, smells, animals and other dogs. Your Cocker may already have a wonderful temperament, but he still needs socialising to avoid him thinking that the world is tiny and it revolves around him, which in turn leads to unwanted adult behaviour traits. Some young Cockers have a natural tendency to be slightly nervous or timid and good socialisation helps them to become confident, more relaxed adults.

The ultimate goal of socialisation is to have a happy, well-adjusted dog that you can take anywhere. Socialisation will give your dog confidence and teach him not to be afraid of new experiences. Ever seen a therapy or service Cocker Spaniel in action and noticed how incredibly well-adjusted to life they are? This is no coincidence. These dogs have been extensively socialised and are ready and able to deal in a calm manner with whatever situation they encounter. They are relaxed and comfortable in their own skin - just like you want your own dog to be.

You have to start socialising your puppy as soon as you bring him home - waiting until he has had all his vaccinations may be leaving it too late.

Start by socialising him around the house and garden and, if it is safe, carry him out of the home environment (but do not put him on the floor or allow him to sniff other dogs until he's got the all-clear after his shots). Regular socialisation should continue until your dog is around 18 months of age.

After that, don't just forget about it. Socialisation isn't only for puppies; it should continue throughout your dog's life. As with any skill, if it is not practised, your dog will become less proficient at interacting with other people, animals, and environments.

Developing the Well-Rounded Adult Dog

Well-socialised puppies usually develop into safer, more relaxed and enjoyable adult dogs. This is because they're more comfortable in a wider variety of situations than poorly socialised canines. Dogs which have not been properly integrated are much more likely to react with fear or aggression to unfamiliar people, dogs and experiences.

Cockers who are relaxed about other dogs, honking horns, cats, cyclists, veterinary examinations, crowds and noise are easier to live with than dogs who find these situations challenging or frightening. And if you are planning on showing your dog or taking part in canine competitions, get him used to the buzz of the events early on. Well socialised dogs also live more relaxed, peaceful and happy lives than dogs which are constantly stressed by their environment. Socialisation isn't an "all or nothing" project. You can socialise a puppy a bit, a lot, or a whole lot. The wider the range of experiences you expose him to when young, the better his chances are of becoming a more relaxed adult.

Don't over-face your little puppy. Socialisation should never be forced, but approached systematically and in a manner that builds confidence and curious interaction. If your pup finds a new experience frightening, take a step back, introduce him to the scary situation much more gradually, and make a big effort to do something he loves during the situation or right afterwards.

For example, if your puppy seems to be frightened by noise and vehicles at a busy road, a good method would be to go to quiet road, sit with dog away from - but within sight of - the traffic. Every time he looks towards the traffic say "YES" and reward him with a treat. If he is still stressed, you need to move further away. When your dog takes the food in a calm manner, he is becoming more relaxed and getting used to traffic sounds, so you can edge a bit nearer - but still just for short periods until he becomes totally relaxed. Keep each session short and positive.

Meeting Other Dogs

When you take your gorgeous and vulnerable little pup out with other dogs for the first few times, you are bound to be a little nervous. To start with, introduce your puppy to just one other dog – one which you know to be friendly, rather than taking him straight to the park where there are lots of dogs of all sizes racing around, which might frighten the life out of your timid little darling. Always make the initial introductions on neutral ground, so as not to trigger territorial behaviour. You want your Cocker to approach other dogs with confidence, not fear.

From the first meeting, help both dogs experience good things when they're in each other's presence. Let them sniff each other briefly, which is normal canine greeting behaviour. As they do, talk to them in a happy, friendly tone of voice; never use a threatening tone. Don't allow them to

sniff each other for too long as this may escalate to an aggressive response. After a short time, get the attention of both dogs and give each a treat in return for obeying a simple command, such as "Sit" or "Stay." Continue with the "happy talk," food rewards and simple commands.

Of course, if you have more than one dog or a number of working Cockers, your puppy will learn to socialise within the pack. However, you should still spend time introducing him to new sights, sounds and animals. Here are some signs of fear to look out for when your dog interacts with other canines:

> Running away
> Freezing on the spot
> Frantic/nervous behaviour, such as excessive sniffing, drinking or playing with a toy frenetically
> A lowered body stance or crouching
> Lying on his back with his paws in the air – this is a submissive gesture
> Lowering of the head, or turning the head away
> Lips pulled back baring teeth and/or growling
> Hair raised on his back (hackles)
> Tail lifted in the air
> Ears high on the head

Some of these responses are normal. A pup may well crouch on the ground or roll on to his back to show other dogs he is not a threat. Try not to be over-protective, your Cocker has to learn how to interact with other dogs, but if the situation looks like escalating into something more aggressive, calmly distract the dogs or remove your puppy – don't shout or shriek. The dogs will pick up on your fear and this in itself could trigger an unpleasant situation.

Another sign to look out for is eyeballing. In the canine world, staring a dog in the eyes is a challenge and may trigger an aggressive response. This is more relevant to adult dogs, as a young pup will soon be put in his place by bigger or older dogs; it is how they learn. The rule of thumb with puppy socialisation is to keep a close eye on your pup's reaction to whatever you expose him to so that you can tone things down if he seems at all frightened.

Always follow up a socialisation experience with praise, petting, a fun game or a special treat. One positive sign from a dog is the play bow, when he goes down on to his front elbows but keeps his backside up in the air. This is a sign that he is feeling friendly towards the other dog and wants to play.

Although Cockers are not naturally aggressive dogs, aggression is often grounded in fear, and a dog which mixes easily is less likely to be aggressive. Similarly, without frequent and new experiences, some Cockers can become timid and nervous when introduced to new experiences. Take your new dog everywhere you can. You want him to feel relaxed and calm in any situation, even noisy and crowded ones.

Take treats with you and praise him when he reacts calmly to new situations. Once he has settled into your home, introduce him to your friends and teach him not to jump up. If you have young children, it is not only the dog who needs socialising! Youngsters also need training on how to act around dogs, so both parties learn to respect the other.

An excellent way of getting your new puppy to meet other dogs in a safe environment is at a puppy class. Ask around locally if any classes are being run. Some vets and dog trainers run puppy classes for very junior pups who have had all their vaccinations. These help pups get used to other dogs of a similar age.

Obedience Training

Training a young dog is like bringing up a child. Put in the effort early on to teach them the guidelines and you will be rewarded with a well-adjusted, sociable individual who will be a joy to live with. Cockers are intelligent, incredibly eager to please and love being with their humans. All of this adds up to one of the easiest breeds of all to train - but only if you are prepared to put in the time too.

Cockers make wonderful companions for us humans, but let yours behave exactly how he wants, and you may well finish up with a wilful, attention-seeking adult. Cockers make such wonderful companions for humans that it becomes all too easy to treat them like a human and spoil them. The secret of good training can be summed up quite simply:

Praise, Patience, Consistency and Plenty of Rewards

Praise and treats are the two prime motivators; training should ALWAYS be reward-based, never punishment-based. Cockers are sensitive critters. Many owners would also say that they have empathy (the ability to understand the feelings of others) and do not respond well to heavy-handed training methods. They are also highly intelligent, making it easy for them to pick up commands - provided you make it clear exactly what you want them to do; don't give conflicting signals.

Psychologist and canine expert Dr Stanley Coren has written a book called ***The Intelligence of Dogs*** in which he ranks 140 breeds. He used "understanding of new commands" and "obey first command" as his standards of intelligence, surveying dog trainers to compile the list. He says there are three types of dog intelligence:

- ➢ Adaptive Intelligence (learning and problem-solving ability). This is specific to the individual animal and is measured by canine IQ tests
- ➢ Instinctive Intelligence. This is specific to the individual animal and is measured by canine IQ tests
- ➢ Working/Obedience Intelligence. This is breed-dependent

The brainboxes of the canine world are the 10 breeds ranked in the 'Brightest Dogs' section of his list. All dogs in this class:

➢ Understand New Commands with Fewer than Five Repetitions
➢ Obey a First Command 95% of the Time or Better

It will come as no surprise to anyone who has ever been into the countryside and seen sheep being worked by a farmer and his right-hand man (his dog) to learn that the Border Collie is the most intelligent of all dogs. The second smartest dog is the Poodle. The second group is called 'Excellent Working Dogs' and in the middle of this group, at Number 18 is the English Cocker Spaniel and at Number 20 is the American Cocker Spaniel. These dogs understand new commands with five to 15 repetitions and obey a first command 85% of the time or better.

By the author's own admission, the drawback of this rating scale is that it is heavily weighted towards obedience-related behavioural traits, which are often found in working dogs, rather than understanding or creativity (found in hunting dogs). As a result, some breeds, such as the Bully breeds (Bulldogs, Mastiffs, Bull Terriers, Pug, Rottweiler, etc.) are ranked quite low on the list due to their stubborn or independent nature.

But as far as Cockers are concerned, it's true to say that you are starting out with a puppy that not only has the intelligence to pick up new commands very quickly, but who also really wants to learn and please you. Three golden rules when training a Cocker are:

1. Training must be reward-based, not punishment based.
2. Keep sessions short or your dog will get bored.
3. Keep sessions fun, give your Cocker a challenge and a chance to shine.

You might also consider enlisting the help of a professional trainer – although that option may not be within the budget of many new owners. If it is, then choose a trainer registered with the Association of Professional Dog Trainers (APDT); you can find details at the back of the book. Make sure the one you choose uses positive reward-based training methods, as the old alpha-dominance theories have largely been discredited.

When you train your dog, it should never be a battle of wills between you and him; it should be a positive learning experience for you both. Bawling at the top of your voice or smacking should play no part in training.

If you have a high spirited, high energy Cocker, you have to use your brain to think of ways which will make training challenging for your dog and to persuade him that what you want him to do is actually what **he** wants to do. He will come to realise that when he does something you ask of him, something good is going to happen – verbal praise, pats, treats, play time, etc. With a strong-willed dog you will need to be firm, but all training should still be carried out using positive techniques.

Establishing the natural order of things is not something forced on a dog through shouting or violence; it is brought about by mutual consent and good training. Like most dogs, Cockers are happiest and behave best when they know and are comfortable with their place in the household.

They may push the boundaries, especially as adolescents, but stick to your rules and everything will run much smoother.

Sometimes your dog's concentration will lapse, particularly with a pup or adolescent dog. Keep training short and fun. If you have adopted an older dog, you can still train him, but it will take a little longer to get rid of bad habits and instil good manners. Patience and persistence are the keys here.

Common Training Questions

1. **At what age can I start training my puppy?** As soon as he arrives home. Begin with a few minutes a day.

2. **How important is socialisation for Cockers?** Extremely, this can't be emphasised enough. Your puppy's breeder should have already begun this process with the litter and then it's up to you to keep it going when the pup arrives home. Up to 16 weeks' old puppies can absorb a great deal of information, but they are also vulnerable to bad experiences. Pups who are not properly exposed to different people and other animals can find them very frightening when they do finally encounter them later in life.

   They may react by cowering, urinating, barking, growling or biting. Food possession can also become an issue with some Cockers. But if they have positive experiences with people and animals before they turn 16 weeks of age, they are less likely to be afraid or to try and establish dominance later. Don't just leave your dog at home in the early days, take him out and about with you, get him used to new people, places and noises. Dogs that miss out on being socialised can pay the price later.

3. **What challenges does training involve?** Chewing is an issue with most puppies. Train your young Cocker only to chew the things you give him – so don't give him your footwear, an old piece of carpet or anything that resembles anything you don't want him to chew. Buy purpose-made long-lasting chew toys.

   Jumping up is another common issue. Cockers love everybody and are so enthusiastic about life, so it's often a natural reaction when they see somebody. You don't, however, want your fully grown dog to jump up on grandma when he has just come back from a romp through the muddy woods. Teach him not to jump up while he is still small.

13 Tips for Training Your Cocker

1. **Start training and socialising early.** Like babies, puppies learn quickly and it's this learned behaviour which stays with them through adult life. Old dogs can be taught new tricks, but it's a lot harder to unlearn bad habits. It's best to start training with a clean slate. Puppy training should start with a few minutes a day from Day One when you bring him home, even if he's only a few weeks old.

2. **Your voice is a very important training tool.** Your dog has to learn to understand your language and you have to understand him. Commands should be issued in a calm, authoritative voice - not shouted. Praise should be given in a happy, encouraging voice,

accompanied by stroking or patting. If your dog has done something wrong, use a stern voice, not a harsh shriek. This applies even if your Cocker is unresponsive at the beginning.

3. **Avoid giving your dog commands you know you can't enforce.** Every time you give a command that you don't enforce, he learns that commands are optional.

4. **Train your dog gently and humanely.** Cockers do not respond well to being shouted at or hit. Keep training sessions short and upbeat so the whole experience is enjoyable for you and him. If obedience training is a bit of a bore, pep things up a bit by 'play training' by using constructive, non-adversarial games.

5. **Begin your training around the house and garden or yard**. How well your dog responds to you at home affects his behaviour away from the home as well. If he doesn't respond well at home, he certainly won't respond any better when he's out and about where there are 101 distractions, such as food scraps, other dogs, people, cats, interesting scents, etc.

6. **Mealtimes are a great time to start training your dog.** Teach him to sit and stay at dinnertime and breakfast, rather than simply putting the dish down and allowing him to dash over immediately. He might not know what you mean in the beginning, so gently place him into the sitting position while you say "Sit." Then place a hand on his chest during the "Stay" command - gradually letting go – and then give him the command to eat his dinner, followed by encouraging praise - he'll soon get the idea.

7. **One command equals one response.** Give your dog only one command - twice maximum - then gently enforce it. Repeating commands or nagging will make your Cocker tune out. They also teach him that the first few commands are a bluff. Telling your dog to **"SIT, SIT, SIT, SIT!!!"** is neither efficient nor effective. Give your dog a single "SIT" command, gently place him in the sitting position and then praise him.

8. **Use your dog's name often and in a positive manner.** When you bring your pup or new dog home, use his name often so he gets used to the sound of it. He won't know what it means in the beginning, but it won't take him long to realise you're talking to him.

DON'T use his name when reprimanding, warning or punishing. He should trust that when he hears his name, good things happen. His name should always be a word he responds to with enthusiasm, never hesitancy or fear. Use the words "No" or "Bad Boy/Girl" in a stern - not shouted - voice instead. Some parents prefer not to use the word "No" with their dog, as they use it often around the human youngsters and it is likely to confuse the young canine! You can make a sound like "ACK!" instead. Say it sharply and the dog should stop whatever it is he is doing wrong – it works for us.

9. **Have a "No" sound.** When a puppy is corrected by his mother – for example if he bites her with his sharp baby teeth – she growls at him to warn him not to do it again. When your puppy makes a mistake, make a short sharp sound like "Ack!" to tell the puppy not to do that again. This works surprisingly well.

10. **Don't give your dog lots of attention (even negative attention) when he misbehaves.** Cockers love their owners' attention. If he gets lots of attention when he jumps up on you, his bad behaviour is being reinforced. If he jumps up, push him away, use the command "No" or "Down" and then ignore him.

11. **Timing is critical to successful training.** When your puppy does something right, praise him immediately. If you wait a while he will have no idea what he has done right. Similarly, when he does something wrong, correct him straight away. For example, if he eliminates in the house, don't shout and certainly don't rub his nose in it; this will only make things worse. If you catch him in the act, use your "No" or "Ack" sound and immediately carry him out of the house. Then use the toilet command (whichever word you have chosen) and praise your pup or give him a treat when he performs. If your pup is constantly eliminating indoors, you are not keeping a close enough eye on him.

12. **Give your dog attention when YOU want to** – not when he wants it. When you are training, give your puppy lots of positive attention when he is good. But if he starts jumping up, nudging you constantly or barking to demand your attention, ignore him. Don't give in to his demands. Wait a while and pat him when you want and after he has stopped demanding your attention.

13. **Start as you mean to go on.** In other words, in terms of rules and training, treat your cute little Cocker as though he were fully grown; introduce the rules you want him to live by as an adult. If you don't want your dog to take over your couch or bed or jump up at people when he is an adult, don't allow him to do it when he is small. You can't have one set of rules for a pup and one set for a fully grown dog, he won't understand. Also make sure that everybody in the household sticks to the same set of rules. Your dog will never learn if one person lets him jump on the couch and another person doesn't.

Remember this simple phrase: **TREATS, NOT THREATS.**

Teaching Basic Commands

Sit - Teaching the Sit command to your Cocker is relatively easy. Teaching a young pup to sit still is a bit more difficult! In the beginning you may want to put your protégé on a lead to hold his attention.

1. Stand facing each other and hold a treat between your thumb and fingers just an inch or so above his head. Don't let your fingers and the treat get any further away or you might have trouble getting him to move his body into a sitting position. In fact, if your dog jumps up

when you try to guide him into the Sit, you're probably holding your hand too far away from his nose. If your dog backs up, you can practise with a wall behind him.

NOTE: It's rather pointless paying for a high quality, possibly hypoallergenic dog food and then filling him with trashy treats. Buy premium treats with natural ingredients which won't cause allergies, or use natural meat, fish or poultry titbits.

2. As he reaches up to sniff it, move the treat upwards and back over the dog towards his tail at the same time as saying "Sit". Most dogs will track the treat with their eyes and follow it with their noses, causing their snouts to point straight up.

3. As his head moves up toward the treat, his rear end should automatically go down towards the floor. TaDa! (drum roll!)

4. As soon as he sits, say "Yes!" give him the treat and tell your dog (s)he's a good boy or girl. Stroke and praise him for as long as he stays in the sitting position. If he jumps up on his back legs and paws you while you are moving the treat, be patient and start all over again. Another method is to put one hand on his chest and with your other hand, gently push down on his rear end until he is sitting, while saying "Sit". Give him a treat and praise, even though you have made him do it, he will eventually associate the position with the word 'sit'.

5. Once your dog catches on, leave the treat in your pocket (or have it in your other hand). Repeat the sequence, but this time your dog will just follow your empty hand. Say "Sit" and bring your empty hand in front of your dog's nose, holding your fingers as if you had a treat. Move your hand exactly as you did when you held the treat.

6. When your dog sits, say "Yes!" and then give him a treat from your other hand or your pocket.

7. Gradually lessen the amount of movement with your hand. First, say "Sit" then hold your hand eight to 10 inches above your dog's face and wait a moment. Most likely, he will sit. If he doesn't, help him by moving your hand back over his head, like you did before, but make a smaller movement this time. Then try again. Your goal is to eventually just say "Sit" without having to move or extend your hand at all.

Once your dog reliably sits on cue, you can ask him to sit whenever you meet and talk to people (admittedly, it may not work, but it might calm him down a bit). The key is anticipation. Give your Cocker the cue before he gets too excited to hear you and before he starts jumping up on the person just arrived. Generously reward your dog the instant he sits. Say "Yes" and give him treats every few seconds while he holds the Sit.

Whenever possible, ask the person you're greeting to help you out by walking away if your dog gets up from the sit and lunges or jumps towards him or her. With many consistent repetitions of this exercise, your dog will learn that lunging or jumping makes people go away, and polite sitting makes them stay and give him attention.

'Sit' is a useful command and can be used in a number of different situations. For example, when you are putting his lead on, while you are preparing his meal, when he returned the ball you have just thrown, when he is jumping up, demanding attention or getting over-excited.

Come - This is another basic command which you can teach right from the beginning. Teaching your dog to come to you when you call (also known as the recall) is an important lesson. A dog who responds quickly and consistently can enjoy freedoms that other dogs cannot.

Although you might spend more time teaching this command to your Cocker than any other, the benefits make it well worth the investment. By the way, "Come" or a similar word is better than "Here" if you intend using the "Heel" command, as these words sound too similar.

No matter how much effort you put into training, no dog is ever going to be 100% reliable at coming when called and especially not an independent-minded Cocker. Dogs are not machines. They're like people in that they have their good days and their bad days. Sometimes they don't hear you call, sometimes they're paying attention to something else, sometimes they misunderstand what you want, and sometimes a Cocker simply decides that he would rather do something else.

Whether you're teaching a young puppy or an older Cocker, the first step is always to establish that coming to you is the best thing he can do. Any time your dog comes to you whether you've called him or not, acknowledge that you appreciate it. You can do this with smiles, praise, affection, play or treats. This consistent reinforcement ensures that your dog will continue to "check in" with you frequently.

1. Say your dog's name followed by the command **"Come!"** in an enthusiastic voice. You'll usually be more successful if you walk or run away from him while you call. Dogs find it hard to resist chasing after a running person, especially their owner.

2. He should run towards you. NOTE: Dogs tend to tune us out if we talk to them all the time. Whether you're training or out for an off-lead walk, refrain from constantly chattering to your dog - no matter how much of a brilliant conversationalist you are! If you're quiet much of the time, he is more likely to pay attention when you call him. When he does, praise him and give him a treat.

3. Often, especially outdoors, a dog will start off running towards you but then get distracted and head off in another direction. Pre-empt this situation by praising your dog and cheering him on when he starts to come to you and before he has a chance to get distracted.

Your praise will keep him focused so that he'll be more likely to come all the way to you. If he stops or turns away, you can give him feedback by saying "Uh-uh!" or "Hey!" in a different tone of voice (displeased or unpleasantly surprised). When he looks at you again, smile, call him and praise him as he approaches you.

Progress your dog's training in baby steps. If he's learned to come when called in your kitchen, you can't expect him to be able to do it straight away at the park or on the beach when he's surrounded by distractions. When you first try this outdoors, make sure there's no one around to distract your dog. It's a good idea to consider using a long training lead - or to do the training within a safe, fenced area. Only when your dog has mastered the recall in a number of locations and in the face of various distractions can you expect him to come to you regularly.

Down - There are a number of different ways to teach this command. It is one which does not come naturally to a young pup, so it may take a little while for him to master. Don't make it a battle of wills and, although you may gently push him down, don't physically force him down against his will. This will be seen as you asserting dominance in an aggressive manner and your Cocker will not respond well.

1. Give the **Sit** command.

2. When your dog sits, don't give him the treat immediately, but keep it in your closed hand. Slowly move your hand straight down toward the floor, between his front legs. As your dog's nose follows the treat, just like a magnet, his head will bend all the way down to the floor.

3. When the treat is on the floor between your dog's paws, start to move it away from him, like you're drawing a line along the floor. (The entire luring motion forms an L-shape).

4. At the same time say "Down" in a firm manner.

5. To continue to follow the treat, your dog will probably ease himself into the Down position. The instant his elbows touch the floor, say "Yes!" and immediately let him eat the treat. If your dog doesn't automatically stand up after eating the treat, just move a step or two away to encourage him to move out of the Down position. Then repeat the sequence above several times. Aim for two short sessions of five minutes or so per day.

If it doesn't work, try using a different treat. And if your dog's back end pops up when you try to lure him into a Down, quickly snatch the treat away. Then immediately ask your dog to sit and try again. It may help to let your dog nibble on the treat as you move it toward the floor. If you've tried to lure your dog into a Down but he still seems confused or reluctant, try this trick:

➢ Sit down on the floor with your legs straight out in front of you. Your dog should be at your side. Keeping your legs together and your feet on the floor, bend your knees to make a "tent" shape
➢ Hold a treat right in front of your dog's nose. As he licks and sniffs the treat, slowly move it down to the floor and then underneath your legs. Continue to lure him until he has to crouch down to keep following the treat
➢ The instant his belly touches the floor, say "Yes!" and let him eat the treat. If your dog seems nervous about following the treat under your legs, make a trail of treats for him to eat along the way

Some dogs find it easier to follow a treat into the Down from a standing position.

➢ Hold the treat right in front of your dog's nose, and then slowly move it straight down to the floor, right between his front paws. His nose will follow the treat

- If you let him lick the treat as you continue to hold it still on the floor, your dog will probably plop into the Down position

- The moment he does, say "Yes!" and let him eat the treat

Many dogs are reluctant to lie on a cold floor. It may be easier to teach yours to lie down on a carpet. The next step is to introduce a hand signal. You'll still reward him with treats, though, so keep them nearby or hidden behind your back.

- Start with your dog in a Sit

- Say "Down"

- Without a treat in your fingers, use the same hand motion you did before

- As soon as your dog's elbows touch the floor, say "Yes!" and immediately get a treat to give him. Important: Even though you're not using a treat to lure your dog into position, you must still give him a reward when he lies down. You want your dog to learn that he doesn't have to see a treat to get one.

Clap your hands or take a few steps away to encourage him to stand up. Then repeat the sequence from the beginning several times for a week or two. When your dog readily lies down as soon as you say the cue and then use your new hand signal, you're ready for the next step. You probably don't want to keep bending all the way down to the floor to make your Cocker lie down.

To make things more convenient, you can gradually shrink the signal so that it becomes a smaller movement. To make sure your dog continues to understand what you want him to do, you'll need to progress slowly.

Repeat the hand signal, but instead of guiding your dog into the Down by moving your hand all the way to the floor, move it almost all the way down. Stop moving your hand when it's an inch or two above the floor. Practice the Down exercise for a day or two, using this slightly smaller hand signal. Then you can make your movement an inch or two smaller, stopping your hand three or four inches above the floor.

After practising for another couple of days, you can shrink the signal again. As you continue to gradually stop your hand signal farther and farther from the floor, you'll bend over less and less. Eventually, you won't have to bend over at all. You'll be able to stand up straight, say "Down," and then just point to the floor.

Your next job is a bit harder - it's to practise your dog's new skill in many different situations and locations so that he can lie down whenever and wherever you ask him to. Slowly increase the level of distraction, for example, first practise in calm places, like different rooms in your house or in your garden, when there's no one else around. Then increase the distractions, practise at home when family members are moving around, on walks and then at friends' houses, too.

Stay - This is a very useful command, but it's not so easy to teach a lively and distracted young Cocker pup to stay still for any length of time. Here is a simple method to get your dog to stay; if you are training a young dog, don't ask him to stay for more than a few seconds at the beginning.

1. This requires some concentration from your dog, so pick a time when he's relaxed and well exercised or just after a game or mealtimes, especially if training a youngster. Start with your dog in the position you want him to hold, either the Sit or Down position.

2. Command your dog to sit or lie down, but instead of giving a treat as soon as he hits the floor, hold off for one second. Then say "Yes!" in an enthusiastic voice and give him a treat. If your dog tends to bounce up again instantly, have two treats ready. Feed one right away, before he has time to move; then say "Yes!" and feed the second treat.

3. You need a release word or phrase. It might be "Free!" or "Here!" or a word which you only use to release your dog from this command. Once you've given the treat, immediately give your release cue and encourage your dog to get up. Then repeat the exercise, perhaps up to a dozen times in one training session, gradually wait a tiny bit longer before releasing the treat. (You can delay the first treat for a moment if your dog bounces up).

4. A common mistake is to hold the treat high and then give the reward slowly. As your dog doesn't know the command yet, he sees the treat coming and gets up to meet the food. Instead, bring the treat toward your dog quickly - the best place to deliver it is right between his front paws. If you're working on a Sit-Stay, give the treat at chest height.

5. When your dog can stay for several seconds, start to add a little distance. At first, you'll walk backwards, because your Cocker is more likely to get up to follow you if you turn away from him. Take one single step away, then step back towards your dog and say "Yes!" and give the treat. Give him the signal to get up immediately, even if five seconds haven't passed. The stay gets harder for your dog depending on how long it is, how far away you are, and what else is going on around him.

    Trainer shorthand is **"distance, duration, distraction."** For best success in teaching a Stay, work on one factor at a time. Whenever you make one factor more difficult, such as distance, ease up on the others at first, then build them back up. That's why, when you take that first step back from your dog, adding **distance,** you should cut the **duration** of the stay.

6. Now your dog has mastered the Stay with you alone, move the training on so that he learns to do the same with distractions. Have someone walk into the room, or squeak a toy or bounce a ball once. A rock-solid Stay is mostly a matter of working slowly and patiently to start with. Don't go too fast, the ideal scenario is that your Cocker never breaks out of the Stay position until you release him.

    If he does get up, take a breather and then give him a short refresher, starting at a point easier than whatever you were working on when he cracked. If you think he's tired or had enough, leave it for the day and come back later – just finish off on a positive note by giving one very easy command you know he will obey, followed by a treat reward.

Don't use the "Stay" command in situations where it is unpleasant for your Cocker. For instance, avoid telling him to stay as you close the door behind you on your way to work. Finally, don't use Stay to keep a dog in a scary situation.

Clicker Training

Clicker training is a method of training that uses a sound - a click - to tell an animal when he does something right. The clicker is a tiny plastic box held in the palm of your hand, with a metal tongue that you push quickly to make the sound.

The clicker creates an efficient language between a human trainer and a trainee. First, a trainer teaches a dog that every time he hears the clicking sound, he gets a treat. Once the dog understands that clicks are always followed by treats, the click becomes a powerful reward.

When this happens, the trainer can use the click to mark the instant the animal performs the right behaviour. For example, if a trainer wants to teach a dog to sit, she'll click the instant his rump hits the floor and then deliver a tasty treat. With repetition, the dog learns that sitting earns rewards.

So the 'click' takes on huge meaning. To the animal it means: "What I was doing the moment my trainer clicked, *that's* what she wants me to do." The clicker in animal training is like the winning buzzer on a game show that tells a contestant he's just won the money! Through the clicker, the trainer communicates precisely with the dog, and that speeds up training.

Although the clicker is ideal because it makes a unique, consistent sound, you do need a spare hand to hold it. For that reason, some trainers prefer to keep both hands free and instead use a one-syllable word like "Yes!" or "Good!" to mark the desired behaviour. In the steps below, you can substitute the word in place of the click to teach your pet what the sound means. It's easy to introduce the clicker to your Cocker. Spend half an hour or so teaching him that the sound of the click means "Treat!" Here's how:

1. Sit and watch TV or read a book with your dog in the room. Have a container of treats within reach.

2. Place one treat in your hand and the clicker in the other. (If your dog smells the treat and tries to get it by pawing, sniffing, mouthing or barking at you, just close your hand around the treat and wait until he gives up and leaves you alone).

3. Click once and immediately open your hand to give your dog the treat. Put another treat in your closed hand and resume watching TV or reading. Ignore your dog.

4. Several minutes later, click again and offer another treat.

5. Continue to repeat the click-and-treat combination at varying intervals, sometimes after one minute, sometimes after five minutes. Make sure you vary the time so that your dog doesn't know exactly when the next click is coming. Eventually, he'll start to turn toward you and look expectantly when he hears the click—which means he understands that the sound of the clicker means a treat is coming his way.

If your dog runs away when he hears the click, you can make the sound softer by putting it in your pocket or wrapping a towel around your hand that's holding the clicker. You can also try using a different sound, like the click of a retractable pen or the word "Yes."

Clicker Training Basics

Once your dog seems to understand the connection between the click and the treat, you're ready to get started.

1. Click just once, right when your pet does what you want him to do. Think of it like pressing the shutter of a camera to take a picture of the behaviour.

2. Remember to follow every click with a treat. After you click, deliver the treat to your pet's mouth **as quickly as possible.**

3. It's fine to switch between practising two or three behaviours within a session, but work on one command at a time. For example, say you're teaching your Cocker to sit, lie down and raise his paw. You can do 10 repetitions of sit and take a quick play break. Then do 10 repetitions of down, and take another quick break. Then do 10 repetitions of stay, and so on. Keep training sessions short and stop before you or your dog gets tired of the game.

4. End training sessions on a good note, when your dog has succeeded with what you're working on. If necessary, ask him to do something you know he can do well at the end of a session.

Collar and Lead Training

You have to train your dog to get used to a collar (or harness) and lead, and then he has to learn to walk nicely on the lead. Teaching these manners can be challenging because many young Cockers are very lively and don't necessarily want to walk at the same pace as you. All dogs will pull on a lead initially. This isn't because they want to show you who is boss, it's simply that they are excited to be outdoors and are forging ahead.

If you are worried about pulling on your Cocker's collar, you might prefer to use a body harness instead. Harnesses work well with some dogs; they take the pressure away from a dog's sensitive neck area and distribute it more evenly around the body. Harnesses with a chest ring for the lead can be effective for training. When your dog pulls, the harness turns him around.

Another option is to start your dog on a padded collar and then change to a harness once he has learned some lead etiquette – although padded collars can be quite heavy. Some dogs don't mind collars; some will try to fight them, while others will slump to the floor like you have hung a two-ton weight around their necks! You need to be patient and calm and proceed at a pace comfortable to him; don't fight your dog and don't force the collar on.

1. The secret to getting a collar is to buy one that fits your puppy now - not one he is going to grow into - so choose a small lightweight one that he will hardly notice. A big collar may be too heavy and frightening. You can buy one with clips to start with, just put it on and clip it together, rather than fiddling with buckles, which can be scary when he's wearing a collar for the first time. Stick to the

principle of positive reward-based training and give a treat once the collar is on, not after you have taken it off. Then gradually increase the length of time you leave the collar on.

IMPORTANT: If you leave your dog in a crate, or leave him alone in the house, take off the collar. He is not used to it and it may get caught on something, causing panic or injury to your dog.

2. Put the collar on when there are other things that will occupy him, like when he is going outside to be with you, or in the home when you are interacting with him. Or put it on at mealtimes or when you are doing some basic training. Don't put the collar on too tight, you want him to forget it's there. Some pups may react as if you've hung a 10-ton weight around their necks, while others will be more compliant. If yours scratches the collar, get his attention by encouraging him to follow you or play with a toy to forget the irritation.

3. Once your puppy is happy wearing the collar, introduce the lead. An extending or retractable one is not really suitable for starting off with, as they are not very strong and no good for training him to walk close. Buy a fixed-length lead. Start off in the house or garden; don't try to go out and about straight away. Think of the lead as a safety device to stop him running off, not something to drag him around with. You want a dog that doesn't pull, so don't start by pulling him around; you don't want to get into a tug-of-war contest.

4. Attach the lead to the collar and give him a treat while you put it on. The minute it is attached, use the treats (instead of pulling on the lead) to lure him beside you, so that he gets used to walking with the collar and lead. As well as using treats you can also make good use of toys to do exactly the same thing - especially if your dog has a favourite. Walk around the house with the lead on and lure him forwards with the toy.

It might feel a bit odd but it's a good way for your pup to develop a positive relationship with the collar and lead with the minimum of fuss. Act as though it's the most natural thing in the world for you to walk around the house with your dog on a lead – and just hope that the neighbours aren't watching! Some dogs react the moment you attach the lead and they feel some tension on it – a bit like when a horse is being broken in for the first time. Drop the lead and allow him to run round the house or yard, dragging it after him, but be careful he doesn't get tangled and hurt himself. Try to make him forget about it by playing or starting a short fun training routine with treats. Treats are a huge distraction for most young Cockers. While he is concentrating on the new task, occasionally pick up the lead and call him to you. Do it gently and in an encouraging tone.

5. The most important thing is not to yank on the lead. If it is gets tight, just lure him back beside you with a treat or a toy while walking. All you're doing is getting him to move around beside you. Remember to keep your hand down (the one holding the treat or toy) so your dog doesn't get the habit of jumping up at you. If you feel he is getting stressed when walking outside on a lead, try putting treats along the route you'll be taking to turn this into a rewarding game: good times are ahead… That way he learns to focus on what's ahead of him with curiosity and not fear.

Take collar and lead training slowly, give your pup time to process all this new information about what the lead is and does. Let him gain confidence in you, and then in the lead and himself. Some dogs can sit and decide not to move. If this happens, walk a few steps away, go down on one knee and encourage him to come to you using a treat, then walk off again. For some pups, the collar and lead can be restricting and they will react with resistance. Some dogs are perfectly happy to walk alongside you off-lead, but behave differently when they have one on. Proceed in tiny steps if that is what your puppy is happy with, don't over face him, but stick at it if you are met with resistance. With training, your puppy **will** learn to walk nicely on a lead; it is a question of when, not if.

Walking on a Lead

There are different methods, but we have found the following one to be successful for quick results. Initially, the lead should be kept fairly loose. Have a treat in your hand as you walk, it will encourage your dog to sniff the treat as he walks alongside. He will not pull ahead as he will want to remain near the treat.

Give him the command **Walk** or **Heel** and then proceed with the treat in your hand, keep giving him a treat every few steps initially, then gradually extend the time between treats. Eventually, you should be able to walk with your hand comfortably at your side, periodically (every minute or so) reaching into your pocket to grab a treat to reward your dog.

If your dog starts pulling ahead, first give him a warning, by saying 'No' or 'Steady', or a similar command. If he slows down, give him a treat. But if he continues to pull ahead so that your arm becomes fully extended, stop walking and ignore your dog. Wait for him to stop pulling and to look up at you. At this point reward him for good behaviour before carrying on your walk.

Be sure to quickly reward him with treats and praise any time he doesn't pull and walks with you with the lead slack. If you have a lively young pup who is dashing all over the place on the lead, try starting training when he is already a little tired - after a play or exercise session – (but not exhausted).

Another way is what dog trainer Victoria Stillwell describes as the Reverse Direction Technique. When your dog pulls, say "Let's Go!" in an encouraging manner, then turn away from him and walk off in the other direction, without jerking on the lead. When he is following you and the lead is slack, turn back and continue on your original way. It may take a few repetitions, but your words and body language will make it clear that pulling will not get your dog anywhere, whereas walking calmly by your side - or even slightly in front of you - on a loose lead will get him where he wants to go.

There is an excellent video (in front of her beautiful house!) which shows Victoria demonstrating this technique and highlights just how easy it is with a dog that's easy to please. It only lasts three minutes and is well worth watching: https://positively.com/dog-behavior/basic-cues/loose-leash-walking.

Puppy Biting

All puppies spend a great deal of time chewing, playing, and investigating objects. All of these normal activities involve them using their mouths and their needle-sharp teeth. Like babies, this is how they investigate the world. When puppies play with people, they often bite, chew and mouth on people's hands, limbs and clothing.

Play biting is normal for puppies; they do it all the time with their littermates. They bite moving targets with their sharp teeth; it's a great game. But when they arrive in your home, they have to be taught that human skin is sensitive and body parts are not suitable biting material. Biting is never acceptable, not even from a small dog.

As a puppy grows and feels more confident in his surroundings, he may become bolder and his bites may hurt someone – especially if you have children or elderly people at home. Make sure every time you have a play session, you have a soft toy nearby and when he starts to chew your hand or feet, clench your fingers (or toes!) to make it more difficult and distract him with a soft toy in your other hand.

Keep the game interesting by moving the toy around or rolling it around in front of him. (He may be too young to fetch it back if you throw it). He may continue to chew you, but will eventually realise that the toy is far more interesting and lively than your boring hand.

If he becomes over-excited and too aggressive with the toy, if he growls a lot, stop playing with him and **walk away**. Although it might be quite cute and funny now, you don't want your Cocker doing this as an adult. Remember, if not checked, any unwanted behaviour traits will continue into adulthood, when you certainly don't want him to bite a child's hand – even accidentally.

When you walk away, don't say anything or make eye or physical contact with your puppy. Simply ignore him, this is extremely effective and often works within a few days. If your pup is more persistent and tries to bite your legs as you walk away, thinking this is another fantastic game, stand still and ignore him. If he still persists, tell him "**No!**" in a very stern voice, then praise him when he lets go. If you have to physically remove him from your trouser leg or shoe, leave him alone in the room for a while and ignore his demands for attention if he starts barking.

You may be surprised to learn that on several lists of dog bites on humans, including one compiled from various resources by the AVMA (American Veterinary Medical Association), Cocker Spaniels feature towards the top of the list http://bit.ly/1jrLz5n. Whether this refers to English as well as American Cockers is not clear.

Jacque Lynn Schultz, CPTD, author and Companion Animal Programs Adviser, National Outreach, Petfinder, says: "The protection of territory is most often seen in males of guarding/herding breeds, such as German Shepherds and Rottweilers, while certain Cocker Spaniels and Labrador Retrievers – females more often than males – put on ferocious displays over toys and chewies, resulting in punishing bites to hands and faces."

Many Cockers are very sensitive and another method which can be very successful is to make a sharp cry of "**Ouch!**" when your pup bites your hand – even when it doesn't hurt. This worked very well for us. Your pup may well jump back in amazement, surprised that he has hurt you. Divert your attention from your puppy to your hand. He will probably try to get your attention or lick you as a way of saying sorry. Praise him for stopping biting and continue with the game. If he bites you again, repeat the process. A sensitive dog will soon stop biting you. You may also think about keeping the toys you use to play with your puppy separate from other toys. That way he will associate certain toys with having fun with you and will work harder to please you.

Cockers love playing and you can use this to your advantage by teaching your dog how to play nicely with you and the toy and then by using play time as a reward for good behaviour.

GENERAL NOTE: If your puppy is in a hyperactive mood or is very tired, he is not likely to be very receptive to training.

CREDIT: With thanks to the American Society for the Prevention of Cruelty to Animals for assistance with parts of this chapter. The ASPCA has a great deal of good advice and training tips on its website at: http://www.aspca.org/pet-care/virtual-pet- behaviourist/dog- behaviour/training-your-dog

Breeders on Training

We asked a number of breeders how easy they thought Cockers were to train and if they had any tips. Here is what they said:

"Very easy, they are quick learners."

"Working Cockers are very clever, they pick things up easily but need the constant attention and brain stimulation to achieve the best results. Everything has to be made into a game or you will find them wandering off to something more interesting. Working Cockers can send themselves mad with boredom if they are not occupied. It would not be a good idea to get a one as a pet to leave at home all day whilst you work. The word 'working' means a lot. Training a Cocker as a hunting dog can take up to a year, it is very complex, there's a lot to learn and a lively dog has to be steadied so that it is safe around guns."

"There are more working Cockers in rescue homes than most other breeds, I believe. New owners do not always understand the exercise regime; obedience is easy if you understand the dog's needs. I exercise mine for an hour a day in 10 minute sessions."

"Cockers are keen to obedience train - although their noses can get in the way. We took Lola to Gundog training at the age of six months and it was staged in a large rabbit-ridden field. It became a little difficult for her to focus on me and not the rabbits!"

"Start when they're young with training; they are like little sponges and will soak everything up. They are such a willing breed and want to please, I have always found them a pleasure and not hard to train."

"Cockers are easy to train, they love to learn."

"Teaching them Sit, Stay and Leave is relatively easy, as is coming when called. BUT they do have a mind of their own and are possibly one of the worst breeds for male deafness if something grabs their attention or their nose on occasions. Boys seem to be worse than girls for that in my experience."

"Not that easy. They have ideas of their own and, as Cesar Millan once said: 'Spaniels always have a Plan B.' But with a sensible approach and a lot of patience they can learn anything. Free running for an hour a day is a must."

"I only have experience with the working type, but have found them to be easy to train. But some have such a strong desire to work (hunt) that they can find it stressful to concentrate on formal obedience training."

"Working are very easy to train, although they WILL do unexpected things, so although they may be trained to walk at heel, I would never trust them to do so where there is danger such as cars. Sometimes their hunting instinct just triggers and they can be off."

We don't do obedience with our working Cockers, but they are bright and easy to train with good working drive and treat/toy motivated. Gundog work is obedience, so are agility and flyball. We give ours five to 10-mile walks a day and/or agility and flyball training. Ours take part in agility, flyball and dock diving" (where dogs compete in jumping for distance or height from a dock into a body of water.

"I find them very eager to please and they love your attention; consistency is the key, keep training sessions short and fun, be repetitive, high praise rather than treats is best. Never lose your cool during training. If training is not going how you want it to then stop and go back to it later otherwise you will do untold damage."

"They are very easy and responsive to train, as long as the whole family is consistent. Cockers are very keen and eager to please their owners."

"They can be more challenging than other breeds of gundogs, however they are keen to learn and want to please. Positive, reward techniques work best for me."

"We can only talk about show type. They are not the easiest breed to obedience train. They are fine with the basic Sit, Down and Stay (to a point), but we would not recommend a Cocker Spaniel for top level obedience competitions. Some of ours will happily stay fairly close by and come back when called off the lead when out on walks, whereas others will put their noses down and disappear as soon as the lead comes off."

"All of our Cocker Spaniels have been very easy to train and eager to learn - unlike our son!"

"Cockers are quite easy to train, but persistence is key as, although they are intelligent, they do have minds of their own! I would thoroughly recommend attending puppy classes as they are great to help socialise your puppy – your local vet should have a list of local classes. As I wanted to work my dog I also invested in gundog training for Spaniels, which was excellent in reinforcing the recall and stay command and in helping me to understand how to work her in the field."

This breeder agrees: "Spaniels love to please and are intelligent little dogs, but can be subject to "selective hearing!" Any distraction can sometimes make them lose concentration. I find they learn very quickly initially, but around six months of age they go through a period of questioning commands and can become a little wilful. Don't give up and you will have a well-trained dog. Puppy training classes can be useful as you can share experiences with other owners, provided your pup doesn't lose concentration when in company!"

"Cockers are fairly easy, it's the people that need to train, not the dogs - and I use to teach obedience!"

"The working lines are generally very intelligent and easy to train, but have an irrepressible amount of drive and energy which must be channelled into a useful purpose, otherwise they will become destructive and often do the 'Wall of Death' in the living room!"

"My experience with working Cockers is that they are very quick learners, but you first have to gain their interest. Building a close bond and being the centre of attention for your Cocker will ultimately make them much more trainable and more willing to please."

"They are highly intelligent and easy to train, but you must know the breed and accept that if yours is a working strain dog, it will need additional stimulation if it won't be working in the field."

One breeder of show Cockers added: "I have found Cockers easy to obedience train, mainly because they are intelligent dogs, very willing to please and also food (treat) driven! My own Cockers love any type of ball toy and quickly learned that they would be rewarded with playtime if they performed a required task. I do believe that exercise is the most important factor in their training; if a dog has boundless energy, he will not be in the right state of mind to follow any training, so exercise first.

"My Cockers are exercised off lead for about an hour first thing in the morning, they have access to a large garden during the day, and I walk them again for about 30 minutes in the afternoon, which is normally their ball playtime. Once it is evening, all they want is the comfort of someone's lap or a sofa - preferably both!"

10. Cocker Spaniel Health

The good news is that the Cocker Spaniel is generally regarded as a healthy breed. In the Kennel Club's Breed Watch, the English Cocker is listed in the healthiest group - Category 1 - with no major points of concern. The American Cocker is in Category 2, see **Chapter 3.** for more details. Responsible breeders are playing their part in producing healthy pups from good breeding stock

However, there is not a single breed without the potential for some genetic weaknesses. Dogs, just like humans, may develop inherited health issues. For example, German Shepherds are more prone to hip problems than some other breeds, and 30% of Dalmatians have problems with their hearing. If you get a German Shepherd or a Dalmatian, your dog will not automatically suffer from these issues, but he or she will statistically be more likely to have them than a breed with no history of the complaint.

Health testing breeding dogs is essential to reduce or eradicate genetic problems, by NOT breeding from dogs which carry the gene or genes for specific health issues. And DNA testing is key to identifying which dogs may pass on diseases. This does not mean that you are 100% guaranteed a healthy dog by choosing a puppy from health-tested parents, but your chances of your puppy having no hereditary problems are greatly increased.

These are the tests to look out for as far as English Cocker Spaniels are concerned; they are fully explained later in this chapter: PRA (eyes), gonioscopy (Glaucoma), the kidney disease FN and hip scores. In the UK these tests are normally carried out by Optigen, the BVA (British Veterinary Association) or Laboklin. In the USA, these will be carried out by OFA, CERF or Optigen. There is also an annual BVA eye examination which tests for cataracts and other eye issues. More recently, Antagene has developed a test for AMS (Acral Mutilation Syndrome) which is affecting some strains of Cocker. For American Cockers the tests are PRA, Glaucoma, retinal dysplasia, hips and the metabolic disorder PFK.

A word of caution: always ask to physically see the relevant health certificates for the parents. Two of our breeders know of separate cases of Cocker puppies from supposedly clear eye-tested dams and sires going blind. Imagine how awful that is for a young dog - and his new owner.

All Kennel Club registered and Assured Breeders have to carry out certain health tests to comply with KC rules. There are, however, moves to improve the rate of testing across the breed generally to eradicate or reduce certain health issues, such as hereditary eye issues or AMS. Breeders of some field trial Cockers often select their breeding stock from champion dogs, and there is still a way to go to get more of these Cockers health tested. For example, 36 elite dogs qualified for the 2016 Cocker Spaniel Championships (for the country's top field trailers). Of these, three-quarters had no health tests whatsoever. Of the others, only one had had the following tests: PRA, FN, Hips and BVA eye, and the rest had fewer tests.

If you are interested in getting a health-tested working dog, a good place to start your search is the Working Cocker Health Screen Directory at www.workingcockerhealthscreendirectory.com. The aim of the Directory is: "To raise awareness of the health issues in the working Cocker by providing a comprehensive guide to the health issues and test available, and facilitating access to other information resources on how to carry out these tests. To support and promote breeders who initiate these tests by providing a directory of breeders and their dogs who initiate these health tests in their breeding programme. And to promote public awareness of these health issues."

Cocker Spaniel Insurance

Another point to consider is insurance for your new puppy or adult dog. The best time to get pet insurance is BEFORE you bring your Cocker home and before any health issues develop. Don't wait until you need to seek veterinary help – bite the bullet and take out annual insurance. If you can afford it, take out life cover. This may be more expensive, but will cover your dog throughout his or her lifetime - including for chronic (recurring and/or long term) ailments, such as ear, eye or joint problems.

Insuring a healthy puppy or adult dog is the only sure-fire way to ensure vets' bills are covered

before anything unforeseen happens - and you'd be a rare owner if you didn't use your policy at least once during your dog's lifetime. Due to the breed's reputation for being relatively healthy, the Cocker Spaniel is not an expensive breed to insure. Basic cover starts at around £10-£15 a month in the UK with Bought By Many, which offers policies from insurers More Than at https://boughtbymany.com/offers/cocker-spaniel-insurance

This company gets groups of single breed owners together, so you have to join the Cocker Spaniel Group, but it claims you'll get a 20% saving on your insurance. We are not on commission - just trying to save you some money – there are numerous companies out there offering pet insurance. Read the small print and the amount of excess; a cheap policy may not always be the best long-term decision.

Of course if you make a claim, your monthly premium will increase, but if you have a decent insurance BEFORE a recurring health problem starts, your dog should continue to be covered if the ailment returns. You'll have to decide whether the insurance is worth the money. On the plus side, you'll have peace of mind if your devoted Spaniel falls ill and you'll know just how much to fork out every month. And with advances in veterinary science, there is so much more vets can do to help an ailing dog - but at a cost. Surgical procedures can rack up bills of thousands of pounds or dollars.

In the US, basic cover starts from around $30-$40 a month for Cockers, depending on where you live and how much excess you're willing to pay. Consumers' Advocate has named the top 10 pet insurance companies, taking into account reimbursement policies, coverage and customers' reviews: 1. Healthy Paws, 2. PetPlan, 3. Trupanion, 4. Embrace, 5. Pets Best, 6. PetFirst, 7. VPI Pet Insurance, 8. Pet Partners, 9. ASPCA Pet Health Insurance, 10. Pet Premium.

Another point to consider is that dogs are at increasing risk of theft by criminals, including organised gangs. With the purchase price of puppies rising, dognapping more than quadrupled in the UK between 2010 and 2015, with around 50 dogs a day being stolen. Some 49% of dogs are snatched from owners' gardens and 13% from people's homes. If you take out a policy, check that theft is included. Although nothing can ever replace your beloved Cocker, a good insurance policy will ensure that you are not out of pocket.

The information in this chapter is not written to frighten new owners, but to help you to recognise symptoms of the main conditions affecting Cocker Spaniels and enable you to take prompt action, should the need arise. There are also a number of measures you can take to prevent or reduce the chances of certain physical and behavioural problems developing, including buying from health-tested stock, keeping your dog's weight in check, regular daily exercise and socialisation.

Three Golden Tips

Tip Number 1: Buy a well-bred puppy

Scientists have come to realise the important role that genetics play in determining a person's long-term health – and the same is true of dogs. This means it's wise to ensure your puppy comes from a reputable Cocker Spaniel breeder. A responsible breeder selects their stock based on:

- **General health and DNA testing of the parents**
- **conformation (physical structure)**
- **temperament**
- **the ability to do a job (with working Cockers)**

Although well-bred Cocker Spaniel puppies are expensive, many breeders do not make a lot of money from their sale, often incurring high bills for health checks, veterinary fees, specialised food, etc. The main concern of a good breeder is to produce healthy puppies with good temperaments and instincts.

It's better to spend time beforehand choosing a puppy which has been properly bred than to spend a great deal of time and money later when your wonderful pet bought from an online advert or pet shop develops health problems due to poor breeding, not to mention the heartache that causes. So spend some time to find the right breeder and read **Chapter 4. Choosing a Puppy** for further information on how to find him or her and the questions to ask.

- Don't buy a puppy from a pet shop. No reputable breeder allows their pups to end up in pet shops
- Don't buy a puppy from a small ad on a general website
- Don't buy a pup or adult dog unseen with a credit card – you are storing up trouble and expense for yourself

Tip Number 2: Get pet insurance as soon as you get your dog

Don't wait until your dog has a health issue and needs to see a vet. Most insurers will exclude all pre-existing conditions on their policies. When choosing insurance, check the small print to make sure that any condition which might occur is covered and that if the problem is recurring, it will continue to be covered year after year. When you are working out costs, factor in the annual or monthly or annual cost of good pet insurance and trips to a vet for check-ups, annual vaccinations, etc.

Tip Number 3: Find a good vet

Ask around your pet-owning friends, rather than just going to the first one you find. A vet that knows your dog from his or her vaccinations as a puppy and then right through their life is more likely to understand your dog and diagnose quickly and correctly when something is wrong. If you visit a big veterinary practice, ask for the vet by name when you make an appointment.

We all want our dogs to be healthy - so how can you tell if yours is? Well, here are some positive things to look for in a healthy Cocker Spaniel.

Signs of a Healthy Cocker

1. **Ears** – If you are choosing a puppy, gently clap your hands behind the pup (not so loud as to frighten him) to see if he reacts. If not, this may be a sign of deafness. Ears are the nemesis for many Cocker Spaniels in terms of keeping them clean and infection free - especially the large droopy ears of the show Cocker. The folded ear flaps can hide dirt and dust and should be inspected regularly for infection or ear mites as part of your normal grooming process. An unpleasant smell, redness, black wax or inflammation are all signs of infection. Some wax inside the ear – usually brown or yellowy - is normal; lots of wax or crusty wax is not. Tell-tale signs of an ear infection are scratching the ears, rubbing them on the carpet or shaking the head a lot, often accompanied by an unpleasant odour around the ears.

2. **Coat and skin** – these are easy-to-monitor indicators of a healthy dog. A Cocker Spaniel's coat, regardless of length, should be silky and smooth to the touch. Dandruff, bald spots, a dull lifeless coat, a discoloured or oily coat, or one which loses excessive hair, can all be signs that something is amiss. Skin should be smooth without redness. (Normal Cocker skin pigment can vary from pale pink to brown, black or mottled, depending on coat colour).

If your dog is scratching, licking or biting himself a lot, he may have a condition which needs addressing before he makes it worse. Open sores, scales, scabs, red patches or growths can be a sign of a problem. Signs of fleas, ticks and other external parasites should be treated immediately. Check there are no small black specks, which may be fleas, on the coat or bedding.

3. **Mouth** – Gums should be a healthy pink or with black pigmentation. A change in colour can be an indicator of a health issue. Paleness or whiteness can be a sign of anaemia or lack of oxygen due to heart or breathing problems. Blue gums or tongue are a sign that your Cocker is not breathing properly. Red, inflamed gums can be a sign of gingivitis or other tooth disease. Again, your dog's breath should smell OK. Young dogs will have sparkling white teeth, whereas older dogs will have darker teeth, but they should not have any hard white, yellow, green or brown bits.

4. **Weight** – Dogs may have weight problems due to factors such as diet, overfeeding, lack of exercise, allergies, diabetes, thyroid or other problems. A general rule of thumb is that your dog's stomach should be above his rib cage when standing, and you should be able to feel his ribs beneath his coat without too much effort. If his stomach hangs below, he is overweight or may have a pot belly, which can also be a symptom of other conditions.

5. **Nose** – a dog's nose is an indicator of health symptoms. It should normally be moist and cold to the touch as well as free from clear, watery secretions. Any yellow, green or foul smelling discharge is not normal - in younger dogs this can be a sign of canine distemper. A Cocker's nose can be black, pink or a similar colour to the coat.

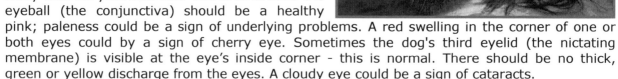

6. **Eyes** – a healthy Spaniel's eyes are dark and shiny with no yellowish tint. The area around the eyeball (the conjunctiva) should be a healthy pink; paleness could be a sign of underlying problems. A red swelling in the corner of one or both eyes could by a sign of cherry eye. Sometimes the dog's third eyelid (the nictating membrane) is visible at the eye's inside corner - this is normal. There should be no thick, green or yellow discharge from the eyes. A cloudy eye could be a sign of cataracts.

7. **Temperature** – The normal temperature of an adult dog is 101°F to 102.5°F. (A human's is 98.6°F). Excited or exercising dogs may run a slightly higher temperature. Anything above 103°F or below 100°F should be checked out. The exceptions are females about to give birth that will often have a temperature of 99°F.

8. **Attitude** – Cockers are known for being "merry" and optimistic. A generally positive attitude is a sign of good health. Cocker Spaniels are engaged, enthusiastic dogs, so symptoms of illness may include one or all of the following: not eating food, a general lack of interest in his or her surroundings, tail not wagging, lethargy and sleeping a lot (more than normal). The important thing is to look out for any behaviour which is out of the ordinary for your individual dog.

9. **Energy** – Cockers Spaniel have medium to high energy levels. Your dog should have good energy levels with fluid and pain-free movements. Lethargy or lack of energy – if it is not the dog's normal character – could be a sign of an underlying problem.

10. **Stools** – poo, poop, business, faeces – call it what you will - it's the stuff that comes out of the less appealing end of your dog on a daily basis! It should be firm and brown, not runny, with no signs of worms or parasites. Watery stools or a dog not eliminating regularly are both signs of an upset stomach or other ailments. If it continues for a day or two, consult your vet. If puppies have diarrhoea they need checking out much quicker as they can soon dehydrate.

11. **Smell** – Your Spaniel should smell like a dog! If there is a musty, 'off' or generally unpleasant smell coming from his body, it could be a sign of yeast infection. There can be a number of reasons for this, often his ears not being cleaned and groomed properly, or occasionally an allergy to a certain type of food. You need to get to the root of the problem.

So now you know some of the signs of a healthy dog – what are the signs of an unhealthy one? There are many different symptoms that can indicate your canine companion isn't feeling great. If you don't yet know your dog, his habits, temperament and behaviour patterns, then spend some time to get acquainted with him.

What are his normal character and temperament? Lively or calm, playful or serious, a joker or an introvert, bold or nervous, happy to be left alone or loves to be with people, a keen appetite or a fussy eater? How often does he empty his bowels, does he ever vomit? (Dogs will often eat grass to make themselves sick, this is perfectly normal and a canine's natural way of cleansing the digestive system).

You may think your Cocker can't talk, **but he can!** If you really know your dog, his character and habits, then he CAN tell you when he's not well. He does this by changing his patterns.

Some symptoms are physical, some emotional and others are behavioural. It's important for you to be able to recognise these changes as soon as possible. Early treatment can be the key to keeping a simple problem from snowballing into a serious illness. If you think your dog is unwell, it is useful to keep an accurate and detailed account of his symptoms to give to the vet, perhaps even take a video of him on your mobile phone. This will help the vet to correctly diagnose and effectively treat your dog.

Four Vital Signs of Illness

1. **Temperature -** A new-born puppy will have a temperature of 94-97ºF. This will reach the normal adult body temperature of 101ºF at about four weeks old. As stated, anything between 100ºF and 103ºF is regarded as normal for an adult dog. The temperature is normally taken via the rectum. If you do this, be very careful. It's easier if you get someone to hold your dog while you do this.

Ear Thermometer

Digital thermometers are a good choice, but **only use one specifically made for rectal use,** as normal glass thermometers can easily break off in the rectum. Ear thermometers are now available (pictured) making the task much easier, although they can be expensive and don't suit all dogs' ears - Walmart has started stocking them.

Remember that exercise or excitement can cause the temperature to rise by 2ºF to 3ºF when your dog is actually in good health, so wait until he is relaxed before taking his temperature. If it is above or below the norms, give your vet a call.

2. **Respiratory Rate** - Another symptom of canine illness is a change in breathing patterns. This varies a lot depending on the size and weight of the dog. An adult dog will have a respiratory rate of 15-25 breaths per minute when resting. You can easily check this by counting your dog's breaths for a minute with a stopwatch handy. Don't do this if he is panting; it doesn't count.

3. **Heart Rate** - You can feel your Cocker Spaniel's heartbeat by placing your hand on his lower ribcage – just behind the elbow. Don't be alarmed if the heartbeat seems irregular compared to a human; it IS irregular in some dogs. Your dog will probably love the attention, so it should be quite easy to check his heartbeat. Just lay him on his side and bend his left front leg at the elbow, bring the elbow in to his chest and place your fingers or a stethoscope on this area and count the beats.

> ➢ **Small dogs have a normal rate of 90 to 140 beats per minute**
> ➢ **Medium-sized dogs have a normal rate of 80 to 120 beats per minute**
> ➢ **Big dogs have a normal rate of 70 to 120 beats per minute**
> ➢ **A young puppy has a heartbeat of around 220 beats per minute**
> ➢ **An older dog has a slower heartbeat**

4. **Behaviour Changes** - Classic symptoms of illness are any inexplicable behaviour changes. If there has NOT been a change in the household atmosphere, such as another new pet, a new baby, moving home, the absence of a family member or the loss of another dog, then the following symptoms may well be a sign that all is not well:

> ➢ Depression
> ➢ Anxiety and/or trembling
> ➢ Falling or stumbling
> ➢ Loss of appetite
> ➢ Walking in circles
> ➢ Being more vocal - grunting, whining and/or whimpering
> ➢ Aggression – Cocker Spaniels are normally extremely friendly
> ➢ Tiredness - sleeping more than normal and/or not wanting to exercise
> ➢ Abnormal posture

Your dog may normally show some of these signs, but if any of them appear for the first time or worse than usual, you need to keep him under close watch for a few hours or even days. Quite often he will return to normal of his own accord. Like humans, dogs have off-days too.

If he is showing any of the above symptoms, then don't over-exercise him, and avoid stressful situations and hot or cold places. Make sure he has access to clean water. There are many other signals of ill health, but these are four of the most important. Keep a record for your vet, if your dog does need professional medical attention, most vets will want to know:

WHEN the symptoms first appeared in your dog

WHETHER they are getting better or worse, and

HOW FREQUENT the symptoms are. Are they intermittent, continuous or increasing?

We have highlighted some of the indicators of good and poor health to help you monitor your dog's wellbeing. Getting to know his or her character, habits and temperament will go a long way towards spotting the early signs of ill health.

Breeders on Health

Health is a clearly an important and topical issue among breeders. Many felt that breeding from non-health tested stock was compromising the future health of the breed. A working Cocker breeder of over 30 years' standing said: "The biggest threat to the breed is the amount of 'pet' people jumping on the Cocker Spaniel's popularity without testing or knowledge of what lies - or potentially lies - behind the lines. In working Cockers at the moment there is a problem with luxating patellas and there appears to be an increase in heart problems as well. There is also a pool of dogs which are potential GPRA carriers/affecteds that are being bred from without Optigen testing."

Chris Warner, of Monwodelea Gundogs, Coventry, UK, who has bred dogs for over 20 years and Cockers since 2010, agrees: "Within the working lines, the lack of health testing for conditions such as Glaucoma, etc. mean people are breeding with no knowledge as to the current health status of the dam or sire. This will possibly lead to unhealthy dogs."

Several people also highlighted the threat caused by unregulated breeders producing crossbreeds, such as the Cockapoo (pictured) and Sprocker, from dogs which have not been tested for genetic issues that they could pass on to their puppies. One breeder added: "The biggest threat to our working Cockers is one or two of the most prominent and successful breeders crossing Cockers with Springers to improve working ability."

Other breeders share their thoughts on health and give prospective owners an idea of what health checks are important when buying a Cocker. Jill Gunn, of Dearganach Working Cockers, Scotland, said: "The main health issues are PRA (Progressive Retinol Atrophy) and FN (Familial Nephropathy), although AMS (Acral Mutilation Syndrome) is creeping into the breed, which is very worrying."

Kennel Club Assured Breeder and veterinary nurse Louise Massey, of Essex, said: "I strongly believe that the only way to eradicate health issues within the breed is to health test breeding stock. At present, only members of the KC Assured Breeder Scheme are required to health test. Within the working world, it is fairly hard to find a pup whose parents have had all the recommended health tests. This could possibly be due to the cost and inconvenience involved with DNA testing.

"I am currently in the process of health testing my 18-month-old working Cocker bitch and it's a complicated situation. Optigen carries out the only KC-approved test for PRA, and the French lab Antagene does AMS and FN testing. Laboklin can send PRA samples to Optigen on a breeder's behalf and can test for FN, but does not offer testing for AMS. It is not overly simple in my opinion! I feel more working folk would be willing to carry out these tests if it were simpler, and then we would see more health-tested working Cockers being used in the field.

"At our practice, we see quite a high number of Spaniels with genetically inherited health issues. The vast majority of those are in 'pet' homes and have been bred from non-health tested stock and bought by people who are generally uninformed about the potential health issues that can arise within the breed. We also see health issues on a daily basis that can be fairly common, such as ear infections, skin issues, keratitis sicca (dry eye) and also behavioural problems.

"I believe there is a huge lack of education with genetically inherited diseases within the breed and it's generally quite hard to reach those owners who are not well informed before they arrive at the practice with their new pups; by which time it's too late."

Helen Marsden, of Finity Cocker Spaniels, Hampshire, UK, breeds show Cockers and said: "As a breeder I am a BIG advocate of health testing. PRA and FN are both hereditary conditions. However, with DNA testing available this should no longer be an issue if buying from reputable breeders. A reputable breeder will also test for Glaucoma (gonioscopy). In addition, yearly eye tests are also undertaken to check for any other conditions, such as entropion, distichiasis, cataracts etc. Hip dysplasia can also affect Cocker Spaniels, and some breeders will have their breeding dogs hip scored. Cockers are also known to suffer with lip fold pyoderma and pancreatitis. The biggest threat to the future of the breed is those breeders who do not health test their dogs. I hear of so many owners buying puppies that sadly fall ill with the genetic conditions that can be avoided through health testing."

One working Cocker breeder with 15 years' experience added: "If people stay with tested parentage, PRA and FN are not the issues they once were. Glaucoma and eye tests are vitally important. Although Glaucoma is not a recommend health test any more, I think it should still be a requirement and will always test mine. Hip scoring is proving to be more of an issue. Hip scoring is a recommendation, but I think should be compulsory."

Caroline Bymolen, Carto Cocker Spaniels, Cambridgeshire, UK, has been a breeder for more than 30 years and has bred only show-type Cockers since 2005. She said: "From a personal point of view, one main issue is ear infections. Because of the way their ears lie, the ear canal doesn't get much ventilation and therefore regular cleaning is essential. Another problem would be loose

bottom eyelids (ectropion), which can increase the risk of eye infections. This is more common in roans and is more prevalent with dogs that have been imported from Europe. Breeders need to be careful of this when importing dogs from overseas."

Show Cocker breeder Robert Baldwin, of Annaru Cocker Spaniels, South Wales, UK, said: "It should be compulsory that all breeders selling Cocker Spaniel puppies have the Optigen PRA and Antagene FN tests done, unless the sire and dam are clear tested."

Eunice Wine, Blackberry Farm Enterprises, Dillwyn, Virginia, USA, has been breeding American Cockers since 2010. Pictured in the pink of condition is Teddy, bred by Eunice. She said: "We have to clean their ears out with a cotton ball and a bit of Opticalm on a regular basis, but our dogs are healthy overall. The Cocker's eyes need regular cleaning and care, especially if you get a dog with 'weepy' eyes. We have had the good fortune to have dogs with healthy eyes, except our eight-year-old who had a cataract in one eye. We also have to refrain from feeding fatty table scraps that will make them overweight and could be bad for their pancreas."

Linda Reed, Of Delindere Cocker Spaniels, Leicestershire, UK, has bred English Cockers for 30 years and American for 20, she added: "In American Cockers, cataracts are the main health issue. With no genetic testing available, control is impossible. Clinical testing is available under the annual BVA scheme but, this test is only really valid for the day it is done; a dog can start to develop cataracts or any other eye defect the following day.

"A popular stud can sire dozens of pups in between clinical tests and be passing the gene on to all of them if he goes down in between tests. This obviously applies to bitches as well, but a bitch would only produce perhaps five or six pups in a litter and should only have one litter in 12 months.

"The other complication is the age of onset with the different types of cataract. Some do not develop until the animal is perhaps five or six years old - or even later than this - so, again, with a prolific stud dog, the amount of pups he could sire would be numerous. Even a bitch at that age could have had three litters and all of these pups would have inherited the gene and perhaps even have been bred from themselves."

The next section looks at some of the most common ailments affecting Cockers, with medical terminology explained in simple terms and symptoms and treatments outlined.

PRA (Progressive Retinal Atrophy)

PRA is the name for several progressive diseases which lead to blindness. First recognised at the beginning of the 20th century in Gordon Setters, this inherited condition has been documented in over 100 breeds. English and American Cocker Spaniels, Labrador Retrievers and Miniature and Toy Poodles are all recognised as being among the breeds which can be affected by the disease.

The specific genetic disorder which can affect Cocker Spaniels is prcd-PRA - progressive rod-cone degeneration PRA. It is sometimes called GPRA - General Progressive Retinal Atrophy. Puppies are born with normal eyesight and, according to The Cocker Spaniel Club, can develop PRA from as early as 18 months to as late as seven years old.

It causes cells in the retina at the back of the eye to degenerate and die, even though the cells seem to develop normally early in life. The rod cells operate in low light levels and are the first to lose normal function, and so the first sign is night blindness. Then the cone cells gradually lose their normal function in full light situations. Most affected dogs will eventually go blind. (Not all retinal disease is PRA and not all PRA is the prcd form of PRA).

If your dog has PRA, you may first notice that he lacks confidence in low light; he is perhaps reluctant to go down stairs or along a dark hallway. He might then start bumping into things, first at night and then in the daytime too. The condition is not painful and the eyes often appear normal - without redness, tearing or squinting. As the disease progresses, you may notice your dog's pupils dilating (becoming bigger) and see the reflection of light from the back of his eyes. The lenses may become opaque or cloudy in some dogs. It's been proven that all breeds tested for prcd-PRA have the same mutated gene, even though the disease may develop at different ages or severities from one breed to another. There is a DNA test which identifies this gene, and it is compulsory for all Cockers from Kennel Club and American Kennel Club breeders. Tested dogs get one of three results:

CLEAR - free from disease

CARRIER - has the gene, is unaffected by it, but could pass the disease on to offspring

AFFECTED - has inherited the disease and could develop PRA.

Ideally, only dogs tested **CLEAR** should be used for breeding. However, if bred, a carrier should only ever be mated with a CLEAR dog or bitch. The gene is 'Autosomal Recessive;' here are the possible outcomes:

Parent clear + parent clear = pups clear

Parent clear + parent carrier = 50% will carry the disease, 50% will be clear

Parent clear + parent affected = 100% will be carriers

Parent carrier + parent clear = 50% will carry disease, 50% will be clear

Parent carrier + parent carrier = 25% clear, 25% affected and 50% carry disease

Parent carrier + parent affected = 50% affected and 50% carry disease

Parent affected + parent clear = 100% will carry disease

Parent affected + parent carrier = 50% affected and 50% carry disease

Parent affected + parent affected = 100% affected

Sadly, there is no cure, but DNA testing all breeding dogs can avoid PRA in future generations. While eyesight is extremely important to dogs, their other senses are more highly developed than in humans and they do not rely as much as we do on our eyes. PRA develops slowly, giving the dog time to adjust to his changing situation. Many blind dogs live happy lives with a little extra help from their owners. If your Cocker Spaniel is affected, it may be helpful to read other owners' experiences of living with blind dogs at www.blinddogs.com.

Another eye disease that can be inherited is Central PRA, now known as RPED (Retinal Pigment Epithelial Dystrophy), which results in loss of central vision, but not total blindness as the dog retains peripheral vision. Scientists believe it is caused by the dog's inability to circulate Vitamin E around his body, and Vitamin E supplements can help affected dogs. As yet there is no DNA test available, however, annual eye testing is recommended.

Primary Glaucoma

Glaucoma is a painful condition that puts pressure on the eye, and if it becomes chronic or continues without treatment, it will eventually cause permanent damage to the optic nerve, resulting in blindness.

A normal eye contains a fluid called aqueous humour to maintain its shape, and the body is constantly adding and removing fluid from inside of the eye to maintain the pressure inside the eye at the proper level. Glaucoma occurs when the pressure inside the eyeball becomes higher than normal. Just as high blood pressure can damage the heart, excessive pressure inside the eye can damage the eye's internal structures. Unless Glaucoma is treated quickly, temporary loss of vision or even total blindness can result.

The cornea and lens inside the eye are living tissues, but they have no blood vessels to supply the oxygen and nutrition they need; these are delivered through the aqueous humour. In Glaucoma, the increased pressure is most frequently caused by this fluid not being able to properly drain away from the eye. Fluid is constantly being produced and if an equal amount does not leave the inner eye, then the pressure starts to rise, similar to a water balloon. As more water is added the balloon stretches more and more. The balloon will eventually burst, but the eye is stronger so this does not happen. Instead the eye's internal structures are damaged irreparably.

Secondary Glaucoma means that it is caused by another problem, such as a wound to the eye. Primary Glaucoma is normally inherited and this is the type of Glaucoma which breeding Cocker Spaniels should be tested for.

Symptoms

Even though a puppy may carry the gene for this disorder, the disease itself does not usually develop until a Cocker Spaniel is at least two or three years old. The dog has to first reach maturity, then live a little longer before the first signs appear.

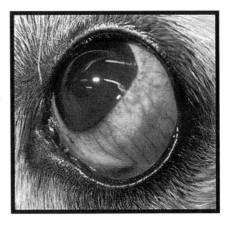

With primary Glaucoma, both eyes are rarely affected equally or at the same time, it usually starts in one eye several months or even years before it affects the second one. Glaucoma is a serious disease and it's important for an owner to be able to immediately recognise initial symptoms. If treatment is not started within a few days - or even hours in some cases - of the pressure increasing, the dog will probably lose sight in that eye. Here are the early signs:

> Pain
> A dilated pupil or one pupil looks bigger than the other
> Rapid blinking
> Red eyeballs
> Cloudiness in the cornea at the front of the eye
> The whites of an eye look bloodshot
> One eye looks larger or sticks out further than the other one
> Loss of appetite, which may be due to headaches
> Change in attitude, less willing to play, etc.

Most dogs will not display all of these signs at first, perhaps just one or two. A dog rubbing his eye with his paw, against the furniture or carpet or your leg is a common - and often unnoticed - early sign. Some dogs will also seem to flutter the eyelids or squint with one eye.

The pupil of the affected eye will usually dilate in the early stages of Glaucoma. It may still react to all bright light, but it will do so very slowly. Remember that Glaucoma, even primary Glaucoma, is usually going to initially affect just one of the eyes. If the pupil in one eye is larger than in the other, something is definitely wrong and it could be Glaucoma.

If you suspect your dog has Glaucoma, get him to the vet as soon as possible, i.e. **immediately,** not the day after, this is a medical emergency. The vet will carry out a manual examination and test your dog's eye pressure using a tonometer on the surface of the eye. There is still a fair chance that the dog may lose sight in this eye, but a much better chance of saving the second eye with the knowledge and preventative measures learned from early intervention.

Treatment will revolve around reducing the pressure within the affected eye, draining the aqueous humour and providing pain relief, as this can be a painful condition for your dog. There are also surgical options for the long-term control of Glaucoma.

As yet it cannot be cured. A genetic predisposition to Glaucoma can, however, be detected by a test called a **gonioscopy**, recommended by the Kennel Club for all breeding dogs, and part of the BVA/KC eye testing scheme. The KC recommends that this be done every three years.

Other Eye Issues

Hereditary Cataracts

These occur in as many as 70 breeds, with the American Cocker Spaniel being one of them. They can develop when the dog is only three to four years old, as well as in middle aged and older dogs, and can affect the entire lens or a localised area. They may develop rapidly over weeks or slowly over years and can occur in one eye before the other.

The specific gene or genes for hereditary cataracts in American Cockers has yet to be identified, which means that there is no DNA test. Dr Gustavo Aguirre of the University of Pennsylvania is leading research, funded by the American Spaniel Club and the American Spaniel Club Foundation, to identify the genetic mutation responsible for hereditary cataracts in (American) Cockers aged four to 10. If you are buying an American Cocker puppy, you should ask to see the parents' current annual eye test certificates, which show that the dog was clear on the day he or she was tested – although they do not guarantee that the dog will not develop cataracts in the future.

Hereditary cataracts are usually first diagnosed when the owner sees their dog bumping into furniture, or when his pupils have changed colour. The vet will refer the pet to the specialist who will carry out the same eye exam that is done for breeding stock. The process is painless and simple, drops are put into the eyes and after a few minutes the dog is taken into a dark room for examination and diagnosis.

Corrective surgery is possible, but it is expensive – it can cost thousands of pounds or dollars - and the dog must be suitable. If you think your Cocker may have cataracts, it is important to get him to a vet as soon as possible.

Early removal of cataracts can restore vision and provide a dramatic improvement in the quality of your dog's life. The only treatment for canine cataracts is surgery (unless the cataracts are caused by another condition like canine diabetes). Despite what you may have heard, laser surgery does not exist for canine cataracts.

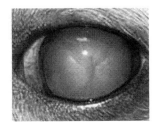 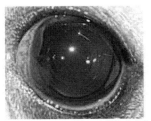

Left: eye with cataracts. Right: same eye with artificial lens

The good news is that surgery is almost always successful, although it can leave the dog with cloudy vision. The dog has to have a general anaesthetic but the operation is often performed on an outpatient basis. The procedure is similar to small incision cataract surgery in people. An artificial lens is often implanted in the dog's eye to replace the cataract lens. Dogs can see without an artificial lens, but the image will not be in focus. Discuss with the vet or ophthalmologist whether your dog would benefit from an artificial lens. Even better news is that once the cataract is removed, it does not recur. However before your dog can undergo this procedure, he has to be fit and healthy and a suitable candidate for surgery.

After the operation, he will probably have to stay at the surgery overnight so that the professionals can keep an eye on him. Once back home, he will have to wear a protective Elizabethan collar, or E collar, for about one to two weeks while his eye is healing. You have to keep him quiet and calm (not always easy with Cockers!) You'll also have to give him eye drops, perhaps four times a day for the first week and then less frequently after that. The success of cataract surgery depends very much on the owner doing all the right things.

There are also other types of cataracts. Congenital cataracts are present at birth and usually occur in both eyes. Despite the dog being born with them, they are not necessarily inherited, as infections or toxins may have caused them in unborn puppies. Developmental (early onset) cataracts occur in puppyhood or adolescence and may be inherited or caused by trauma, diabetes mellitus, infection or toxins. Senile (late onset) cataracts affect dogs over six years of age and occur much less frequently in dogs than in humans.

Retinal Dysplasia

This is an inherited disease which affects American Cocker Spaniels, but not English Cockers. Retinal dysplasia is a disorder in which the cells and layer of retinal tissue at the back of the eye do not develop properly. One or both eyes may be affected. It can be detected by a vet using an ophthalmoscope when the puppy is six weeks old or even younger. The retina looks like layers of folded tissue rather than one flat layer.

There are different types of the condition; American Cockers can have Focal and Multifocal Retinal Dysplasia, which appear as streaks and dots in the central retina. Some dogs have no symptoms, while more severely affected puppies may have symptoms such as a reluctance to walk into dark areas, bumping into things and obvious sight problems. There is sadly no treatment for the condition, which ultimately results in partial or total blindness. Ask the breeder if there is any history of retinal dysplasia in her bloodlines.

Entropion

This is a condition in which the edge of the lower eyelid rolls inward, causing the dog's fur to rub the surface of the eyeball, or cornea. In rare cases the upper lid can also be affected, and one or both eyes may be involved. This painful condition is thought to be hereditary and is more commonly found in dog breeds with wrinkled faces, although other affected breeds include Spaniels, Poodles and Labrador Retrievers.

The affected dog will scratch at his painful eye with his paws and this can lead to further injury. If your dog is to suffer from entropion, he will usually show signs at or before his first birthday. You will notice that his eyes are red and inflamed and they will produce tears. He will probably squint.

The tears typically start off clear and can progress to a thick yellow or green mucus. If the entropion causes corneal ulcers, you might also notice a milky-white colour develop. This is caused by increased fluid which affects the clarity of the cornea. For your poor dog, the irritation is constant. Imagine how painful and uncomfortable it would be if you had permanent hairs touching your eyes. It makes my eyes water just thinking about it.

It's important to get your dog to the vet as soon as you suspect entropion before he scratches his cornea and worsens the problem. The condition can cause scarring around the eyes or other issues which can affect a dog's vision if left untreated. A vet will make the diagnosis after a painless and relatively simple inspection of your dog's eyes. But before he or she can diagnose entropion, they will have to rule out other issues, such as allergies, which might also be making your dog's eyes red and itchy.

In young dogs, some vets may delay surgery and treat the condition with medication until the dog's face is fully formed to avoid having to repeat the procedure at a later date. In mild cases, the vet may successfully prescribe eye drops, ointment or other medication. However, the most common treatment for more severe cases is a fairly straightforward surgical procedure to pin back the lower eyelid. Discuss the severity of the condition and all the options before proceeding to surgery.

Ectropion

Ectropion is sometimes called 'droopy eyelid'. The lower lids are loose and actually turn outwards, causing a drooping of the eyelid's margins. One or both eyes may be involved. It can occur in any breed, but it is known to be inherited in American Cocker Spaniels (pictured), Saint Bernards, Mastiffs and Bloodhounds.

As the lower lid sags downward, the underlying conjunctiva (the mucous membrane that covers the front of the eye and lines the inside of the eyelids) is exposed. This forms a pouch or pocket, allowing pollens, grasses, dust and all sorts of unwanted debris to accumulate and rub against the sensitive conjunctiva. This constantly irritates the dog and leads to increased redness and watering of the eye.

Many dogs live normal lives with ectropion, but some develop repeated eye infections due to the dirt, dust, etc. constantly getting into the eye. Some dogs require no treatment; however, if eye irritations or infections develop, you should consult a vet. Mild cases can be treated with eye drops or ointment to alleviate irritations and/or infections when they occur. Severe cases may require surgery to remove excess tissue, which tightens the lids and removes the abnormal pocket.

Distichiasis

Distichiasis is the medical term for eyelashes irritating a dog's eyes. With this condition small eyelashes abnormally grow on the inner surface or the very edge of the eyelid, and both upper and lower eyelids may be affected. Some breeds, such as Cocker Spaniels, Golden Retrievers, French Bulldogs, Boxers and Pekingese, are affected more than others, suggesting that it is an inherited trait.

The affected eye becomes red, inflamed, and may develop a discharge. The dog will typically squint or blink a lot, just like a human with a hair or other foreign matter in the eye. The dog will often rub his eye against furniture, other objects or the carpet. In severe cases, the cornea can become ulcerated and it looks blue. If left, the condition usually worsens and severe ulcerations and infections develop, which can lead to blindness. The dog can make the condition worse by scratching or rubbing his eyes.

Treatment usually involves surgery or electro- or cryo-epilation, where a needle is inserted into the hair follicle and an ultra-fast electric current is emitted. This current produces heat which destroys the stem cells responsible for hair growth. This procedure may need to be repeated after several months because all of the abnormal hairs may not have developed at the time of the first treatment -although this is not common with dogs older than three years.

If surgery is performed, the lid is actually split and the areas where the abnormal hairs grow are removed. Both treatments require anaesthesia and usually result in a full recovery. After surgery, the eyelids are swollen for four to five days and the eyelid margins turn pink. Usually they return to their normal colour within four months. Antibiotic eye drops are often used following surgery to prevent infections.

Cherry Eye

Humans have two eyelids, but dogs have a third eyelid, called a nictating membrane. This third eyelid is a thin, opaque tissue with a tear gland which rests in the inner corner of the eye. Its purpose is to provide additional protection for the eye and to spread tears over the eyeball.

Usually it is retracted and therefore you can't see it, although you may notice it when your dog is relaxed and falling asleep. When the third eyelid becomes visible it may be a sign of illness or a painful eye. Cherry Eye is a medical condition, officially known as 'nictitans gland prolapse', or prolapse of the gland of the third eyelid.

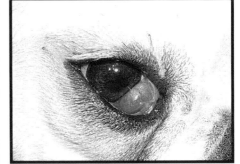

Cocker Spaniels can be susceptible to this, although it is not known whether the condition is inherited, along with other breeds such as the Bulldog, Beagle, Bloodhound, Boston Terrier, Bull Terrier, Lhasa Apso, Saint Bernard and Shar-Pei.

The exact cause of cherry eye is not known, but it is thought to be due to a weakness of the fibrous tissue which attaches the gland to the surrounding eye. This allows the gland to fall down, or prolapse. Once this has happened and the gland is exposed to the dry air and irritants, it can become infected and/or begin to swell. There is sometimes a mucous discharge and if the dog rubs or scratches it, he can further damage the gland and even possibly create an ulcer on the surface of the eye.

The main visible symptom is a red, often swollen, mass in the corner of one or both eyes, which is often first seen in young dogs up to the age of two years. It can occur in one or both eyes and may be accompanied by swelling and/or irritation. Although it may look sore, it is not a painful condition for your dog.

At one time, it was popular to surgically remove the gland to correct this condition. While this was often effective, it could create problems later on. The gland of the third eyelid is very important for producing tears, without which dogs could suffer from 'dry eye', also known as keratoconjunctivitis sicca (KCS). These days, removing the gland is not considered a good idea.

A far better and straightforward option is to surgically reposition the gland by tacking it back into place with a single stitch that attaches the gland to the deeper structures of the eye socket. There is also another type of operation during which the wedge of tissue is removed from directly over the gland. Tiny dissolving stitches are used to close the gap so that the gland is pushed back into place.

After surgery the dog may be placed on antibiotic ointment for a few days. Mostly, surgery is performed quickly and for most dogs that's the end of the matter. However, a few dogs do have a recurrence of cherry eye. The eye should return to normal after about seven days, during which time there may be some redness or swelling.

If the affected eye suddenly seems uncomfortable or painful for your dog, or you can see protruding stitches, then take him back to the vet to get checked out. Other options include anti-inflammatory eye drops to reduce the swelling and manually manipulating the gland back into place.

Sometimes a dog will develop cherry eye in one eye and then the condition will also appear some time later in the other eye. If you have a young dog diagnosed with cherry eye, discuss with your vet whether to delay surgery a few weeks or months to see if the second eye is affected. This will save the dog being anesthetised twice and will also save you money.

Dry Eye (Keratoconjunctivitis sicca)

KCS is the technical term for a condition also known as 'dry eye' caused by not enough tears being produced. With insufficient tears, a dog's eyes can become irritated and the conjunctiva appears to be red.

The eyes typically develop a thick, yellowy discharge. Infections are common as tears also have anti-bacterial and cleansing properties, and inadequate lubrication allows dust, pollen and other debris to accumulate. The nerves of these glands may also become damaged.

In many cases the reason for dry eye is not known, other times it may be caused by injuries to the tear glands, eye infections, reactions to drugs, an immune reaction or even the gland of the third eyelid being surgically removed by mistake. Left untreated, the dog will suffer painful and chronic eye infections. Repeated irritation of the cornea results in severe scarring, and ulcers may develop which can lead to blindness.

Treatment usually involves drugs; cyclosporine, ophthalmic ointment or drops being the most common. In some cases another eye preparation – Tacrolimus - is also used and may be effective when cyclosporine is not. Sometimes artificial tear solutions are also prescribed. In very severe cases, an operation can be performed to transplant a salivary duct into the upper eyelid, causing saliva to drain into and lubricate the eye. This procedure is rarely used, but is an option.

Familial Nephropathy (FN)

Familial Nephropathy is an inherited disease that leads to kidney failure and death in young dogs, and both show and working Cockers can be carriers of the genetic mutation responsible. American Cockers are not affected.

Great strides have been made to reduce the incidence of this disease over the last 30 years, particularly by the UK's Cocker Spaniel Club, alongside research carried out in the USA. There is a reliable DNA test which accurately identifies affected dogs. This can be used by breeders to effectively eliminate undesirable disease genes in their stock.

According to Antagene, the company which carries out the testing, about 11% of English Cocker Spaniels in Europe are carriers of the disease. Without testing, an unsuspecting breeder can mate a male carrier and a female carrier without knowing it and produce a litter containing affected puppies. A carrier will pass FN on to 50% of his or her puppies.

All Kennel Cub Assured Breeders have to have this test on their breeding dogs. Results show whether the dog is Clear, Carrier or Affected. The gene is recessive and if one parent has a Clear result, the puppy will not inherit the disease, although he could be a carrier. If you are buying an English Cocker puppy, ask to see the parents' certificates for FN.

Sadly, the disease usually affects puppies and young dogs between the age of six months and two years.

Symptoms are:

> Excessive thirst
> Excessive urine
> Weight loss
> A slowdown in growth
> Reduced appetite
> Vomiting and diarrhoea

All these are signs of the kidney ceasing to function, leading to the death of the dog.

PFK Deficiency

PFK (Phosphofructokinase) Deficiency is a genetic metabolic disorder affecting American Cocker Spaniels and their offspring, but not English Cockers. It prevents the glucose metabolising into energy. Phosphofructokinase is the name of the enzyme responsible for this metabolic action.

The technical description of PFK is 'an autosomal recessive genetic disease.' This means that dogs which are carriers show no signs of PFK deficiency, but can pass the gene on to their puppies, thereby spreading the disease. Some 10% of American Cockers are thought to be affected.

Symptoms vary depending on how serious the condition is, but typical signs are:

➢ An intolerance to exercise
➢ Lethargy or general weakness
➢ Muscle wasting and cramping
➢ Blood in the dog's urine (haematuria)
➢ Fever
➢ Depression
➢ Pale gums

Affected dogs have persistent mild anaemia (low levels of red blood cells), but can usually compensate for this. They also have intermittent bouts of red blood cell breakdown (haemolysis), when they become lethargic and weak and may even bleed. This usually happens after intense exercise, excessive barking or panting. The dog's gums are pale or jaundiced and he usually has a high fever. You may notice your dog's urine is brown, this is due to blood breakdown products in the urine and during these bouts the dog needs to see a vet.

The vet will examine the dog and take blood tests before diagnosing PFK Deficiency. There is no specific treatment, but the condition can be managed with veterinary help. You have to play your part by keeping on the lookout for symptoms and avoiding certain situations, such as increased stress for your dog, strenuous exercise, excitement that causes lots of barking and hot conditions.

There is a DNA test to detect the disease, but neither the KC nor American Kennel Club stipulate that this is compulsory.

Hip Dysplasia

Canine Hip Dysplasia (CHD) is the most common cause of hind leg lameness in dogs; dysplasia means 'abnormal development'. It is also the most common heritable orthopaedic problem seen in dogs, affecting virtually all breeds, but is more common in large breeds. The condition develops into degenerative osteoarthritis of the hip joints.

CHD is known in Cocker Spaniels - both English and American –some 6.4% of American Cockers and 5.6% of English Cockers tested by the OFA in the USA had abnormal hips.

The hip is a ball and socket joint. Hip dysplasia is caused when the head of the femur (thigh bone) fits loosely into a shallow and poorly developed socket in the pelvis. Most dogs with dysplasia are born with normal hips, but due to their genetic make-up - and sometimes other factors such as diet and exercise - the soft tissues that surround the joint develop abnormally.

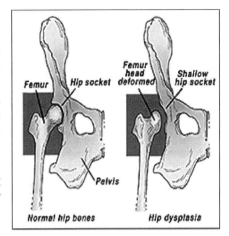

The joint carrying the weight of the dog and becomes loose and unstable, muscle growth lags behind normal growth and is often followed by degenerative joint disease or osteoarthritis, which is the body's attempt to stabilise the loose hip joint. Early diagnosis gives your vet the best chance to tackle the problem as soon as possible, minimising the chance of arthritis developing. Symptoms range from mild discomfort to extreme pain. A puppy with canine hip dysplasia often starts to show signs between five and 13 months old.

The right hand side of our picture shows a shallow hip socket and a deformed femur head, causing hip dysplasia. The healthy joint is on the left.

Symptoms

> Lameness in hind legs, particularly after exercise
> Difficulty or stiffness when getting up or climbing uphill
> A 'bunny hop' gait
> Dragging the rear end when getting up
> Waddling rear leg gait
> A painful reaction to stretching the hind legs, resulting in a short stride
> A side-to-side sway of the croup (area above the tail) with a tendency to tilt the hips down if you push down on the croup
> A reluctance to jump, exercise or climb stairs

Causes and Triggers

Canine hip dysplasia is usually inherited, but there are also factors which can trigger or worsen the condition, including:

> Extended periods without exercise – or too much vigorous exercise - especially when your dog is growing
> Overfeeding, especially on a diet high in protein and calories
> Excess calcium, also usually due to overfeeding
> Obesity

Advances in nutritional research have shown that diet plays an important role in the development of hip dysplasia. Feeding a high-calorie diet to growing dogs can trigger a predisposition to hip dysplasia, as the rapid weight gain places increased stress on the hips. During their first year of life, Cocker Spaniel puppies should be fed a diet that contains the right amount of calories, minerals and protein, thereby reducing the risk of hip dysplasia. Ask your breeder or vet for advice on the best diet.

Exercise may be another risk factor. Dogs that have a predisposition to the disease may have an increased chance of getting it if they are over-exercised at a young age. Young Spaniels are very lively and it's tempting to give them lots of exercise to help them burn off steam, but caution must be exercised. See **Chapter 9. Exercise and Training** for more information. The key is moderate, low impact exercise for fast-growing young dogs. Activities which strengthen the gluteus muscles, such as running and swimming, are probably a good idea. Whereas high impact activities that apply a lot of force to the joint, such and jumping and catching Frisbees, is not recommended with young Cockers.

Treatment and Prevention

As with most conditions, early detection leads to a better outcome. Your vet will take X-rays to make a diagnosis. Treatment is geared towards preventing the hip joint getting worse and decreasing pain. Various medical and surgical treatments are now available to ease the dog's discomfort and restore some mobility. Treatment depends upon several factors, such as the dog's age, how bad the problem is and, sadly, how much money you can afford to spend on treatment.

Management of the condition usually consists of restricting exercise, keeping body weight down and then managing pain with analgesics and anti-inflammatory drugs. As with humans, cortisone injections may sometimes be used to reduce inflammation and swelling. Cortisone can be injected directly into the affected hip to provide almost immediate relief for a tender, swollen joint. In severe cases, surgery may be an option, especially with older dogs.

Ideally, both the dam and sire of your puppy should have been 'hip scored' and the results available for you to see, although this may not always be the case. Thirty years ago the Kennel Club and British Veterinary Association (BVA) set up a hip screening programme for dogs in the UK, which tests them using radiology and gives them a rating or 'hip score'. In the USA the OFA (Orthopedic Foundation for Animals) administers the tests.

In the USA it is compulsory for both English and American Cockers to have a hip evaluation before they can qualify for a CHIC (Canine Health Information Centre) number. Veterinary MRI and radiology specialist Ruth Dennis, of the Animal Health Trust, states: *"For dogs intended for breeding, it is essential that the hips are assessed before mating to ensure that they are free of dysplastic changes or only minimally affected."*

However, it is only recommended for English Cockers and not mentioned at all for American Cockers by the UK's Kennel Cub. Some British breeders involved in this book have said they think hip scoring and luxating patella tests should be compulsory in the UK, as they believe these ailments are actually more common in Cockers than some others for which testing is compulsory.

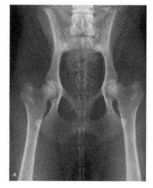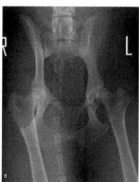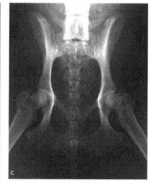

In these X-rays, Figure A (left) is the healthy hip, Figure B shows lateral tilting, C shows outward rotation

The test is a one off X-ray done by any vet under anaesthetic, usually performed before the dog reaches 18 months old. This is then submitted to a KC panel of assessors. The hip score is the total number of points given for nine points examined by X-ray. The best score for each hip is 0 and the worst is 53 and, as a dog has two hips, the total score will be between 0 and 106.

In the UK, the current cost of a hip score is around £57; the cost of a joint hip and elbow test is £105. The tests are much cheaper in the US: hip testing costs $35 for an individual pup or $90 for the whole litter, and $40 for a joint hip and elbow test.

The current Breed Mean Score (BMS, i.e. average) for Cocker Spaniels is 13. This is one point lower than three years previously, which shows that hip testing is slowly helping to reduce the problem. Responsible breeders should only breed from stock that has a hip score below 13. When buying a pup, ask to see the original hip score certificate. If the breeder does not own the stud dog, a photocopy of his results should also be available. The same applies with elbow tests outlined below.

Elbow Dysplasia

Elbow Dysplasia (ED) simply means 'abnormal development of the elbow.' It affects many breeds and is thought to be on the increase in the canine population. It is more commonly seen in large breed fast-growing puppies, but some Cocker Spaniels are also affected. It starts in puppyhood and affects the dog for the rest of his life.

There are a number of causes, but the biggest one is thought to be genetic, with the disease being passed on from dam or sire to puppy. And it is a combination of genes, rather than a single gene, which causes ED. Dogs who show no symptoms can still be carriers of the disease. Other factors such as rate of growth, diet and level of exercise may influence the severity of the disease in an individual dog, but they cannot prevent it or reduce the potential of the dog to pass it on to offspring.

Many bones in a new-born puppy are not a single piece of bone, but several different pieces with cartilage in between. This is especially true of long limb bones. As the puppy grows, the cartilage changes into bone and several pieces of bone fuse together forming one entire bone. For instance, the ulna, a bone in the forearm, starts out as four pieces that eventually fuse into one bone.

Elbow dysplasia occurs when certain parts of the joint develop abnormally as a dog grows. Some parts of the joint may have abnormal development, resulting in an uneven joint surface, inflammation, lameness and arthritis. It eventually results in elbow arthritis which may be associated with joint stiffness (reduced range of motion) and lameness.

The most notable symptom is a limp. Your Cocker may hold his leg out away from his body while walking, or even lift a front leg completely, putting no weight on it. Signs may be noted as early as four months old and many dogs will go through a period between six months and a year old when symptoms will be at their worst. After this, most will occasionally show less severe symptoms. As yet there is no DNA test for Elbow Dysplasia. Vets diagnose the condition by taking X-rays of the affected joint or joints.

Treatment

Treatment varies depending on the exact cause of the condition. A young dog is usually placed on a regular, low-impact exercise programme - swimming can be a good exercise. Owners must carefully manage their dog's diet and weight. Oral or injected medication such as non-steroid anti-inflammatory drugs (NSAIDS) may be necessary to make him more comfortable, prescribed to reduce pain and inflammation.

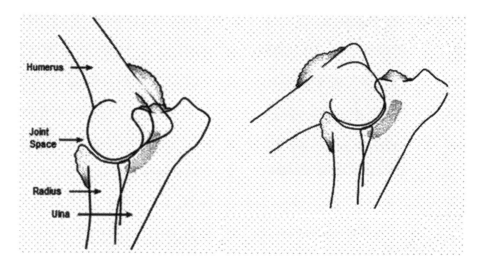

Osteoarthritic changes to the shape and structure of the elbow joint. The shaded areas on figure 4a (left, extended elbow) and 4b (right, flexed elbow) represent the changes to bone and cartilage as a result of UAP and other forms of elbow dysplasia.
Images courtesy of the British Veterinary Association.

After the age of 12 to 18 months, the dog's lameness becomes less severe and some individuals function very well. Elbow dysplasia is a lifelong problem, although some can be very effectively helped with surgery. In most cases, degenerative joint disease (arthritis) will occur as the dog gets older, regardless of the type of treatment.

Luxating Patella

Luxating patella, also called 'floating kneecap,' 'trick knee' or 'slipped stifle' is a painful condition similar to a dislocated kneecap. It is often congenital (present from birth) and typically affects small and miniature breeds, although some Cockers can also suffer from the complaint. OFA (Orthopedic Foundation of America) statistics show that the American Cocker is ranked Number Four out of all breeds for the problem in the USA, with one in seven dogs being affected. Around 2% of English Cockers tested in the USA were sufferers. Currently testing is not routinely carried out on breeding stock in the UK - although several breeders we contacted felt that it should be – but it is compulsory for AKC English Cockers in the USA.

Symptoms

A typical sign would be if your dog is running across the park when he suddenly pulls up short and yelps with pain. He might limp on three legs and then after a period of about 10 minutes, drop the affected leg and start to walk normally again. If the condition is severe, he may hold up the affected leg for a few days. Sometimes an owner may hear a 'pop' when the dog is being handled as the kneecap pops out of its normal position.

The condition can be seen as early as eight to 10 weeks old in a puppy, but is more often seen once the dog is over six months of age. Dogs that have a luxating patella on both hind legs may change their gait completely, dropping their hindquarters and holding the rear legs further out from the body as they walk. In the most extreme cases they might not even use their rear legs, but walk like a circus act by balancing on their front legs so their hindquarters don't touch the ground. Genetics, injury and malformation during growth can all cause this problem. Because the

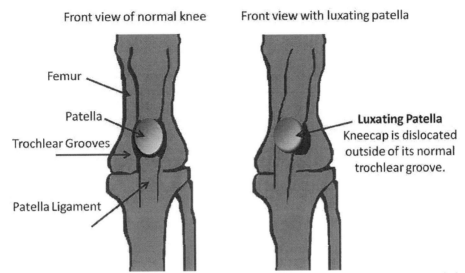

Front view of normal knee   Front view with luxating patella

Femur

Patella

Trochlear Grooves

Patella Ligament

Luxating Patella
Kneecap is dislocated
outside of its normal
trochlear groove.

most common cause is genetics, a dog with luxating patella should not be used for breeding. If you are buying a puppy, ask if there is any history in either parent.

A groove in the end of the femur (thigh bone) allows the knee cap to glide up and down when the knee joint is bent, while keeping it in place at the same time. If this groove is too shallow, the knee cap may luxate – or dislocate. It can only return to its natural position when the quadricep muscle relaxes and increases in length, which is why a dog may have to hold his leg up for some time after the dislocation. Sometimes the problem can be caused by obesity, the excess weight putting too much strain on the joint – another good reason to keep your dog's weight in check.

Treatment

There are four grades of patellar luxation, from Grade I, which causes a temporary lameness in the joint, to Grade IV, in which the patella cannot be realigned manually, and which makes the dog look bow-legged. If left untreated, the groove will become even shallower and the dog will become progressively lamer, with arthritis prematurely affecting the joint. This will cause a permanently swollen knee and reduce your dog's mobility. It is therefore important to get your dog in for a check-up with the vet ASAP if you suspect he may have a luxating patella.

In severe cases, surgery is an option, although this should not be undertaken lightly. The groove at the base of the femur may be surgically deepened to better hold the knee cap in place. This operation is known as a **trochlear modification**. The good news is that dogs generally respond well, whatever the type of surgery, and are usually completely recovered within one to two months.

Acral Mutilation Syndrome (AMS)

This is a relatively rare disease which has recently been discovered in some strains of English Cocker Spaniels, as well as other breeds such as Springer Spaniels, French Spaniels and some Pointers. The French laboratory Antagene has developed a DNA test for the gene and UK breeders of working strains are increasingly testing their dogs for the disease. According to Antagene, some 7% of Cockers - one in 14 - are carriers.

This extremely distressing condition usually shows itself when the dog is aged between three and 12 months. It causes the dog to self-mutilate by licking and biting his paws, resulting in him chewing off claws, and even toes and footpads in extreme cases. Affected pups are often smaller than unaffected littermates. The first signs are the dog over-grooming himself, licking his pads and causing ulcers and bleeding. Affected dogs walk on their severely mutilated feet without showing pain or lameness.

The technical description of AMS is 'an autosomal recessive genetic sensory neuropathy', which means that it is a recessive condition caused by a genetic fault in the nervous system. Sadly, there is neither treatment nor cure and affected dogs are put to sleep once diagnosed.

Chronic Pancreatitis

According to the Cocker Spaniel Club, some Cockers suffer from an unusual form of chronic pancreatitis, which is inflammation of the pancreas. It results in bouts of sickness, diarrhoea and abdominal pain and, in some dogs, the development of diabetes mellitus. One of our breeders had a dog die of the illness.

The pancreas is a V-shaped organ located behind the stomach and the first section of the small intestine, the duodenum. It has two main functions: it aids the metabolism of sugar in the body by producing insulin, and it helps the digestion of nutrients by producing enzymes. These enzymes help the body digest and absorb nutrients from food.

Acute pancreatitis is a sudden onset of pancreatic inflammation. Chronic pancreatitis means recurring, and this is the type which can affect some Cockers. In effect, dogs with chronic pancreatitis have multiple attacks of acute pancreatitis. This is a complicated illness. It is more common in older dogs, overweight dogs and females. There are many factors which can contribute to its development, such as:

> Certain medications
> Liver disease
> Metabolic disorders including hyperlipidaemia (high amounts of fatty acids in the blood) and hypercalcaemia (high amounts of calcium in the blood)
> Hormonal diseases such as Cushing's Disease, hypothyroidism and diabetes mellitus
> Obesity -overweight dogs appear to be more at risk
> Nutrition: dogs with high fat diets, dogs who have recently eaten rubbish or have been fed table scraps and dogs who 'steal' or are fed greasy 'people food' appear to have a higher incidence of the disease
> Genetics
> Infection
> Toxins
> Abdominal surgery, trauma to the abdomen (e.g. being hit by a car), shock or other conditions that could affect blood flow to the pancreas
> Previous pancreatitis

Symptoms

Symptoms may range from mild to very severe, some are similar to those of other diseases. They include:

- ➤ Stopping eating and drinking
- ➤ Upset stomach and abdominal pain
- ➤ Swollen abdomen
- ➤ Unusual posture, such as arching of the back
- ➤ Vomiting
- ➤ Diarrhoea
- ➤ Restlessness
- ➤ Gagging
- ➤ Fever

Animals with more severe disease can develop heart arrhythmias (irregular heartbeat), sepsis (body-wide infection), difficulty breathing and a life-threatening condition called disseminated intravascular coagulation (DIC), which results in multiple haemorrhages.

If the inflammation is severe, organs surrounding the pancreas could be 'auto digested' by pancreatic enzymes released from the damaged pancreas and become permanently damaged. Dogs with chronic pancreatitis may show signs similar to those in acute pancreatitis, but they are often milder, and severe complications are less likely.

Diagnosis and Treatment

To diagnose pancreatitis, other causes of the symptoms must be ruled out. The vet will ask for a history of your dog and then make a thorough physical exam and take a complete blood count to check for infection, anaemia and other blood issues. He will probably also do the following tests: electrolytes, specific pancreas tests, X-ray, Ultrasound and urinalysis. The goals of treatment are to rehydrate the dog, provide pain relief, control vomiting, provide nutritional support and prevent complications.

Dehydration and electrolyte imbalances are common, so extra fluids are often given either by injection or intravenously, depending on how severe the condition is. If vomiting is severe, food, water and oral medications are stopped for at least 24 hours. Depending upon the dog's response, food can be started again after a day or more. The dog is generally fed small meals of a bland, easily digestible, high-carb, low-fat food. In some cases it may be necessary to use tube feeding.

If the pancreatitis was caused by a medication, this should be stopped. If it was caused by a toxin, infection or other condition, the vet will start the appropriate treatment for the underlying condition. In rare cases where there are intestinal complications or the development of a pancreatic abscess, surgery may be necessary.

Prognosis (Outlook)

Pancreatitis can be unpredictable. Chronic pancreatitis can lead to diabetes mellitus and/or pancreatic insufficiency, also called 'maldigestion syndrome.' In pancreatic insufficiency, the nutrients in food are passed straight through the body undigested. A dog with this disease often has a ravenous appetite, diarrhoea and weight loss. Even though he is eating, he could literally starve to death.

Treatment for pancreatic insufficiency is lifelong and expensive, but it is possible. The dog's digestive enzymes are replaced through a product processed from the pancreases of pigs and cattle which contain large quantities of the digestive enzymes. A change in diet with added nutritional supplements may also be necessary.

Good habits can go a long way in preventing pancreatitis, as well as many other health conditions. Pancreatitis is often found in dogs that have eaten foods with a high fat content. The best way to ensure that your dog is a lower risk is to feed him a healthy, low fat diet. Since obese dogs are commonly afflicted with pancreatitis, a **regular exercise** routine is also important.

Pancreatitis is a degenerative, self-fuelling illness that can eventually cause irreversible damage to your dog's system. Since the symptoms of pancreatitis will usually begin long before serious damage, it is important to identify the symptoms and start treatment as soon as possible.

Hypothyroidism

Hypothyroidism is a common hormonal disorder in dogs and is due to an under-active thyroid gland. The gland (located on either side of the windpipe in the dog's throat) does not produce enough of the hormone thyroid, which controls the speed of the metabolism. Dogs with very low thyroid levels have a slow metabolic rate. It usually happens in middle-aged dogs of both sexes aged four to eight and in medium to large breeds, including some English and American Cockers.

The symptoms are often non-specific and quite gradual in onset, and they may vary depending on breed and age. Most forms of hypothyroidism are diagnosed with a blood test.

Common Symptoms and Treatment

Symptoms are:

 ➢ High blood cholesterol
 ➢ Lethargy
 ➢ Hair Loss
 ➢ Weight gain or obesity
 ➢ Dull, dry coat or excessive shedding
 ➢ Hyper pigmentation or darkening of the skin, seen in 25% of cases
 ➢ Intolerance to cold, seen in 15% of dogs with the condition

Although hypothyroidism is a type of auto-immune disease and cannot be prevented, symptoms can usually be easily diagnosed and treated. Most affected dogs can be well-managed on thyroid hormone replacement therapy tablets. The dog is placed on a daily dose of a synthetic thyroid hormone called thyroxine (levothyroxine). He is usually given a standard dose for his weight and then blood samples are periodically taken to check his response and the dose is adjusted accordingly.

Depending upon the dog's preferences and needs, the medication can be given in different forms; a solid tablet, or a liquid or gel that can be rubbed into the dog's ears. Treatment is lifelong. In some less common situations, surgery may be required to remove part or all of the thyroid gland.

Another treatment is radioiodine, where radioactive iodine is used to kill the overactive cells of the thyroid. While this is considered one of the most effective treatments, not all animals are suitable and lengthy hospitalisation is often required. Happily, once the diagnosis has been made and treatment has started, whichever treatment your dog undergoes, the majority of symptoms disappear.

By the way, **Hyper**thyroidism (as opposed to **hypo**thyroidism) is caused by the thyroid gland producing **too much** thyroid hormone. It's quite rare in dogs, more often seen in cats. A common symptom is the dog being ravenously hungry, but losing weight.

NOTE: Cockers are also thought to be one of the breeds with an increased chance of being affected by autoimmune disorders. Under normal circumstances the dog's immune system recognises tissues and cells that are part of itself, and the immune system only produces antibodies against foreign cells. However, sometimes the immune system produces antibodies which attack the dog's own body tissues. These are called 'autoantibodies' and the result is called an autoimmune disease. The reasons are as yet not fully understood.

Autoimmune diseases can result in a wide range of symptoms and a number of treatments, depending on the exact cause. According to Provet Healthcare: "The prognosis is always guarded, with only fair to poor chances of long term survival without treatment. However some dogs respond well to therapy."

Epilepsy

Thanks to **www.canineepilepsy.co.uk** for assistance with this article. If your Cocker Spaniel has epilepsy, we recommend reading this excellent website to gain a greater understanding of the illness.

Cocker Spaniels have a slightly higher risk than average of having epilepsy. The characteristics of genetic epilepsy tend to show up between 10 months and three years of age, but dogs as young as six months or as old as five years can show signs.

Anyone who has witnessed their dog having a seizure (convulsion) knows how frightening it can be. Seizures are not uncommon in dogs, but many dogs only ever have one. If your dog has had more than one seizure, it may be that he or she is epileptic. Just as with people, there are medications to control seizures in dogs, allowing them to live more normal lives.

Epilepsy means repeated seizures due to abnormal activity in the brain and is caused by an abnormality in the brain itself. It can affect any breed of dog and in fact affects around four or five dogs in every 100. In some breeds it can be hereditary. If seizures happen because of a problem somewhere else in the body, such as heart disease (which stops oxygen reaching the brain), this is not epilepsy. Your vet may do tests to try to find the reason for the epilepsy, but in many cases no cause can be identified.

Symptoms

Some dogs seem to know when they are about to have a seizure and may behave in a certain way. You will come to recognise these signs as meaning that a seizure is likely. Often dogs just seek out their owner's company and come to sit beside them when a seizure is about to start. Once the seizure starts, the dog is unconscious – he cannot hear or respond to you. Most dogs become stiff, fall onto their side and make running movements with their legs. Sometimes they will cry out and may lose control of their bowels or bladder. Most seizures last between one and three minutes - **it is worth making a note of the time the seizure starts and ends** because it often seems that a seizure goes on for a lot longer than it actually does.

Afterwards dogs behave in different ways. Some just get up and carry on with what they were doing, while others appear dazed and confused for up to 24 hours afterwards. Most commonly, dogs will be disorientated for only 10 to 15 minutes before returning to their old self. They often have a set pattern of behaviour that they follow - for example going for a drink of water or asking to go outside to the toilet. If your dog has had more than one seizure, you may well start to notice a pattern of behaviour which is typically repeated.

Most seizures occur while the dog is relaxed and resting quietly. It is very rare for one to occur while exercising. They often occur in the evening or at night. In a few dogs, seizures seem to be triggered by particular events or stress. It is common for a pattern to develop and, should your dog suffer from epilepsy, you will gradually recognise this as specific to your dog.

The most important thing is to **stay calm**. Remember that your dog is unconscious during the seizure and is not in pain or distressed. It's likely to be more distressing for you than him. Make sure he is not in a position to injure himself, for example by falling down the stairs, but otherwise do not try to interfere with him. Never try to put your hand inside his mouth during a seizure or you are very likely to get bitten.

Seizures can cause damage to the brain and if your dog has repeated occurrences, it is likely that further seizures will occur in the future. The damage caused is cumulative and after a lot of seizures there may be enough brain damage to cause early senility (with loss of learned behaviour and housetraining or behavioural changes).

It is very rare for dogs to injure themselves during a seizure. Occasionally they may bite their tongue and there may appear to be a lot of blood, but's unlikely to be serious; your dog will not swallow his tongue. If it goes on for a very long time (more than 10 minutes), his body temperature will rise, which can cause damage to other organs such as the liver and kidneys and brain. In very extreme cases, some dogs may be left in a coma after severe seizures. If you can, record your dog's seizure on a mobile phone, as it will be most useful in helping the vet.

When Should I Contact the Vet?

Generally, if your dog has a seizure lasting more than five minutes, or is having more than two or three a day, you should contact your vet. When your dog starts fitting, make a note of the time. If he comes out of it within five minutes, allow him time to recover quietly before contacting your vet. It is far better for him to recover quietly at home rather than be bundled into the car and carted off to the vet right away.

However, if your dog does not come out of the seizure within five minutes, or has repeated seizures close together, contact your vet immediately, as he or she will want to see your dog as soon as possible. If this is his first seizure, your vet may ask you to bring him in for a check-up and some routine blood tests. Always call your vet's practice before setting off to be sure that there is someone there who can help when you arrive.

There are many things other than epilepsy which cause seizures in dogs. When your vet first examines your dog, he or she will not know whether your dog has epilepsy or another illness. It's unlikely that the vet will see your dog during a seizure, so it is **vital** that you're able to describe in some detail just what happens. You might want to make notes or record it on your mobile phone.

Your vet may need to run a range of tests to ensure that there is no other cause of the seizures. These may include blood tests, possibly X-rays, and maybe even a scan (MRI) of your dog's brain. If no other cause can be found, then a diagnosis of epilepsy may be made. If your Cocker Spaniel already has epilepsy, remember these key points:

- ➢ **Don't change or stop any medication without consulting your vet**
- ➢ **See your vet at least once a year for follow-up visits**
- ➢ **Be sceptical of 'magic cure' treatments**

Remember, live **with** epilepsy not **for** epilepsy. With the proper medical treatment, most epileptic dogs have far more good days than bad ones. Enjoy all those good days.

Treatment

It is not usually possible to remove the cause of the seizures, so your vet will use medication to control them. Treatment will not cure the disease, but it will manage the signs – even a well-controlled epileptic will have occasional seizures. As yet there is no cure for epilepsy, so don't be tempted with 'instant cures' from the internet.

There are many drugs used in the control of epilepsy in people, but very few of these are suitable for long-term use in a dog. Two of the most common are Phenobarbital and Potassium Bromide (some dogs can have negative results with Phenobarbital). There are also a number of holistic remedies advertised, but we have no experience of them or any idea if any are effective. Many epileptic dogs require a combination of one or more types of drug to achieve the most effective control of their seizures. Treatment is decided on an individual basis and it may take some time to find the best combination and dose of drugs for your pet. You need patience when managing an epileptic pet. It is important that medication is given at the same time each day.

Once your dog has been on treatment for a while, he will become dependent on the levels of drug in his blood at all times to control seizures. If you miss a dose of treatment, blood levels can drop and this may be enough to trigger a seizure. Each epileptic dog is an individual and a treatment plan will be designed specifically for him. It will be based on the severity and frequency of the seizures and how they respond to different medications.

Keep a record of events in your dog's life, note down dates and times of episodes and record when you have given medication. Each time you visit your vet, take this diary along with you so he or she can see how your dog has been since his last check-up. If seizures are becoming more frequent, it may be necessary to change the medication. The success or otherwise of treatment may depend on YOU keeping a close eye on your Cocker Spaniel to see if there are any physical or behavioural changes.

It is rare for epileptic dogs to stop having seizures altogether. However, provided your dog is checked regularly by your vet to make sure that the drugs are not causing any side effects, there is a good chance that he will live a full and happy life. Visit www.canineepilepsy.co.uk for more information.

Heart Problems

Heart problems are relatively common among the canine population in general. Heart failure, or **congestive heart failure (CHF)**, occurs when the heart is not able to pump enough blood around the dog's body.

The heart is a mechanical pump. It receives blood in one half and forces it through the lungs, then the other half pumps the blood through the entire body. The two most common forms of heart failure in dogs are Degenerative Valvular Disease (DVD) and Dilated Cardiomyopathy (DCM), also known as an enlarged heart.

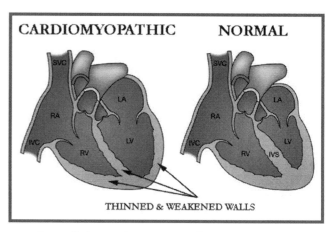

According to Provet Healthcare, Cockers are one of the more common breeds to present at vets with DCM, which often affects male dogs aged between four and six years. Some Cockers can also suffer from **Pulmonic Stenosis,** which is a congenital narrowing in the region of the pulmonary valve. However, most dogs don't require any medical treatment. Smaller breeds more often suffer from mitral valve disease.

In people, heart disease usually involves the arteries that supply blood to the heart muscle becoming hardened over time, causing the heart muscles to receive less blood than they need. Starved of oxygen, the result is often a heart attack. In dogs, hardening of the arteries (arteriosclerosis) and heart attacks are very rare. However, heart disease is quite common.

In dogs, heart disease is often seen as heart failure, which means that the muscles 'give out.' This is usually caused by one chamber or side of the heart being required to do more than it is physically able to do. It may be that excessive force is required to pump the blood through an area and over time the muscles fail.

Unlike a heart attack in humans, heart failure in the dog is a slow insidious process that occurs over months or years. In these cases, once symptoms are noted, they will usually worsen over time until the dog requires treatment.

Symptoms

> **Tiredness**
> **Decreased activity levels**
> **Restlessness,** pacing around instead of settling down to sleep
> **Intermittent coughing** - especially during exertion or excitement. This tends to occur at night, sometimes about two hours after the dog goes to bed or when he wakes up in the morning. This coughing is an attempt to clear fluid in the lungs and is often the first clinical sign of a valve disorder. As the condition worsens, other symptoms may appear:
> **Lack of appetite**
> **Rapid breathing**
> **Abdominal swelling (due to fluid)**
> **Noticeable loss of weight**
> **Fainting (syncope)**
> **Paleness**

Diagnosis and Treatment

If your dog is exhibiting a range of the above symptoms, the vet may suspect congestive heart failure. He will carry out tests to make sure. These may include listening to the heart, chest X-rays, blood tests, electrocardiogram (a record of your dog's heartbeat) or an echocardiogram (ultrasound of the heart).

If the heart problem is due to an enlarged heart (DCM) or valve disease, the condition cannot be reversed. Instead, treatment focuses on managing the symptoms with various medications, which may change over time as the condition worsens. The vet may also prescribe a special low salt diet for your dog, as sodium (found in salt) determines the amount of water in the blood. The amount of exercise will also have to be controlled. There is some evidence that vitamin and other supplements may be beneficial, discuss this with your vet.

The prognosis for dogs with congestive heart failure depends on the cause and severity, as well as their response to treatment. Sadly, CHF is progressive, so your dog can never recover from the condition. But once diagnosed, he can live a longer, more comfortable life with the right medication and regular check-ups.

Heart Murmurs

Heart murmurs are not uncommon in dogs. Our dog was diagnosed with a Grade 2 murmur several years ago and, of course, your heart sinks when the vet gives you the terrible news. But once the shock is over, it's important to realise that there are several different severities of the condition and, at its mildest, it is no great cause for concern.

Our dog is 11 now and, as the saying goes: "fit as a butcher's dog," with seemingly no signs of the heart murmur (except through the vet's stethoscope). However, we are always on alert for a dry, racking cough, which is a sign of fluid in the lungs. So far it hasn't happened, touch wood.

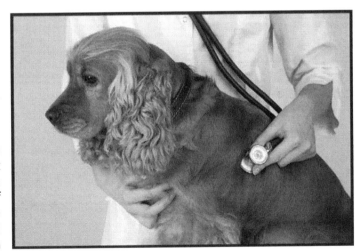

Literally, a heart murmur is a specific sound heard through a stethoscope, it results from the blood flowing faster than normal within the heart itself or in one of the two major arteries. Instead of the normal 'lubb dupp' noise, an additional sound can be heard that can vary from a mild 'pshhh' to a loud 'whoosh'.

The different grades are:

- ◆ **Grade 1**—barely audible
- ◆ **Grade 2**—soft, but easily heard with a stethoscope
- ◆ **Grade 3**—intermediate loudness; most murmurs which are related to the mechanics of blood circulation are at least grade III
- ◆ **Grade 4**—loud murmur that radiates widely, often including opposite side of chest
- ◆ **Grades 5 and Grade 6**—very loud, audible with stethoscope barely touching the chest; the vibration is also strong enough to be felt through the animal's chest wall

Murmurs are caused by a number of factors; it may be a problem with the heart valves or could be due to some other condition, such as hyperthyroidism, anaemia or heartworm. In puppies, there are two major types of heart murmurs, and they will probably be detected by your vet at the first or second vaccinations. The most common type is called an innocent "flow murmur." This type of murmur is soft - typically Grade 2 or less - and is not caused by underlying heart disease. An innocent flow murmur typically disappears by four to five months of age.

However if a puppy has a loud murmur - Grade 3 or louder - or if the heart murmur is still easily heard with a stethoscope after four or five months of age, the likelihood of the puppy having an underlying congenital (from birth) heart problem becomes much higher. The thought of a puppy having congenital heart disease is worrying, but it is important to remember that the disease will not affect all puppies' life expectancy or quality of life.

A heart murmur can also develop suddenly in an adult dog with no prior history of the problem. This is typically due to heart disease that develops with age. In toy and small breeds, a heart murmur may develop in middle-aged to older dogs due to an age-related thickening and degeneration of one of the valves in the heart, the mitral valve. (This is the type our dog has). This thickening of the valve prevents it from closing properly and as a result it starts to leak, this is known as mitral valve disease. The more common type of heart disease affecting larger dog breeds in middle age is Dilated Cardiomyopathy (DCM).

Canine Diabetes

Cocker Spaniels are not regarded as one of the breeds having an increased risk of contracting canine diabetes. However, it can affect dogs of all breeds, sizes and both genders and obese dogs more than ones of a normal weight. There are two types:

> ➤ *diabetes mellitus*
> ➤ *diabetes insipidus*

Diabetes mellitus (sugar diabetes) is the most common form and affects one in 500 dogs. Thanks to modern veterinary medicine, the condition is now treatable and need not shorten a dog's lifespan or interfere with his quality of life. Diabetic dogs undergoing treatment now have the same life expectancy as non-diabetic dogs of the same age and gender.

However, if left untreated, the disease can lead to cataracts, increasing weakness in the legs (neuropathy), other ailments and even death. In dogs, diabetes is typically seen anywhere between the ages of four to 14, with a peak at seven to nine years.

Both males and females can develop it; unspayed females have a slightly higher risk. The typical canine diabetes sufferer is middle-aged, female and overweight, but there are also juvenile cases.

Diabetes insipidus is caused by a lack of vasopressin, a hormone which controls the kidneys' absorption of water. *Diabetes mellitus* occurs when the dog's body does not produce enough insulin and cannot successfully process sugars. Dogs, like us, get their energy by converting the food they eat into sugars, mainly glucose. This glucose travels in the dog's bloodstream and individual cells then remove some of that glucose from the blood to use for energy. The substance that allows the cells to take glucose from the blood is a protein called *insulin.*

Insulin is created by beta cells that are located in the pancreas, next to the stomach. Almost all diabetic dogs have Type 1 diabetes; their pancreas does not produce any insulin. Without it, the cells have no way to use the glucose that is in the bloodstream, so the cells 'starve' while the glucose level in the blood rises. Your vet will use blood samples and urine samples to check glucose concentrations in order to diagnose diabetes. Early treatment helps to prevent further complications developing.

Symptoms of Diabetes Mellitus

> ➢ Extreme thirst
> ➢ Excessive urination
> ➢ Weight loss
> ➢ Increased appetite
> ➢ Coat in poor condition
> ➢ Lethargy
> ➢ Vision problems due to cataracts

Some diabetic dogs go blind. Cataracts may develop due to high blood glucose levels causing water to build up in the eyes' lenses. This leads to swelling, rupture of the lens fibres and the development of cataracts. In many cases, the cataracts can be surgically removed to bring sight back to the dog. Vision is restored in 75% to 80% of diabetic dogs that undergo cataract removal. However, some dogs may stay blind even after the cataracts are gone, and some cataracts simply cannot be removed. Blind dogs are often able to get around surprisingly well, particularly in a familiar home.

Treatment and Exercise

Treatment starts with the right diet. Your vet will prescribe meals low in fat and sugars. He will also recommend medication. Many cases of canine diabetes can be successfully treated with diet and medication. More severe cases may require insulin injections. In the newly-diagnosed dog, insulin therapy begins at home.

Normally, after a week of treatment, you return to the vet who will do a series of blood sugar tests over a 12-14 hour period to see when the blood glucose peaks and when it hits its lows. Adjustments are then made to the dosage and timing of the injections. Your vet will explain how to prepare and inject the insulin. You may be asked to collect urine samples using a test strip of paper that indicates the glucose levels in urine.

If your dog is already having insulin injections, beware of a 'miracle cure' offered on some internet sites. It does not exist. There is no diet or vitamin supplement which can reduce your dog's dependence on insulin injections because vitamins and minerals cannot do what insulin does in the dog's body. If you think that your dog needs a supplement, discuss it with your vet first to make sure that it does not interfere with any other medication.

Managing your dog's diabetes also means managing his activity level. Exercise burns up blood glucose the same way that insulin does. If your dog is on insulin, any active exercise on top of the insulin might cause him to have a severe low blood glucose episode, called 'hypoglycaemia'.

Keep your dog on a reasonably consistent exercise routine. Your usual insulin dose will take that amount of exercise into account. If you plan to take your dog out for some extra demanding exercise, such as running round with other dogs, give him only half of his usual insulin dose.

Tips

➢ You can usually buy specially formulated diabetes dog food from your vet

➢ You should feed the same type and amount of food at the same time every day

➢ Most vets recommend twice-a-day feeding for diabetic pets. It is OK if your dog prefers to eat more often

➢ If you have other pets in the home, they should also be placed on a twice-a-day feeding schedule, so that the diabetic dog cannot eat from their bowls. Help your dog to achieve the best possible blood glucose control by not feeding him table scraps or treats between meals

➢ Watch for signs that your dog is starting to drink more water than usual. Call the vet if you see this happening, as it may mean that the insulin dose needs adjusting. Remember these simple points:

Food raises blood glucose

Insulin and exercise lower blood glucose

Keep them in balance

For more information on canine diabetes visit **www.caninediabetes.org**

Canine Cancer

This is the biggest single killer of dogs of whatever breed and will claim the lives of one in four dogs. It is the cause of nearly half the deaths of all dogs aged 10 years and older, according to the American Veterinary Medical Association.

Symptoms

Early detection is critical, and some things to look out for are:

➢ Swellings anywhere on the body
➢ Lumps in a dog's armpit or under his jaw
➢ Sores that don't heal
➢ Bad breath
➢ Weight loss
➢ Poor appetite, difficulty swallowing or excessive drooling
➢ Changes in exercise or stamina level

"I DON'T SEE TABLE SCRAPS."

➤ Laboured breathing
➤ Change in bowel or bladder habits

If your dog has been spayed or neutered, the risk of certain cancers decreases. These cancers include uterine and breast/mammary cancer in females, and testicular cancer in males (if the dog was neutered before he was six months old). Along with controlling the pet population, spaying is especially important because mammary cancer in female dogs is fatal in about 50% of all cases.

Diagnosis and Treatment

Just because your dog has a skin growth doesn't mean that it's cancerous. As with humans, tumours may be benign (harmless) or malignant (harmful).

Your vet will probably confirm the tumour using X-rays, blood tests and possibly ultrasounds. He or she will then decide whether it is benign or malignant via a biopsy in which a tissue sample is taken from your dog and examined under a microscope. If your dog is diagnosed with cancer, there is hope. Advances in veterinary medicine and technology offer various treatment options, including chemotherapy, radiation and surgery. Unlike with humans, a dog's hair will not fall out with chemotherapy.

Canine cancer is growing at an ever-increasing rate. One of the difficulties is that your pet cannot tell you when a cancer is developing, but if cancers can be detected early enough through a physical or behavioural change, they often respond well to treatment.

Over recent years, we have all become more aware of the risk factors for human cancer. Responding to these by changing our habits is having a significant impact on human health. For example, stopping smoking, protecting ourselves from over-exposure to strong sunlight and eating a healthy, balanced diet all help to reduce cancer rates. We know to keep a close eye on ourselves, go for regular health checks and report any lumps and bumps to our doctors as soon as they appear. Increased cancer awareness is definitely improving human health. The same is true with your dog.

While it is impossible to completely prevent cancer from occurring, a healthy lifestyle with a balanced diet and regular exercise can help to reduce the risk - as can being aware of any new lumps and bumps on your dog's body and any changes in his behaviour. The success of treatment will depend on the type of cancer, the treatment used and how early the tumour is found. The sooner treatment begins, the greater the chances of success.

One of the best things you can do for your dog is to keep a close eye on him for any tell-tale signs. This shouldn't be too difficult and can be done as part of your regular handling and grooming. If you notice any new bumps, for example, monitor them over a period of days to see if there is a change in their appearance or size. If there is, then make an appointment to see your vet as soon as possible. It might only be a cyst, but better to be safe than sorry.

Research into earlier diagnosis and improved treatments is being conducted at veterinary schools and companies all over the world. Advances in biology are producing a steady flow of new tests and treatments which are now becoming available to improve survival rates and canine cancer care. If your dog is diagnosed with cancer, do not despair, there are many options and new, improved treatments are constantly being introduced.

Our Happy Ending

We know from personal experience that canine cancer can be successfully treated if it is diagnosed early enough. Our dog was diagnosed with T-cell lymphoma when he was four years old. We had noticed a black lump on his anus which grew to the size of a small grape. We took him to the vet within the first few days of seeing the lump and, after a test, he was diagnosed with the dreaded T-cell lymphoma. This is a particularly nasty and aggressive form of cancer which can spread to the lymph system and is often fatal for dogs.

As soon as the diagnosis was confirmed, our vet Graham operated and removed the lump. He also had to remove one of his anal glands, but as dogs have two this was not a serious worry. Afterwards, we were on tenterhooks, not knowing if another lump would grow or if the cancer had already spread to his lymph system.

After a few months, Max had another blood test and was finally given the all-clear. Max is now happy, healthy and 11 years old. We were very lucky. I would strongly advise anyone who suspects that their dog has cancer to get him or her to your local vet as soon as possible.

Disclaimer: The author of this book is not a veterinarian. This chapter is intended to give owners an indication of some of the illnesses which may affect their dog or dogs and the symptoms to look out for. If you have any concerns regarding the health of your dog, our advice is always the same: consult a veterinarian.

11. Skin and Allergies

Allergies are a growing concern for owners of many breeds. Visit a busy vet's surgery these days – especially in spring and summer – and it's likely that one or more of the dogs will be there because of some type of sensitivity. When bred from good stock, Cockers are generally healthy dogs with not too many allergies and skin problems reported. However, log on to any online Cocker Spaniel forum and you'll see there are plenty of itchy dogs out there – and ear infections can be a recurring problem within the breed.

Some breeds are more prone to develop issues, and while the Cocker is not particularly regarded as one of them, any individual dog can have issues. Skin conditions, allergies and intolerances are on the increase in the canine world as well as the human world. How many children did you hear of having asthma or a peanut allergy when you were at school? Not many, I'll bet, yet allergies and adverse reactions are now relatively common – and it's the same with dogs. As yet the reasons are not clear; it could be to do with breeding, but there is no clear scientific evidence to back this up.

This is a complicated topic and a whole book could be written on this subject alone. While many dogs have no problems at all, some suffer from sensitive skin, allergies, yeast infections and/or skin disorders, causing them to scratch, bite or lick themselves excessively on the paws and other areas. Symptoms may vary from mild itchiness to a severe reaction.

Only a handful of this book's contributing breeders have come across problems. Working Cocker breeder Andy Platt, of Scotland, said: "Some Cockers are prone to nettle rash, which can be treated with antihistamines. Fox (sarcoptic) mange can also be a problem as Cockers love hunting through thick cover. This can easily be treated with Aludex or Advocate if identified early enough."

Another working breeder said: "I have found a couple of my lemon roans to have dust mite allergies and they have been the ones needing regular ear care. I have also had a Cocker (white and black ticked) to have an allergy to lamb." A third working Cocker breeder with two decades of experience agreed: "More Cockers do seem to have an intolerance of dust mites, resulting in constant itching and nibbling of the feet, as well as ear issues. Another issue is bad teeth; for some reason lots of Cockers have bad teeth."

Another working breeder added: "I have experienced hair loss on one dog; there were no obvious reasons for this. Washing the dog in a dermatological antiseptic shampoo prescribed by the vet allowed the hair to grow back."

A highly experienced show breeder has come across an entirely different problem: "The main issue we have come across is when there is an infection with the skin just below the bottom jaw line. This is sometimes known as 'Cocker mouth'. To help prevent this, keep the area clipped short (we use a #40 clipper blade) and keep the area clean. Hibiscrub is freely available and is an excellent product."

If you haven't already bought your puppy, skin issues would be one topic to ask the breeder about. One quite common condition - particularly among show Cockers - is ear infections due to their long, floppy Spaniel ears – more about these later.

As with humans, the skin is the dog's largest organ. It acts as the protective barrier between your dog's internal organs and the outside world; it also regulates temperature and provides the sense of touch. Surprisingly, a dog's skin is actually thinner than ours, and it is made up of three layers:

1. **Epidermis** or outer layer, the one that bears the brunt of your dog's contact with the outside world. Humans have between 10 to15 layers in the stratum corneum (outer part of the epidermis) and canines have about five. As well as thin skin, dogs' pH is more alkaline, making their skin not only delicate, but susceptible to absorbing undesirable toxins, etc.

2. **Dermis** is the extremely tough layer mostly made up of collagen, a strong and fibrous protein. This is where blood vessels deliver nutrients and oxygen to the skin, and it also acts as your dog's thermostat by allowing his body to release or keep in heat, depending on the outside temperature and your dog's activity level

3. **Subcutis** is a dense layer of fatty tissue that allows your dog's skin to move independently from the muscle layers below it, as well as providing insulation and support for the skin

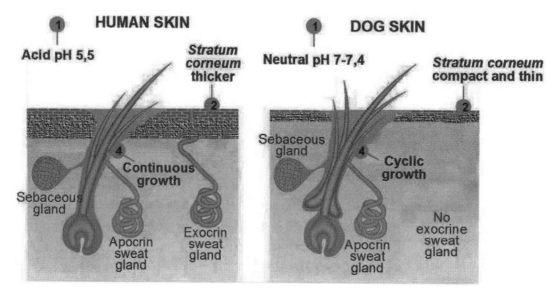

Human allergies often trigger a reaction within the respiratory system, causing us to wheeze or sneeze, whereas allergies or hypersensitivities in a dog often cause a reaction in his or her **skin.**

Skin can be affected from the **inside** by things that your dog eats or drinks.

Skin can be affected from the **outside** by fleas, parasites, inhaled or contact allergies triggered by grass, pollen, man-made chemicals, dust, mould etc. These environmental allergies are especially common in some Terriers as well as the Miniature Schnauzer, Bulldog and certain other breeds.

Skin problems may be the result of one or more of a wide range of causes - and the list of potential remedies and treatments is even longer. It's by no means possible to cover all of them in this chapter. The aim here is to give a broad outline of some of the ailments most likely to affect Cockers and how to deal with them. We have also included remedies tried with some success by ourselves (our dog has skin issues) and other owners of dogs with skin problems, as well as advice from a holistic specialist.

Like all dogs, Cockers can suffer from food allergies or intolerances as well as environmental allergies. Canine skin disorders are a complex subject. Some dogs can run through fields and brush, dig holes and roll around in the grass with no after-effects at all. Others may spend more time indoors and have an excellent diet, but still experience severe itching.

Pictured are Tracey Simpson's Bravialis Gundogs Betty and Jack, aged nearly two, who can run across the moors all day long without any problems at all.

This information is not intended to take the place of professional help. We are not animal health experts and you should always contact your vet as soon as your dog appears physically unwell or uncomfortable. This is particularly true with skin conditions:

If a vet can find the source of the problem early on, there is more chance of successfully treating it before it has chance to develop into a more serious condition with secondary issues.

There is anecdotal evidence from some owners that switching to a raw diet or raw meaty bones diet can significantly help some dogs with skin issues as well as those with food intolerances or allergies. See **Chapter 7. Feeding a Cocker** for more information.

One of the difficulties with this type of ailment is that the exact cause is often difficult to diagnose, as the symptoms may also be common to other issues. If environmental allergies are involved, some specific tests are available costing hundreds of pounds or dollars. You will have to take your vet's advice on this, as the tests are not always conclusive and if the answer is dust or pollen, it can be difficult to keep your lively dog away from the triggers while still having a normal life - unless you and your Cocker spend all your time in a spotlessly clean city apartment (which is, frankly, unlikely!) It is often a question of managing a skin condition, rather than curing it.

Skin issues and allergies often develop in adolescence or early adulthood, which may be anything from a few months to two or three years old. Our dog Max was perfectly normal until he reached two when he began scratching, triggered by environmental allergies - most likely pollen. He's now 11 and over the years he's been on various different remedies which have all worked for a time. As his allergies are seasonal, he normally does not have any medication between October and March. But come spring and as sure as daffodils are daffodils, he starts scratching again. Luckily, they are manageable and Max lives a happy, normal life.

Allergies and their treatment can cause a lot of stress for dogs and owners alike. The number one piece of advice is that if you suspect your Cocker has an allergy or skin problem, try to deal with it right away - either via your vet or natural remedies – before the all-too-familiar scenario kicks in and it develops into a chronic (recurring and long term) condition.

Whatever the cause, before a vet can diagnose the problem you have to be prepared to tell him or her all about your dog's diet, exercise regime, habits, medical history and local environment. He or she will then carry out a thorough physical examination, possibly followed by further (expensive) tests, before treatment can be prescribed. You'll have to decide whether these tests are worth it and whether they are likely to discover the exact root of the problem.

Types of Allergies

'*Canine dermatitis*' means inflammation of a dog's skin and it can be triggered by numerous things, but the most common by far is allergies. Vets estimate that one in four dogs at their clinics is there because of some kind of allergy.

Symptoms

- ➢ Chewing on paws
- ➢ Rubbing the face on the carpet
- ➢ Scratching the body
- ➢ Scratching or biting the anus
- ➢ Itchy ears, head shaking
- ➢ Hair loss
- ➢ Mutilated skin with sore or discoloured patches or hot spots

A Cocker who is allergic to something will show it through skin problems and itching; your vet may call this '*pruritus'*. It may seem logical that if a dog is allergic to something he inhales, like certain pollen grains, his nose will run; if he's allergic to something he eats, he may vomit, or if allergic to an insect bite, he may develop a swelling. But in practice this is seldom the case. The skin is an organ and with dogs it is this organ which is often affected by allergies. So instead, he will have a mild to severe itching sensation over his body and maybe a chronic ear infection.

Dogs with allergies often chew their feet until they are sore and red. You may see your Cocker rubbing his face on the carpet or couch or scratching his belly and flanks. Because the ear glands produce too much wax in response to the allergy, ear infections can occur, with bacteria and yeast - which is a fungus - often thriving in the excessive wax and debris.

But your Cocker doesn't have to suffer from allergies to get ear infections, the lack of air flow under the floppy, hairy ears make the breed prone to the condition. By the way, if your dog does develop a yeast infection and you decide to switch to a grain-free diet, try and avoid those which are potato-based, as these contain high levels of starch.

Holistic vet Dr Jodie Gruenstern says: "Grains and other starches have a negative impact on gut health, creating insulin resistance and inflammation. It's estimated that up to 80% of the immune system resides within the gastrointestinal system; building a healthy gut supports a more appropriate immune response. The importance of choosing fresh proteins and healthy fats over processed, starchy diets (such as kibble) can't be overemphasized."

An allergic dog may cause skin lesions or 'hot spots' by constant chewing and scratching. Sometimes he will lose hair, which can be patchy, leaving a mottled appearance. The skin itself may be dry and crusty, reddened, swollen or oily, depending on the dog. It is very common to get secondary bacterial skin infections due to these self-inflicted wounds. An allergic dog's body is reacting to certain molecules called 'allergens.' These may come from:

- ➤ Trees
- ➤ Grass
- ➤ Pollens
- ➤ Foods and food additives, such as specific meats, grains or colourings
- ➤ Milk products
- ➤ Fabrics, such as wool or nylon
- ➤ Rubber and plastics
- ➤ House dust and dust mites
- ➤ Mould
- ➤ Flea bites
- ➤ Chemical products used around the house

These allergens may be **inhaled** as the dog breathes, **ingested** as the dog eats or caused by **contact** with the dog's body when he walks or rolls. However they arrive, they all cause the immune system to produce a protein (IgE), which causes various irritating chemicals, such as histamine, to be released. In dogs these chemical reactions and cell types occur in sizeable amounts only within the skin, hence the scratching.

Inhalant Allergies (Atopy)

The most common allergies in dogs are inhalant and seasonal (at least at first, some allergies may worsen). Substances which can cause an allergic reaction in dogs are similar to those causing problems for humans. While any dog can suffer from them, some breeds may have a higher incidence of them and there is some evidence that this includes the American Cocker (pictured).

A clue to diagnosing these allergies is to look at the timing of the reaction. Does it happen all year round? If so, this may be mould, dust or some other trigger which is permanently in the environment. If the reaction is seasonal, then pollens may well be the culprit.

A diagnosis can be made by allergy testing - either a blood or skin test where a small amount of antigen is injected into the dog's skin to test for a reaction. The blood test can give false positives, so the skin test is many veterinarians' preferred method.

Whether or not you take this route will be your decision; allergy testing is not cheap, it takes time and may require your dog to be sedated. And there's also no point doing it if you are not going to go along with the recommended method of treatment afterwards, which is immunotherapy, or **'hyposensitisation',** and this can also be an expensive and lengthy process.

It consists of a series of injections made specifically for your dog and administered over weeks or months to make him more tolerant of specific allergens. It may have to be done by a veterinary dermatologist if your vet is not familiar with the treatment. Vets in the US claim that success rates can be as high as 75% of cases. These tests work best when carried out during the season when the allergies are at their worst. But before you get to this stage, your vet will have had to rule out other potential causes, such as fleas or mites, fungal, yeast or bacterial infections and hypothyroidism. Due to the time and cost involved in skin testing, most mild cases of allergies are treated with a combination of avoidance, fatty acids and antihistamines.

Environmental or Contact Irritations

These are a direct reaction to something the dog physically comes into contact with. It could be as simple as grass, specific plants, dust or other animals. If the trigger is grass or other outdoor materials, the allergies are often seasonal. The dog may require treatment - often tablets, shampoo or localised cortisone spray - for spring and summer, but be perfectly fine with no medication for the other half of the year. This is the case with our dog. (Pictured are dust mites).

If you suspect your Cocker may have outdoor contact allergies, here is one very good tip guaranteed to reduce his scratching: get him to stand in a tray or large bowl of water on your return from a walk. Washing his feet and under his belly will get rid of some of the pollen and other allergens, which in turn will reduce his scratching and biting. This can help to reduce the allergens to a tolerable level. Other possible triggers include dry carpet shampoos, caustic irritants, new carpets, cement dust, washing powders or fabric conditioners. If you wash your dog's bedding or if he sleeps on your bed, use a fragrance-free - if possible, hypoallergenic - laundry detergent and avoid fabric conditioner.

The irritation may be restricted to one part of the dog – e.g. the underneath of the paws or belly - which has touched the offending object. Symptoms are skin irritation - either a general problem or specific hotspots - itching (pruritis) and sometimes hair loss. Readers sometimes report to us that their dog will incessantly lick one part of the body, often the paws, anus, belly or back.

Flea Bite Allergies

These are a very common canine allergy and affect dogs of all breeds. To compound the problem, many dogs with flea allergies also have inhalant allergies. Flea bite allergy is typically seasonal, worse during summer and autumn – peak time for fleas - and is worse in warmer climates where fleas are prevalent.

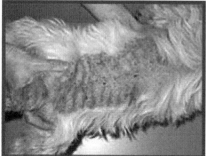

This type of allergy is not the flea itself, but to proteins in flea saliva, which are deposited under the dog's skin when the insect feeds. Just one bite to an allergic dog will cause intense and long-lasting itching. If affected, the dog will try to bite at the base of his tail and scratch a lot. Most of the damage is done by the dog's scratching, rather than the flea bite, and can result in his fur falling out or skin abrasions.

Some Cockers will develop hot spots. These can occur anywhere, but are often along the back and base of the tail. Flea bite allergies can only be totally prevented by keeping all fleas away from the dog. Various flea prevention treatments are available – see the section on **Parasites**. If you suspect your dog may be allergic to fleas, consult your vet for the proper diagnosis and medication.

Diet and Food Allergies

Food is the third most common cause of allergies in dogs. Cheap dog foods bulked up with grains and other ingredients can cause problems. Some dogs have problems with wheat and other grains. If you feed your dog a dry commercial dog food, make sure that it's a high quality, preferably hypoallergenic, one and that the first ingredient listed on the sack is meat or poultry, not grain.

Without the correct food, a dog's whole body - not just his skin and coat - will continuously be under stress and this manifests itself in a number of ways. The symptoms of food allergies are similar to those of most allergies:

> ➢ Itchy skin affecting primarily the face, feet, ears, forelegs, armpits and anus
> ➢ Excessive scratching
> ➢ Chronic or recurring ear infections
> ➢ Hair loss
> ➢ Hot spots
> ➢ Skin infections that clear up with antibiotics, but return after the antibiotics have finished
> ➢ Possible increased bowel movements, maybe twice as many as normal

The bodily process which occurs when an animal has a reaction to a particular food agent is not very well understood. As many other problems can cause similar symptoms to food allergies (and also the fact that many sufferers also have other allergies), it is important that a vet identifies and treats any other problems before food allergies are diagnosed. Atopy, flea bite allergies, intestinal parasite hypersensitivities, sarcoptic mange and yeast or bacterial infections can all cause similar symptoms. This can be an anxious time for owners as vets try one thing after another to get to the bottom of the allergy.

The normal method for diagnosing a food allergy is elimination. Once all other causes have been ruled out or treated, then a food trial is the next step – and that's no picnic for owners either. See **Chapter 7. Feeding a Cocker** for more information. As with other allergies, dogs may have short-term relief by taking fatty acids, antihistamines, and steroids, but removing the offending items from the diet is the only permanent solution.

Acute Moist Dermatitis (Hot Spots)

Acute moist dermatitis or 'hot spots' are not uncommon. A hot spot can appear suddenly and is a raw, inflamed and often bleeding area of skin. The area becomes moist and painful and begins spreading due to continual licking and chewing. They can become large, red, irritated lesions in a short pace of time. The cause is often a local reaction to an insect bite; fleas, ticks, biting flies and even mosquitoes have been known to cause acute moist dermatitis. Other causes of hot spots include:

> ➢ Allergies - inhalant allergies and food allergies
> ➢ Mites
> ➢ Ear infections
> ➢ Poor grooming
> ➢ Burs or plant awns
> ➢ Anal gland disease
> ➢ Hip dysplasia or other types of arthritis and degenerative joint disease

Diagnosis and Treatment - The good news is that, once diagnosed and with the right treatment, hot spots disappear as soon as they appeared. The underlying cause should be identified and treated, if possible. Check with your vet before treating your Cocker for fleas and ticks at the same time as other medical treatment (such as anti-inflammatory medications and/or antibiotics), as he or she will probably advise you to wait.

Treatments may come in the form of injections, tablets or creams – or your dog might need a combination of them. Your vet will probably clip and clean the affected area to help the effectiveness of any spray or ointment and your poor dog might also have to wear an E-collar until the condition subsides, but usually this does not take long.

Parasites

Demodectic Mange

Demodectic mange is also known as red mange, follicular mange or puppy mange. It is caused by the tiny mite Demodex canis – pictured - which can only be seen through a microscope. The mites actually live inside the hair follicles on the bodies of virtually every adult dog, and most humans, without causing any harm or irritation. In humans, the mites are found in the skin, eyelids and the creases of the nose … try not to think about that!

The demodectic mite spends its entire life on the host dog. Eggs hatch and mature from larvae to nymphs to adults in 20 to 35 days and the mites are transferred directly from the mother to the puppies within the first week of life by direct physical contact. Demodectic mange is not a disease of poorly kept or dirty kennels. It is generally a disease of young dogs with inadequate or poorly developed immune systems (or older dogs suffering from a suppressed immune system).

Vets currently believe that virtually every mother carries and transfers mites to her puppies, and most are immune to the mite's effects, but a few puppies are not and they develop full-blown mange. They may have a few (less than five) isolated lesions and this is known as localised mange

– often around the head. This happens in around 90% of cases, but in the other 10% of cases, it develops into generalised mange which covers the entire body or region of the body. This is most likely to develop in puppies with parents that have suffered from mange. Most lesions in either form develop after four months of age. It can also develop around the time when females have their first season, typically around nine months old, and may be due to a slight dip in the bitch's immune system.

Symptoms – Bald patches are usually the first sign, usually accompanied by crusty, red skin which sometimes appears greasy or wet. Usually hair loss begins around the muzzle, eyes and other areas on the head. The lesions may or may not itch. In localised mange, a few circular crusty areas appear, most frequently on the head and front legs of three to six-month-old puppies. Most will self-heal as the puppies become older and develop their own immunity, but a persistent problem needs treatment.

With generalised mange there are bald patches over the entire coat, including the head, neck, body, legs, and feet. The skin on the head, side and back is crusty, often inflamed and oozes a clear fluid. The skin itself will often be oily to touch and there is usually a secondary bacterial infection. Some puppies can become quite ill and can develop a fever, lose their appetites and become lethargic. If you suspect your puppy has generalised demodectic mange, get him to a vet straight away.

There is also a condition called pododermatitis, when the mange affects a puppy's paws. It can cause bacterial infections and be very uncomfortable, even painful. The symptoms of this mange include hair loss on the paws, swelling of the paws (especially around the nail beds) and red/hot/inflamed areas which are often infected. Treatment is always recommended, and it can take several rounds to clear it up.

Diagnosis and Treatment – The vet will normally diagnose demodectic mange after he or she has taken a skin scraping. As these mites are present on every dog, they do not necessarily mean the dog has mange. Only when the mite is coupled with lesions will the vet diagnose mange. Treatment usually involves topical (on the skin) medication and sometimes tablets. Localised demodectic mange often resolves itself as the puppy grows.

If the dog has just one or two lesions, these can usually be successfully treated using specific creams and spot treatments. With generalised demodectic mange, treatment can be lengthy and expensive. The vet might prescribe Amitraz anti-parasitic dips every two weeks. This is an organophosphate available on prescription under the name Aludex (UK) or Mitaban (USA). Owners should always wear rubber gloves when treating their dog, and it should be applied in an area with adequate ventilation. It should also be noted that **some dogs – especially Toy breeds - can react to this**, so check very carefully with your vet as to whether it will be suitable for your Cocker.

Most dogs with the severe form of the condition need from six to 14 dips every two weeks. After the first three or four dips, your vet will probably take another skin scraping to check that the mites have gone. Dips continue for one month after the mites have disappeared, but dogs shouldn't be considered cured until a year after their last treatment.

Other options include the heartworm treatment Ivermectin. This isn't approved by the FDA for treating mange, but is often used to do so. It is usually given orally every one to two days, or by injection, and can be effective. **Again, some dogs react badly to it.** Another drug is Interceptor (Milbemycin oxime), which can be expensive as it has to be given daily. However, it is effective on up to 80% of the dogs who did not respond to Mitaban dips – but should be given with caution to pups under 21 weeks of age. Discuss all options fully with your vet before starting treatment, as some of these chemicals can cause side effects in certain dogs.

There are also a number of holistic remedies, including aloe vera, lemon and garlic, apple cider vinegar, honey, yoghurt and olive oil. We have no personal experience as to how effective they are, but there is plenty of anecdotal evidence that holistic remedies work in certain cases. Whatever option you choose, act promptly, to avoid the dreaded full-blown mange developing; it is a terrible and painful ailment for a dog.

Dogs that have the generalised condition may have underlying skin infections, so antibiotics are often given for the first several weeks of treatment. Because the mite flourishes on dogs with suppressed immune systems, you should try to get to the root cause of immune system disease, especially if your dog is older when he or she develops demodectic mange.

Sarcoptic Mange

Also known as canine scabies, this is an inflammatory disease caused by various types of the demodex mite. This microscopic parasite can cause a range of skin problems such as hair loss and severe itching, and in some cases problems with the immune system. The mites can infect other animals such as foxes and cats, with each species having a slightly different parasite. The human version is called scabies.

Cockers, especially working dogs, can be susceptible as they can catch the parasite from close contact with foxes, fox dens and fox poo. Fox mange is less severe (for a dog) than the dog mite, but it still causes severe itching for the affected dog, who will scratch and bite himself.

The mites burrow into the dog's skin and live for up to 22 days in cool, moist environments. At normal room temperature they live from two to six days, preferring to live on parts of the dog with less hair. These are the areas you may see him scratching, although it can spread throughout the body in severe cases.

Diagnosing canine scabies can be somewhat difficult, and it is often mistaken for inhalant allergies. The most common way is for the vet to take a skin scraping from the dog and analyse it under a microscope.

Once diagnosed, there are a number of effective treatments, including selamectin (Revolution), a topical solution applied once a month which also provides heartworm prevention, flea control and some tick protection. Various Frontline products are also effective – check with your vet for the correct ones. As with demodectic mange, washes and dips may also be necessary - in some cases the dog is completely clipped for the dip to have maximum effect.

It may take between four and six weeks for a complete course of treatment. During this time, try and limit other dog's contact with the infected dog, as mange is highly infectious. Most cases clear up with veterinary treatment, but in extreme cases, the dog may have to be quarantined.

Sarcoptic mange is highly infectious, as the mites move quickly from one animal to the next. As well as catching it from foxes, dogs can also pick it up at kennels, veterinary surgeries, the local park, the dog groomer's or anywhere where there are lots of other dogs. Because your Cocker does not have to come into direct contact with an infected dog to catch scabies, it is difficult to completely protect him. If your dog is affected, make sure his bedding is clean, avoid washing powders and other chemicals. A healthy immune system can help prevent the recurrence of the problem, and a good diet can go some way towards prevention.

Fleas

When you see your dog scratching and biting, your first thought is probably: "He's got fleas!" and you may well be right. Fleas don't fly, but they do have very strong back legs and they will take any opportunity to jump from the ground or another animal into your Cocker's lovely warm coat. You can sometimes see the fleas if you part your dog's fur.

And for every flea that you see on your dog, there is the awful prospect of hundreds of eggs and larvae in your home if your Cocker lives indoors. So if your dog is unlucky enough to catch fleas, you'll have to treat your environment as well as your dog in order to completely get rid of them. The best form of cure is prevention. Vets recommend giving dogs a preventative flea treatment every four to eight weeks. This may vary depending on your climate, the season - fleas do not breed as quickly in the cold - and how much time your dog spends outdoors.

Once-a-month topical (applied to the skin) insecticides - like Frontline, Advocate and Advantix - are the most commonly used flea prevention products on the market. You part the skin and apply drops of the liquid on to a small area on your dog's back, usually near the neck. Some kill fleas and ticks, and others just kill fleas - check the details.

It is worth spending the money on a quality treatment, as cheaper brands may not rid your dog completely of fleas, ticks and other parasites. Sprays, dips, shampoos and collars are other options, as are tablets and injections in certain cases, such as before your dog goes into boarding kennels or has surgery. Incidentally, a flea bite is different from a flea bite allergy.

NOTE: There is considerable anecdotal evidence from dog owners of various breeds that the US flea and worm tablet **Trifexis** may cause severe side effects in some dogs. You may wish to read some owners' comments at: www.max-the-schnauzer.com/trifexis-side-effects-in-schnauzers.html

Ticks

A tick is not an insect, but a member of the arachnid family, like the spider. There are over 850 types of them, divided into two types: hard shelled and soft shelled. Ticks don't have wings - they can't fly, they crawl. They have a sensor called Haller's organ which detects smell, heat and humidity to help them locate food, which in some cases is a Cocker. A tick's diet consists of one thing and one thing only – blood! They climb up onto tall grass and when they sense an animal is close, crawl on him.

Ticks can pass on a number of diseases to animals and humans, the most well-known of which is Lyme Disease, a serious condition which causes lameness and other problems. Spaniels which spend a lot of time outdoors in high risk areas, such as woods and moorland, can have vaccinations against Lime Disease, but they are not cheap.

If you do find a tick on your dog's coat and are not sure how to get it out, have it removed by a vet or other expert. Inexpertly pulling it out yourself and leaving a bit of the tick behind can be detrimental to your dog's health. Prevention treatment is similar to that for fleas. If your Cocker has particularly sensitive skin, he might do better with a natural flea or tick remedy.

Heartworm

Heartworm is a serious and potentially fatal disease affecting pets in North America and many other parts of the world. It is caused by foot-long worms (heartworms) that live in the heart, lungs and associated blood vessels of affected pets, causing severe lung disease, heart failure and damage to other organs in the body.

The dog is a natural host for heartworms, which means that heartworms living inside the dog mature into adults, mate and produce offspring. If untreated, their numbers can increase; dogs have been known to harbour several hundred worms in their bodies. Heartworm disease causes

lasting damage to the heart, lungs and arteries, and can affect the dog's health and quality of life long after the parasites are gone. For this reason, prevention is by far the best option and treatment - when needed - should be administered as early as possible.

The mosquito (pictured) plays an essential role in the heartworm life cycle. When a mosquito bites and takes a blood meal from an infected animal, it picks up baby worms which develop and mature into 'infective stage' larvae over a period of 10 to 14 days. Then, when the infected mosquito bites another dog, cat or susceptible wild animal, the infective larvae are deposited onto the surface of the animal's skin and enter the new host through the mosquito's bite wound. Once inside a new host, it takes approximately six months for the larvae to develop into adult heartworms. Once mature, heartworms can live for five to seven years in a dog.

In the early stages of the disease, many dogs show few or no symptoms. The longer the infection persists, the more likely symptoms will develop. These include:

> A mild persistent cough
> Reluctance to exercise
> Tiredness after moderate activity
> Decreased appetite
> Weight loss

As the disease progresses, dogs may develop heart failure and a swollen belly due to excess fluid in the abdomen. Dogs with large numbers of heartworms can develop sudden blockages of blood flow within the heart leading to the life-threatening caval syndrome. This is marked by a sudden onset of laboured breathing, pale gums and dark, bloody or coffee-coloured urine. Without prompt surgical removal of the heartworm blockage, few dogs survive.

Although more common in south eastern USA, heartworm disease has been diagnosed in all 50 states. And because infected mosquitoes can fly indoors, even dogs that spend much time inside the home are at risk. For that reason, the American Heartworm Society recommends that you get your dog tested every year and give your dog heartworm preventive treatment for 12 months of the year.

Thanks to the American Heartworm Society for assistance with the section

---

Ringworm

This is not actually a worm, but a fungus and is most commonly seen in puppies and young dogs. It is highly infectious and often found on the face, ears, paws or tail. The ringworm fungus is most prevalent in hot, humid climates but, surprisingly, most cases occur in autumn and winter. Ringworm infections in dogs are not that common; in one study of dogs with active skin problems, less than 3% had ringworm.

Ringworm is transmitted by spores in the soil and by contact with the infected hair of dogs and cats, which can be typically found on carpets, brushes, combs, toys and furniture. Spores from infected animals can be shed into the environment and live for over 18 months, but fortunately most healthy adult dogs have some resistance and never develop symptoms.

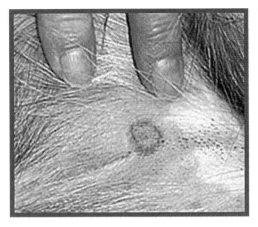

The fungi live in dead skin, hairs and nails - and the head and legs are the most common areas affected. Tell-tale signs are bald patches with a roughly circular shape (see photo). Ringworm is relatively easy to treat with fungicidal shampoos or antibiotics from a vet.

Humans can catch ringworm from pets, and vice versa. Children are especially susceptible, as are adults with suppressed immune systems and those undergoing chemotherapy. Hygiene is extremely important. If your dog has ringworm, wear gloves when handling him and wash your hands well afterwards. And if a member of your family catches ringworm, make sure they use separate towels from everyone else or the fungus may spread. (As an adolescent I caught ringworm from horses at stables where I worked at weekends - much to my mother's horror - and was treated like a leper by the rest of the family until it had cleared up!)

Seborrhoea

This is a common skin condition in dogs that causes flaky skin (dandruff) and greasiness of the skin and hair. Seborrhoea causes the dog's skin to give off a smelly, waxy, greasy substance that clumps up in the ears, under the belly and armpits, elbows, and around the ankles. Dogs may scratch at the affected areas, causing bleeding, crusting, hair loss and secondary infections due to skin damage.

There may also be an alteration of sebaceous gland secretions. Sebaceous glands are found in or near hair follicles and their normal function is to enrich the skin with oily secretions.

There are two common types of seborrhoea: oily (oleosa) and dry (sicca), which results in scaly skin. The majority of dogs have a combination of both. There are also two separate causes: primary seborrhoea is genetic-based, while secondary seborrhoea results from injury to the skin caused by things such as parasites, allergies, food disorders and hormonal issues like hypothyroidism. Cocker Spaniels are thought to be one of the breeds at a higher risk than average of suffering from seborrhoea, along with Springer Spaniels, Bassett Hounds, Dachshunds, Doberman Pinschers, German Shepherds, Irish Setters, Labrador Retrievers, Poodles, Shar Peis, and Westies.

The condition cannot usually be cured; treatment may last for the lifetime of the dog and is centred on managing the symptoms. If there is an underlying cause - such as allergies, then this also has to be tackled, along with any yeast or bacterial infections which are often present. The vet might also recommend an omega-3 fatty acid supplement, which may seem odd as the dog often already has a greasy coat, but fatty acids are essential for normal skin cell function and do actually help.

Interdigital Cysts

If you've ever noticed a fleshy red lump between your dog's toes that looks like an ulcerated sore or a hairless bump, then it may well be an interdigital cyst - or 'interdigital furuncle' to give the condition its correct medical term.

More commonly seen in breeds such as the Bulldog, these can be very difficult to get rid of, since they are not the primary issue, but often a sign of some other condition. Actually they are not cysts, but the result of **furunculosis**, a condition of the skin which clogs hair follicles and creates chronic infection. They can be caused by a number of factors, including allergies, obesity, poor foot conformation, mites, yeast infections, ingrowing hairs or other foreign bodies, and obesity.

These nasty-looking bumps are painful for your dog and will probably cause him to limp. Vets might recommend a whole range of treatments to get to the root cause of the problem. It can be extremely expensive if your dog is having a barrage of tests or biopsies and even then you are not guaranteed to find the underlying cause. The first thing he or she will probably do is put your dog in an E-collar to stop him licking the affected area, which will never recover properly as long as he's constantly licking it. This again is stressful for your dog. Here are some remedies your vet may suggest:

> ➢ Antibiotics and/or steroids and/or mite killers
> ➢ Soaking his feet in Epsom salts twice daily to unclog the hair follicles
> ➢ Testing him for allergies or thyroid problems
> ➢ Starting a food trial if food allergies are suspected
> ➢ Shampooing his feet
> ➢ Cleaning between his toes with medicated (benzoyl peroxide) wipes
> ➢ Referring him to a veterinary dermatologist
> ➢ Surgery

If you suspect your Cocker has an interdigital cyst, take him to the vet for a correct diagnosis and then discuss the various options. A course of antibiotics may be suggested initially, along with switching to a hypoallergenic diet if a food allergy is suspected. If the condition persists, many owners get discouraged, especially when treatment may go on for many weeks.

Before you resort to any drastic action, first try soaking your dog's affected paw in Epsom salts for five or 10 minutes twice a day. After the soaking, clean the area with medicated wipes, which are antiseptic and control inflammation. In the US these are sold under the brand name Stridex pads in the skin care section of any grocery, or from the pharmacy. If you think the cause may be an environmental allergy, wash your dog's paws and under his belly when you return from a walk, this will help to remove pollen and other allergens from his body.

Surgery can be effective, but it is a drastic option and although it might solve the immediate problem, it will not deal with whatever is triggering the interdigital cysts in the first place. Not only is healing after this surgery a lengthy and difficult process, it also means your dog will never have the same foot as before - future orthopaedic issues and a predisposition to more cysts are a couple of possible scenarios. All that said, your vet will understand that interdigital cysts aren't so simple to deal with, but they are always treatable. Get the right diagnosis as soon as possible, limit all offending factors and give medical treatment a good solid try before embarking on more drastic cures.

Bacterial infection (Pyoderma)

Pyoderma literally means 'pus in the skin' (yuk!) and fortunately this condition is not contagious. Early signs of this bacterial infection are itchy red spots filled with yellow pus, similar to pimples or spots in humans. They can sometimes develop into red, ulcerated skin with dry and crusty patches.

Pyoderma is caused by several things: a broken skin surface, a skin wound due to chronic exposure to moisture, altered skin bacteria, or poor blood flow to the skin. Dogs have a higher risk of developing an infection when they have a fungal infection or an endocrine (hormone gland) disease such as hyperthyroidism, or have allergies to fleas, food or parasites.

Pyoderma is often secondary to allergic dermatitis and develops in the sores on the skin which happen as a result of scratching. Puppies often develop 'puppy pyoderma' in thinly-haired areas such as the groin and underarms. Fleas, ticks, yeast or fungal skin infections, thyroid disease, hormonal imbalances, heredity and some medications can increase the risk. If you notice symptoms, get your dog to the vet quickly before the condition develops from **superficial pyoderma** into **severe pyoderma**, which is extremely unpleasant and takes a lot longer to treat.

Bacterial infection, no matter how bad it may look, usually responds well to medical treatment, which is generally done on an outpatient basis. Superficial pyoderma will usually be treated with a two to six-week course of antibiotic tablets or ointment. Severe or recurring pyoderma looks awful, causes your dog distress and can take months of treatment to completely cure. Medicated shampoos and regular bathing, as instructed by your vet, are also part of the treatment. It's also important to ensure your dog has clean, dry, padded bedding.

Ear Infections

Due to the physical structure of the Spaniel, ear infections can be the Cocker's Achilles' heel. American and English show Cockers are more susceptible than working Cockers, which have shorter, lighter ears.

Infection of the external ear canal (outer ear infection) is called otitis externa and is one of the most common types seen. The fact that your dog has recurring ear infections does not necessarily mean that his ears are the source of the problem – although they might be.

One common reason for them in Cockers is moisture in the ear canal, which in turn allows bacteria to flourish there. However, some Cockers with chronic or recurring ear infections have inhalant or food allergies or low thyroid function (hypothyroidism). Sometimes the ears are the first sign of allergy. The underlying problem must be treated or the dog will continue to have chronic ear problems. Tell-tale signs include your dog shaking his head, scratching or rubbing his ears a lot, or an unpleasant odour coming from the ears.

If you look inside the ears, you might notice a reddy brown, blackish or yellow discharge, it may also be red and inflamed with a lot of wax. Sometimes a dog may appear depressed or irritable; ear infections are painful. In chronic cases, the inside of his ears may become crusty or thickened. Dogs can have ear problems for many different reasons, including:

> ➢ Allergies, such as environmental or food allergies
> ➢ Ear mites or other parasites
> ➢ Bacteria or yeast infections

- ➢ Injury, often due to excessive scratching
- ➢ Hormonal abnormalities, e.g. hypothyroidism
- ➢ The ear anatomy and environment, e.g. excess moisture
- ➢ Hereditary or immune conditions and tumours

In reality, many Cockers have ear infections due to the structure of the ear. The long, hairy ears often prevent sufficient air flow inside the ear. This can lead to bacterial or yeast infections - particularly if there is moisture inside. These warm, damp and dark areas under the ear flaps provide an ideal breeding ground for bacteria. Most Cockers love swimming and this is not thought to cause ear infections.

Treatment depends on the cause and what – if any - other conditions your dog may have. Antibiotics are used for bacterial infections and antifungals for yeast infections. Glucocorticoids, such as dexamethasone, are often included in these medications to reduce the inflammation in the ear. Your vet may also flush out and clean the ear with special drops, something you may have to do daily at home until the infection clears.

A dog's ear canal is L-shaped, which means it can be difficult to get medication into the lower (horizontal) part of the ear. The best method is to hold the dog's ear flap with one hand and put the ointment or drops in with the other, if possible tilting the dog's head away from you so the liquid flows downwards **with gravity**. Make sure you then hold the ear flap down and massage the medication into the horizontal canal before letting go of your dog, as the first thing he will do is shake his head – and if the ointment or drops aren't massaged in, they will fly out.

Nearly all ear infections can be successfully managed if properly diagnosed and treated. But if an underlying problem remains undiscovered, the outcome will be less favourable. Deep ear infections can damage or rupture the eardrum, causing an internal ear infection and even permanent hearing loss. Closing of the ear canal (*hyperplasia* or *stenosis*) is another sign of

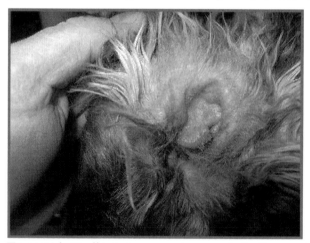

severe infection. Most extreme cases of hyperplasia will eventually require surgery as a last resort; the most common procedure is called a 'lateral ear resection'.

Our dog had a lateral ear resection some three years ago following years of recurring ear infections and the growth of scar tissue. It was surgery or deafness, the vet said. We opted for surgery and our dog has been free of ear infections ever since. However, it is an **extremely** painful procedure for the dog and should only be considered as a very last resort. The photo shows a Cocker Spaniel with a severe ear infection.

To avoid or alleviate recurring ear infections, check your dog's ears and clean them regularly. Hair should be regularly plucked from inside your Cocker's ears – either by you or a groomer, or both. If your Cocker is one of the very many who enjoys swimming, great care should be taken to ensure the inside of the ear is thoroughly dry afterwards - and after bathing at home. There is more information in **Chapter 12. Grooming.**

When cleaning or plucking your dog's ears, be very careful not to put anything too far down inside. Visit YouTube to see videos of how to correctly clean without damaging them. In a nutshell, DO NOT use cotton buds, these are too small and can damage the ear. Some owners recommend regularly cleaning the inside of ears with cotton wool and a mixture of water and white vinegar once a week or so. If your dog appears to be in pain, has smelly ears, or if his ear canals look inflamed, contact your vet straight away. If you can nip the first infection in the bud, there is a chance it will not return. If your dog has a ruptured or weakened eardrum, ear cleansers and medications could do more harm than good. Early treatment is the best way of preventing a recurrence.

There is a good veterinary website here: http://animalpetdoctor.homestead.com/ears.html which describes the different causes, severity and possible treatments for ear infections.

Canine Acne

Acne is not uncommon and - just as with humans - generally affects teenagers, often between five and eight months of age with dogs. It occurs when oil glands become blocked causing bacterial infection and these glands are most active in teenagers.

Acne is not a major health problem as most of it will clear up once the dog becomes an adult, but it can recur. Typical signs are pimples, blackheads or whiteheads around the muzzle, chest or groin. If the area is irritated, then there may some bleeding or pus that can be expressed from these blemishes.

Hormonal Imbalances

These occur in dogs of all breeds. They are often difficult to diagnose and occur when a dog is producing either too much (hyper) or too little (hypo) of a particular hormone. One visual sign is often hair loss on both sides of the dog's body. The condition is not usually itchy. Hormone imbalances can be serious as they are often indicators that glands which affect the dog internally are not working properly. However, some types can be diagnosed by special blood tests and treated effectively.

Some Allergy Treatments

Treatments and success rates vary tremendously from dog to dog and from one allergy to another, which is why it is so important to consult a vet at the outset. Earlier diagnosis is more likely to lead to a successful treatment. Some owners whose dogs have recurring skin issues find that a course of antibiotics or steroids works wonders for their dog's sore skin and itching. However, the scratching starts all over again shortly after the treatment stops.

Food allergies require patience, a change of diet and maybe even a food trial, and the specific trigger is notoriously difficult to isolate – unless you are lucky and hit on the culprit straight away. With inhalant and contact allergies, blood and skin tests are available, followed by hypersensitisation treatment. However, these are expensive and often the specific trigger for many dogs remains unknown. So the reality for many owners of Cockers with allergies is that they manage the ailment with various medications and practices, rather than curing it completely.

Our Personal Experience

After corresponding with numerous other dog owners and consulting our vet, Graham, it seems that our experiences with allergies are not uncommon.

This is borne out by the dozens of dog owners who have contacted our website about their pet's allergy or sensitivities. Our dog was perfectly fine until he was about two years old when he began to scratch a lot. He scratched more in spring and summer, which meant that his allergies were almost certainly inhalant or contact-based and related to pollens, grasses or other outdoor triggers.

One option was for Max to have a barrage of tests to discover exactly what he was allergic to. We decided not to do this, not because of the cost, but because our vet said it was highly likely that he was allergic to pollens. If we had confirmed an allergy to pollens, we were not going to stop taking him outside for walks, so the vet treated him on the basis of seasonal inhalant or contact allergies, probably related to pollen.

As mentioned, one method is to have a shallow bath or hose outside and to rinse the dog's paws and underbelly after a walk in the countryside. This is something our vet does with his own dogs and has found that the scratching reduces as a result. Regarding medications, Max was at first put on to a tiny dose of Piriton, an antihistamine for hay fever sufferers (prescribed in the millions for humans and canines) and for the first few springs and summers, this worked well.

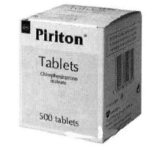

Allergies can often change and the dog can also build up a tolerance to a treatment, which is why they can be so difficult to treat. This has been the case with our dog over the past nine years. The symptoms change from season to season, although the main ones remain and they are general scratching, paw biting and ear infections. One year he bit the skin under his tail a lot (near the anus) and this was treated effectively with a single steroid injection followed by spraying the area with cortisone once a day at home for a period. This type of spray can be very effective if the itchy area is small, but no good for spraying all over a dog's body.

A few years ago Max started nibbling his paws for the first time - a habit he persists with - although not to the extent that they become red and raw. Over the years we have tried a number of treatments, all of which have worked for a while, before he comes off the medication in autumn for six months when plants and grasses stop growing outdoors. He manages perfectly fine the rest of the year without any treatment.

If we were starting again from scratch, knowing what we know now, I would investigate a raw diet, if necessary in combination with holistic remedies. Our dog is now 11; we feed him a high quality hypoallergenic dry food. His allergies are manageable, he loves his food, is full of energy and otherwise healthy, and so we are reluctant to make such a big change at this point in his life.

According to Graham, more and more dogs are appearing in his waiting room every spring with various types of allergies. Whether this is connected to how we breed our dogs remains to be seen. One season he put Max on a short course of steroids. These worked very well for five months, but steroids are not a long-term solution, as prolonged use can cause organ damage.

Another spring Max was prescribed a non-steroid daily tablet called Atopica, sold in the UK only through vets. (The active ingredient is **cyclosporine**, which suppresses the immune system. Some dogs can get side effects, although Max didn't, and holistic practitioners believe that it is harmful to the dog). This treatment was expensive, but initially extremely effective – so much so that we thought we had cured the problem completely. However, after a couple of seasons on cyclosporine he developed a tolerance to the drug and started scratching again.

A few years ago he went back on the antihistamine Piriton, a higher dose than when he was two years old, and this worked very well again. One advantage of this drug is that is it manufactured

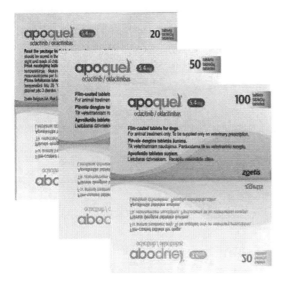

by the million for dogs and is therefore very inexpensive. In the meantime, we were returning to the vet's periodically for ear drops for recurring ear infections.

In 2013 the FDA approved **Apoquel** (oclacitinib) to control itching and inflammation in allergic dogs. In some quarters it has been hailed '**a wonder drug**' for canine allergies. In fact it has proved so popular in the UK and North America that there has been a shortage of supply, with the manufacturers not being able to produce it fast enough.

We have tried it with excellent results. There was some tweaking at the beginning to get the daily dose right, but it really has proved effective for us. Max still scratches, but not so much – all dogs scratch a bit - and he is still on Apoquel today for six months of the year. Normally dogs start with a double dose for 10 days to suppress the allergic reaction and then go on to a single tablet a day mixed into one of their feeds. The tablets cost around £1 or $1.50 each, so it's not cheap.

Many vets recommend adding fish oils (which contain Omega-3 fatty acids) to a daily feed to keep your dog's skin and coat healthy all year round – whether or not he has problems. We add a liquid supplement called Yumega Plus, which contains Omegas 3 and 6, to one of his two daily feeds all year round and this definitely seems to help his skin.

In the past when the scratching has got particularly bad, we have bathed Max in an antiseborrhoeic shampoo (called Malaseb) twice a week for a limited time. This also helped, although this has not been necessary since he started on the Apoquel.

The main point is that most allergies are manageable. They may change throughout the life of the dog and you may have to alter the treatment. Our Max still scratches, but not as much as when he was younger. He may have allergies, but he wouldn't miss his walks for anything and, all in all, he is one contented canine. We've compiled some anecdotal evidence from our website from owners of dogs with various allergies. Here are some of their suggestions for alleviating the problems:

Bathing - Bathing your dog using shampoos that break down the oils which plug the hair follicles. These shampoos contain antiseborrhoeic ingredients such as benzoyl peroxide, salicylic acid, sulphur or tar. One example is Sulfoxydex shampoo, which can be followed by a cream rinse such as Episoothe Rinse afterwards to prevent the skin from drying out. Do not bathe your dog too often, unless instructed to do so by the vet, as it washes away natural oils in the skin.

Dabbing – Using an astringent such as witch hazel or alcohol on affected areas. We have heard of zinc oxide cream being used to some effect. In the human world, this is rubbed on to mild skin abrasions and acts as a protective coating. It can help the healing of chapped skin and nappy rash in babies. Zinc oxide works as a mild astringent and has some antiseptic properties and is safe to use on dogs, **as long as you do not allow the dog to lick it off**.

Daily supplements - Vitamin E, vitamin A, zinc and omega oils all help to make a dog's skin healthy. Feed a daily supplement which contains some of these, such as fish oil, which provides omega.

Here are some specific remedies from owners. We are not endorsing them; we're just passing on the information. **Check with your vet before trying any new remedies.**

A medicated shampoo with natural tea tree oil has been suggested by one owner. Some have reported that switching to a fish-based diet has helped lessen scratching. Ann G. said: "Try Natural Balance Sweet Potato and Fish formula. My dog Charlie has skin issues and this food has helped him tremendously! Plus he LOVES it!" Others have suggested home-cooked food is best, if you have the time to prepare the food.

This is what another reader had to say: "My eight-month-old dog also had a contact dermatitis around his neck and chest. I was surprised how extensive it was. The vet recommended twice-a-week baths with an oatmeal shampoo. I also applied organic coconut oil daily for a few weeks. This completely cured the dermatitis. I also put a capsule of fish oil with his food once a day and continue to give him twice-weekly baths. His skin is great now."

Several owners have tried coconut oil with some success. Here is a link to an article on the benefits of coconut oils and fish oils: www.cocotherapy.com/fishoilsvsvirginoil_coconutoil.htm Check with your vet first.

The Holistic Approach

As canine allergies become increasingly common, more and more owners of dogs with allergies and sensitivities are looking towards natural foods and remedies to help deal with the issues. Some are finding that their dog does well for a time with injections or medication, but then the symptoms slowly start to reappear. A holistic practitioner looks at finding the root cause of the problem and treating that, rather than just treating the symptoms.

Dr Sara Skiwski is a holistic vet working in California. She writes here about canine environmental allergies: "Here in California, with our mild weather and no hard freeze in Winter, environmental allergens can build up and cause nearly year-round issues for our beloved pets. Also seasonal allergies, when left unaddressed, can lead to year-round allergies. Unlike humans, whose allergy symptoms seem to affect mostly the respiratory tract, seasonal allergies in dogs often take the form of skin irritation/inflammation.

"Allergic reactions are produced by the immune system. The way the immune system functions is a result of both genetics and the environment: Nature versus Nurture. Let's look at a typical case. A puppy starts showing mild seasonal allergy symptoms, for instance a red tummy and mild itching in Spring. Off to the vet!

"The treatment prescribed is symptomatic to provide relief, such as a topical spray. The next year when the weather warms up, the patient is back again - same symptoms but more severe this time. This time the dog has very itchy skin. Again, the treatment is symptomatic - antibiotics, topical spray (hopefully no steroids), until the symptoms resolve with the season change. "Fast forward to another Spring... in the third year, the patient is back again but this time the symptoms last longer, (not just Spring but also through most of Summer and into Fall). By Year Five, all the symptoms are significantly worse and are occurring year round.

"This is what happens with seasonal environmental allergies. The more your pet is exposed to the allergens they are sensitive to, the more the immune system over-reacts and the more intense and long-lasting the allergic response becomes. What to do?

"In my practice, I like to address the potential root cause at the very first sign of an allergic response, which is normally seen between the ages of six to nine months old. I do this to circumvent the escalating response year after year. Since the allergen load your environmentally-sensitive dog is most susceptible to is much heavier outdoors, I recommend two essential steps in managing the condition. They are vigilance in foot care as well as fur care.

"What does this mean? A wipe down of feet and fur, especially the tummy, to remove any pollens or allergens is key. This can be done with a damp cloth, but my favorite method is to get a spray bottle filled with Witch Hazel and spray these areas. First, spray the feet then wipe them off with a cloth, and then spray and wipe down the tummy and sides. This is best done right after the pup has been outside playing or walking.

"This will help keep your pet from tracking the environmental allergens into the home and into their beds. If the feet end up still being itchy, I suggest adding foot soaks in Epsom salts."

Dr Skiwski also stresses the importance of keeping the immune system healthy by avoiding unnecessary vaccinations or drugs: "The vaccine stimulates the immune system, which is the last thing your pet with seasonal environmental allergies needs. I also will move the pet to an anti-inflammatory diet. Foods that create or worsen inflammation are high in carbohydrates. An allergic pet's diet should be very low in carbohydrates, especially grains. Research has shown that 'leaky gut,' or dysbiosis, is a root cause of immune system overreactions in both dog and cats (and some humans).

"Feed a diet that is not processed, or minimally processed; one that doesn't have grain and takes a little longer to get absorbed and assimilated through the gut. Slowing the assimilation assures that there are not large spikes of nutrients and proteins that come into the body all at once and overtax the pancreas and liver, creating inflammation.

"A lot of commercial diets are too high in grains and carbohydrates. These foods create inflammation which overtaxes the body and leads not just to skin inflammation, but also to other inflammatory conditions, such as colitis, pancreatitis, arthritis, inflammatory bowel disease and ear infections. Also, these diets are too low in protein, which is needed to make blood. This causes a decreased blood reserve in the body and in some of these animals this can lead to the skin not being properly nourished, starting a cycle of chronic skin infections which produce more itching."

After looking at diet, check that your dog is free from fleas and then these are some of her suggested supplements:

> **Raw (Unpasteurised) Local Honey** - an alkaline-forming food containing natural vitamins, enzymes, powerful antioxidants and other important natural nutrients, which are destroyed during the heating and pasteurisation processes.

Raw honey has anti-viral, anti-bacterial and anti-fungal properties. It promotes body and digestive health, is a powerful antioxidant, strengthens the immune system, eliminates allergies, and is an excellent remedy for skin wounds and all types of infections. Bees collect pollen from local plants and their honey often acts as an immune booster for dogs living in the locality.

Dr Skiwski says: "It may seem odd that straight exposure to pollen often triggers allergies, but that exposure to pollen in the honey usually has the opposite effect. But this is typically what we see. In honey, the allergens are delivered in small, manageable doses and the effect over time is very much like that from undergoing a whole series of allergy immunology injections."

➢ **Mushrooms -** make sure you choose the non-poisonous ones! Dogs don't like the taste, so you may have to mask it with another food. Medicinal mushrooms are used to treat and prevent a wide array of illnesses through their use as immune stimulants and modulators, and antioxidants. The most well-known and researched are reishi, maitake, cordyceps, blazei, split-gill, turkey tail and shiitake.

The mushrooms stabilise mast cells in the body, which have the histamines attached to them. Histamine is what causes much of the inflammation, redness and irritation in allergies. By helping to control histamine production, the mushrooms can moderate the effects of inflammation and even help prevent allergies in the first place.

WARNING! Mushrooms can interact with some over-the-counter and prescription drugs, so do your research as well as checking with your vet first.

➢ **Stinging Nettles** - contain biologically active compounds that reduce inflammation. Nettles have the ability to reduce the amount of histamine the body produces in response to an allergen. Nettle tea or extract can help with itching. Nettles not only help directly to decrease the itch, but also work overtime to desensitise the body to allergens, helping to reprogramme the immune system.

➢ **Quercetin** – is an over-the-counter supplement with anti-inflammatory properties. It is a strong antioxidant and reduces the body's production of histamines.

➢ **Omega-3 Fatty Acids** - these help decrease inflammation throughout the body. Adding them into the diet of all pets - particularly those struggling with seasonal environmental allergies – is very beneficial. If your dog has more itching along the top of their back and on their sides, add in a fish oil supplement. Fish oil helps to decrease the itch and heal skin lesions. The best sources of Omega 3s are krill oil, salmon oil, tuna oil, anchovy oil and other fish body oils, as well as raw organic egg yolks. If using an oil alone, it is important to give a vitamin B complex supplement.

➢ **Coconut Oil** - contains lauric acid, which helps decrease the production of yeast, a common opportunistic infection. Using a fish body oil combined with coconut oil before inflammation flares up can help moderate or even suppress your dog's inflammatory response.

Dr Skiwski adds: "Above are but a few of the over-the-counter remedies I like. In non-responsive cases, Chinese herbs can be used to work with the body to help to decrease the allergy threshold even more than with diet and supplements alone. Most of the animals I work with are on a program of Chinese herbs, diet change and acupuncture.

"So, the next time Fido is showing symptoms of seasonal allergies, consider rethinking your strategy to treat the root cause instead of the symptom."

With thanks to Dr Sara Skiwski, of the Western Dragon Integrated Veterinary Services, San Jose, California, for her kind permission to use her writings as the basis for this section.

This chapter has only just touched on the complex subject of skin disorders. As you can see, the causes and treatments are many and varied. One thing is true; if your Cocker has a skin issue, seek a professional diagnosis as soon as possible - whatever the condition - before attempting to treat it yourself and before the condition becomes entrenched.

Early diagnosis and treatment can sometimes nip the problem in the bud. Some skin conditions cannot be completely cured, but they can be successfully managed, allowing your Cocker to live a happy, pain-free life.

If you haven't got your puppy yet, ask the breeder if there is a history of skin issues in her bloodlines. Once you have your dog, remember that a good quality diet and attention to cleanliness and grooming go a long way in preventing and managing canine skin problems and ear infections.

12. Grooming

Cockers have many advantages over other breeds: they adapt to a variety of roles, from family pet to working gundog, they generally get along with everybody and other dogs, they like children, they can work as therapy dogs, and they are eager to please their owners, which makes them easier than many breeds to train and housetrain. These are just a few of their outstanding qualities.

However, one of the downsides of owning a Spaniel is that they can be pretty high maintenance when it comes to grooming – especially if yours is a show-type, which has a longer, denser coat and longer ears than a working Cocker.

Officially, Cockers have a single coat which is flat and silky, although some breeders with dogs with heavier coats believe it seems more like a double coat. The amount of coat and shedding varies greatly from one Cocker to the next and one bloodline to the next. However, show Cockers have more 'feathering' and their coat is longer and denser than that of a working Cocker. American Cockers have been bred for even longer coats. While some Cockers are heavy shedders, others appear to lose little hair.

Experienced show breeder Linda Reed said: "Show Cockers will develop a heavy undercoat which is what we 'strip' out. Show Cockers need - and are bred for - a heavier coat. For obvious reasons, the working Cockers do not need the heavy coat and tend to be bred away from coat."

Country Durham breeder Julie Summers added: "I have seven Cockers, all pure working strain and I find dogs with the tan gene almost seem to have a completely different coat. It's more like a double than a single coat; my gold girl hardly has any fur in comparison with them."

Other factors affecting shedding are age, allergies, sudden changes in temperature and nutrition. A healthy skin and coat generally mean less shedding, which can be managed with regular (i.e. more than once a week) grooming sessions and occasional baths with a canine shampoo. A high quality diet helps, and some owners have found that feeding hypoallergenic kibble or a raw diet improves skin and reduces shedding. Adding a once-daily squirt or spoonful of Omega 3 oil to a feed is also beneficial.

Whatever type of Cocker you have, they all love running through the mud and undergrowth with their noses to the ground – not to mention swimming - and so may not be the best choice if you are particularly house-proud. All Cockers need regular home grooming and show Cockers need trips to your local groomer, unless you learn to hand strip or clip. If you do decide to trim your pet Cocker yourself, invest in a high quality set of clippers (rather than a cheap set), it will save you money in the long run.

Routine grooming sessions help your dog to look and feel his best. They also allow you to examine his coat, ears, teeth, eyes and nails for signs of infection, ticks, fleas and other problems. With a show-type or American Cocker, you cannot simply leave the coat untrimmed, it will become matted. There are some truly awful photos on the internet of Cocker Spaniels whose owners have neglected their grooming. If you have a working Cocker which spends a lot of time outdoors, you also need to be vigilant and check for anything which might have got caught in his coat.

Anyone thinking of showing their Cocker should have the coat hand stripped. Clipped (shaved) coats are not acceptable in the show ring. If your dog is simply a pet, you might consider having him clipped to keep the coat short, particularly in summer as some Cockers with dense coats can feel the heat (others are unaffected); the decision is yours. Our photo shows a pet show Cocker being trimmed with clippers.

Hand stripping gives a more natural look and feel to the coat, while clipping is an easy way of keeping a pet Cocker with a thick coat in trim. Depending on the amount of coat your dog has, trimming should take place every two to three months - although some show types may need a trim as often as every month. If you use a professional groomer, get your dog used to the experience when young, otherwise the first visit will be very stressful for an adult dog. Many groomers offer reduced puppy rates.

Regular brushing at home removes dead hair and skin, stimulates blood circulation and spreads natural oils throughout the coat, helping to keep it in good condition. If brushed regularly, your dog shouldn't need a bath more than once every few weeks or months – unless he has a skin condition, is particularly dirty or is bound for the show ring. Time spent grooming is also time spent bonding with your dog; it is this physical and emotional inter-reliance which brings us closer to our pets.

If you do notice an unpleasant smell from your dog and he hasn't been rolling in something unmentionable, then he may have an ear or yeast infection which will require a visit to the vet (or his anal glands may need squeezing). The breed's long, droopy ears might be great for trapping scent when retrieving, but they can be a real pain when it comes to maintenance. All types of Spaniel are prone to ear infections, so regular inspections are a must to nip any potential issues in the bud.

Finally, few breeds can boast such a wide range of acceptable colours and markings. According to The Cocker Spaniel Club, this is due to the fact that originally some people preferred a solid coloured dog as they felt it was better camouflaged, others preferred parti-coloured dogs (white and one other colour) so the dog was more easily seen and less likely to be injured, while others believed that top performance in certain field tasks was linked to coat colour.

The solid colours are: Black, Liver (also called Chocolate), Red and Golden. Sometimes a solid has a white mark or marks on the chest and this is perfectly acceptable. Within the other colours, roan is a popular marking; it means that the coat has a main colour thickly interspersed with hairs of another colour. White is a rare solid colour, in fact the dog is usually Black and White, Orange and White or Lemon and White with just a few flecks of marking. White Spaniels are thought to be more prone to deafness and are not generally encouraged.

The roans are: Blue Roan, Liver Roan - sometimes called Chocolate Roan or even Red Roan - Orange Roan and the more unusual Lemon Roan, where the colour is carried by a recessive gene. The parti colours are: Black and White (ticked with flecks of black), Liver and White (with flecks of brown) Orange and White (with flecks of orange) and Lemon and White (with flecks of lemon). Any of the 'and White' coloured dogs can have a tan mask and trim. It's interesting that new-born pups show no ticking, but that it develops within a few weeks.

A well-groomed Cocker is a joy to behold; here are some general tips for keeping yours in tip top condition.

Ear Cleaning

Ear infections (otitis externa) are a common problem. Vets estimate that up to 20% of the canine population is affected – and the incidence is even higher for Cocker Spaniels. The Cocker's ear canals, surrounded by lots of hair, are generally warm and moist under the ear flap, making them a haven for bacteria.

Hearing is very important to your dog and an infection is not only extremely painful if left untreated, but can also spread to the middle or inner ear causing more serious issues, such as damage to the dog's nerves and/or balancing mechanism. In severe cases of recurring infections the dog can go deaf or require an operation to change the shape of his ear canal (called a lateral ear resection).

You can regularly pluck - or ask your groomer to pluck – some of the hair inside the ear flap. If you do this yourself, don't overdo it. Keep an eye out for redness or inflammation of the ear flap or inner ear. Ask your groomer for tips. If your dog is not being shown, you can also ask your groomer to trim the inside of the ear flap. Cleaning ears and allowing adequate air circulation is especially important for breeds with long or floppy ears.

Check and clean the inside of your Cocker's ears regularly (once or twice a fortnight) and from time to time use an ear cleansing solution. Squeeze a few drops of cleanser into the ear canal. If you can, tilt your dog's head so the ear canal is pointing downwards, allowing gravity to help distribute the solution. Massage the base of the ear for 15 seconds before allowing him to shake his head. Then dry the inside of the ear flap with cotton wool and gently wipe out any dirt and waxy build up in the ear canal.

Another method is to use a baby wipe regularly to gently remove dirt and wax. In both cases it is important to only clean as far down the ear canal as you can see to avoid damaging the eardrum.

NOTE: If your dog swims, you should dry the inside of his ears afterwards to help prevent infection.

As well as an unpleasant smell, other signs of ear infections are: your dog scratching his ears or shaking his head a lot, rubbing his ears on the carpet, or the inside of the ear looks red and/or dark coloured wax is present. In any of these cases, consult your vet ASAP, as simple routine cleaning won't clear it up - and ear infections are notoriously difficult to rid the dog of once he's had one.

The trick is to keep your dog's ears clean and free from too much hair right from puppyhood and hope that he never gets an ear infection.

Bathing

A dirty coat or skin can cause irritation, leading to scratching and excessive shedding. With bathing, it's all a question of getting the balance right, and this will to some extent depend on how much outdoor exercise your Cocker gets, what sort of areas he's exercised in and what his natural skin condition is like.

Don't bathe your dog too often as it will cause his coat to dry out; certainly not more than once a month unless you are showing your Cocker, in which case most show owners also use a conditioner after the shampoo. The exceptions would be if he has been rolling in or eating something disgusting, in which case he might need an extra wash as a dirty coat can also lead to bacterial infections.

A dog's coat has a different pH to human hair so, if you use shampoo, only use one recommended for dogs, as human shampoos can lead to skin problems and coat damage. If your dog has any sign of skin problems or allergies, select a **medicated** shampoo (such as Malaseb) with antibacterial, antifungal or anti-itching (antihistamine) properties; it will help to get rid of bacteria and fungi without damaging the coat. If your dog does have skin or shedding issues, your vet will be able to recommend a suitable medicated shampoo. They are also widely available in pet stores and online.

Cockers' ear canals are prone to infections, so it's a good idea to put a cotton wool ball in each ear before bathing - make sure you do this gently and do not force the cotton wool into the ear canal – and don't forget to remove them afterwards or your Cocker will appear even deafer than usual to your commands! You must also be extremely careful with the eyes, especially if you use a shampoo.

As with all things Cocker, there is a wide variation on how your dog will react to having a bath – some love the attention, while others hate the experience. Make sure you get everything ready before you start and keep your dog's collar on so you have something to hold on to. You can wash your dog in a bowl, the kitchen sink, the family bath or outdoors, it doesn't matter. If it's the sink, make sure he can't jump out and injure himself, and if it's the bath, put a non-slip mat in the bottom.

The Cocker is a pretty hardy breed and often a rinse down outside with a hose pipe is enough to clean a dog's coat after a particularly muddy walk. However, attention should always be paid to the ears – wetness inside the ear flaps provides ideal conditions for bacteria.

Spray water from the neck down to the tail until the coat is completely soaked, avoid wetting the face if you can, but gently wash the ear flaps without getting water in the ear canals. If you use a shampoo, work it into your dog's body and legs, not forgetting underneath, and, if it's medicated, you may have to leave it on for a few minutes. This is not easy with a lively Cocker, so keep a firm hold - it DOES get better as they get more used to it – especially if they get a treat at the end of the ordeal. Our dog hates being bathed and races round the house like a lunatic afterwards, as though he has just miraculously escaped the most horrific death by drowning in three inches of water!

Rinse your dog thoroughly on top, underneath, on the legs, etc., making sure all of the soap is out of the coat. Use your hand to squeegee excess water off the coat before putting him on an old towel on the floor and towelling him dry - again, be careful with the eyes. Then stand back as he shakes and gets his revenge by soaking you too! Dry the coat as much as possible and don't forget to remove the cotton wool balls if you've used them.

Teeth Cleaning

Veterinary studies show that by the age of three, 80% of dogs exhibit signs of gum disease, and Cockers are more prone to dental problems than some other breeds. Symptoms include yellow and brown build-up of tartar along the gum line, red inflamed gums and persistent bad breath. You can give your dog a daily dental treat, such as Dentastix, to help keep his mouth and teeth clean, but you should also consider brushing your Cocker's teeth.

It shouldn't be a chore, but a pleasant experience for both of you. Take things slowly in the beginning, give him lots of praise and many dogs will start looking forward to teeth brushing sessions. Use a pet toothpaste (the human variety can upset a canine's stomach); many have flavours which your dog will find tasty. The real benefit comes from the actual action of the brush on the teeth. Various brushes, sponges and pads are available; the choice depends on factors such as the health of your dog's gums, the size of his mouth and how good you are at teeth cleaning!

Get your dog used to the toothpaste by letting him lick some off your finger. If he doesn't like the flavour, try a different one. Continue this until he looks forward to licking the paste – it might be instant or take days. Put a small amount on your finger and gently rub it on one of the big canine teeth at the front of his mouth. Then get him used to the toothbrush or dental sponge you will be using, praise him when he licks it – do this for several days. The next step is to actually start brushing. Talk to your Cocker in an encouraging way and praise him when you're finished.

Lift his upper lip gently and place the brush at a 45º angle to the gum line. Gently move the brush backwards and forwards. Start just with his front teeth and then gradually do few more. You don't need to brush the inside of his teeth as his tongue keeps them relatively free of plaque. Cockers love games and, with a bit of encouragement and patience, it can become a fun task for both of you. There are various videos on YouTube which demonstrate how to clean a dog's teeth.

Nail Trimming

Nails must be kept short for the paws to remain healthy. Long nails interfere with the dog's gait, and can make walking awkward or painful. They can also break easily. This usually happens at the base of the nail, where blood vessels and nerves are located and results in a trip to the vet's. If you can hear the nails clicking on the floor, they're too long. Dogs which are exercised on hard surfaces such as pavements (sidewalks) naturally wear down their nails more quickly than dogs which are exercised on soft surfaces such as grass.

You can ask your groomer to trim your dog's nails. If you do it yourself, you will need specially designed clippers. Most have safety guards to prevent you from cutting the nails too short. You want to trim only the ends, before the 'quick,' which is a blood vessel inside the nail. (It is also where we get the expression 'cut to the quick' from). You can see where the quick ends on a white nail, but not on a dark nail. Clip only the hook-like part of the nail that turns down. It's fair to say that many dogs dislike having their nails trimmed!

You can make it a painless procedure by getting him used to having his paws handled in puppyhood. Start trimming gently, a nail or two at a time, and your dog will learn that you're not going to hurt him.

If you accidentally cut the quick, stop the bleeding with some styptic powder. Another option is to file your dog's nails with a nail grinder tool. Some dogs may have tough nails which are hard to trim and this may be less stressful for your dog, with less chance of pain or bleeding. It may take a little while for your dog to get used to the sound of the grinder, so start with very short sessions. If you find it impossible to clip your dog's nails, or you are at all worried about doing it, take him to a vet or a groomer.

Eyes - If your dog's eye(s) has a discharge, if they get a little sticky, or if he has dried deposits in the corner of his eyes, clean them gently with damp cotton wool. Do not use anything else unless instructed to do so by your vet.

Anal Glands – The two anal glands are located on each side of your dog's anus (butt). They give off a scent when your dog has a bowel movement. Squeezing them is normally done if you take your dog to a groomer's, as the glands can get full. If you notice your dog dragging himself along on his rear end or licking or scratching his anus, he may have impacted anal glands - or he may have worms or allergies. Either way, he needs some attention!

Breeders on Grooming

We asked breeders for any grooming advice and these were their responses:

Show Cockers

Caroline Bymolen: "We always bath our dogs the night before a show, so that could be every other week. Those not being shown are bathed around every three weeks unless, of course, one of them has an accident in which case we bath as required. The dogs with the fullest coats are groomed daily, whereas those with shorter coats or those which have been clipped out are groomed weekly. Shedding with show Cockers can be a problem if they are with a show coat, but with regular grooming this is not a problem as any loose hair is combed out. As we carry out all of our own grooming, trimming, stripping and clipping, we do not visit a groomer. Those who cannot do this themselves should visit a groomer every six to eight weeks."

Andrew Height: "Grooming is near enough a daily event. Bathing is as and when; they are bathed if they get really dirty. They are also bathed prior to going to a Championship Show, but not always prior to an Open Show. Regular grooming helps to keep the mud and dirt out of their coats. In our experience, bitches tend to shed their coat after their first season, then it takes forever to grow back. Luckily, they do not shed after their next season!"

Christine Grant: "I groom my Cockers about once a week, or more if they have any twigs, etc., in their coats. I only bath them when I really need to. I don't visit a groomer as I do it myself about every two to three months. My dogs certainly do shed quite a bit, perhaps an incredibly house-proud owner would be advised to choose a breed that sheds less."

David Matthews: "Grooming is ongoing for the show ring, as is bathing for shows. For a pet, I'd say two or three times a year for a trim and bathing as necessary."

Jane Minikin: "They are groomed daily, which reduces shedding, and bathed as necessary - sometimes this is daily in winter after muddy walks, but less so in summer. I prefer to keep the coats on my Cockers, but if you do not want to spend a long time grooming, then it is easier to have them clipped out and you can vary the grade of clip depending on the time of year."

Lynne Waterhouse: "As my Cockers spend a lot of exercise time in muddy woods and water, I tend to keep their coats quite short and they are clipped every four to six weeks with baths, more frequently when mud and smells dictate it! I would recommend daily grooming, which benefits the majority of coats."

Wendy Tobijanski: "I brush daily and bath once a week. I trim all my own dogs, but you would take a pet to the groomer's about every six weeks."

Rachel Appleby: "I have six Cockers, so groom (trim) my own every five to six weeks to keep their coats under control. They are bathed when necessary."

Linda Reed (who breeds English and American Cockers): "Bitches if not spayed will shed after every season. I trim and bath all our show dogs every week. The English pet Cockers visit a groomer's every 10 to12 weeks and the Americans every six to eight weeks." Pictured is Linda's Delindere Dare t'Be Different, sporting a wonderful coat.

Eunice Wine, of Virginia, USA, also breeds American Cockers and said: "The Cocker Spaniel's long coat needs regular, trimming, brushing and baths. This coat needs to be clipped in the warm summer months for the comfort of the dog. The face needs trimming often around the eyes so they can see properly and the eyes themselves need regular cleaning and care, especially if you get a dog with 'weepy' eyes."

Working Cockers

Andy Platt: "I very rarely bath them, so as not to destroy their natural oil. Their ears are deburred weekly."

Barry Hutchinson: "They are bathed very rarely, if at all. I do not condone the displacement of the natural oils and structure of dogs' coats, particular those that live and work outdoors. Kennel dogs shed less than their house-dwelling counterparts."

Alan and Carole Pitchers: "Ours visit the groomer's every 10 weeks, and we brush the dogs regularly. Our dogs do not really get bathed at home unless they have visited the boggy pond on their walk."

Billie Cheeseman: "As mine are workers, their hair is quite short, so they do not need to visit the groomer's. I periodically scissor-trim their ears, feathers and feet, roughly every six weeks. I use a 'Coat King' rake monthly during the summer to keep their ear hair free of mats and then use it when they come home with burrs, etc. They shed a lot! Regular use of a de-shedding tool like a Furminator (pictured) can help."

Chris Warner: "I groom them as and when required if the coat becomes clogged. I do my own grooming and clipping and do not bath them unless they have rolled in something - fox poo seems to be their favourite!"

Christine Thomas: "Working Cockers don't need much grooming, unlike the show type. I just trim the undercarriage and back of legs in the winter because of the mud. They get washed underneath a lot as they run around in wet mud, but rarely do I use shampoo, as that tends to strip them of their natural moisture. They do shed a fair bit; I have a hard floor throughout downstairs and the hair accumulates, but I prefer that to visiting a groomer and having matted fur."

Jill Gunn: "They get a daily brush; one bitch gets bathed once every three to four months and one gets clipped out and bathed at the groomer's as she is spayed and has grown a very woolly coat, so needs clipping through the winter working season. Both bitches cast (moult) a minimum amount. One dog doesn't cast a hair, he never has and so is clipped every three months all year round, otherwise his coat can get seriously long and he can easily overheat in warm temperatures when working (i.e. on a grouse moor in August) or his coat weighs him down when picking up in water."

Jo Oxley: "My working dogs have shorter and less dense fur on their ears than the show type. Owners should pay special attention to their fluffy feet – especially when the grass is long and full of seeds, as they can pick up seed between their pads and toes. If this is not noticed they can be forced under the skin and cause pain and infection. Some owners have their Cockers trimmed or shaved; as mine have fine silky coats I have only to comb them. The more they are combed, the easier and finer the coat. They do get 'dreadlocks' behind the ears if left unattended for a couple of weeks."

Tracey Simpson: "They visit a groomer once a year for the winter coat to be taken off."

Julie Summers: "I use a stripper comb and do the dogs every other day as part of our bonding time together. I will trim their feathers and ears so there is no need to go to the groomer's. I find that if Cockers have had their coat cut right down, their fur does not grow back very well." Pictured is one of Julie's working Cockers in action.

Kerena Marchant: "Rupert, one of my workers, is more like a show Cocker with regards to his coat and is hand stripped four times a year. The other two go about three times a year for bath and 'trouser trim' and nails."

Wendy Roberts: "Lola hardly shed before she had puppies, now both she and Charlie shed quite a lot. I have tried not to get them trimmed too often, but trims (only their feathers, some back and ears usually) every three months do help to control their shedding. Most often they are hosed down after the dog walk and regularly brushed - at least weekly."

Manda Smith: "They are usually groomed once a week and bathed about once a month, but neutered animals may need more unless clipped off as the coat changes, it gets fluffy and thick and mats easily. They do shed quite a lot and the hair can be difficult to remove from bedding, etc. Mine don't visit a groomer as I'm able to groom and trim them myself. Pet dogs, especially if neutered, would need a groomer about every six weeks."

As you can see, grooming isn't just about giving your dog the odd tickle with a brush. Hopefully yours will thrive without too much extra maintenance, but some Cockers do require that little extra bit of care - and it's up to you to give it. It's all part of the bargain when you decide that the Cocker is the dog for you.

13. The Birds and the Bees

Judging by the number of questions our website receives from owners who ask about their dog's reproductive cycle and breeding their dogs, there is a lot of confusion about the canine facts of life out there. Some owners want to know whether they should mate their dog, while others ask at what age they should consider having their dog spayed (females) or neutered (males).

Owners of bitches often ask when and how often she will come on heat and how long it will last. Sometimes they want to know how you can tell if a female is pregnant or how long a pregnancy lasts. So here, in a nutshell, is a short chapter on the Cocker Spaniel facts of life.

Should I Breed From My Cocker Spaniel?

The short and simple answer is: Unless you know exactly what you are doing or have a mentor, **leave it to the experts.** You need specialist knowledge to successfully breed healthy Cocker Spaniels to type - whether it's show or working.

The rising popularity and cost of puppies is tempting more people to consider breeding their dogs. Puppies from good breeders with proven track records cost many hundreds of pounds or dollars – sometimes more. But anyone who thinks it is easy money should bear in mind that responsible Cocker Spaniel breeding is an expensive and time-consuming business when all the fees, DNA and health tests, care, nutrition, medical expenses and - in the case of working dogs - training, have been taken into account.

You can't just put any two dogs together and expect perfect, healthy Cocker Spaniels every time; successful breeding is much more scientific than that. A good breeder is one whose main aim is to produce healthy puppies with good temperaments and physical structures - and with working Cockers, the instincts to do a job well. This does not happen by accident or happy coincidence.

If you are determined to breed from your dog, you must first learn a lot. Perhaps one of the best ways to go about it is to find a mentor, somebody who has a lot of experience with show or working Cockers and who is prepared to share their knowledge. Another way to learn more is to visit shows, see the dogs in action and talk to their breeders and handlers. If it's show Spaniels you're interested in, look for a Kennel Club registered or Assured Breeder near you - see the back of this book for details. If it's the working dog that lights your fire, visit field trials and tests and talk to people there. You can find a list of field trials organised by the UK's Cocker Spaniel Club on their website at: www.thecockerspanielclub.co.uk/fieldtrials.htm.

In the US visit www.fieldcockers.com for details of events, or The English Cocker Spaniel Club of America at www.ecsca.info. Breeders of (American) Cocker Spaniels in the States can be found online at http://marketplace.akc.org/puppies/cocker-spaniel, and the American Spaniel Club has a list of breeders at www.asc-cockerspaniel.org/index.php/breeders.html - although it's up to you to do your research.

Ask one of these people to become a mentor. And the marvels of modern technology mean that you can visit online Cocker Spaniel forums where other owners are willing to share their experiences, regardless of where you live. If you have provisionally selected a breeder, ask other owners if anyone already has one of their puppies. Before you think of breeding from your dog, ask yourself these questions:

1. **Did you get your Cocker from a good, responsible breeder?** Dogs sold in pet stores and on general sales websites are seldom good specimens and can be unhealthy.

2. **Are your dog and his or her close relatives free from a history of eye, kidney and other genetic ailments which can affect Cockers?** Have you got the relevant certificates for your dog and seen those for his or her parents? Progressive Retinal Atrophy Progressive Rod Cone Degeneration (prcd-PRA) can be passed on to puppies if the parents aren't clear, as can Glaucoma, hip problems and other issues.

3. **Does your Cocker Spaniel have a good temperament? Does he or she socialise well with other dogs, animals and people?** Take your puppy or adult dog to training classes where the instructor can help you evaluate the dog's temperament. Dogs with poor temperaments should not be bred from, regardless of how good they look or how well they work.

4. **Does your dog conform to the standard/type?** A show Cocker should conform to the Kennel Club or AKC standard - see **Chapter 3**. for details. A working dog may not exactly conform to the breed standard, but will have a good pedigree of proven, healthy ancestors. Do not breed from a dog which is not a good specimen, hoping that somehow the puppies will turn out better. They won't. Talk with experienced breeders and ask them for an honest assessment of your dog

5. **Is your female two years old or older and at least in her second heat cycle?** Females should not be bred until they are fully physically mature, when they are able to carry a litter to term and are robust enough to whelp and care for a litter. Even then, not all females are suitable. Some are simply poor mothers who don't care for their puppies - which means you have to do it – some others may not be able to produce enough milk.

6. **Do you understand COI and its implications?** COI stands for Coefficient of Inbreeding. It calculates how closely the ancestors are related to each other. Ideally, the COI should be calculated over at least 10 generations with fully complete pedigrees. Typical values for a brother and sister or parent and child are 25%; half-brother and

sister, or grandfather and grandchild, 12.5%, etc. The lower the result, the better. See **Chapter 3. Breed Standard** for more information.

7. **Are you financially able to provide good veterinary care for the mother and puppies - particularly if complications occur?** Have you considered these costs: DNA and health testing, medical care and vets' fees, supplements, whelping equipment, vaccinations and worming, extra food and stud fees? Health can be expensive, and that's in addition to routine veterinary care and the added costs of pre-natal care and immunisations for puppies. What if your female needs a Caesarean section (C-section) or the puppies need emergency treatment - can you afford the bills? If you are not prepared to make a financial commitment to a litter that could end up costing you a significant amount of money, then do not breed from your Cocker.

8. **Have you got the indoor space?** The mother and puppies will need their own space in your home, which will become messy as new-born pups do not come into this world housetrained. It should also be warm and draught-free.

9. **Do you have the time to provide full-time care for the mother and puppies if necessary?** Caring for the mother and new-borns is a 24/7 job in the beginning, particularly the first couple of weeks or so.

10. **Will you be able to find good homes for however many puppies there should be and will you be prepared to take them back if necessary?** This is an important consideration for good breeders, who will not let their precious puppies go to any old home. They want to be sure that the new owners will take good care of their Cocker Spaniels for their lifetime.

Responsible breeding is backed up by genetic information and screening as well as a thorough knowledge of the desired traits of the Cocker Spaniel. It is definitely not an occupation for the uninformed. Breeding is not just about the look of the dog; health and temperament are important factors too, along with instinct for a working dog. Many dog lovers do not realise that the single most important factor governing health and certain temperament traits is genetics.

Having said that, experts are not born, they learn their trade over several years. Anyone who is seriously considering getting into Cocker Spaniel breeding should first spend time researching the breed and its genetics. Make sure you are going into breeding for the right reasons.

Don't do it to make money or to get puppies just like your perfect Cocker Spaniel, and certainly not to show the kids "the miracle of birth." If you are determined to go into breeding, then do so for the right reason. Learn all you can beforehand, read books, visit dog shows, make contact with established breeders and make sure you have a good vet on hand.

Useful resources are the Kennel Club's www.thekennelclub.org.uk/services/public/mateselect **Mate Select** which provides health related information about individual dogs that you may be considering. Another source of free information is the new **Kennel Club Academy** which has produced a series of films on pre-breeding considerations. Further Breeder Education resources are being developed on all aspects of dog breeding, rearing and owning dogs.

Committed breeders use their skills and knowledge to improve the breed by producing healthy pups with good traits – are you up to the task?

Working Cocker breeder Carole Pitchers, of Alcarbrad Cocker Spaniels, Essex, UK, explains how she first got involved with breeding: "I grew up around Labradors as my father was, and still is, very keen on shooting. My father bred the occasional litter from his Labradors, and I was very keen to help out – even from the age of five. I gained invaluable experience watching him around the puppies from their birth, through weaning and eventually on to their new homes. I experienced the highs and the lows with him. When my husband, Alan, and I decided to breed our first litter, I was able to draw on all of all of my experiences." Pictured is the Pitchers' Bradley's Kentucky Woman (Kimber).

"During the first whelp I was confident as I still had my dad with us, in the background, just in case! I am also lucky to have a good friend who is an ex-veterinary nurse who was also on hand. Although our first whelp was long and protracted, everything turned out well and no-one was needed, but to have people on standby was a great relief. I think mentoring is a great idea.

"The following are a list of questions that I have asked colleagues at work who are thinking about breeding from their dogs – the first question usually stops them dead in their tracks:

1) Sometimes whelping can go wrong - are you prepared to take the risk that your bitch may die during whelping?
2) In the event of the bitch (or puppies) needing urgent veterinary treatment, can you afford this?
3) How are you going to ensure the puppies (and the bitch) receive all the care and attention they require? (I ask this question when people are working full-time and have no support from other people).
4) How are you going to ensure that the puppies go to suitable homes?
5) If you are unable to sell all of your puppies, are you prepared to look after the dogs long-term?

6)   If an owner of one of your puppies decides they have made the wrong decision, or cannot care for the animal in the future, are you prepared to have the animal back?

"Our four litters have been between five and eight puppies. They have all been hard work - any litter is hard work. We insist the puppies are brought up in the house amongst the family and we employ a strict hygiene regime. We also socialise the pups, interacting with them and playing with them and their toys."

Carole added: "The biggest threat to future health is indiscriminate breeding." And Helen Marsden, of Finity Cocker Spaniels, Hampshire, UK, agrees: "The one biggest threat to the future of the breed is those breeders who do not health test their dogs."

Billie Cheeseman, of BarleyCourt Spaniels, Hertfordshire, UK, adds: "Having a litter of puppies is not for the faint-hearted. There are many things that can go wrong, researching things like pyometra, mastitis, calcium deficiency and uterine inertia are vital to being able to step in if needed and take mum and pups to the vet's in time for help. From four weeks of age it is a constant battle to keep them and their area clean, and even the small things like getting wormer down puppies can be tricky, as they somehow manage to spit it back out."

Females and Heat

Just like all other animal and human females, a female Cocker Spaniel has a menstrual cycle - or to be more accurate, an oestrus cycle. This is the period when she is ready (and willing!) for mating and is more commonly called **heat** or being **on heat**, **in heat** or **in season**.

A female Cocker Spaniel has her first cycle from about six to nine or 12 months old. She will generally come on heat every six to eight months, though it may be even longer between cycles, and the timescale becomes more erratic with old age. It can also be irregular with young dogs when cycles first begin.

Heat will last on average from 12 to 21 days, although it can be anything from just a few days up to four weeks. Within this period there will be several days which will be the optimum time for her to get pregnant. This middle phase of the cycle is called the *oestrus*. The third phase, called *diestrus*, then begins. During this time, her body will produce hormones whether or not she is pregnant. Her body thinks and acts like she is pregnant. All the hormones are present; only the puppies are missing. This can sometimes lead to what is known as a 'false pregnancy'.

Breeders normally wait until a female has been in heat at least twice before breeding from her. Many believe that around two years old is the right age for a first litter as a pregnancy draws on her calcium reserves which she needs for her own growing bones. Also, some dogs are relatively slower to reach maturity than others. Responsible breeders limit the number of litters from each female, as overbreeding can take too heavy a toll on her body.

While a female is on heat, she produces hormones which attract male dogs. Because dogs have a sense of smell hundreds of times stronger than ours, your girl on heat is a magnet for all the males in the neighbourhood. They may

congregate around your house or follow you around the park, waiting for their chance to prove their manhood – or mutthood in their case.

Don't expect your precious little Cocker princess to be fussy. Her hormones are raging when she is on heat and during her most fertile days, she is ready, able and ... very willing! Keep her on a lead at all times when she is on heat. As your female approaches the optimum time for mating, you may notice her tail bending slightly to one side. She will also start to urinate more frequently. This is her signal to all those virile male dogs out there that she is ready for mating.

The first visual sign you may notice is when she tries to lick her swollen rear end – or vulva, to be more precise. She will then bleed, this is sometimes called spotting. It will be a light red or brown at the beginning of the heat cycle. Some bitches can bleed quite heavily, this is normal. But if you have any concerns about her bleeding, contact your vet to be on the safe side. She may also start to "mate" with your leg or other dogs. These are all normal signs of heat.

Breeding requires specialised knowledge on the part of the owner, but this does not stop a female on heat from being extremely interested in attention from any old mutt. To avoid an unwanted pregnancy, you must keep a close eye on your female and not allow her to freely wander where she may come into contact with other dogs when she is on heat.

Carole adds: "When in season, bitches should not even be left in the back garden unattended, no matter how secure you think you garden is. The dog will find a way in, or the bitch a way out. I have heard of a bitch who stood for a dog - even though they were separated by a chain-link fence!"

Unlike women, female dogs do not go through the menopause and can have puppies even when they are quite old. However, a litter for an elderly Cocker Spaniel can also result in complications.

If you don't want your female to get pregnant, you should have her spayed. In the UK, Europe and North America, rescue groups, animal shelters and humane societies urge dog owners to have their pets spayed or neutered to prevent unwanted litters which contribute to too many animals in the rescue system or, even worse, euthanasia. Normally all dogs from rescue centres and shelters are spayed or neutered. Many breeders also encourage the early spaying and neutering of pets if they are not to be shown or worked – and some may even specify it in the puppy's sale contract.

Pregnancy

Dogs of all shapes and sizes are all one species. So whether you have a Cocker Spaniel, a St Bernard or a Miniature Pinscher, a pregnancy will normally last for 61 to 65 days - typically 63 days. Sometimes pregnancy is referred to as the "gestation period."

After mating it is recommended that the bitch is taken for a pre-natal check-up The vet should answer any questions, such as the type of food, supplements, care and physical changes in you female. A female Cocker may have anything from one to 10 pups, but often has around six. There is a blood test available which measures levels of **relaxin**. This is a hormone produced by the ovary and the developing placenta, and pregnancy can be detected by monitoring relaxin levels as early as three weeks after mating. The levels are high throughout pregnancy and then decline rapidly after the female has given birth.

A vet can usually see the puppies using Ultrasound from around the same time. X-rays also give the breeder an idea of the number of puppies and help to give the vet more information, particularly useful if the bitch has previously had whelping problems. Here are some of the signs of pregnancy:

➢ After mating, many females become more affectionate. (However, some will become uncharacteristically irritable and maybe even a little aggressive)

➢ The female may produce a slight clear discharge from her vagina about one month after mating

➢ Three or four weeks after mating, a few females experience morning sickness – if this is the case, feed little and often. She may seem more tired than usual

➢ She may seem slightly depressed and/or show a drop in appetite. These signs can also mean there are other problems, so you should consult your vet

➢ Her teats (nipples) will become more prominent, pink and erect 25 to 30 days into the pregnancy. Later on, you may notice a fluid coming from them

➢ After about 35 days, or seven weeks, her body weight will noticeably increase

➢ Her abdomen will become noticeably larger from around day 40, although first-time mums and females carrying few puppies may not show as much

➢ Many pregnant females' appetite will increase in the second half of pregnancy

➢ Her nesting instincts will kick in as the delivery date approaches. She may seem restless or scratch her bed or the floor

➢ During the last week of pregnancy, females often start to look for a safe place for whelping. Some seem to become confused, wanting to be with their owners and at the same time wanting to prepare their nest. Even if the female is having a C-section, she should still be allowed to nest in a whelping box with layers of newspaper, which she will scratch and dig as the time approaches

If your female becomes pregnant – either by design or accident - your first step should be to consult a vet.

False Pregnancies

As many as 50% or more of intact (unspayed) females may display signs of a false pregnancy. In the wild it was common for female dogs to have false pregnancies and to lactate (produce milk). This female would then nourish puppies if their own mother died.

False pregnancies occur 60 to 80 days after the female was in heat - about the time she would have given birth – and are generally nothing for an owner to worry about. The exact cause is unknown. However, hormonal imbalances are thought to play an important role. Some dogs show symptoms within three to four days of spaying. Typical symptoms include:

➢ Mothering or adopting toys and other objects
➢ Making a nest
➢ Producing milk (lactating)
➢ Appetite fluctuations
➢ Barking or whining a lot
➢ Restlessness, depression or anxiety
➢ Swollen abdomen
➢ She might even appear to go into labour

Try not to touch your dog's nipples, as touch will stimulate further milk production. If she is licking herself repeatedly, she may need an Elizabethan collar (or E-collar, a large plastic collar from the vet) to minimise stimulation.

Under no circumstances should you restrict your Cocker's water supply to try and prevent her from producing milk. This is dangerous as she can become dehydrated.

Some unspayed bitches may have a false pregnancy with each heat cycle. Spaying during a false pregnancy may actually prolong the condition, so better to wait until the false pregnancy is over and then have her spayed to prevent it happening again.

False pregnancy is not a disease, but an exaggerated response to normal hormonal changes. Owners should be reassured that even if left untreated, the condition almost always resolves itself.

However, if your female appears physically ill or the behavioural changes are severe enough to worry you, visit your vet. He or she may prescribe tranquilisers to relieve anxiety, or diuretics to reduce milk production and relieve fluid retention.

In rare cases, hormone treatment may be necessary. Generally, dogs experiencing false pregnancies do not have serious long-term problems, as the behaviour disappears when the hormones return to their normal levels in two to three weeks.

One exception is pyometra, a disease mainly affecting unspayed middle-aged females, caused by a hormonal abnormality. Pyometra follows a heat cycle in which fertilisation did not occur and the dog typically starts showing symptoms within two to four months. The signs are excessive drinking and urination, with the female trying to lick a white discharge from her vagina. She may also have a slight temperature. If the condition becomes severe, her back legs will become weak, possibly to the point where she can no longer get up without help.

Pyometra is serious if bacteria take a hold, and in extreme cases it can be fatal. It is also relatively common and needs to be dealt with promptly by a vet, who will give the dog intravenous fluids and antibiotics for several days. In most cases this is followed by spaying.

Spaying

Spaying is the term used to describe the removal of the ovaries and uterus (womb) of a female dog so that she cannot become pregnant. Although this is a routine operation, it is major abdominal surgery and she has to be anaesthetised. A popular myth is that a female should have her first heat cycle before she is spayed, but this is not the case. Even puppies can be spayed. Consult your vet for the optimum time, should you decide to have your dog done. Note that if she is on heat or nearing her heat cycle, your dog cannot be spayed.

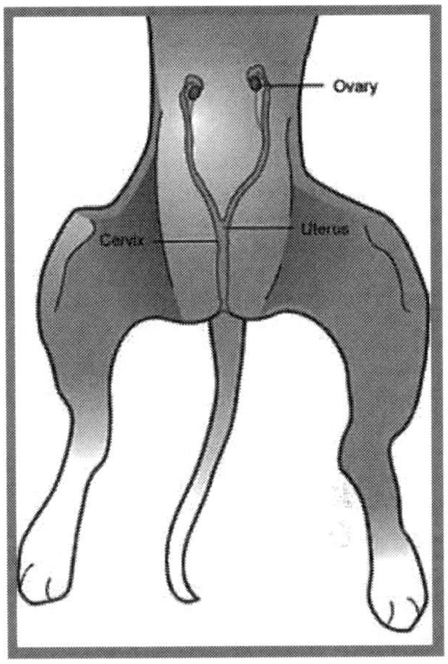

If spayed before her first heat cycle, one of the advantages is that your dog will have an almost zero risk of mammary cancer (the equivalent of breast cancer in women). Even after the first heat, spaying massively reduces the risk of this cancer. The American College of Veterinary Surgeons (ACVS) says: "Mammary tumors are more common in female dogs that are either not spayed or were spayed after two years of age. The risk of a dog developing a mammary tumor is 0.5% if spayed before their first heat (approximately six months of age), 8% after their first heat, and 26% after their second heat."

Some females may put on weight easier after spaying and will require slightly less food afterwards. As with any major procedure, there are pros and cons.

Spaying is a much more serious operation for a female than neutering is for a male. This is because it involves an **internal** abdominal operation, whereas the neutering procedure is carried out on the male's testicles, which are outside his abdomen.

For:

➢ Spaying prevents infections, mammary cancer and other diseases of the uterus and ovaries

➢ It reduces hormonal changes which can interfere with the treatment of diseases like diabetes or epilepsy

➢ Spaying can reduce behaviour problems, such as roaming, aggression to other dogs, anxiety or fear

➢ It eliminates the risk of the potentially fatal disease pyometra (a secondary infection that occurs as a result of hormonal changes in the female's reproductive tract), which affects unspayed middle-aged females

➢ A spayed dog does not contribute to the pet overpopulation problem.

Against:

➢ Complications can occur, including an abnormal reaction to the anaesthetic, bleeding, stitches breaking and infections. This is not common

➤ Occasionally there can be long-term effects connected to hormonal changes. These may include weight gain, urinary incontinence or less stamina and these problems can occur years after a female has been spayed

➤ Older females may suffer some urinary incontinence, but it only affects a very few spayed females. Discuss it with your vet

➤ Cost (this is a rough estimate, vets' practices vary greatly). This can range from £100 to £300 in the UK and $160 - $480 in the USA.

If you talk to your vet or a volunteer at a rescue shelter, they will say that the advantages of spaying far outweigh any disadvantages. When you take your female Cocker Spaniel puppy for her vaccinations, you can discuss with the vet at what age spaying should be considered.

Neutering

Neutering male dogs involves castration; the removal of the testicles. This can be a difficult decision for some owners, as it causes a drop in the pet's testosterone levels, which some humans – males in particular! - feel affects the quality of their dog's life.

Fortunately, dogs do not think like people and male dogs do not miss their testicles or the loss of sex. We decided to have our own dog, Max, neutered after he went missing three times on walks – he ran off on the scent of a female on heat. Fortunately, he is micro-chipped and has our phone number on a tag on his collar and we were lucky that he was returned to us on all three occasions. He hasn't run off since being neutered.

Unless you specifically want to breed from your dog, or he has a special job, neutering is recommended by animal rescue organisations and vets. Even then, Guide Dogs for the Blind, Hearing Dogs for Deaf People and Dogs for the Disabled are routinely neutered and this does not impair their ability. There are countless unwanted puppies, especially in the US, many of which are destroyed. There is also the problem of a lack of knowledge from the owners of some breeding dogs, resulting in the production of puppies with congenital health or temperament problems.

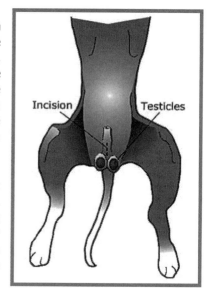

Neutering is usually performed around puberty, i.e. about six months old. It can, however, be done at any age over eight weeks, provided both testicles have descended. The operation is a relatively straightforward procedure. Dogs neutered before puberty tend to grow a little larger than dogs done later. This is because testosterone is involved in the process which stops growth, so the bones grow for longer without testosterone.

The neutering operation for a male is much less of a major operation than spaying for a female, and complications are less common and less severe. Although he will feel tender afterwards, your dog should return to his normal self within a couple of days. When he comes out of surgery, his scrotum (the sacs which held the testicles) will be swollen and it may look like nothing has been done! But it is normal for these to slowly shrink in the days following surgery. Here are the main pros and cons:

For:

> Behaviour problems such as aggression and wandering off are reduced
> Unwanted sexual behaviour, such as mounting people or objects, is reduced or eliminated
> Testicular problems such as infections, torsion (painful rotation of the testicle) are eradicated. Neutering also significantly reduces the number of cases of testicular cancer
> Prostate disease, common in older male dogs, is less likely to occur
> A submissive entire (uncastrated) male dog may be targeted by other dogs. After he has been neutered, he will no longer produce testosterone and so will not be regarded as much of a threat by the other males, so he is less likely to be bullied
> A neutered dog is not fathering unwanted puppies

Against:

> As with any surgery, there can be bleeding afterwards, you should keep an eye on him for any blood loss after the operation. Infections can also occur, generally caused by the dog licking the wound, so try and prevent him doing this. If he persists, use an E collar. In the **vast majority** of cases, these problems do not occur
> Some dogs' coats may be affected, but supplementing their diet with fish oil can compensate for this
> Cost. This starts at around $130 in the US, £80 in the UK

Myths - Here are some common myths about neutering and spaying:

Neutering or spaying will spoil the dog's character - There is no evidence that any of the positive characteristics of your dog will be altered. He or she will be just as loving, playful and loyal. Neutering may reduce aggression or roaming, especially in male dogs, because they are no longer competing to mate with a female.

A female needs to have at least one litter - There is no proven physical or mental benefit to a female having a litter. Pregnancy and whelping (giving birth to puppies) can be stressful and can have complications. In a false pregnancy, a female is simply responding to the hormones in her body.

Mating is natural and necessary - Dogs are not humans, they do not think emotionally about sex or having and raising a family. Because Cocker Spaniels like the company of humans so much, we tend to ascribe human emotions to them. Unlike humans, their desire to mate or breed is entirely physical, triggered by the chemicals called hormones within their body. Without these hormones – i.e. after neutering or spaying – the desire disappears or is greatly reduced.

Male dogs will behave better if they can mate - This is simply not true; sex does not make a dog behave better. In fact it can have the opposite effect. Having mated once, a male may show an increased interest in females. He may also consider his status elevated, which may make him harder to control or call back.

To recap: You many have the most wonderful Cocker Spaniel in the world, but only enter the world of canine breeding if you have the right knowledge and motivation. Don't do it just for the money or the cute factor. Breeding poor examples only brings heartache for everyone in the long run when health or other issues develop. If your dog is purely a pet and not bound for the show ring, field trials or other events, consider having him neutered or her spayed.

14. Cocker Spaniel Rescue

Are you thinking of adopting a Cocker Spaniel from a rescue organisation? What could be kinder and more rewarding than giving a poor, abandoned dog a happy and loving home for the rest of his life?

Not much really; adoption saves lives. The problem of homeless dogs is truly depressing. It's a big issue in Britain, but even worse in the US, where the sheer numbers in kill shelters is hard to comprehend. Randy Grim states in "Don't Dump The Dog" that 1,000 dogs are being put to sleep every hour in the States.

According to Jo-Anne Cousins, former Executive Director at IDOG, who has spent many years involved in US canine rescue, the situations leading to a dog ending up in rescue can be summed up in one phrase: 'Unrealistic expectations.'

She said: "In many situations, dog ownership was something that the family went into without fully understanding the time, money and commitment to exercise and training that it takes to raise a dog. While they may have spent hours on the internet pouring over cute puppy photos, they probably didn't read any puppy training books or look into actual costs of regular vet care, training and boarding."

That lack of thought was highlighted in a story which recently appeared in the Press in my Yorkshire home town. A woman went shopping in a retail centre on Christmas Eve. She returned home with a puppy she had bought on impulse for £700 ($1,050). The pup was in a rescue shelter two days later.

One reason some Cockers end up in rescue shelters is that potential owners do not always realise that Spaniels were bred to work and still have those instincts. The UK's CAESSR (Cocker and English Springer Spaniel Rescue) says: "Spaniels, like most working dogs, need both mental and physical exercise to keep them happy and fulfilled. They are not a breed that will be happy with a ten-minute walk round the block and are likely to develop behavioural problems if not given the mental and physical activity that they need."

The RSPCA adds: "Even the 'merry Cocker' will be unhappy if it's not given everything it needs to be happy and healthy, for example space and opportunity to play. Make sure you're prepared to meet a puppy's needs.

"Before you buy one of the Cocker Spaniel puppies you may have seen advertised, think carefully about the commitment you are about to make. Every puppy requires regular ongoing training and, despite their reputation for being easy to train, every Cocker Spaniel puppy is unique and will learn at his or her own unique pace. And like any breed, without regular walks and enough to do, your Cocker puppy could become bored and develop behavioural problems, such as destructive behaviour."

The breed's parent club, The Cocker Spaniel Club, has a Re-homing and Rescue Scheme run by volunteers throughout the UK.

The club says: "A rescue Cocker Spaniel is not necessarily a dog recovered from a life threatening situation, but a dog that has had another owner prior to adoption. These dogs are rehomed for many reasons. Sometimes the reasons are personal (allergies, bereavement, divorce/separation, work commitments) but there is a time when the reason is with the dog himself (behavioural problems like barking, chewing, disobedience). Some behavioural problems can be caused by the mismanagement of a dog as a youngster and with time and guidance the problems could be remedied. Occasionally, puppies are available, but usually most of the rescue Cocker Spaniels are adults."

Common reasons for rehoming a dog include:

> The dog has too much energy, needs too much exercise, knocks the kids over and jumps on people
> A change in the owner's personal circumstances – such as a divorce or change of home or job
> The dog is growling and/or nipping
> It chews or eats things it shouldn't
> It makes a mess in the house
> It needs way more time and effort than the owner is able or prepared to give

There is, however, a ray of sunshine for some of these dogs. Every year many thousands of people in the UK, North America and countries all around the world adopt a rescue dog and the story often has a happy ending.

The Cocker Spaniel Club Scheme, like other Spaniel rescue organisations, tries to make prospective new adopters as aware as possible of potential problems: "Giving a home to an unwanted dog can be emotionally, physically and financially challenging. It can also be very rewarding, and the home you offer may help to convert a canine delinquent into the perfect pet.

"Some re-homed/rescue Cocker Spaniels can be insecure at first and may like to sleep with a comfort item in their bed (an old, worn item of clothing and/or cuddly toy).

"It is advisable to establish house rules in a kind, but consistent, manner from Day One, don't keep changing commands or sleeping arrangements and don't allow things 'just for now'.

"Cocker Spaniels which have lived in kennels for a long time may experience problems with housetraining. Treat this and other behaviour problems from his past sympathetically but firmly - and immediately. You cannot 'make up to him' for the previous experience the dog has endured. Positive, reward-based training, which encourages him to want to please you, is the most reliable method. Seek guidance from a local dog training club or your Area Representative.

"If a Cocker Spaniel has been badly treated in his previous home, he may have short or long term health problems. You may need to work closely with a vet, so make sure you register with one as soon as possible. Veterinary insurance may be advisable immediately, as it may be difficult to get this arranged if the dog develops long term health problems later.

"Your re-homed/rescue Cocker Spaniel may seem to settle down with no difficulties, but then develop unexpected behavioural problems some time later. See this as part of his adapting to a new life rather than a personal failure or rejection. Continue your usual training routine and seek advice from your Area Representative or local dog training club if you need extra help or support."

The Dog's Point of View...

But if you are serious about adopting a Cocker, then you should do so with the right motives and with your eyes wide open. If you're expecting a perfect dog, you could be in for a shock. Rescue dogs can and do become wonderful companions, but much of it depends on you. Cockers are people-loving dogs. Some of them in rescue centres are traumatised. They don't understand why they have been abandoned by their beloved owners and may arrive at your home with problems of their own until they adjust to being part of a loving family again. Ask yourself a few questions before you take the plunge and fill in the adoption forms:

> ➤ Are you prepared to accept and deal with any problems - such as bad behaviour, timidity, chewing, aggression, jumping up, submissive urination or making a mess in the house - which a Cocker may display when initially arriving in your home?
> ➤ How much time are you willing to spend with your new pet to help him integrate back into normal family life?
> ➤ Can you take time off work to be at home and help the dog settle in at the beginning?
> ➤ Are you prepared to take on a new addition to your family that may live for another 10 years or more?
> ➤ Are you prepared to stick with the dog even if he develops behavioural or health issues later?

Think about the implications before taking on a rescue dog - try and look at it from the dog's point of view. What could be worse for the unlucky dog than to be abandoned again if things don't work out between you?

Other Considerations

Adopting a rescue dog is a big commitment for all involved. It is not a cheap way of getting a Cocker and shouldn't be viewed as such. It could cost you several hundred pounds – or dollars. You'll have adoption fees to pay and often vaccination and veterinary bills as well as worm and flea medication and spaying or neutering. Make sure you're aware of the full cost before committing.

Some rescue Cockers have had difficult lives. You need plenty of time to help them rehabilitate. Some may have initial problems with housetraining. Others may need socialisation with people and/or other dogs. If you are serious about adopting, you may have to wait a while until a suitable dog comes up. One way of finding out if you, your family and home are suitable is to volunteer to become a foster home for one of the rescue centres. Fosters offer temporary homes until a forever home becomes available It's a shorter term arrangement, but still requires commitment and patience.

And it's not just the dogs that are screened - you'll have to undergo a screening by the rescue organisation. Rescue groups and shelters have to make sure that prospective adopters are suitable and they have thought through everything very carefully before making such a big decision. It would be a tragedy for the dog if things did not work out. To try and combat this, most rescue groups will ask a raft of personal questions – some of which may seem intrusive.

If you are serious about rescuing a Cocker, you will have to answer them. Here is the information required on the Spaniel Aid Adoption Form at http://spanielaid.co.uk/adoption-application:

➢ Name, address, age
➢ Your work hours
➢ Type of property you live in
➢ The height of your garden fence at its lowest point
➢ Details of any other pets
➢ Details of who lives in your house
➢ Whether you have any previous experience with Spaniels
➢ Whether you are able to train a dog to obey basic commands
➢ Details of the dog training methods you employ
➢ Any other details

A chat with the charity's administrators is then organised, followed by a chat with the dog's foster carer, then a meeting for all family members and your other dogs at the foster home. There will then be an inspection visit to your home and, if all goes well, you will then pay the adoption fee. Some rescue organisations also ask for personal references. If you are not prepared to go through all of this, you may have to reconsider whether rescuing a Cocker is the right path for you.

The Cocker Spaniel Club asks other questions, such as whether you prefer a "show-type - a family pet" or "working Cocker – a very active dog." It also wants to know where the dog will be left during the day or night, whether anyone in the family has allergies, how long and how far you would walk the dog, if you've ever had a dog with behavioural problems and, if so, how you resolved them, whether you have a holiday planned and if the dog will be going with you, whether you know of a good boarding kennel and if you are registered with a vet.

Rescue dogs are usually spayed or neutered before adoption, if they are not, it is likely there will be a clause in the adoption contract which states that you agree not to breed from the dog.

Maxine Shaverin was a founder member of Spaniel Aid and gave this interview: "There are numerous reasons for Spaniels ending up in rescue. Not being able to cope was sadly common, but not just the usual 'wrong choice of breed,' but also older kids getting a dog and then leaving home and not being able to take the dog. We did get a fair share of owner sickness-related relinquishments too.

"There may have been slightly more workers than show, more Springers than Cockers. The workers and Springers tended to be relinquished more for not being able to cope and behavioural issues. Liaising with others in rescue, the longer legged, thinner Cockers (more so workers but also the show-types) tend to be more sensitive, highly strung and prone to behavioural issues."

She added some advice for prospective owners: "Given that Cockers are gundogs and love hunting, crawling around in mud, wet paws and chasing birds, new owners have to be prepared for accidents (and vet bills) and dirty carpets and furniture. The breed's stubbornness can lead to obedience issues from time to time. Generally easy to train, the Cocker can often suffer from 'male deafness' as my vet diagnosed. Again, you have to be prepared for this and not OCD about having the perfectly clean sofa all the time.

"Cockers can also be an extremely difficult breed for the first 12 to 18 months in terms of chewing, separation anxiety and activity levels; they are inquisitive and stubborn too. They become the perfect pet afterwards, but some will cause havoc in the meantime. Can the potential owner cope with that?

"Most workers are going to need more exercise and mental stimulation than most show types. If you're thinking about a worker because you have an active lifestyle, do think very carefully about whether your lifestyle is **that** active every day of the week, and remember that a show Cocker also enjoys very long walks and running with the owner, etc., too. They go until you stop.

"Older people should ask how they are going to look after the dog in 10 years' time, do they have family who can help if need be? And, if they are older and missing having a dog, they should

consider an older dog - there are so many 'oldies' out there who would welcome being a lap dog in their later years. Yes, you might have less time left and it's very hard when you lose them, but think how much an older dog will enrich the older owner's life and match their lifestyle.

"They are frequently very much 'want to be with you' dogs and that can be hard work too. If a younger person is looking to buy, they should ask themselves if they are of an age where they are going to go to university, are they relying on parents to doggy sit whilst living at home, are they planning or thinking about going into the armed forces etc.? They must think about how they are going to care for the dog long term.

"Obviously I would recommend the breed to everyone, as Cockers can be perfect with children and their 'needy' manner frequently means that they are very happy to fit into routines - mine have never got me up at 6am to go for a walk. They are happy to go when I am - that is if I am not dragging them out from under the duvet!"

Rescue Organisations

There are a number of rescue organisations in the UK and North America, often run by volunteers who give up their time to help dogs in distress. There are also online Cocker forums where people sometimes post information about a dog which needs rehoming. Even if you don't want to rehome a Cocker Spaniel, there are other ways in which you can help these worthy organisations.

In the UK, there are a number of Cocker-specific rescue organisations, including:

- o   The Cocker Spaniel Club Re-homing and Rescue Scheme - www.thecockerspanielclub.co.uk/rescue.htm

- o   Kennel Club Cocker Spaniel rescue -

www.thekennelclub.org.uk/services/public/findarescue/Default.aspx?breed=2052

- o Spaniel Aid (Cocker and English Springer) - http://spanielaid.co.uk

- o Cocker and English Spaniel Rescue - http://www.caessr.org.uk

- o Working Cocker Spaniel Rescue - www.workingcockerspanielrescue.co.uk

- o Northern English Cocker Spaniel Rescue - www.necsr.co.uk

- o Cheshire Pet Charity Network
     http://thecheshirepetcharitynetwork.co.uk/the-charities/cocker-english-springer-spaniel-rescue

There are also some general canine websites which act as a portal for rescue organisations with Cockers to rehome. Always do your research beforehand. They include:

- o www.manytearsrescue.org
- o www.rspca.org.uk/findapet/rehomeapet
- o www.dogsblog.com/category/english-cocker-spaniel
- o www.homes4dogs.co.uk
- o www.greenleafanimalrescue.org.uk
- o www.rainrescue.co.uk/rehoming/dog-rehoming

In the USA, there are numerous regional Cocker Spaniel rescue organisations, mostly rehoming American Cockers, as well as organisations such as:

- o American Cocker Spaniel Rescue - www.acsrwa.org

- o Cocker Spaniel Rescue Network - www.cockerspanielrescue.org

- o The English Cocker Spaniel Club of America rescue - http://ecscahealthandrescue.org

- o English Cocker Spaniel groups are listed at http://englishcockerspaniel.rescueshelter.com

- o Second Chance Cocker Rescue - http://secondchancecockerrescue.org

There are also general websites, such as www.petfinder.com and www.adoptapet.com

This is by no means an exhaustive list, but it does cover some of the main organisations involved. If you do visit these websites, you cannot presume that the descriptions are 100% accurate. They are given in good faith, but ideas of what constitutes a 'medium-sized' or 'lively' dog may vary. Some dogs advertised may have other breeds in their genetic make-up (although not often with the Cocker-specific rescues). It does not mean that these are necessarily worse dogs, but if you are attracted to the breed for its temperament and other assets, make sure you are looking at a Cocker.

NEVER get a dog from eBay, Craig's List, Gumtree or any of the other general advertising websites which sell old cars, washing machines, golf clubs etc. You might think you are getting a cheap Cocker Spaniel, but in the long run you will pay the price. If the dog had been well bred and properly cared for, he or she would not be advertised on a website such as this. If you buy or get a free one, you may be storing up a whole load of trouble for yourselves in terms of health and/or behaviour issues, due to poor breeding and environment.

If you haven't been put off with all of the above..... Congratulations, you may be just the family or person that poor homeless Cocker is looking for!

If you can't spare the time to adopt - and adoption means forever - you might want to consider fostering. Or you could help by becoming a fundraiser to generate cash to keep these very worthy rescue groups providing such a wonderful service. However you decide to get involved,

Good Luck!

Saving one dog will not change the world,
But it will change the world for one dog

15. Caring for Older Dogs

Cocker Spaniels are generally healthy and active dogs that live life to the full. Lifespan varies from one individual to another and is affected by factors such as bloodlines, general health, environment, lifestyle and diet. According to the breeders involved in this book, a typical lifespan may be anything from 10 to 15 years, with a few dogs having longer or shorter lives. Four of our breeders reported owning or knowing of Cockers who reached the ages of 17 to 19, but these are exceptions rather than the rule.

Many Cockers remain fit and active well into their twilight years, but eventually all dogs – even lively Cocker Spaniels –slow down.

At some point your old dog will start to feel the effects of ageing. Physically, joints may become stiffer and organs, such as heart or liver, may not function as effectively. On the mental side - just as with humans - your dog's memory, ability to learn and awareness will all start to dim.

Your faithful companion might become a bit grumpier, stubborn or a little less tolerant of lively dogs and children. You may also notice that he doesn't see or hear as well as he used to. On the other hand, your old friend might not be hard of hearing at all. He might have developed that affliction common to many older dogs – ours included - of selective hearing.

Our 11-year-old Max has bionic hearing when it comes to the word 'Dinnertime' whispered from 30 feet away, yet seems strangely unable to hear the commands 'Come' or 'Down' when we are right in front of him!

You don't have to mollycoddle your ageing Spaniel, but you can help ease him or her into old age gracefully by keeping an eye out for any changes and taking action to help as much as possible. This might involve a visit to the vet for supplements and/or medications, modifying your dog's environment, changing the food and slowly reducing the amount of daily exercise. Much depends on the individual dog. Just as with humans, a dog of ideal weight that has been active and stimulated throughout his or her life is likely to age slower than an overweight couch potato.

We normally talk about dogs being old when they reach the last third of their lives. This varies greatly from dog to dog and bloodline to bloodline. Some Cockers may start to show signs of ageing as young as seven or eight years old, while others will still be fit in mind and body when several years older.

Keeping Cockers at that optimum weight is challenging - and important – as they age. Their metabolisms slow down, making it easier to put on the pounds unless their daily calories are reduced. At the same time, extra weight places additional, unwanted stress on joints and organs, making them have to work harder than they should.

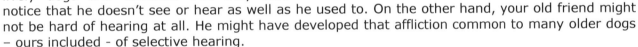

Physical and Mental Signs of Ageing

If your Cocker is in or approaching the last third of his life, here are some signs that his body is feeling its age:

➢ He gets up from lying down more slowly and he goes up and down stairs more slowly. He can no longer jump on to the couch or bed. These are all signs that his joints are stiffening, often due to arthritis

➢ He has generally slowed down and no longer seems as keen to go out on his walks. He tires more easily on a walk

➢ He doesn't want to go outside in bad weather

➢ He has the occasional 'accident' (incontinence) inside the house

➢ He is getting grey hairs, particularly around the muzzle

➢ He has put on a bit of weight

➢ He urinates more frequently

➢ He drinks more water

➢ He gets constipated

➢ The foot pads thicken and nails may become more brittle

➢ He has one or more lumps or fatty deposits on his body. Our dog Max developed two on his head recently and we took him straight to the vet, who performed an operation to remove them. They were benign (harmless), but you should always get them checked out ASAP in case they are an early form of cancer

➢ He can't regulate his body temperature as he used to and so feels the cold and heat more

➢ He doesn't hear as well as he used to

➢ His eyesight may deteriorate – if his eyes appear cloudy he may be developing cataracts and you should see your vet as soon as you notice the signs

➢ He has bad breath (halitosis), which could be a sign of dental or gum disease. Some Cockers are prone to poor dental health. Brush his teeth regularly and give him a daily dental stick, such as Dentastix or similar. If the bad breath persists, get him checked out by a vet

➢ If he's inactive he may develop callouses on the elbows, especially if he lies down on hard surfaces – although this is more common with larger breeds

It's not just your dog's body which deteriorates, his mind does too. It's all part of the normal ageing process. Here are some symptoms. Your dog may display some, all or none of these signs of mental deterioration:

- His sleep patterns change, an older dog may be more restless at night and sleepy during the day, and sleeps deeper

- He barks more

- He stares at objects or wanders aimlessly around the house

- He forgets or ignores commands or habits he once knew well, such as housetraining and recall

- He displays increased anxiety, or aggressiveness

- Often Cockers may become more clingy and dependent on you, which may result in separation anxiety, while a few may become less interested in human contact

Understanding the changes happening to your dog and acting on them compassionately and effectively will help ease your dog's passage through his or her senior years. Your dog has given you so much pleasure over the years, now he or she needs you to give that bit of extra care for a happy, healthy old age. You can also help your Cocker to stay mentally active by playing gentle games and getting new toys to stimulate interest.

Helping Seniors

The first thing you can do is monitor your dog and be on the lookout for any changes in actions or behaviour. Then there are lots of things you can do for him.

Food and Supplements - As dogs age they need fewer calories, so many owners switch to a food specially formulated for older dogs. These are labelled 'Senior,' ' Ageing' or 'Mature.' Check the labelling; some are specifically for dogs aged over eight, others may be for 10 or 12-year-olds. If you are not sure if a senior diet is necessary for your dog, talk to your vet the next time you are there for annual vaccinations or a check-up. Remember, if you do change the brand, switch the food gradually over a week to 10 days. Unlike with humans, a dog's digestive system cannot cope with sudden changes of diet.

Consider feeding your Cocker a supplement, such as Omega-3 fatty acids for the brain and coat, or one to help joints. There are also medications and homeopathic remedies to help relieve anxiety. Again, check with your vet before introducing anything new.

Exercise - Take the lead from your dog, if he doesn't want to walk as far, then don't. But if your dog doesn't want to go out at all, you will have to coax him out. ALL senior dogs need some physical exercise to keep their joints moving and to exercise their heart and lungs.

Environment - Make sure your dog has a nice soft place to rest his old bones, which may mean adding an extra blanket to his bed. This should be in a place which is not too hot or cold, as he may not be able to regulate his body temperature as well as when he was younger. If his eyesight is failing, move obstacles out of his way, reducing the chance of injuries.

Jumping on and off furniture or in or out of the car is high impact for old joints and bones. He may need a helping hand on to and off the couch or your bed (if he's allowed up there) and maybe a ramp or step to get in and out of the car. Make sure he has plenty of time to sleep and is not pestered and/or bullied by younger dogs, other animals or young children.

Weight - No matter how old your Cocker is, he still needs a waist! Maintaining a healthy weight with a balanced diet and regular, gentler exercise are two of the most important things you can do for your dog.

Consult a Professional - If your dog is showing any of the following signs, get him checked out by your vet:

> ➤ Increased urination or drinking - this can be a sign of something amiss, such as reduced liver or kidney function, Cushing's Disease or Diabetes

> ➤ Constipation or not urinating regularly could be a sign of something not functioning properly with the digestive system or organs

> ➤ Incontinence, which could be a sign of a mental or physical problem

> ➤ Cloudy eyes, which could be cataracts

> ➤ Lumps or bumps on the body -which are most often benign, but can occasionally be malignant (dangerous)

> ➤ Decreased appetite – loss of appetite is often a sign of an underlying problem

> ➤ Excessive sleeping or a lack of interest in you and his or her surroundings

> ➤ Diarrhoea or vomiting

> ➤ A darkening and dryness of skin that never seems to get any better - this can be a sign of hypothyroidism

> ➤ Any other out-of-the-ordinary behaviour for your dog. A change in patterns or behaviour is often your dog's way of telling you that all is not well

---

The Last Lap

Huge advances in veterinary science have meant that there are countless procedures and medications which can prolong the life of your dog, and this is a good thing. But there comes a time when you have to let go. If your dog is showing all the signs of ageing, has an ongoing medical condition from which he or she cannot recover, or is showing signs of pain, mental anxiety or distress and there is no hope of improvement, then the dreaded time has come to say goodbye.

You owe it to him or her. There is no point keeping an old dog alive if all they have to look forward to is pain and death.

I'm even getting upset as I write this, as I think of parting from my 11-year-old dog not too many years into the future, as well as the wonderful dogs we have had in the past. But we have their lives in our hands and we can give them the gift of passing away peacefully and humanely at the end when the time is right.

Losing our beloved companion, our best friend, our sporting buddy, a member of the family, is truly heart-breaking for many owners. But one of the things we realise at the back of our minds when we get that lively little puppy is the pain that comes with it; knowing that we will live longer than him or her and that we will probably have to make this most painful of decisions at some point. It's the worst thing about being a dog owner.

If your Cocker has had a long and happy life, then you could not have done any more. You were a good owner and your dog was lucky to have you. Remember all the good times you have had together. And try not to rush out and buy another dog; wait a while to grieve for your Cocker. Assess your current life and lifestyle and, if your situation is right, only then consider getting another dog and all that that entails in terms of time, commitment and expense. Cockers are sensitive, often intuitive, creatures. One coming into a happy, stable household will get off to a much better start in life than a dog entering a home full of grief.

Whatever you decide to do, put the dog first.

What the Cocker Experts Say

Let's not dwell on the end stages of our dog's life, but focus on what we can do to keep him or her fit and healthy as the years roll by. This is the breeders' advice:

Hobby breeder Maxine Shaverin, of Lancashire, has owned Cockers for more than 20 years, including Tanya (pictured, aged 15), who lived to almost 17 years old: "I continued to feed her Skinners Maintenance, although this was supplemented with sardines, chicken and rice or pasta if required. I gave glucosamine chondroitin 500mg, and then 1000mg, daily - but a good brand, not Holland and Barrett.

"In her latter months she didn't like knowing I was there but not in sight. She did also get more fussy over her food. Now, whether that was opportunity, knowing that if she refused her kibble she would get chicken, I don't know - although it wouldn't surprise me! Ear infections become more frequent as they become less mobile and when she was 16, she had more severe and frequent stomach upsets, so I always kept Pro-Kolin in for that purpose.

"My advice is to try and keep your dog mobile for as long as you can. Don't hesitate to give pain relief for arthritis – they hate not going out - and look at hydrotherapy when they do slow down; maintaining muscle strength helps to keep them mobile for longer. Get footstools, etc. so that they can still be independent and enjoy the comforts that they have been used to previously, like the sofa or the bed, but you need to look after their joints more and prevent injury. Let them tell you when walks need to be shorter and less demanding, but then drive them somewhere new where they can have a little mooch and enjoy new sniffs."

KC Assured Breeder Peter Harvey, of Grannus (show) Cocker Spaniels, Somerset, said that he looks to change a dog's diet at around seven or eight years of age, and then feeds chicken and boiled rice with vegetables and a senior mixer. Supplements are only added on veterinary advice.

He added: "As they get older, they tend to be "lap dogs" and follow you around; they want to be with you all the time. Physical issues may include poor eyesight, joints (mainly hips), poor hearing, warts, being overweight and lack of bladder control. Dental care needs to be more regular. Be patient, give them all the love and attention they want and keep them clean. Take your time with old dogs, be slow and gentle and give them soft, chewy treats."

Jacquie Ward, of Breezybrook Gundogs, Bedfordshire, says: "My working Cockers are kept very fit - especially during the winter months - as they are working on shoots; their main role being picking up. One would expect them to age quicker, but I find that keeping them lean keeps them younger for longer. I only change their diet in late old age - probably 12 to 13 years - and I don't necessarily use a senior diet but I look for a higher protein, lower fat diet with high meat content and no cereal. They need higher protein to aid in tissue repair.

"I feed my older Cockers Fish 4 Dogs Salmon complete food. It has a high meat (fish) content and no cereal. The protein is 26%. I add salmon oil to their diet to help with their joints. If they show any signs of joint pain or stiffness, I use Lintbells Yumove tablets."

Pictured is Jacquie's Cressett Chocolate Drop of Breezybrook (Chocolate) aged 14 retrieving a pheasant. Chocolate had three litters and was still fit and working until she had a stroke and was put to sleep aged 15 years and six months. She had no supplements and was still on an ordinary adult diet. At 15 years old she was placed third in the Gamekeepers' Class at Crufts, with the judge commenting on her 'super movement!'

"The only behavioural changes I have found is they may steady up and they start to become hard of hearing, but this may be attributable to a life on the shooting field without hearing protection. The advice I would give is keep your dog lean; dogs were never designed to be fat. This reduces pressure on joints and helps keep them mobile. Also, especially for those that work their dogs, dry them off after getting wet and use a coat to warm them. This all helps to prevent arthritis and stiff joints."

Andrew Height, of Fourtails Cocker Spaniels, Cambridgeshire, says: "Cocker Spaniels become veterans in the Kennel Club's eyes at the age of seven, but I think every dog has a different 'age' threshold. We have one that is just coming up to 11 years and though she has slowed down a bit, she still loves life. I would say that 10 is probably the time when they may become 'old'.

"We feed her with food that contains less fat as we do not want her overweight. She still has treats, but on a limited basis. She also gets a supplement for her joints and bones. We noticed that she was getting stiff and starting to limp, so checked with our vet and there was nothing wrong but age. Since we put her on the supplement, she has stopped limping and lost all of the stiffness. It's good stuff!

"We have had no major old age health issues with any of ours. Our old girl tends to sleep more, but apart from that, there's no real change, she's still friendly and demanding fuss. My advice is to keep an eye out for them when they get older. Don't be obsessive, but watch them more than the youngsters. Allow them more leeway, as in shorter walks, maybe. Each individual dog has its own ways - keep looking at them."

Gail Parsons, of Gaiter (show) Cocker Spaniels, Sussex: "Cracker - pictured - is 12, going on 13, and he's been on Arden Grange Senior food for three years. He has a garlic pill every day (as do all my dogs) and half a glucosamine tablet. I haven't come across any particular health issues; he still chases a ball with the others, but he does sleep more now.

"Behaviourally, he's still the same but, like any other breed, they start to hear less and see less - unless it's a biscuit of course! As they age, don't walk them too far - especially in winter - and if they get wet, make sure they are completely dry when you get home - and give them lots of TLC."

Christine Grant, of Rostreigan (show) Cocker Spaniels, Hampshire, adds: "I have not come up against any health issues which are particularly associated with older Cockers myself, although they can become a little more grumpy, and less tolerant of a bouncy puppy, for instance. They sleep more, similar to a puppy, and are perhaps a bit more set in their ways."

Nicola Hunter, of Pursley Gundogs, Hertfordshire: "I'd say Cocker Spaniels become senior dogs at around nine years old. My older Cockers have the same working dog food as my younger ones. I am lucky enough to be able to keep them working throughout the majority of their lives. The older dogs have a tin of sardines or oily fish regularly, I find this keeps them supple. I also use food with a joint supplement included during the shooting season.

"I find if they are kept working and their weight is kept down, then Spaniels cope very well with old age. The biggest problem is persuading them to take life a little easier! I have known Cockers live to 18 and have personally had them live to 15."

Dutch international show breeder Haja van Wessem, of Speggle-Waggel Cocker Spaniels, Wassenaar: "I change the diet to one with less protein; I feed raw meat and dry dog food with salmon oil. Regarding health, the ears should always be checked at any age. Teeth are more prone to get covered with tartar when they get older and this could damage the gums, so they must be cleaned regularly. Sometimes older dogs get 'dry eye' when they do not produce enough tears any more and artificial teardrops should be applied. Also the folds in the underjaw must be kept clean and dry to prevent eczema or bacterial infections.

"An older dog sleeps more and sometimes they do not like to be disturbed. I felt with my oldies that they needed my company more than when they were young; sort of seeking reassurance that I am still there. My advice with older dogs is to love them, spoil them and have a little patience. They are not as quick and alert as they used to be and dementia in a dog does occur, but never forget the pleasure and love they gave you in their more active lifetime."

Jackie Hornby, of Jacmist Cockers, Bedfordshire, gives Joint Aid fish oil to her older dogs and continues to feed them a raw diet. She says: "Watch the digestion and stools as these can change, and arrange check-ups with the vet to monitor their general condition. Little lumps and cysts or warts can appear through the coat, and nails need trimming more often if they go down on their pasterns. Keep them out of draughty places as it can affect the joints. Old dogs can bark more, I think it's because their hearing is not as good. The appetite can change if the sense of smell is going, and they sleep longer and deeper."

Caroline Bymolen, Carto (show) Cocker Spaniels, Cambridgeshire: "As we feed raw, we continue with the same diet, but care should be taken on the amount given as they may be less active. We also give a multi-vitamin supplement. Some older dogs can develop skin issues or have problems with teeth, and some can develop small growths under the skin which tend to be benign. Behavioural changes very much depend on the individual, but in general they become less active and will come to a halt on long walks. (Stock photo).

"My advice is to keep a closer eye on them. Reduce their food intake if they become less active; a fat Cocker won't live as long as one of the correct weight. Try and keep teeth free from too much tartar and if they do develop growths that appear and enlarge quickly, take them to the vet. Generally, don't let them take advantage and pull the wool over your eyes - an old Cocker is not necessarily a sick Cocker!"

Wendy Tobijanski, of Janski Cocker Spaniels, Shropshire, has been breeding English and American Cockers for 40 years. She says: "I feed my old dogs the same as the others. I don't see the need to change the diet if the dog continues to thrive; just watch their weight. I do add cod liver oil and a glucosamine and chondroitin supplement if they seem a bit stiff or struggling to jump up on the sofa.

"When I groom my dogs, I check for any lumps and bumps or signs of cancer and watch out for eye problems too. Old dogs generally slow down, but often introducing a puppy works wonders and gives them a new lease of life. I advise owners to enjoy your time with them and to seek veterinary help if you find any changes in health or behaviour."

Kate McBride, of Ferebim Cockers Lincolnshire and Limousin: "All my Cockers sadly have died at 12 years of age; they have all been really active dogs right up till that awful day. Lily, my old lady I have here at the moment (pictured) loves life and has the usual Cocker response to life, which is to fling herself headlong into any fun going.

"However, Lily recently showed signs of struggling to walk up hills. She needed carrying and struggled to jump on the sofa - a very unheard of situation. A bit of research flagged up how great turmeric mixed into 'golden paste' was. So we made up this mixture and six months down the line Lily no longer needs to be carried up hills - she runs up and woofs at our slowness, and the sofa is no longer a problem.

"I feel so very privileged to have got to know my dogs for such a short space of time, but really would love to have them with me for longer. Their crazy love of life and ability to turn any situation into one of fun and mayhem is a great joy and so infectious. My dogs have a huge energy and passion for living. They love food, learning new things, walks, sniffing - Oh how they love to sniff! All walks are done with the head down and tails held high and wagging. Did I mention food, cuddles and being with the family all the time?!"

NB Turmeric is a blood thinner, so check with your vet if you are thinking of giving it to your dog.

---

16. Cockers in Action

I can't think of another breed which is as versatile as the Cocker Spaniel. If there is one word which keeps cropping up when discussing this little Spaniel, it is "adaptable". The Cocker's combination of intelligence, eagerness to please, highly developed sense of smell and work ethic create a unique dog which excels in so many different fields.

Cockers are hugely popular as family pets, they are good with children, adults and other dogs, they make excellent gundogs and field triallers, they shine at Flyball and agility, in the showing world only four dogs have ever won the prestigious 'Best in Show' at Crufts more than once, and three of them were Cockers. And if all that wasn't enough, the Cocker Spaniel is also one of the few breeds which make excellent assistance and therapy dogs - whether it is helping to improve the lives of autistic children, deaf people or the elderly, or working alongside police and customs officers as sniffer dogs.

In this chapter we have asked several experts in their fields to tell their personal stories. Their love of their dogs shines through and the result is a wonderful tribute to this remarkable breed.

A Clean Sweep

By Richard Preest

The sport of field trialling is highly competitive and many of the top handlers are people who work full-time with gundogs. Head Gardener **Richard Preest** tells the remarkable story of how he started out from scratch and 10 years later achieved the ultimate accolade with his dog, Centrewalk Sweep. The duo followed in the footsteps of legendary handlers and dogs to win the 86th Cocker Spaniel Championships in 2016.

"Unlike many dog men and trainers who have been around dogs from an early age, my life with dogs started quite late. I was never allowed a dog as a child, and it was not until I married that I got my first one, a lively black show Cocker called Bonnie that we loved. Sadly, she collapsed with a heart attack when she was about seven years old.

The Duchess of Beaufort, for whom I work as Head Gardener on the Badminton Estate, told me she had a friend looking to rehome a nine-month-old working Cocker. So we became the owners of Storm, a handsome blue roan. I decided to use him for what he was bred for, and so set about training him for the field.

I must have watched a video called 'Basic Training for a Working Cocker Spaniel' by Carl and Mark Colclough a million times, and I actually trained Storm to a pretty good standard. I started taking him beating and picking up on the Badminton Estate. Sadly, Storm developed cancerous tumours and at only four we had to have him put to sleep, which was heart-breaking. I'll never forget that day.

My next pup was Sky, a lemon and white Cocker bought from Laurence Dewis in Coventry. I followed the same route I'd taken with Storm and worked him on the Estate shoot. Around this time, my wife, Suzie, said she'd like a dog of her own and found a newspaper ad, it read: "Blue roan working Cocker Spaniel bitch, two and a half years old, £100."

We bought Daisy and as we left, the lady said she had a pedigree if I wanted it, so we took that home too. At that time I knew nothing about pedigrees, although I remember noticing that one of her grandparents, Larford Cateran, had won the Championships and there were a few other FTCHs (which I now know means Field Trial Champion) scattered about in the pedigree.

The following season, while picking up behind my boss, the Duke of Beaufort, Sky pulled off a really eye-catching retrieve of a wounded cock pheasant over a stream and a wall. I didn't realise the Duke was watching and when Sky returned with the bird, he said: "It was worth coming out today just to watch that, you should trial that dog, Richard." I asked him what he meant and he explained about field trials, where you compete against others with your dog. Having always played lots of sport and having a competitive edge, it appealed to me, so I thought I'd go along and watch one. I went to watch a Novice Cocker Trial held by the Bristol & West Gundog Society.

Probably like most people when they watch one for the first time, I thought: "That's easy enough: hunt your dog, find a pheasant and retrieve it. My dog can do that." However, you soon learn that it's far from easy and a very, very steep learning curve to reach field trial standard. It's even harder to actually win one - especially with a half-trained dog, which is what most of us beginners turn up with at our first trial. But I have the Duke to thank for giving me that first prod.

I bred a litter from Daisy with a novice dog from John Cook and kept a pup, Flint, with field trials in mind. I trained him as I had the others and ran him in my first event at West Morden, Dorset, in 2006 under Judges Peter Clulee and Walter Harrison. I remember pulling up at the meet as nervous as anything, but fellow competitor Ron James, who has since become a good friend, introduced himself and me to a few others. I finished fourth and remember thinking: "If this is what finishing fourth feels like, heaven knows what it must feel like to win!"

I ran Flint too many times in quick succession without ironing out a few little errors - as much on my part as his - and spoilt him. He became 'trial-wise', a phrase you'll hear if you ever get involved in the sport. He had several awards without winning, so I decided to sell him to a friend who takes him shooting regularly, loves him to bits and Flint has a wonderful life.

I had definitely been bitten by the trialling bug. I'd learned a lot running Flint and was ready to try again. This time I got serious, did some research and mated Daisy with a dog that had won the Championships, FTCH Danderw Druid. I also applied to the Kennel Club for a kennel name: Centrewalk.

I kept a bitch pup this time, Centrewalk Daydream - we called her Freckle (pictured). I followed my same training methods and she looked very good from the start, with bags of speed and drive and very clever. I was out training with another good friend, Andy Fisher, and he said she could be a champion. I remember laughing and saying it would be nice just to win a Novice Trial.

She was ready to run in 2007 and finished fourth in her first trial at the Shaftesbury Estate, followed by a close second in her second trial. Her first win came in her next event at Badminton in the Bristol and West Novice Cocker. It felt amazing, I had reached that first goal. The judges that day - Jeremy Organ and Ben Randall - were very complimentary about Freckle. I then spent the rest of that season either getting close to winning my first Open Stake, or being put out. I just couldn't get it quite right.

I was lucky enough to be invited on a training day with Will Clulee, of Poolgreen Gundogs. Will gave me some good advice on handling her and at the end of the day told me she'd be a Champion, no problem! He gave me the confidence to stick with it, and said to get Freckle right for the next season. He was so right about her.

The following season Freckle won her first two Open Stakes. She beat two of top handler Ian Openshaw's dogs in a three-dog run-off for first place: FTCH Chyknell Lilly and - one of the best bitches I'd seen - FTCH Chyknell Iris. This was a real feather in my cap and it had proved Freckle was seriously good and had qualified us for the Championships for the first time. A week later she won again at the Cocker Club Open Stake at Hamptworth to make her up to Field Trial Champion.

Between the two wins my Dad died and it was the most up and down I have ever felt in my life.

We went to Ford and Etal in Northumberland for the Championships in January 2010, but sadly nerves got the better of me and Freckle, and she unfortunately boiled over and spoilt her chance. The following season she won her third Open very quickly to qualify again for the Championship, held at the Queensberry Estate in Drumlanrig, Scotland. This time she went very well, I was mentally more prepared and she finished fourth.

After this I decided to retire her and concentrate on her offspring. Having qualified her two pups, I thought I'd give her one more go in the last qualifier of that season and she finished a close second on the back of no training at all. That was the end of her trialling career and she now lives with good friend Rosemary Price picking up in Devon. She has the best retirement home I could have wished for; she has a lovely life and is very happy.

I have kept three of Freckle's offspring and all of them are now Field Trial Champions – or FTCHs. They are Centrewalk Moonshell (Pixie), FTCH Centrewalk Piccolo (Rosie) and, of course, FTCH Centrewalk Sweep (Sweep - pictured). Pixie has qualified for the Cocker Spaniel Championship three times, as has Sweep, and Rosie twice to date. All have been awarded Diplomas.

With Freckle I was still a novice, but with Sweep I was a more experienced handler and realised right from the early days of training that he had potential. In the end, he was good enough to go all the way and win the 2016 Championship, held on the beautiful Dunira Estate in Perthshire, Scotland. Competition for the title is very strong. The Championship involves the top 30-odd Cocker Spaniels in the country, which have all first had to qualify at regional field trials around Britain.

During the event, Sweep was able to demonstrate all the attributes required in a Field Trial Champion. He showed pace, drive, style, game finding ability, good marking and retrieving and steadiness. And on this particular occasion, he also showed stamina on his first run and the natural ability to work the wind; essential if a dog is to be a good game finder.

I feel very lucky to have had the success I have had with my dogs in a relatively short space of time and hope it will inspire more people to come into what is a fabulous sport to be involved in. My aim for the future is to continue to enjoy training and competing with dogs that I have bred and also to help a few people along the way to enjoy working their dogs; be it in field trials or in the shooting field."

A Life with Show Cockers

By Linda Reed

Linda, of Delindere Cocker Spaniels, Leicestershire, UK, has a wealth of experience with both English and American Cockers, having owned, bred, showed and judged them for several decades.

"I acquired my first English Cocker more than 35 years ago quite by accident. A friend of my mum's had a couple of Cockers that she showed a little – a dog and a bitch – and, in a moment of madness, she allowed them into the garden together when the bitch was in season! Nine weeks later a litter of seven was born; blue roans and black and whites.

I had wanted a dog as a family pet for a long time and as soon as I saw them, I knew this was the breed for me. So a few weeks later my first dog, Gyp, a black and white English Cocker, came to me. It did not take long to realise what a fun loving, happy, outgoing and loving breed Cockers are. Gyp's breeder encouraged me to show him, so I entered my first event. It was a Limit Show, where the Kennel Club limit the number of classes and exhibitors have to be members of the organising society. As with so many of us with our first show dog, it soon became evident that Gyp was not that good – but the showing bug bit!

I was also determined that I was going to have a dog good enough to win with, and my ultimate goal was to breed something that could win. (Pictured is Linda's Delindere Wanna B'The One JW - Gracie).

About 10 years after showing English Cockers with moderate success, someone came to my local ring training with a four-month-old red and white American Cocker puppy. I vowed there and then that one day I would have one. About four years later – and after much research and searching - my first American puppy arrived, a red and white bitch, Cassie, show name Mygilie Muscarat from Delindere.

We had a wonderful time in the ring, mainly at Open Show level, with Best Puppy in Show wins followed by group wins, Best in Show and Reserve Best in Show awards. It just made sense to breed from Cassie as she was a winner herself, and put an own-bred puppy in the ring. So I did.

English and American Cockers are quite different breeds in lots of ways. They look different; they have different natures and require different methods of trimming for show. Americans are quite independent and can easily entertain themselves with toys and can, at times, be quite vocal. An English Cocker prefers to be entertained either by his owner or a playmate. English Cockers are, perhaps, more loving and more destructive as pups. But as gundogs, both breeds should have fantastic temperaments.

My first serious English show bitch was Zoe, a blue purchased in the mid-80s, show name Bullpark Vogue with Delindere. She had been chosen by her breeder as the pick of the litter and was to be retained. However, at the time the breeder was having personal problems, which included moving house, so she had to let Zoe go. As the breeder knew me and knew I would show Zoe, she allowed me to take her.

Zoe was the one that gave me many firsts: Best Puppy in Show, Best in Show at Open Show level and my first Crufts qualification. She went on to gain a fifth and Very Highly Commended (VHC) in her class at Crufts. She produced my first homebred puppy to follow in her mother's 'paw prints'. At the time I did not think things could get any better – I was on Cloud Nine!

I was really fortunate to get my first serious show girl in the way that I did, as generally most newcomers would perhaps purchase an eight-week-old puppy. Buying a pup at this age for show is a tricky business as there are things that can 'go wrong'. Be wary of the breeder stating that a pup is 'show quality' at eight weeks; the most a pup can be at that age is 'show potential'. Also be wary of any breeder that cannot produce any relevant health testing certificates for both parents - particularly eye test certificates.

If possible, find a breeder that might be happy to run a pup on for you until he or she is four to five months old, as at this age the new teeth will be through and the dog's general showmanship will be more evident. Does she (or he) carry herself well on the move, does she move true and is she happy around strangers and confident around other dogs? If you are lucky enough to find a breeder happy to do this, you need to be prepared to pay for it.

Normally, with a first show dog, Open Shows are where you would go to learn the ropes. However, there are a lot of people who happen to buy a pup with a 'famous' affix that go straight to Championship Shows expecting the dog to win at this level and qualify for Crufts at their first show. (Pictured is German Junior Champion Rauberleins Samba Pa Ti, owned in partnership by Linda and her good friend Elaine Thomas).

All shows - whether All-Breed Open Shows, Breed Club Open Shows, Group Open Shows, General Championship Shows, Group Championship Shows or Breed Club Championship Shows - are open to all. Crufts is the only show you have to qualify for and this can only be done in certain classes at Championship Shows, which is why a lot of newcomers tend to go straight for Championship Shows - whether or not the dog or they are ready for that level of competition. Classes are either age-related or for dogs that have won a number of Firsts at either Open Shows or Championship Shows.

I always advise newcomers at ring training to attend several local Open Shows to start their pup's show career. A new exhibitor in a large class at a busy Championship Show is not a good idea. Just finding your bench can be frustrating, and a long journey with a pup that has perhaps not travelled well can be a recipe for disaster. You need to be calm and relaxed to show dogs, as your mood can very easily travel down the lead to the dog.

The social side of the show scene is great as you will see the same exhibitors week after week and many good friendships develop. Everybody in the same breed knows everybody to some degree. One week you can be competing against someone you might be showing under (as a judge) the next. I was first asked to judge English Cockers about 20 years ago, then American Cockers shortly after that.

To be asked to judge is an honour and privilege as show committees are usually made up of people who have been around in their respective breeds for many years and have much experience. When I was offered that first Open Show judging appointment, I was thrilled and naturally accepted. When my first Championship Show appointment came along, I was on Cloud Nine again for many weeks!

When judging, I hope to find a dog that in my opinion fits the breed standard as I interpret it. I like a feminine bitch and a handsome dog and they certainly have to be enjoying their time in the ring, showing this in the way they move with a constantly wagging tail. They must also be

generally fit, strong and in good coat. English Cockers are one of the hardest breeds to keep in show trim as they are one of the few that are totally hand stripped. Hand stripping is not easy as it is very time consuming, and a show Cocker needs this doing regularly to keep the coat down. Americans are slightly easier as there is more clipper work and scissoring, but obviously have a heavier, more profuse coat. To trim an American correctly is an art and takes many months to master.

Show Cockers, both American and English, do need to be trimmed and bathed weekly, whether or not they are to be shown, otherwise you will regret it - particularly if they are allowed to get wet while exercising. Their long coats can and do mat very easily when wet.

A good healthy diet is important also as what 'goes in' shows on the outside; a coat needs to be fed well to grow well. Plenty of exercise and fresh air is also important – a healthy dog is a happy dog. (Linda is pictured with Delindere She's a Moody Blu – Maisie - and Delindere Nordic Maid - Phoebe).

Dog showing can and does take over your life, is time consuming and expensive, but so rewarding and enjoyable. I cannot imagine ever being without dogs or dog showing - dogs are my life, they keep you fit and healthy. (You can't be ill when you have animals to care for!)

You plan every aspect of your life around your dogs and dog shows. Your garden has to be large enough for kennels and runs, you buy a car big enough to transport your dogs, plus their cages and trolley, to shows. You plan your holidays around litters and you even have a three-piece suite the same colour as the dogs to disguise the dog hair!"

Agility and Flyball

By Kerena Marchant

Many Cockers, especially those from working stock, excel at canine competitions. Here Kerena Marchant, of Sondes Cocker Spaniels, Surrey, explains some of the ins and outs of the sport.

"Cocker Spaniels have always been a part of our family. My grandfather enjoyed shooting and his Cockers were a firm part of our family history and identity. After my husband died, my Mum decided to give my five-year-old dog-mad son, Jordan, his own dog to help him through his grief, and so it was that Rupert (Pays D Amour des Sondes) entered our lives.

Like most working Cockers, Rupert was a live wire and it wasn't long before he and his young owner were booked into weekly child-friendly obedience classes where they built a strong bond and excelled. After an agility demonstration at the club, Jordan was hooked and joined a local agility club, aged six.

Rupert was crazy, an agility course was like a theme park to him, but there was such a bond. He and Jordan soon became a partnership and, after a year of training, entered their first show. Now, 10 years later, it is no surprise that Rupert's agility career has taken him right to the top, including an individual gold medal for England at the Open Junior Agility championships. Our photograph shows a young Jordan with Rupert.

Those years from 2006 onwards also saw a huge uptake of working Cockers on the British agility circuit, with Cockers doing well in medium and, later, over the small heights - even holding their own against the increasing number of Collies in the medium height with their speed, drive, and agility. They were frequently called up to join the England squad in the medium and small categories of the FCI (Fédération Cynologique Internationale) European Open and World Agility Open Championships. By 2013 there was the first Cocker Spaniel Agility Champion, working Cocker, Ag. Ch. Octertyre Bonnie Heather handled by Charlotte Harding.

Due to their desire to please, high treat motivation, speed and drive, Cockers are easily trainable for agility. Agility is obedience under speed, with the dog having to negotiate a course consisting of jumps, tyres, tunnels, weaves and contact equipment such as the seesaw, A-frame and dog walk. It takes about a year to train a dog, depending on the aptitude of the dog and handler, to compete safely over all those obstacles.

Cockers can be sensitive little dogs and need plenty of praise, play and treat motivation at training so it is always fun. If they are pushed too far too fast, they can lose confidence and shut down or seek distractions and sniff. As they have good noses, they can be distracted by smells, but good training and strong work drive overrides this.

The growing success of Cockers in agility and other dog sports has seen a number of specialist breeders breeding Cockers for sporting homes. Sports breeders aim to breed Cockers with an aptitude for dog sports. They tend to breed from high drive dogs from top sporting and working lines with good temperaments. Health testing is a must as dogs that do sport need to be healthy with good hips. As KC (Kennel Club) registration is a requirement for participation in sports, most litters are KC registered. Due to restrictions on competing with docked dogs in some countries and the specific sports market, these Cockers are usually left undocked. The Cockers bred for dog sports tend to be smaller as, due to their conformity, Cockers do better over the lower jump heights.

Not long after Jordan and Rupert started competing, we got Magic, (Bryning Makin Magic for Sondes AWS). Magic came from the Bryning line of Cockers bred for sport, with an undocked tail. More importantly, his breeder promoted health testing and he came to us from parents who were health tested. Both Magic's parents did Flyball and were listed among the top 10 Flyball Cockers at the time.

Magic (pictured) was quite large - exactly 17" - with amazing speed and a long stride. He was well able to hold his own against the Collies in medium agility, taking my son to the top Grade 7, winning gold, silver and bronze for England at Junior International agility championships and gaining his Silver Agility Warrant. Alongside that he became my Flyball dog.

Flyball is a relay where the dogs race in a four-strong team to trigger a box and retrieve a tennis ball, then race back and exchange it for another toy. The retrieving skill of Cockers is one reason why they are quite prolific in British Flyball. Another is that in British Flyball Association Flyball (BFA), like NAFA (The North American Flyball Association), the team jump at the height of the smallest dog in the team.

Thus a small, fast Cocker gives the larger fast Collies or Whippets a lower height and enables the team to run faster, so Cockers are sought after dogs in the UK. Our current team, Wicked, has six Cockers, (five working and one show Cocker) and other teams have similar numbers. However, the Cambridgeshire Canines are the British team that really do fly the Cocker flag. They have 11 Cockers and breed working Cockers under the Tottlefields affix. They have even run a fast Flyball team consisting of four Cockers called the Cambridgeshire Cockups!

Crufts Flyball, which is run under separate KC rules, doesn't use height dogs and runs under a single height, which was formerly 12", but has now been reduced to 10". As it was dominated by Border Collies, the KC introduced a rule that you have to have a dog in the team that isn't a Collie. This was where Magic, our large, fast Cocker came into his own, competing with the Dream Team South East at Crufts in 2010 over 12" alongside Collies. Cockers are quite easy to train for Flyball, with their love of retrieving, treat motivation and natural speed. It takes about a year to bring a Cocker from basic training to open competition.

Again, like agility, it's best not to take a Cocker too far too fast as they can get in over their heads and lose confidence. They can have some "span-head" moments, so a team sense of humour is essential when a Cocker follows some ducks in flight instead of the jumps or takes a pit stop by some spectators eating burgers!

There is no doubt that Cockers are likely to dominate agility and Flyball over the next decade. Our young Cocker, The Ghost (Tottlefields Totally Go For Sondes), came from the Tottlefields affix. He is the great nephew of Magic and boasts three generations of health-tested parents. He is much smaller than Rupert and Magic, but just as fast. He has a promising future as a height dog in our current Flyball team, Wicked, and as an agility dog.

Dog sports are at the heart of our family life. Doing sports takes your relationship with your dog onto a deeper level. The bond between you and your dog is so strong that on an agility course you are of one mind. In Flyball you are part of a team with total trust in the other dogs and handlers. For the dogs it's an enrichment and they greet the sight of their agility and Flyball leads, collars and harnesses with excitement on show days. It's so easy to get hooked into this way of life however old or young you are. It's a life of weekends away with your dogs and family in the open air doing something you love that bonds you.

Come to a show and watch - most public dog shows hold agility and Flyball shows - and have a go. You never know, you could start a new way of life and move your dog ownership onto a deeper level dog ownership!"

Prospective Flyballers can find their local clubs by looking on the web pages of the national Flyball organisations such as the BFA, British Flyball Association or NAFA North American Flyball Association.

The Kennel Clubs of countries usually list their registered agility clubs that prospective handlers can join, as do agility web pages such as Agilitynet and various Facebook agility pages. Pictured is Dream Team South East at Crufts, with Kerena and Magic far right. Here are some useful websites:

British Agility Clubs http://agilitynet.co.uk/clutch/clubs.htm

The kennel Club agility page www.thekennelclub.org.uk/activities/agility

American Kennel Club agility page www.akc.org/events/agility

The Gundog Agility League www.gundog-agility.co.uk

The Cocker Spaniel Database www.cockerspanieldatabase.info

An Eventful Journey

By Stewart North

Kennel Club Assured Breeder Stewart North is a professional gundog trainer based in Leicestershire. He has decades of experience and has won 12 Field Trials and more than 100 Working Test Awards; most of them have been with Labrador Retrievers. A few years ago he turned his attention to Cocker Spaniels. This is his story.

"My journey to the UK's 2016 Cocker Spaniel Championship started in 2009 when I was introduced to a Cocker called Bramble owned by a training client, Paul Toseland of Lincolnshire. Paul had been on a graded training programme I had created for novice gundog handlers, and Bramble progressed with excellent results to a Grade 4 level, the highest novice level at that time. I was so impressed by the dog that we discussed the possibility of running her in working tests and field trials.

I sought advice from a well-known Cocker handler Simon Tyers, who had been at the top of the working Cocker world for some years. I had met Simon while competing at the Kennel Club Working Tests with a Labrador Retriever and was eager to demonstrate Bramble's abilities, so showed her off to Simon in some woodland cover.

Much to my surprise, Simon remarked that, despite her abilities, she would never win because her tail was too short! I was somewhat perplexed by such a comment: "What on Earth has that got to do with winning?" I asked.

Simon replied: "Running a Cocker is nothing like the Retriever world. Although a Cocker must complete a retrieve, 80% of the marks are awarded for the dog's hunting ability. The dog needs to demonstrate, pace, style and drive, and the way it hunts is very important. By removing such a large proportion of the tail, the owner has robbed the dog of its potential style."

At the time, I did not understand that logic and returned Bramble to the owner, advising that her potential to do well was not as good as I had initially thought, but said that if she ever had pups, I would buy one. In August 2011, Bramble (Enginebank Pepsi) produced six pups to FTCH Timsgary Barlow.

I collected my first working Cocker puppy two months later, a solid black I named Pip (Toadsspannel Foxey at Northglen), pictured. Despite arriving with the cash to pay for her, Paul refused it and we agreed to a training arrangement or future pup! It was not too long before I discovered Pip's excellent ability to learn; she has always been eager to please and highly intelligent.

At nine months old I entered her in the Kennel Club Novice AV Spaniel Working Test and, although we did not feature in the awards that day, she received the highest hunting marks out of the 20 dogs competing and gained the 'The Hunter' title from the judge of the day, recorded on the Paul French video. A few weeks later Pip gained her first Working Test award in both the Puppy and Novice classes, and also put in a very good performance in the Open Class.

I quickly discovered that too many working tests was not producing the type of working Cocker I wanted, but found them a useful experience to learn the dos and don'ts.

At 16 months of age, I entered Pip in her first Field Trial event and came fourth - we were very close to winning at one stage, but won no further awards that season. In 2013 and 2014 Pip showed her potential and went on to win her first Novice Field Trial, after gaining several awards. She didn't quite get there until January 2015, when she proved herself a worthy winner of the London Cocker Spaniel Club AV Novice Field Trial in difficult cover against several English Springer Spaniels - always a big ask in the Spaniel world.

Eight months of training followed before I entered her in her first Open Cocker Field Trial at Preston, held by the North Western Counties Field Trial Society. Unbelievably, she won and qualified for the 2016 Cocker Championship.

The emotions on that day were so high. We trainers talk about potential, but actually delivering a first class performance on the day is not that easy, especially when you are competing with the very best handlers in the UK, many of whom have qualified for the Championship on numerous occasions.

It just goes to show that with the right dog and many months and years of hard work, the dizzy heights of the very top can be achieved. We didn't go on to win at the 2016 Cocker Championships

– Richard Preest and Centrewalk Sweep came away with the title - but it was an incredible journey and a hugely enjoyable experience.

I have this basic advice for anyone thinking of training a working Cocker: Most puppy buyers choose a pup based on price, location, sex and colour without considering temperament, health and exercise. Very few buyers research the breeder and their dogs before viewing puppies. Acting on impulse is one sure way of making the wrong decision! Asking to see the Dam, SIRE and previous progeny will give you a much better indication of what your future pup will turn out to be.

After making that decision...If you want a good hunting working Cocker then the best advice I can give is not to start too early with obedience training. A puppy needs to be well socialised with people and other dogs, too much leash work, sit/stay and steadiness work can decrease the drive and confidence of a young dog.

FTW TOADSSPANNEL FOXEY AT NORTHGLEN

Allow the pup to grow up without too much discipline, concentrate on play-retrieve and recall-reward, then at about nine months of age the proper training can start. Visit a local trainer or experienced gundog handler to get a feel for the environment, teaching methods and - most importantly - the bond between dog and handler.

Far too many working Cockers end up in rescue homes due to irresponsible breeders, and buyers who have not researched the breed...Please do your homework."

Bringing the 'Best Dog' Home

By Peter Harvey

Kennel Club Assured Breeder Peter Harvey, of Grannus Cocker Spaniels, Somerset, shares his enthusiasm for the breed and gives an insight into the world of showing Cocker Spaniels.

"We got our first Cocker, Olive, more than 20 years ago. We couldn't help but fall in love with everything she did - good and bad: here's your shoe (chewed), there's a present for you under the stairs, here's a puddle! She became an instant family member.

Watching TV programmes and reading books got me interested in showing, so we contacted the Kennel Club and started looking for a breeder. It became my ambition to show and my choice of puppy was a solid black. I wanted to find out if we could be a team and together reach the heights others do. The breeder checked us out and we checked out the breeder. At eight weeks old there is no guarantee that the dog would achieve anything, it was up to me to train us both... and then hope! Bella (pictured overleaf) arrived and we haven't looked back since.

Before choosing a puppy, you MUST always see the puppies with the dam and - if possible - the sire in their normal environment. Look at how they interact with each other, how they walk and play. Pick them up, how much do they weigh? They should be stocky with a good thickness of bone. Are they clean, are their eyes bright, can they hear you? Always look at the paperwork: Kennel Club papers, pedigree, breeder's early care record, vet's report, puppy contract and insurance. Ask about after-sale care and contact with the breeder and returning the pup if there is a problem. Always check out the breeders, I always ask any potential new owner to contact the Kennel Club for my details and get back to me if they are happy with what they have discovered. I haven't had a dog back.

Showing Cocker Spaniels for the first time is nerve racking: "That one moves very well." "WOW, look at the coat on this one." "She stands on her own!" "I love the feet on that golden and look at that black one." "See how round that one's head is." Why doesn't my girl…move/stand/shine like that?"

You marvel at how experienced show people control their dogs as they do, how they manage to get them to look so wonderful and make them look like they are floating around the ring. And how do they get the dog to let the judge examine her like that, without so much as a murmur?

These are just one per cent of the thoughts that go through your head when you visit a show for the first time. The standard of dogs highlights the dedication and attention to detail that reputable breeders put in before a litter is even produced, followed by all the training, feeding and love the dogs subsequently receive.

When you are considering a dog for showing, all aspects of the sire and dam should be examined, such as health and health screening, pedigree, age and achievements. No breeder knows 100% whether any of the litter will be good enough for the show ring. I ask several other breeders to look at my litter and give their opinions during the first eight weeks (which is the earliest they can go to new homes), which helps me decide which, if any, I will keep and train on.

Training and Grooming

During the first eight weeks ALL of my puppies go through more than 50 activities every week to help with their development. (These activities can be found in the KC Puppy Handbook). As the breeder, I keep a record of everything and pass on the complete details of how and when to do things to the new owner.

'Bringing on' a potential show puppy can take several hours a day, depending upon how well the puppy - and handler - progress. This includes regular walking (which every dog needs, although not too much with young puppies), and by that I mean show walking. For the show ring, your Cocker has to learn how to walk, run, stop and stand, i.e. be placed in a stance which enhances his or her profile. The dog must be able to move elegantly, perfectly and without a stutter, as if floating around the ring. There must be no hint of pigeon toe or bow legs. All of this requires a lot of time and patience on the part of both dog and handler.

Then there's table training. Dogs are placed on a table to enable the judge to 'go over' the dog with ease to check for all the breed requirements and any faults. And you'll need a table to get the dog used to being groomed and judged. It is very important to get a show puppy used to being groomed, as grooming for show dogs is specialised. It's not like visiting your local grooming parlour, and at first it seems strange to a young puppy. The coat needs to be 'trained', i.e. guided to become naturally flat. It is NEVER clipped for the show ring.

This is very time consuming, involving an hour or two daily at different stages of the puppy's development, using various tools and techniques. Cockers are hand stripped, using finger and thumb to remove puppy coat and unsightly hairs. Their feet require attention so that they look 'cat-like' and several different types of scissors and brushes are also used. All knots must be removed carefully by easing them out without hurting the puppy or cutting them out - this would easily be noticed and look unsightly.

Knots appear spontaneously and occur almost everywhere, especially in and under the Cocker's 'skirt', ears, tail and nether regions. Each knot can take up to 10 minutes to remove, always take your time and be gentle and patient. The areas inside the dog's ears, teeth, nether regions and in between the pads need regular checking and cleaning, and don't forget the anal glands - but seek help and advice before attempting anything in this area! The puppy needs to get used to having his or her entire body touched, as all judges will do this to ensure the dog is healthy and conforms to the breed standard. Judges don't want to be bitten while 'going over' the exhibit, so every chance you get, ask other people to handle your puppy; the more he or she gets used to this, the more relaxed your puppy will be at a show.

Before every show my Cockers are washed, dried and groomed. Every dog is different and requires attention in different areas, which could take half an hour each to complete. This includes each ear/foot/leg, head and tail, and then you have the coat - sides, back, chest, hind, skirt – as well as the mouth, eyes and teeth. I do all of this on a regular basis to minimise the amount of work needed before shows; it also means my dogs don't have a single marathon grooming session, which could be stressful.

Food is another important point to consider for a show Cocker, all show breeders have their own ideas. I give mine a variety of different food, depending on what I think each one needs; it may be tinned, chicken/rice, complete and/or mixer biscuits. In terms of the shows themselves, there are three main types.

Fun or Companion Shows are for anyone and any dog to enter, often held in aid of charity. They include fun classes like Prettiest Face, Best Condition, and may also include pedigree classes. I and many other breeders enter these shows to help train puppies and juniors and as a fun day out for our other dogs.

I remember the first Companion Show I took Bella to, I wanted to see what it was like to try to learn from it. Not knowing anything, I saw some people sitting by the ring with trolleys, cages, tables and five dogs. I asked them what I had to do to enter. They looked at me and Bella, pointed to a tent and said: "The fun desk is over there." I replied: "She's a pedigree!"

With a surprised look they said: "She's a mess, you can't take her in looking like THAT! Let me take a look at her." We put Bella on the table, then to my horror, out came scissors, brushes, combs and a host of tools I had never seen before. "She's in good shape," they said: "Let's tidy her up for you." Within half an hour she looked wonderful and they taught me very quickly how to handle her. We came away with a third place – WOW, what a thrill! And made some very good friends.

They helped me learn everything I needed to know and do: grooming, handling lessons, all the paperwork and where the local dog training classes were. We entered another show, and the winner was announced: "It's the black Cocker Spaniel!" Over the years we had many successes, including several Best of Breed and Best in Show. After the last win we filled our car with her dog food winnings. Bella passed away a few years ago, but we still have some of her offspring.

Open Shows are for Kennel Club-registered pedigree entrants only and all entrants must abide by the KC rules and regulations. This is where we 'cut our teeth' in the showing world. Around 90% of the people are breeders and know what they are doing; they dress and act accordingly. In some classes we have been placed (which is from first to fifth position) and other times we have got nowhere - the judge has the final word. Not everyone may agree with the judge's decision, but there is always another show and another judge, and we all learn from the experience, sometimes more training, grooming, feeding or dieting is needed. Anyway, at the end of the day, the 'Best Dog' always goes home with me – and that's my dog!

Championship Shows are like Open Shows, but the entrants are 'benched' (pictured). They have their own three-sided area in which they must be kept unless they are being exercised or shown. We may bring a crate to keep them in for safety and security. These shows are open to the public, therefore everything has to be thief and tamper-proof. Challenge Certificates (CCs) are awarded at most of these shows and at a few Open Shows, which can lead to the titles every show breeder aspires to. Cocker Spaniel classes are normally large and being placed first to third qualifies your dog for Crufts, the ultimate dog show. The atmosphere at Crufts is electric; everyone is hoping to win. Tens of thousands of dogs enter, but only one achieves top spot. Winning even a single class puts you on an all-time high for weeks.

My girls are too old to breed with now – Happy Retirement! - so I am looking for another puppy to bring on, show and, as long as she is completely healthy and screen check cleared, hopefully to breed with. I'm not in a rush; I'm taking my time to find the right one. We will work together as a team and, I hope, enjoy some success in the ring. Whatever happens, I will still bring my Best Dog home."

A New Lease of Life

The Cocker Spaniel's bond with its humans and eagerness to please them is second to none. Combined with a sharp intellect and ability to learn quickly, these traits have made the Cocker one of the few breeds suited to therapy and assistance work. Here are two stories from the UK charity Hearing Dogs for Deaf People.

Beth and Biscuit

Cocker Spaniel Biscuit has transformed Beth Bates' life. She has helped Beth, 54, of West Yorkshire, to resume a normal life after illness - and has been the inspiration for a new career as a dog groomer.

Seven years ago, Beth woke up to discover she couldn't hear anything. It followed a series of ear infections and a bout of viral meningitis several years earlier, leaving her with permanent nerve damage and deafness. "It happened overnight and it was a complete shock," said Beth, who works as a part-time healthcare assistant.

She lost confidence and became isolated at home, not wanting to go out without her husband, Phillip. Then two-and-a-half years ago, after a four-year wait, Beth was introduced to Biscuit, a black Cocker Spaniel who had been trained by Hearing Dogs for Deaf People.

And it was love at first sight.

"There was a connection straight away when I was first introduced to Biscuit at Hearing Dogs," said Beth, a mother of two. "There is a very close bond between us; she follows me everywhere - even to the toilet! She has completely transformed my life. I feel more confident now, I've taken up golf again and I'm out and about everywhere. She has given me a new lease of life."

Biscuit nudges Beth with her nose to alert her to the doorbell, phone or smoke alarm. When the alarm clock rings she jumps on the bed. Two years also she averted a potential fire by nudging Beth to make her go to the kitchen. When Beth opened the door she discovered the kitchen was filled with smoke after inadvertently leaving the grill on.

Beth has always enjoyed taking care of Biscuit and now it has led to a new career, as she has just set up a new dog grooming business, Kutz 4 Muttz. She has taken a training course, converted her garage into a grooming parlour and has a growing list of clients - many of them owners of Cocker Spaniels.

Beth said: "I've got Biscuit to thank for setting me on this path. I really love grooming and combing her and now I'm fully qualified as a groomer. I'm really excited about the business. A lot of dogs are nervous with a groomer; I want to create a bond with the dog and to make the experience as pleasant as possible."

Biscuit is a show Cocker and was donated to Hearing Dogs by breeder Margaret Burnham, also of West Yorkshire. Margaret and Beth have become friends through Hearing Dogs and have been on two coach holidays together. When Margaret saw Biscuit helping Beth, she was moved to tears. She has since donated another dog.

Brenda and Yogi

Brenda underwent brain surgery at the age of 61 and woke to discover she had lost her hearing. Her whole life was turned upside down and she didn't even want to leave her home. But her life has been transformed again thanks to her hearing dog, Yogi! This is Brenda's story in her own words:

"Several years ago I was deafened after having surgery to remove a brain tumour and a cyst. I never realised the impact being deaf would make to my life.

"I never realised losing one of my senses would affect me so much – I completely lost my confidence and didn't want to meet with people. I was a teacher in a large comprehensive school and, of course, I had to leave my job.

"It got to the stage that I didn't even want to leave the house. I struggled to speak to people. There was an incident when I went to the supermarket and someone said 'excuse me,' but because I hadn't heard them, they drove their trolley into the back of me. It was terrible.

"However, on a visit to the Audiology Department in the local hospital I read a notice which was to change my life for the better – it was about Hearing Dogs for Deaf People. "The audiologist came to call me into her office and asked if I had ever had a dog. She persuaded me to apply and sent my hearing test results to see if I could be accepted as a recipient.

"About a week later I was visited by a Hearing Dogs representative and a wonderful journey began which would improve my life – and that of my husband's – greatly.

"We were later introduced to a black and white Cocker Spaniel called Sedge. He was wonderful and through him my quality of life was completely restored. We had him for about 12-and-a-half years until he unfortunately passed away. We still miss him greatly.

"We now have another Cocker Spaniel, Yogi (pictured). I feel I've gotten my confidence back and now when I go to the supermarket with Yogi, people see his coat and they ask me what he does to help me. Everyone talks to me now and they all want to say hello to Yogi. When I take him to the shops, it takes us ages to get around because people are always stopping us to talk to him.

"He is loved by everyone. He comes with me to chapel, and if I don't take him with me, the others will ask, 'Where is Yogi?' I think he's more popular than me!

"Yogi just makes friends wherever he goes. We really wouldn't be without him. Hearing Dogs have given me my quality of life back, and I love Yogi to bits."

Hearing Dogs for the Deaf, set up in 1982, trains dogs to alert deaf people to sounds they can't hear. The dogs also help bring independence, companionship and confidence to deaf people.

It takes around 18 months to train a hearing dog and costs tens of thousands of pounds. The charity currently has around 900 dogs in the UK. Visit www.hearingdogs.org.uk for more information or to make a donation.

Useful Contacts

UK: www.thekennelclub.org.uk/services/public/acbr/Default.aspx?breed=Spaniel+(Cocker) Kennel Club Cocker Spaniel breeders

www.thecockerspanielclub.co.uk The Cocker Spaniel Club (UK)

www.champdogs.co.uk/breeds/cocker-spaniel/breeders Champdogs Cocker Spaniel breeders (UK)

www.working cockerhealthscreendirectory.com Working Cocker Health Screen Directory

wwww.cockerspaniel-info.org.uk The Cocker Spaniel Breed Council

ww.cockerspanieldatabase.info Pedigrees and health information

www.apdt.co.uk Association of Pet Dog Trainers UK

USA: http://marketplace.akc.org/puppies/cocker-spaniel American Kennel Club (American) Cocker Spaniel breeders

http://marketplace.akc.org/puppies/english-cocker-spaniel American Kennel Club English Cocker Spaniel breeders

www.asc-cockerspaniel.org/index.php/breeders.html American Spaniel Club

www.ecsca.info/index.php/breeders/breeder-listing English Cocker Spaniel Club of America

www.fieldcockers.com Field trials for English Cocker Spaniels

www.apdt.com Association of Pet Dog Trainers USA

OTHERS: www.cappdt.ca Canadian Association of Professional Pet Dog Trainers

www.dogfoodadvisor.com Useful information on grain-free and hypoallergenic dog foods

www.akcreunite.org Helps find lost or stolen dogs in USA, register your dog's microchip

There are also a number of Cocker Spaniel internet forums and Facebook groups which are a good source of information from other owners.

List of Contributors

Breeders (in alphabetical order)

Alan & Carole Pitchers, Alcarbrad Cocker Spaniels, Essex

Andy Platt, Nithvalley Gundogs, Scotland http://nithvalley-gundogs.weebly.com

Barry Hutchinson, Brynovation Gundogs, Gloucestershire www.brynovationgundogs.co.uk

Billie Cheeseman, BarleyCourt Spaniels, Hertfordshire http://barleycourtspaniels.wix.com

Caroline Bymolen, Carto Cocker Spaniels, Cambridgeshire

Chris Warner, Monwodelea Gundogs, Coventry

Christine & Dave Grant, Rostreigan Cocker Spaniels, Hampshire

Christine Thomas, Dodfordhills Spaniels, Worcestershire

David & Alison Matthews, Tojamatt Cockers, Nottinghamshire

Debra Ralston, Staffordshire

Eunice Wine, Blackberry Farm Enterprises, Virginia, USA

Gail Parsons, Gaiter Cocker Spaniels, Sussex

Haja van Wessem, Speggle-Waggel Cocker Spaniels, The Netherlands www.spegglewaggel.com

Helen Marsden, Finity Cocker Spaniels, Hampshire www.finitydogs.co.uk

Jackie Hornby, Jacmist Cocker Spaniels, Bedfordshire

Jacquie Ward, Breezybrook Gundogs, Bedfordshire www.breezybrookgundogs.co.uk

Jane Minikin, North Yorkshire

Jane Seekings, Dorset

Jill Gunn, Dearganach Working Cockers, Scotland www.dearganachworkingcockers.co.uk

Jo Oxley, Looseminxjoy Working Cocker Spaniels, Norfolk

Julie & Darren Summers, Summervilles Gundogs, County Durham www.summervillesgundogs.com

Kate McBride, Ferebim Cockers, Lincolnshire & Limousin

Keith Henderson, Owencraig Cocker Spaniels, Dunfermline, Scotland

Kerena Marchant, Sondes Cocker Spaniels, Surrey

Kirsten Strachan, Lorne Working Cockers, Perthshire, Scotland

Linda Reed, Delindere (English & American) Cocker Spaniels, Leics. www.delindere.f9.co.uk

Louise Massey, Essex

Lynne Waterhouse, Lyfora Cocker Spaniels, Berkshire

Manda & Jacquie Smith, Tassietay Working Cocker Spaniels, Kent http://tassietaywcs.tripod.com

Maxine Shaverin, Lancashire

Michelle Mills, Bryntail Gundogs, Powys, Wales

Nicola Hunter, Pursley Gundogs, Hertfordshire

Pat & Andrew Height, Fourtails (show) Cocker Spaniels, Cambridgeshire

Peter Harvey & Nikki Arnold, Grannus Cocker Spaniels, Somerset

Rachel Appleby, Cockerbye Cocker Spaniels, Lincolnshire

Robert & Ruth Baldwin, Annaru Cocker Spaniels, South Wales www.annaru-cockerspaniels.co.uk

Stewart North, Northglen Labradors & Cockers, Leicester

Tracey Simpson, Bravialis Gundogs, North Yorkshire http://bravialisgundogs.com

Wendy Roberts, Cheshire

Wendy Tobijanski, Janski Cocker Spaniels, Shropshire

Other Contributors

Richard Preest, Centrewalk Cocker Spaniels, Gloucestershire

Dr Sara Skiwski, The Western Dragon holistic veterinary practice, San Jose, California, USA

Extra photography: http://ruralshots.com and www.guywoodland.co.uk

Cover shot www.warrenphotographic.co.uk

Disclaimer

This book has been written to provide helpful information on Cocker Spaniels. It is not meant to be used, nor should it be used, to diagnose or treat any medical condition. For diagnosis or treatment of any animal medical problem, consult a qualified veterinarian. The author is not responsible for any specific health or allergy conditions that may require medical supervision and is not liable for any damages or negative consequences from any treatment, action, application or preparation, to any animal or to any person reading or following the information in this book. The views expressed by contributors to this book are solely personal and do not necessarily represent those of the author. References are provided for informational purposes only and do not constitute endorsement of any websites or other sources.

Author's Note: For ease of reading, the masculine pronoun 'he' is often used to represent both male and female dogs.

Printed in Great Britain
by Amazon